Disneyland Hotel

The Early Years, 1954-1988

Donald W. Ballard

Cover design: Christine Sparks • www.sparksarts.com Layout by:

Parks Printing www.parksprinting.com

Set in Century 725BT, Century Old Style, Times New Roman
New Press Eroded by Galdino Otten

Printed in Korea.
Revised Second Edition, February 2021

Soft Cover ISBN: 978-1-7326020-9-0

Library of Congress Control Number: 2020945243

Visit www.theoldmillpress.com

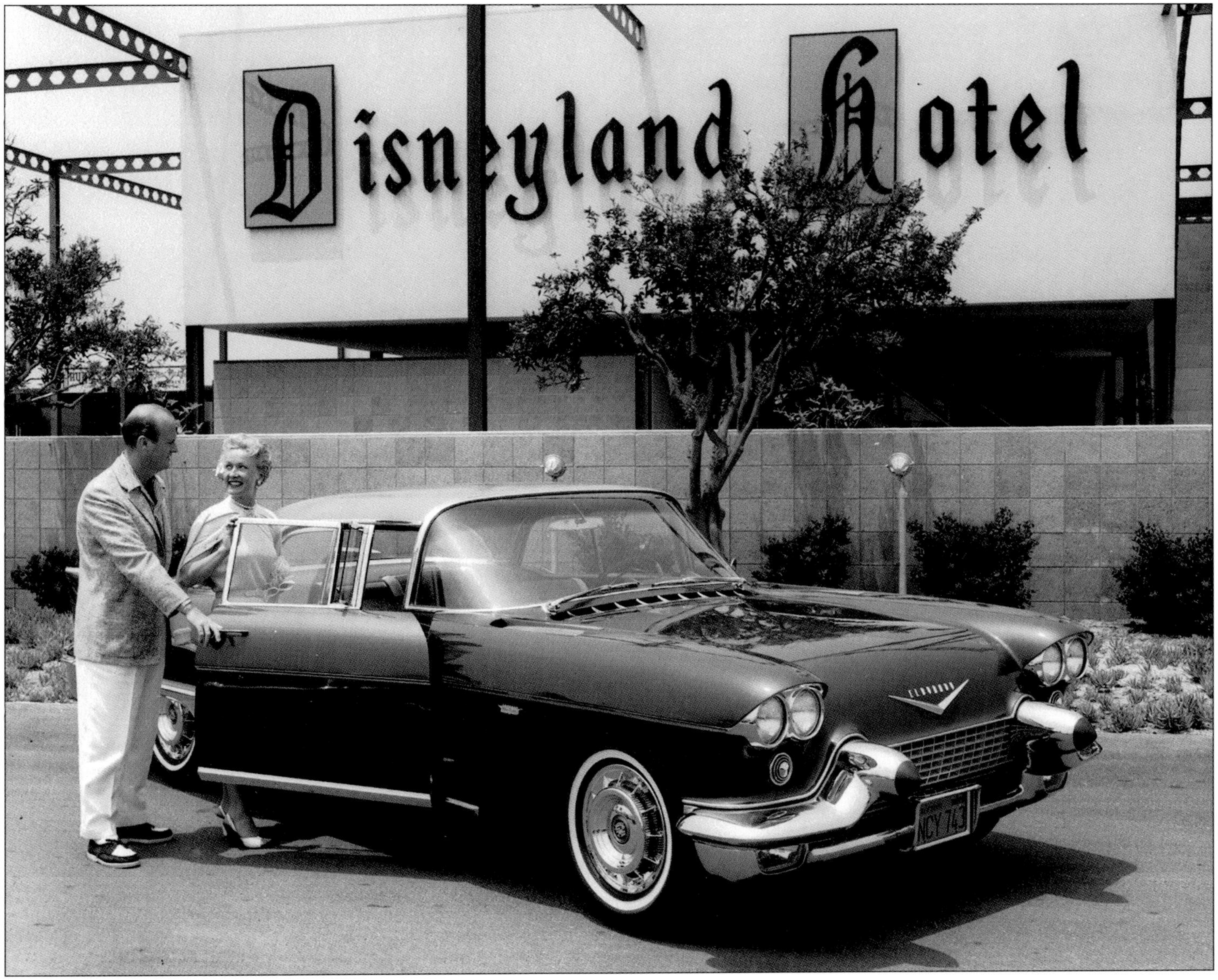

Jack and Bonita Wrather with their hand-built, limited edition 1957 Cadillac El Dorado Brougham.

Table of Contents

Dedication

This book is dedicated to Disney Legends Jack and Bonita Wrather, two visionaries who provided countless hours of recreation, entertainment and enjoyment to millions of people from around the world.

To my wife Lorrie who showed me the true meaning of love.

To Alfred Nicholson & Kurt Weber who were instrumental in making the Disneyland Hotel into a Magical place. Rest in Peace.

To Tony Bruno whom I think the world of.

You are cordially invited...

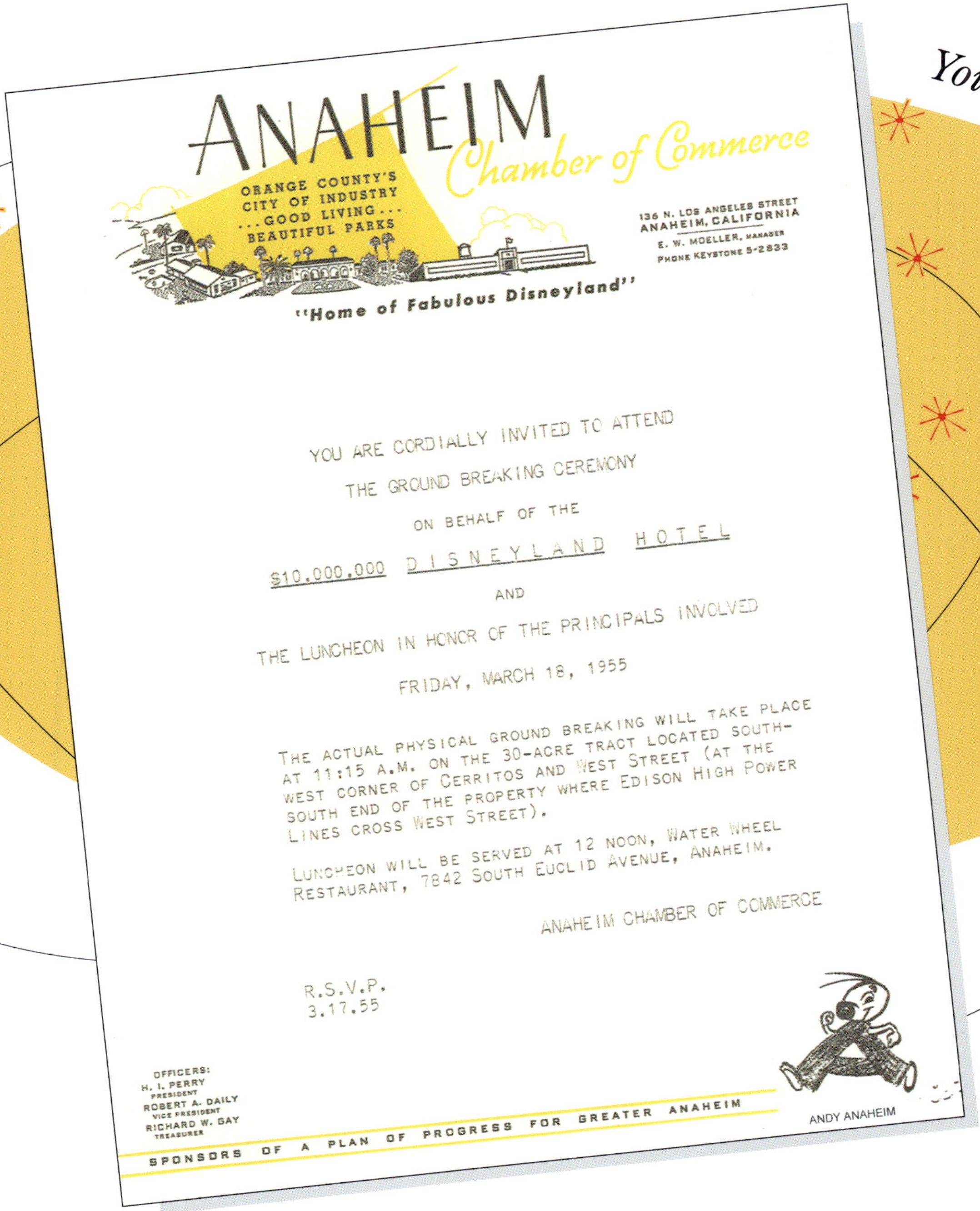

ANAHEIM Chamber of Commerce

ORANGE COUNTY'S CITY OF INDUSTRY ...GOOD LIVING... BEAUTIFUL PARKS

136 N. LOS ANGELES STREET
ANAHEIM, CALIFORNIA
E. W. MOELLER, MANAGER
PHONE KEYSTONE 5-2833

"Home of Fabulous Disneyland"

YOU ARE CORDIALLY INVITED TO ATTEND

THE GROUND BREAKING CEREMONY

ON BEHALF OF THE

$10,000,000 D I S N E Y L A N D H O T E L

AND

THE LUNCHEON IN HONOR OF THE PRINCIPALS INVOLVED

FRIDAY, MARCH 18, 1955

THE ACTUAL PHYSICAL GROUND BREAKING WILL TAKE PLACE AT 11:15 A.M. ON THE 30-ACRE TRACT LOCATED SOUTH-WEST CORNER OF CERRITOS AND WEST STREET (AT THE SOUTH END OF THE PROPERTY WHERE EDISON HIGH POWER LINES CROSS WEST STREET).

LUNCHEON WILL BE SERVED AT 12 NOON, WATER WHEEL RESTAURANT, 7842 SOUTH EUCLID AVENUE, ANAHEIM.

ANAHEIM CHAMBER OF COMMERCE

R.S.V.P.
3.17.55

OFFICERS:
H. I. PERRY
PRESIDENT
ROBERT A. DAILY
VICE PRESIDENT
RICHARD W. GAY
TREASURER

ANDY ANAHEIM

SPONSORS OF A PLAN OF PROGRESS FOR GREATER ANAHEIM

Introduction

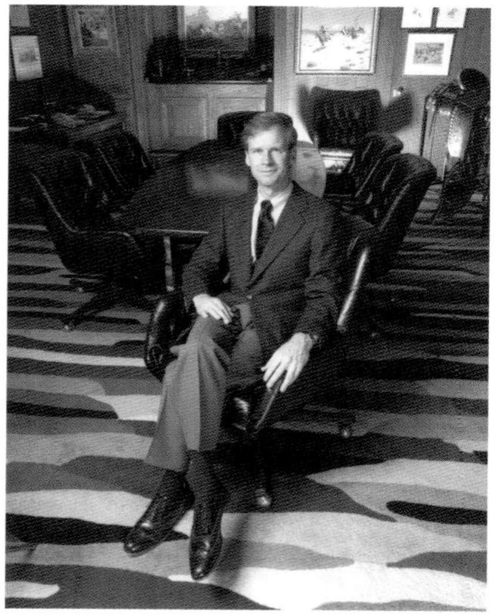

Christopher Wrather

My first impressions of the Disneyland Hotel were through the eyes of a four-year old. There was the seemingly endless drive from our home across Hollywood and down the exciting Hollywood Freeway. There was the striking exposed girder construction of the Hotel's main building. As is often the case with children, the little memories survive best: pancakes at the Coffee Shop, hamburgers served on grilled parmesan french bread at the Gourmet Restaurant, the small "trick" we children were allowed to buy at the Arcade's novelty store to make departure more palatable. As I grew, there was that most memorable moment when we were allowed to go to Disneyland on our own, riding the famous tram, and later, the Monorail.

The Disneyland Hotel presaged many future developments in the way Americans entertain themselves. My Dad understood that the landscape of entertainment was changing, calling his era the "age of frantic relaxation". Originally conceived as lodging for the main event, Disneyland, the Hotel was designed by architects experienced in the movie business and soon was helping to pioneer new forms of dining as entertainment, shopping as entertainment, and the use of a waterfront setting which anticipated the later emergence of waterfront festival shopping centers that became so popular in many urban renewals.

My father had the notion that business should be fun. He liked making money, but it wasn't his main motivation. He entertained himself while he entertained others. He had more fun with the Disneyland Hotel than with any other investment. If he was feeling blue on a weekend he would jump into his car and drive, unannounced, to the Hotel and just walk around. This drove Hotel management crazy. One such trip ended in the dismissal of the Hotel's current general manager when my Dad found that the petunias in the flower beds of his beloved Garden Rooms had been allowed to wither. It was a symbol to him of the manager's failure to grasp basic principles, as well as a personal affront!

I thank the author for his dedicated work to preserve the history of this important piece of twentieth century American culture.

Christopher Wrather
Los Alamos, California
April 2005

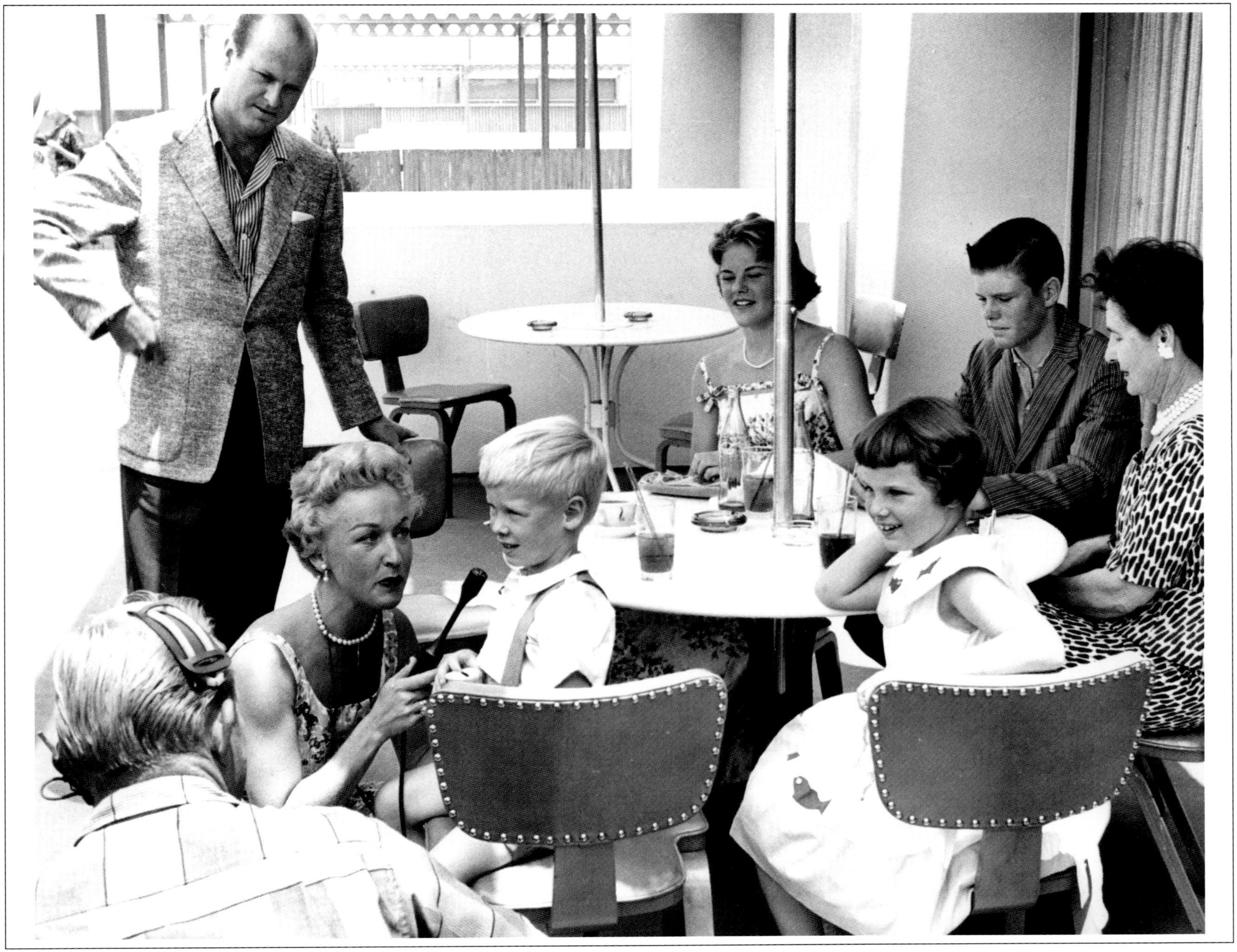

The Wrather family on their second floor balcony at the Disneyland Hotel. Bonita Wrather is interviewing her youngest child Christopher while the rest of the family looks on. Also pictured is Jack Wrather's mother Mazie seated far right.

The Disneyland Hotel: The Early Years, 1954-1988

By
Donald W. Ballard

Foreword:

Today's Disneyland Hotel is a far different facility than the Disneyland Hotel originally opened in October of 1955. Over the past decades, millions of guests have found countless pleasures there and have created many lasting family memories. Over the years, returning guests have been witness to an ever changing and expanding complex of buildings. As with Disneyland, the Park, the Disneyland Hotel has never stopped growing and improving.

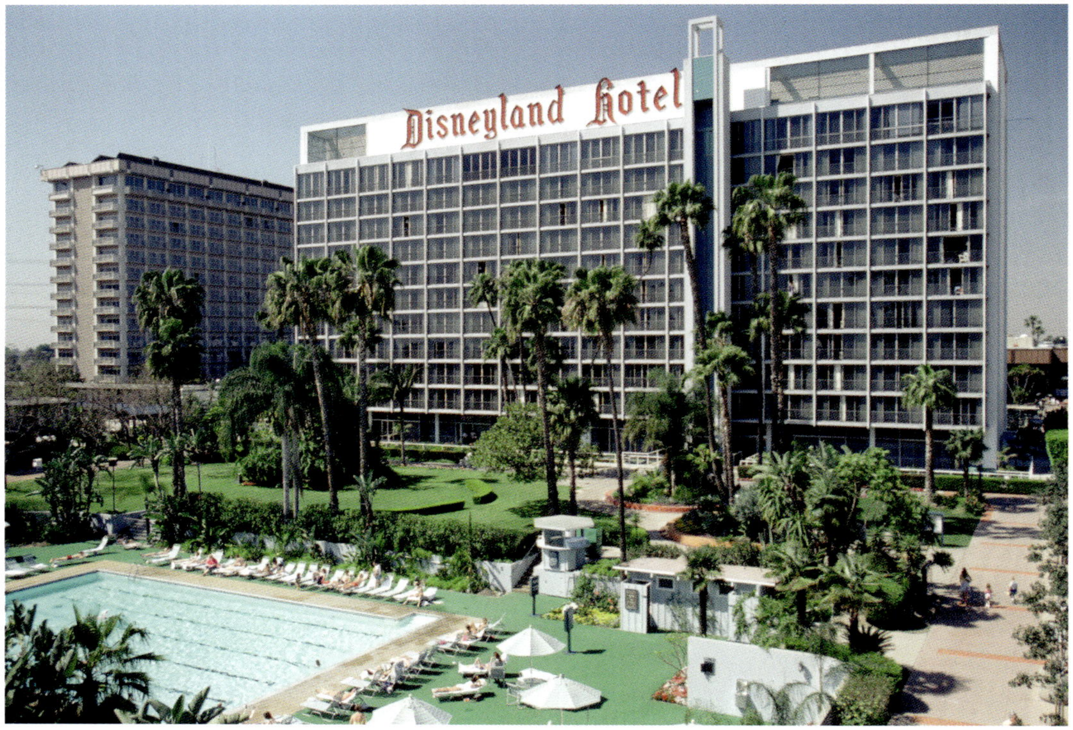

The beautiful Disneyland Hotel.

The following is an attempt to view the early years of the Disneyland Hotel in its historical perspective...in words and through photographs. First, an over-view of the evolution of the community of Anaheim and of Walt Disney's search for a location for Disneyland will set the stage for the eventual building of the Disneyland Hotel. Next, the lives of the two most influential developers of the Hotel will be explored. [To some, it may come as a surprise to discover that this was not Walt Disney's hotel...not that he did not have an influence upon its creation.] Finally, a look at the growth of the Hotel during its first three decades hopefully will bring back many happy memories for those who have been guests there. For those who did not have that pleasure, hopefully these pages will provide a clear picture of the early history of the Disneyland Hotel.

ANAHEIM & WALT DISNEY

The town of Anaheim was established in 1857 as a colony of German farmers and vintners, becoming the first settlement in Southern California of non-Spanish origin. The first two families to take up residence were the Hammes and the Rehms. While native Californians referred to the area as "Campo Aleman" (German field), the city's name was a combination of "Ana" from the nearby Santa Ana River and "heim," the German word for home. Thus, Anaheim was their home by the river. In praise of the new settlement's name, the *Los Angeles Star* of January 30, 1858 wrote: "...not only euphonious, but expressive. It is suggestive of the most pleasing associations, reminding one of the wide-spreading and lightly cultivated wineyards [*sic*] of the Fatherland." For the next quarter century, grapes (and the wine they produced) were the primary industry of the Anaheim colony. By 1861, 400,000 vines of the Criolla grape (developed in Mexico) had been planted and in that year produced 75,000 gallons of wine.

In 1884, 1.25-million gallons of wine were produced. However, that success came to an abrupt end when an agricultural blight in 1885 began destroying the vineyards. The *Anaheim Gazette* (first published on October 29, 1870) reported in an 1886 article that "vines which appeared vigorous and healthy...are beginning to shrivel and dry, and the berries are dropping off." In the end, 25,000-acres of grape vines perished, and along with them the economic base of Anaheim was shattered.

Area farmers experimented with a variety of other crops (sugar beets, lemons, apricots) but had limited success. In the 1880's, walnuts provided some economic relief. Chili peppers also became a productive crop for a few decades. At one time, Orange County would produce almost every chili pepper grown in California. Chili weevils would destroy that industry in the 1920's.

The most successful attempt to find a substitute for the ruined grape crop would prove to be the orange. Dr. William N. Hardin of Anaheim is credited with planting from seed the first Valencia orange grove in the county in 1870. Because of its late growing season, its juiciness, its lasting taste, and its ability to be shipped long distances, this variety of orange would soon erase almost all economic effects from the grape blight. By 1923, there would be 37,528-acres of orange groves in Orange County, producing 4.3-million boxes of oranges. By 1938 (the peak year for the orange crop in the county), 67,536-acres produced 9.3-million boxes of Valencias. It seemed that an agricultural future for the area was assured.

At the time that Anaheim was incorporated in 1876, it had a population of 881 and became the first incorporated city in what would later become Orange County. Anaheim immediately became the second largest city (next only to Los Angeles) in the county. [Until 1889, today's Orange County area would be a part of Los Angeles County.] In 1887, the Santa Fe Railroad linked Anaheim's citrus growers with the East, providing vital markets for their crops. At the turn of the century, the city had 1,565 residents. By 1920, the population had grown to 5,526, with agriculture still being the area's primary economic base. Due to the post-World War I population and housing boom in Southern California, Anaheim would nearly double in size during the next four years.

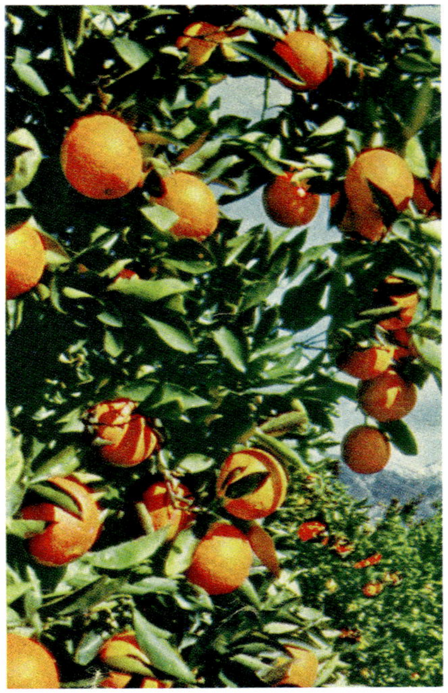

Orange County, California.

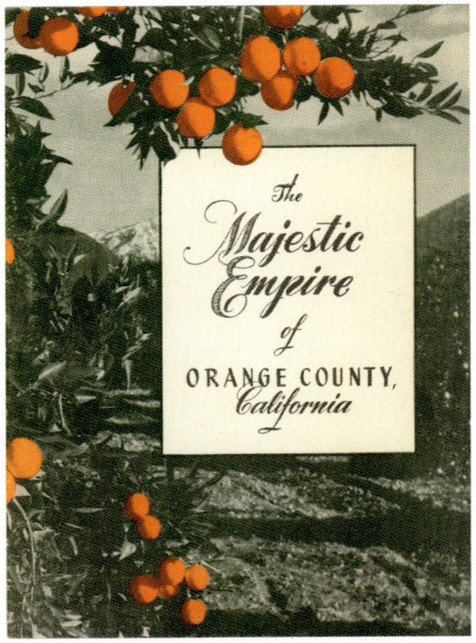

Anaheim's small town life-style continued throughout the first half of the twentieth century. By 1950, the population had grown to 14,556; and the sleepy, little community was about to undergo tremendous changes.

During the late 1940's and the early 1950's, the State of California experienced its third major population explosion. The first had occurred in the late 1840's with the discovery of gold at Sutter's mill near Sacramento. The second happened in the late 1800's when rate wars between the Southern Pacific and the Santa Fe railroads made it much faster and more affordable for almost anyone to travel west to California. With fares as low as a single dollar from Kansas City to Los Angeles, Easterners flocked to California to buy land and to establish businesses. The economic and industrial boom following World War II had sparked California's most recent wave of growth up to that time.

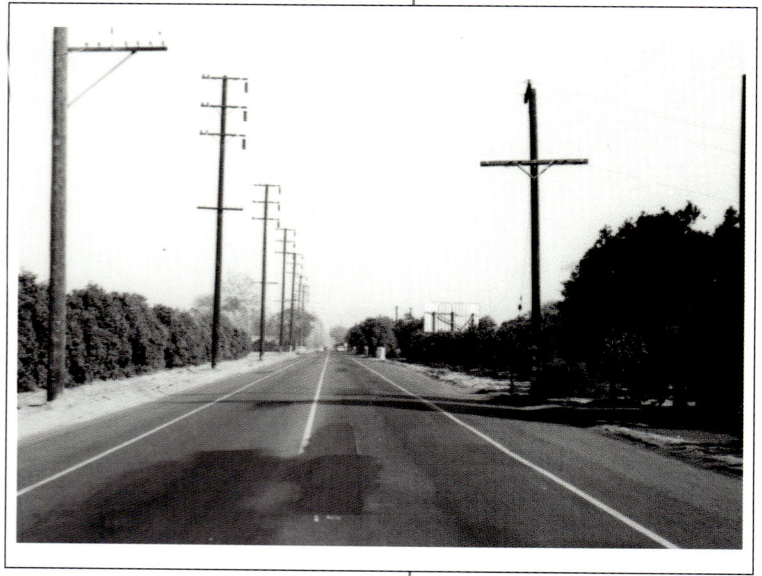

Katella and Walnut, Anaheim 1950s.

That post-war period witnessed a great industrial push that reinvigorated the state's economy. All over Southern California, sprawling growth developed in the form of new businesses, modern freeways, and housing developments. Spawned by a tidal wave of optimism, this new growth spread at an alarming rate. Farms and pastures were transformed, seemingly overnight, into new towns and towns grew into cities. With this new affluence came leisure time to build family relationships and to enjoy the bounties of the good life. In the Los Angeles area, people took to the roads with a newfound freedom. One such person was Walt Disney.

Walt Disney's dreams were like few others' dreams. Walt could conceive an idea, keep it to himself, and nurture it for years before acting upon it. It is known that before World War II, Walt had referred to a "magical little park." But like so many other plans at the Studio, the war put the idea of a park on hold for most of that decade. His idea had been to create a park for the entire family, a unique playground where a family could find happiness together and where they could escape the pressures of every day life. Walt was not impressed with the ordinary city parks or the traditional amusement parks. Perhaps from the first day that he had moved into his new studio in Burbank in 1940, Walt had eyed a vacant strip of weed-covered land across Riverside Drive just south of the Studio (the acreage that in 1994 became the site of the new $52-million Disney Animation building).

After the war, his plan for a family park was revived. At first, he thought of calling it Mickey Mouse Park and began having plans created for an area of approximately 8-acres. The park would feature activities that an entire family could enjoy. One concept map included a farm for small animals. He would stock a lake with fish so that parents and their children could sit on the banks and enjoy a pleasant time together. He would put an island in the middle of that lake and allow the children to explore its caves, bridges, and waterfalls. He would have boats for guests to row around the lake and by which to travel back and forth from the island. He would build a carousel and a bandstand, simulating a small town square at the turn of the century. There would be a miniature train circling the entire park. Trains being one of Walt Disney's favorite hobbies and passions, it was only natural that there would have to be a train or two in his dream park. In its early stages, the park had been budgeted at $10,000.

As planning continued, that miniature train changed into a full-sized, narrow gauge steam railroad. Other ideas included an old-fashioned circus, a county fair, a Mississippi steamboat, a Victorian village, a Western town, a covered bridge, a picnic area...and the ideas kept filling more and more sheets of paper. An internal office memo from Walt in August of 1948 stated, "...no roller coaster or other rides in the cheap thrill category." At another time Walt had commented to Harper Goff (who would later work on designs for Main Street, U.S.A. and for the Jungle Cruise), "I don't want to just entertain kids with pony rides and swings. I want them to learn something about their heritage."

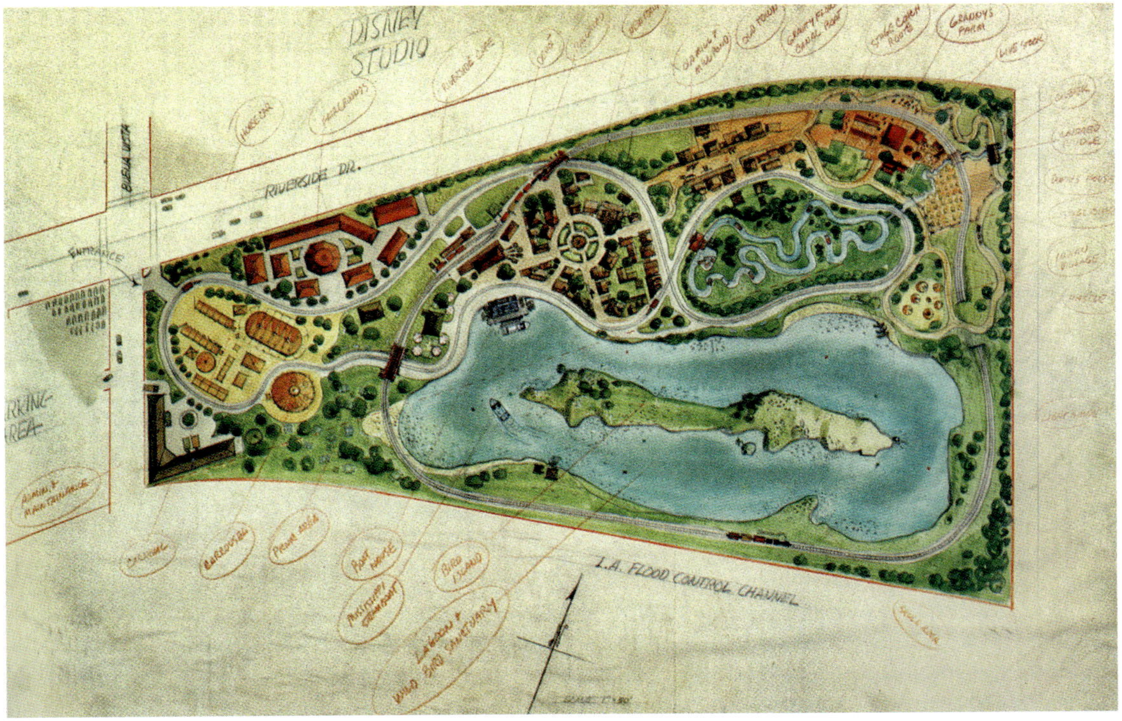

An early concept drawing of Disneyland.

As with most things that Walt Disney touched, the ideas kept growing and soon the park was projected to cover the entire 11-acres that he owned of the 16-acres across the street. John Hench (who started at Disney as a storyman in 1939 and who in 1972 became executive vice-president of WED) recalled Walt's early fascination with the park idea. "I remember several Sundays seeing Walt across the street.... And I'd see him out there, stepping things off, in the weed filled lot, standing, visualizing, all by himself. I knew what he was doing." The internal memo from August of 1948 is the first document that describes a themed park that somewhat can be recognized as the beginnings of the park as it would finally develop. By 1951, the name for the park had changed from Mickey Mouse Park to Disneyland, and the ideas were continuing to multiply.

Soon Walt's plans encompassed the entire 16-acre lot. There were several problems facing the continuation of planning for a park in Burbank...and they were all governmental problems. The U.S. Army Corps of Engineers had jurisdiction over a portion of the property along the Los Angeles River for flood-control purposes. The State of California had a claim upon another section of the land for the proposed Ventura Freeway. Finally, before Walt could hope to do anything, he would have to win support from the City of Burbank for purposes of re-zoning the land.

Before he could meet with the City Council, the news leaked to the press. The *Burbank Daily Review* for Thursday, March 27, 1952, broke the news of Disney's plans with the front page headline: "Walt Disney Make-Believe Land Project Planned Here: $1,500,000 Dreamland to Rise On Site in Burbank." In the article, Walt was quoted: "Disneyland will be something of a fair, an exhibition, a playground, a community center, a museum of living facts, and a showplace of beauty and magic."

The more he worked, the bigger the project grew. Walt wanted to have dedicated, themed areas within his park. One area would be dedicated to the American frontier. Another area would explore the world of tomorrow with rocket ships and flights into outer space. Walt soon realized that the original Burbank site would not be large enough to accommodate all of his plans and dreams for a family park.

One day, taking a break from work, Walt jumped into his car and drove toward the newly constructed Santa Ana Freeway. He then headed south, away from the smoggy city and away from the congestion...toward the blue sky and the white clouds. His journey ended in Orange County. It was like being transported back to the days of his youth in the Midwest. Before him were miles of open farmland, and the smell of orange blossoms filled the air. The skyline was dominated by tall eucalyptus trees that shaded the groves of oranges. An occasional farmhouse or barn was all he could see of habitation. This was so much like his boyhood home of Marceline, Missouri. Years later, Walt would recall, "I first saw the [possible] site for Disneyland back in 1953. In those days, it was all flat land--no rivers, no mountains, no castles or rocket ships--just orange groves and a few acres of walnut trees." Here, in the middle of the orange groves in Anaheim, Walt Disney had found the place where perhaps he could build his magical park.

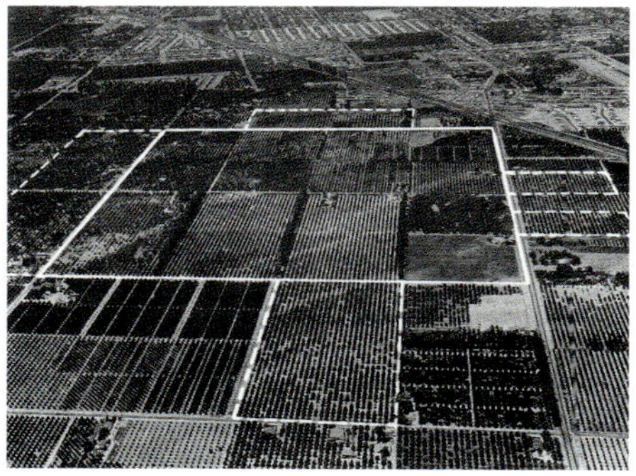

The proposed Disneyland site just prior to construction.

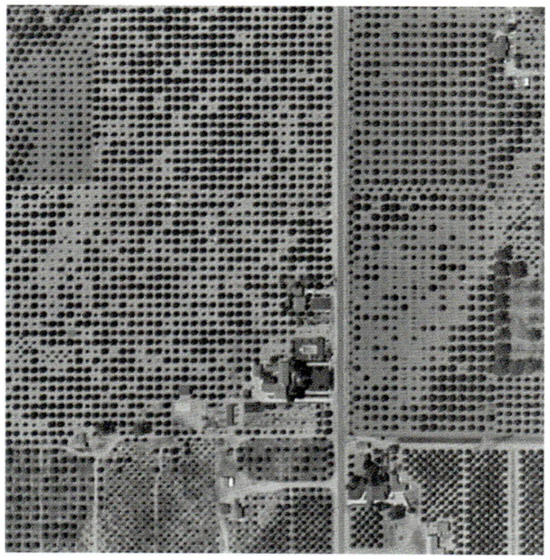

Hotel grounds close up.

In December of 1952, Walt had created Walt Disney, Inc. for the purpose of designing and building his dream. [This would later become WED Enterprises, WED standing for Walter Elias Disney] Before Disneyland was completed, Walt would pour almost all of his personal assets into this project. He sold or mortgaged all of his personal properties (except for the family home on Carolwood Drive in the Los Angeles suburb of Holmby Hills). He borrowed against his own life insurance policy to build the steam trains for the Park. Studio employees also contributed what they could. By opening day, he would be personally in debt for $100,000. Walt would later reflect that "It's no secret we were sticking just about every nickel we had on the chance that people would really be interested in something totally new and unique in the field of entertainment." At that time, the Studio was heavily in debt as a result of the depressed foreign box office revenues during World War II. Had the park venture failed, it is highly likely that such a disaster would have meant the end of the Studio.

Earlier, Walt's planning had reached a stage that required the hiring of an architect. Harper Goff suggested the firm of William L. Pereira and Charles Luckman to create the master plan for the park. Luckman recalled that in April of 1952, he was invited to the Disney Studios for lunch with Walt Disney in his private office. As the meal was served, Walt began to weave his tale of the magical kingdom he was planning. Luckman was so totally engrossed by the descriptions being verbally displayed before him that he only later realized that he had not touched a bite of his meal. "Walt, I've never heard anything as exciting in my life. It's wholly unbelievable and yet I know you can do it." When asked where he planned to build his park, Walt rose, led Luckman to the windows, and pointed to a small vacant lot just to the south of the studio property. When Luckman suggested that that area might be too small to hold all of Walt's ideas, Disney just laughed and added, "You and Bill [Pereira] can do it. Go back to your office and get started on a master plan right away."

A month later, Luckman presented to Disney a plan for a seven-acre site. When Walt agreed that the proposed site was too small, Luckman immediately pulled out a master plan for a ten-acre site. More months passed, and Walt's dreams were demanding more and more land...twenty-acres, thirty-acres, fifty-acres. Almost from the beginning, Walt's ideas and the architects' concepts failed to match. Walt became increasingly dissatisfied with the master plans being presented to him. One evening at a party, Walt discussed those frustrations with his long-time friend and architect, Welton Becket. Analyzing Walt's situation, Becket finally suggested, "Walt, no one can design Disneyland for you; you'll have to do it yourself." As a result, in May of 1953, Walt rejected their master plan and Pereira and Luckman were relieved of their task, they were fired. One should not feel sorry for them. Soon they would have a new employer (Jack Wrather) and a new project (the Disneyland Hotel).

Disney openly sought others to help him with the financing of his dream. As the visions for Disneyland expanded, so did the costs of building it. What had started in the 1940's as a $10,000 family park next to the Studio had quickly ballooned into a major project, estimated at over $4-million. Walt, with the sound financial advice of his brother Roy, realized that he would need to find major financial support to finish the project. The Disney brothers took a gamble and ventured into the newest area of entertainment media.

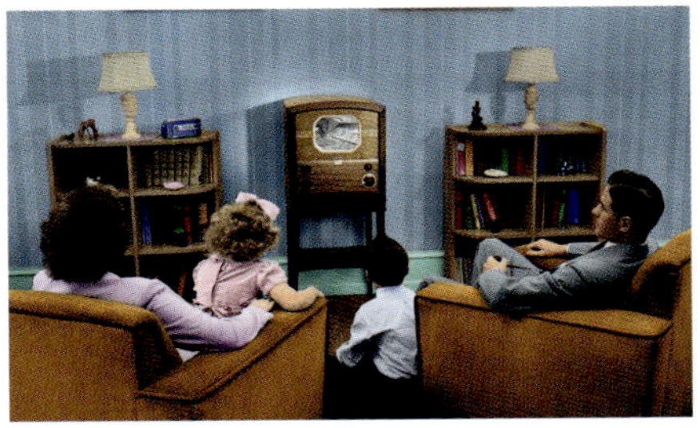

1950's family enjoying television.

By the beginning of the 1950's, the total number of television sets in homes across the United States finally had reached the 10-million mark, and sales had increased to a million new sets per year. Soon, Walt Disney would utilize that ever-growing audience not only for the promotion of each of his latest movie releases, but he would ingeniously use the new medium to create a pre-opening interest in and excitement about his biggest gamble, his Park.

While most Hollywood studio heads feared the advent of television and what it might do to their profits and to the motion picture industry as a whole, Walt Disney saw television as an opportunity to further his visions. Walt once remarked, "I saw that if I was ever going to have my park, here, at last was the way to tell millions of people about it--with TV." It would then fall to Walt's brother Roy to fashion a deal.

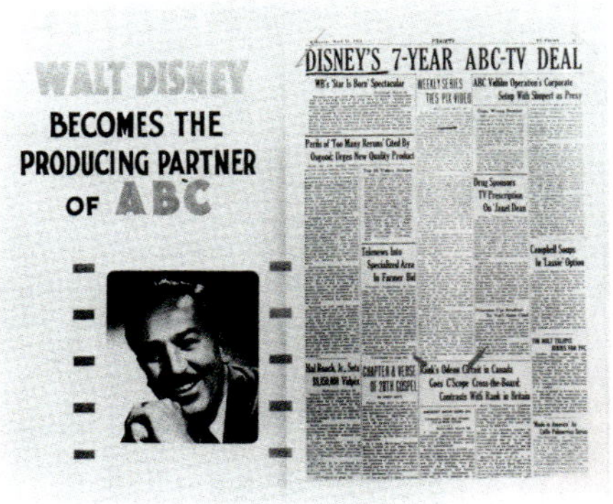

New Partners.

On Monday, September 28, 1953, Roy Disney flew to New York with maps, concept paintings, and descriptions of Disneyland, much of which having been created in a frantic 42-hour period that weekend by Herb Ryman (who would later design Sleeping Beauty Castle) with Walt looking over his shoulder, giving directions and moral support. The Columbia Broadcasting System (CBS) showed no interest in the project. At General Foods, there was interest but only if Walt first produced a "pilot" episode. Roy had to explain that Walt's policy was, "We don't make samples." Next, the National Broadcasting Company (NBC) was interested in the park but seemed more interested in obtaining Disney films for broadcast. However, negotiations went nowhere. The executives kept referring to Disneyland as "Walt's fairground." Those men in suits with big offices high up in skyscrapers could not seem to grasp the concept of Walt's family park. Walt commented, "I could never convince the financiers that Disneyland was feasible, because dreams offer too little in collateral." Later that same day in frustration, Roy called a friend Leonard Goldenson, the head of ABC. ABC was the least attractive possibility since it continually finished a very distant third in the ratings. ABC was the brunt of numerous jokes. On his top-rated television show, comedian Milton Berle had quipped, "In case [the Russians] drop the [atomic] bomb, go to ABC; they've never had a hit." ABC was desperate to obtain a hit program that could give the troubled network a boost.

The fledgling American Broadcasting Company agreed to invest $500,000 and become a partner in the Park. The network would also guarantee $4.5-million in loans to cover construction costs. In return, ABC received a

34.48-percent stake in Disneyland, Inc., which Walt had formed in 1951. A seven year contract required Walt to produce for ABC a weekly, one-hour television program, which also was to be called *Disneyland*.

Concerning the benefits of his entry into this new medium, Walt Disney said, "Every time I got to thinking of television, I would think of this park. Instead of considering TV a rival, when I saw it I said, 'I can use that...here's the way I'll get my park going.' It's natural for me to tie in with television."

After the contracts were finalized and signed, a United Press International wire-story of March 30, 1954 read: "Hollywood--Walt Disney's movie studio confirmed today it planned a partnership with the American Broadcasting Co., making it the first major film studio to enter the television field." The story went on to indicate that the budget for Disneyland Park by then had climbed to $6-million. With ABC's financial backing assured, the Bank of America (a long time backer of Disney dreams) at last agreed to help in the financing of Disneyland, despite the bankers' lack of confidence in the potential success of such an untested project.

Walt used the first telecast of his weekly program to introduce his dream park to a national audience on Wednesday evening (7:30 eastern) October 27, 1954. The first episode was titled *The Disneyland Story*, with one of the highlights being the displaying of a huge wall map of Disneyland painted by Peter Ellenshaw (Disney's renowned matte painter). Over the next eight months, Walt kept the viewers informed about the progress of the construction of Disneyland by using a portion of several of his weekly programs to hype his project. *A Progress Report* and *A Further Report on Disneyland* gave viewers updates on the building of the Park. *Disneyland* was seen on 153 stations in the United States and 15 stations in Canada. During its first season on ABC, the weekly program was seen by an audience that frequently numbered over 40-million viewers.

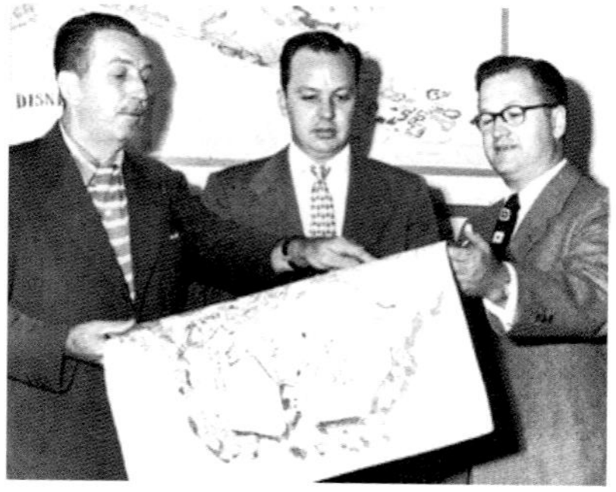

Walt Disney with SRI's C.V. Wood and Harrison Price.

While at the same time financial negotiations were taking shape, Walt continued to be confident that Southern California was the ideal place to build his park, but Anaheim was not the only site considered. Disney had been offered an option on land, a former police pistol range, in the San Fernando Valley near Canoga Park. While he was not certain about many things, of one thing Walt was certain: NOT the beach. He realized that a beachfront park would limit the possible access routes. Most former beach parks had earned a bad reputation. Walt was adamant that he did not want people coming into his park in bathing suits.

To be certain of finding the ideal location, Walt and Roy contracted the Stanford Research Institute (SRI) to conduct the needed surveys. SRI was a projects consulting firm founded in 1946, and it quickly had gained a sterling reputation for its work. [SRI was/is not affiliated with Stanford University.] In April of 1953, Harrison "Buzz" Price (co-director of SRI with C. V. Wood) was called to the Disney Studio for discussions. After listening intently to Walt's plans, Price suggested a two-part study: a 10-week survey to determine the proper location for the park and a 4-month feasibility analysis of both public and private attractions and parks (in other words, will it succeed financially?). Roy was impressed with Price and authorized the payment of the $32,000 fee.

In his own way, Walt Disney already had been doing that same type of research for years. Ever since he had begun contemplating a Disney park, he had prowled through zoos of the United States and Europe, intrigued with their layouts and their methods of crowd control. At one time while planning another trip to Europe, Walt's wife

Lillian snapped that if he intended to tour more zoos, she was not going. Walt had been on the right track, for in its final report SRI stated that the San Diego Zoo had proven to be the most fertile source of information for its nation-wide feasibility study.

In 1950, while in Europe with his close friend Art Linkletter, Walt was most impressed by Tivoli Gardens (Copenhagen, Denmark) for its cleanliness, its flowers and landscaping, its illuminations at night, and its ability to bring joy to visitors. [The director of Tivoli would later be brought to California so as to obtain his insights and advice on Disneyland.] In a later conversation with Harper Goff, Walt stated that he wanted Disneyland to be a combination of an American Tivoli, Henry Ford's Greenfield Village (Dearborn, Michigan), and Colonial Williamsburg (Virginia). In Walt's personal research, he and Goff had ventured to Knott's Berry Farm on the Sunday afternoon just before Christmas of 1953. There the two men stood around in the Ghost Town, studying the movements of the crowds.

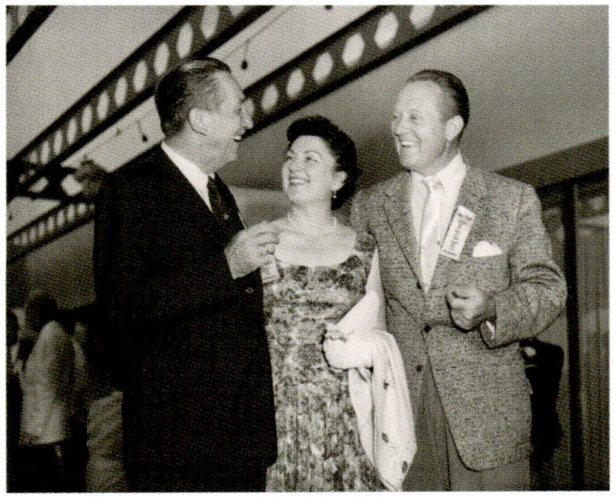

Walt Disney with Art & Lois Linkletter.

In an attempt to discover the chances for success of his family park, Disney had sent staff members to the annual convention of amusement park owners, held in Chicago in November of 1953. Many of the owners and operators turned out to be Walt's harshest critics. They were the most indifferent to and the most skeptical of the Disneyland project. One amusement park owner stated, "All of that money just for theming and landscaping? Walt's got to be kidding. It'll never go." Others predicted that, without a roller coaster or a Ferris wheel and without a dart game or a ring toss, the public just would not come. Walt should stay with what he knew, cartoons. The Walt Disney Productions Board of Directors complained to Walt that the Disney Studio was not in the amusement park business. Walt replied, "We are not in the amusement park business; we are in the entertainment business." He went on to explain his idea of Disneyland: "There's nothing like it in the entire world. I know because I've looked. That's why it will be great…because it will be unique-a totally new concept in entertainment."

Temperature averages, wind velocities, smog and fog levels, topography, road and freeway access, utilities, taxes, local building codes, local governments' support of businesses were studied in forty potential locations in and around the Los Angeles area. To add to Walt's dislike of the beach for his park, SRI further ruled out such places as Santa Monica and Long Beach due to fog and lower temperatures. Chavez Ravine lost out due to the lack of enough flat land, a demand of Walt's for his trains. The police pistol range near Canoga Park was rejected because of 15-degrees higher summer temperatures and winter temperatures 10-degrees below other potential sites. Lack of freeway access (just in its infancy in the 1950's) also eliminated many of the investigated locations.

On August 28, 1953, Walt and Roy Disney drove to the Los Angeles offices of SRI in the Pacific Finance Building to receive SRI's Final Report. A birth rate study had indicated that the center of population in Southern California was gradually moving south and east. [SRI was extremely accurate in its findings since by the 1970's that population center had moved to Fullerton, a mere four miles from Disneyland.] Due to its temperate climate, lack of scorching afternoon heat, and the absence of fog, SRI had selected Anaheim as the ideal site for the building of the park. Of special note were the soon to be completed sections of freeway at Anaheim. Interstate-5 (the Santa Ana Freeway) was then being completed, and it cut through the heart of Anaheim. SRI even suggested a number of possible sites, just off that exit, the Disney's might consider purchasing. That new highway would be in stark contrast to the past. A long time resident of the area recalled that at the beginning of the twentieth century "the road to Anaheim was just a couple of ruts zig zagging this way and that--not straight like it is now. At some seasons of the year the sunflowers grew so tall and so close to the road that they would touch your hat when driving by. It was a half a day's drive to go to Anaheim and back." All that was quickly being altered.

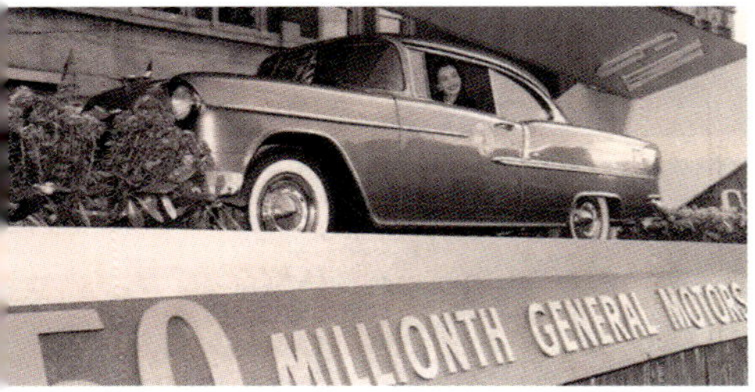

General Motors milestone.

By the 1950's, the United States was beginning to experience the freedoms and changes brought by the affluence of the post-war era and by the increasing availability of automobiles now that steel was no longer a wartime rationed commodity. General Motors drove its 50-millionth automobile off the assembly line...helping to make it the first company ever to post annual sales of more than $1-billion. Added to those facts, freeways in California were beginning to connect the small, agricultural communities with downtown Los Angeles. Now it would only be a 45-minute drive from Los Angeles to Anaheim. The freeway would also bring more residents into Orange County, and the weather in that area was ideal for attracting tourists.

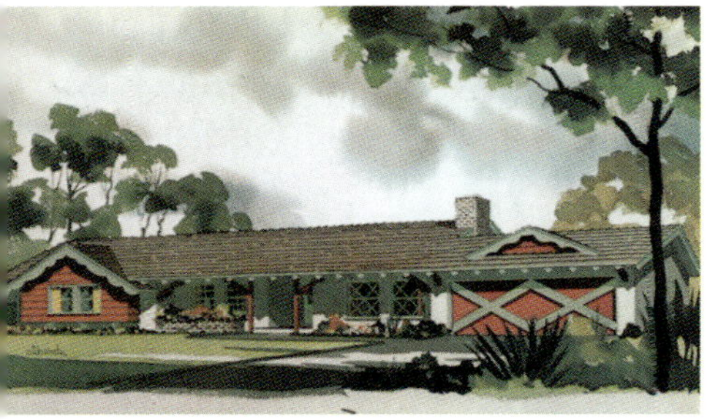

The suburban life & the American Dream.

All the necessary factors seemed to be present in Anaheim for the success of Walt Disney's latest dream. The Disney Studios had already become involved with the city of Anaheim when in the early 1950's, artists from the Studio volunteered to help in the designing of floats for the city's annual October parade, thereby creating for Disney a favorable reputation within that community. Anaheim's first Halloween Parade had been presented in 1924, started mainly as an attempt to reduce the pranks of the city's youth (soaping store windows, overturning outhouses, placing buggies on barn roofs). Over the years, the festival would continue to grow, becoming the "Greatest Night Pageant west of the Mardi Gras." By the 1950's, the parade was drawing over 150,000 spectators.

Finally, SRI estimated a reasonable "start-up cost" for the park to be $11-million. Roy Disney was so impressed by C. V. Wood and his report that Wood was hired as executive vice-president of Disneyland in charge of building the park. [Wood left Disneyland in 1956 to form his own marketing research, design, engineering, and construction company for leisure industry firms.]

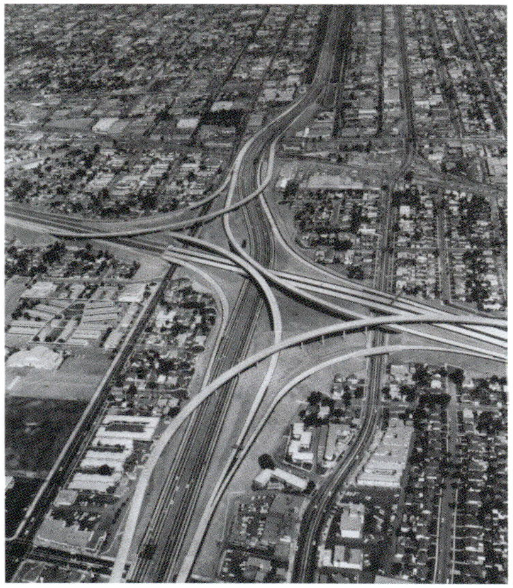

The new freeway system.

At first, Anaheim's city officials had been hesitant about the project. The mayor was the most skeptical, not wanting "no honky-tonk" enterprise in his city. Walt Disney went to work selling the idea that his park would be different than the ordinary amusement parks and carnivals (too often dirty and too often easy prey for the criminal element). Anaheim's Mayor Charles Pearson was concerned that Disneyland would also be dirty, littered with peanut shells, and full of the usual riff-raff. Walt explained to the mayor and the councilmen that there would be strict rules in a Disney park, thereby assuring that the city officials were comfortable with his plans. Walt Disney's park would have a family atmosphere, and cleanliness would be a top priority. Only shelled peanuts and no chewing gum would be sold within the park. Mayor Pearson's objections quickly were put to rest. [Pearson served as Anaheim's mayor from 1939 until his resignation in 1959.]

The acquisition of land was the immediate priority. That process was not to be without problems. One of the proposed sites was too close to a rundown cemetery, and Walt rejected it. One possible deal fell through when a real estate agent overheard a city official in a restaurant discussing the Disney plans. The agent quickly purchased parcels of that land and offered it for resale at outrageous prices. By early 1954, six different sites in and around Anaheim had been rejected. Even the final site had a few problems. First, the desired properties lay outside the city limits, and an unpredictable annexation vote would have to be held. Second, Cerritos Avenue cut through the middle of the proposed park's acreage. The willingness of Anaheim's city officials to do almost anything for Disney was expressed by City Administrator Keith Murdock: "After all this effort, we weren't going to let an arterial highway stand in our way." Thus, Cerritos was closed on that land slated to become Disneyland. Eventually, using "dummy" buyers to prevent the skyrocketing of land prices, the Disneys purchased 270-acres from seventeen families (at an average cost of $4,500 per acre). That land was covered mostly with orange groves, walnut trees, and sweet potato patches.

The plan for the construction of Disneyland in Anaheim was announced on April 2, 1954. Opening day was projected to be July 17, 1955. This date was critical to the park's success. During the early 1950's, August was the prime vacation time for American tourists. A July opening would allow Disneyland to cash in on the peak summer tourist trade. Due to labor problems and to difficulties in closing escrow on several parcels of property, the beginning of construction was delayed until summer--with ground finally being broken on July 21, 1954. While construction proceeded at a furious pace, Walt plugged his park through his highly successful, weekly television show, *Disneyland*. Time-lapse photography was used to show the progress of the construction. The final budget for Disneyland would be over $17-million. This would create yet another problem. Walt was out of cash and had no budget to finance an up-scale hotel where his guests could stay if they desired to visit the park for more than just one day or if they had to travel from long distances. Thus entered Jack Wrather, the prime developer of the Disneyland Hotel.

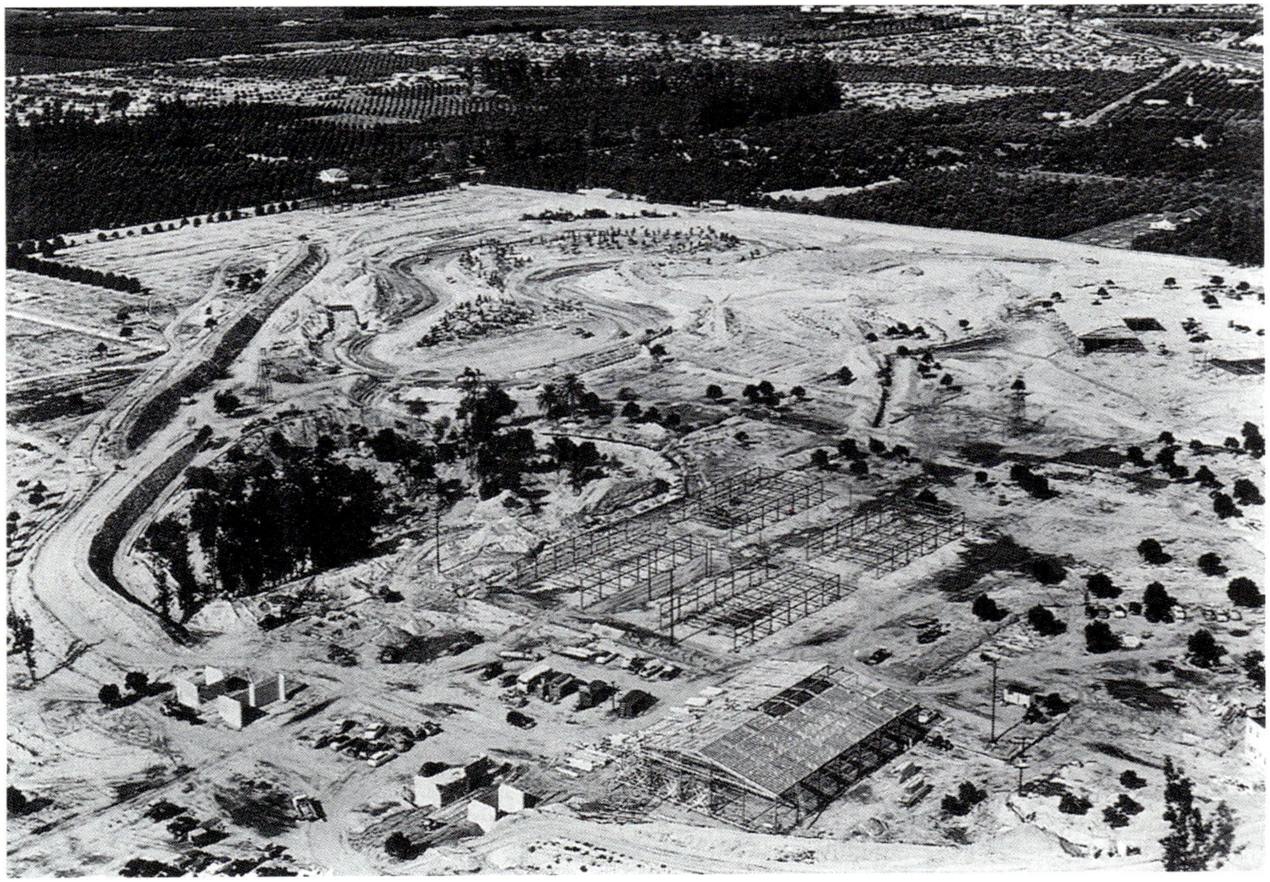

An aerial view of construction underway on Disneyland.

JACK WRATHER

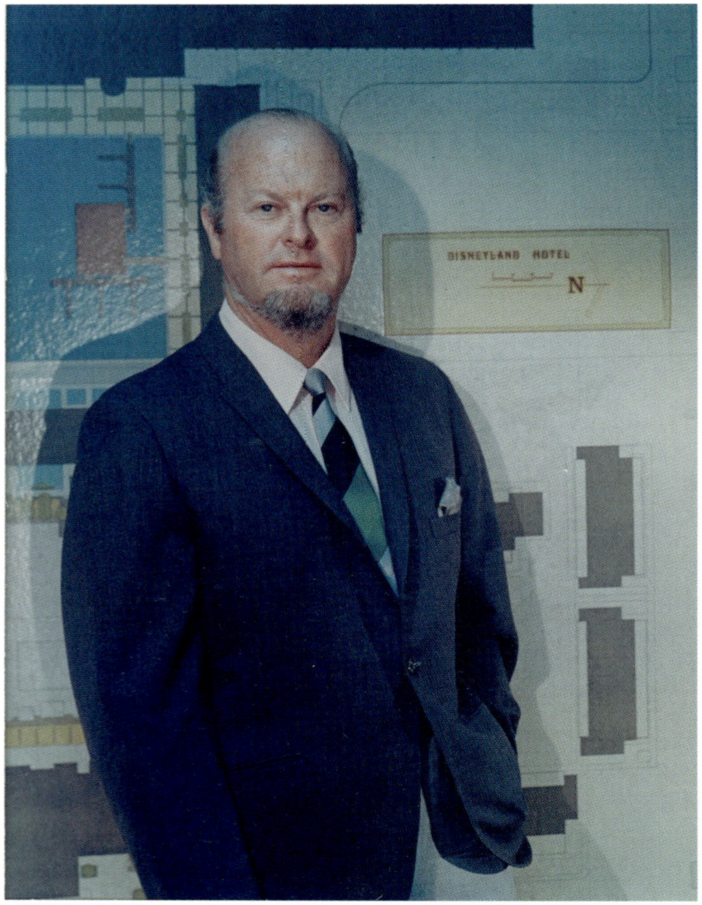

Jack Wrather.

John (Jack) Devereaux Wrather, Jr. was born in Amarillo, Texas on May 24, 1918. He was the son of Mazie (Cogdell) and John Devereaux Wrather, Sr. He attended the University of Texas from which he graduated cum laude, receiving his Bachelor of Arts degree in 1939. On July 31, 1941, he married Molly O'Daniel, the daughter of then Texas Governor Wilbert Lee (Pappy) O'Daniel. O'Daniel invited everyone in the state to come to the wedding at the Governor's Mansion. A crowd estimated at 25,000 cheered as Molly and Jack took their vows. The marriage was not fated to last, and Molly filed for divorce in 1945, with the ensuing court battles lasting until as late as 1952. During their brief marriage, Mollie presented Jack with two children, Jack D. III and Molly.

After college, Jack worked at various jobs in the oil industry...pipeline walker, wildcatter, and construction supervisor for various refineries. He also became an independent oil producer in Texas, Indiana, and Illinois. When his father fell ill in 1940, Jack took control of the family's oil interests. Under his skilled leadership, the Wrather Petroleum Company was expanded into a highly successful business.

In 1942, Wrather entered the United States Marine Corps. Trained in Quantico, Virginia, Jack rose to the rank of Commanding Officer of Aviation Training Squadron 131 prior to being sent overseas. During 1944-1945, Jack saw action in the Solomon Islands and the Philippines. For his service, he received three combat stars. He was released from duty in December of 1945 with the rank of Captain (retiring from the Marine Corps Reserves in 1950 with the rank of Major).

In 1946, Jack relocated to California, convinced that the entertainment industry would experience huge growth in the post-war era and would be a profitable investment. "After being away four and a half years," he explained, 'you get a little nervous and want to change your way of life." There he met and married actress Bonita Granville in 1947. She had been a famous child star in the 1930's and 1940's. The Wrathers built a home in the Los Angeles suburb of Holmby Hills in 1951. They would continue to reside in that home throughout their lives. Their marriage would produce two more children, Linda and Christopher.

From that point on in his life, Jack began to diversify his financial holdings (acquiring at least 25% interest in 45 companies) and entered into the motion picture business, creating Jack Wrather Pictures, Inc. and Freedom Productions. Between 1946 and 1955, Wrather produced feature films for Eagle Lion, Warner Brothers, Allied Artists, and United Artists. Wrather's films included *The Guilty* (1946), *High Tide* (1947), *Perilous Waters*

(1947), *Strike It Rich* (1948), *Guilty of Treason* (1949), *The Lone Ranger* (1955), *The Lone Ranger and the Lost City of Gold* (1958), *The Magic of Lassie* (1978), and *The Legend of the Lone Ranger* (1981).

Jack entered into television in 1951 by forming Wrather Television Productions. He met and formed a partnership with Helen Marie Alvarez of San Diego, and formed Wrather-Alvarez Broadcasting, Inc.

Helen Alvarez's interest in the media came naturally since she was the sister of the legendary Southern California television and radio pioneer Jim Harmon. As early as 1944, she had expressed an interest in television. She pioneered early studies of television's possibilities in 1946, spending every weekend visiting various stations operating throughout the United States. She read every book concerning television and took correspondence courses in electronic engineering. She met George Cameron (a wealthy Texas oil man) and John Hill (a super salesman) who both wished to invest capital in a new enterprise. The trio immediately began to formulate plans to construct a television station in Tulsa, Oklahoma. With FCC approval in hand, Miss Alvarez became president of station KOTV in 1949 with John Hill acting as commercial manager. Cameron was busy with his oil dealings and mostly stayed away from Tulsa. The station took to the airwaves on October 15, 1949. Under Miss Alvarez, the station flourished. There was no question that Miss Alvarez was solely responsible for the emergence of television in northeastern Oklahoma. At the nation's peak of interest in television, the station changed hands as Jack Wrather purchased the station. Because the Wrathers knew nothing about the management of a television station, they requested that Miss Alvarez continue with the management of the station. Alvarez would later be a partner with Jack Wrather in the earliest stages of the development, building and operation of the Disneyland Hotel. Though from all accounts, Alvarez acted mostly as a silent partner with respect to the operation of the Hotel. She first visited the Disneyland site shortly after Jack in the fall of 1954.

Being a true entrepreneur, Wrather established television syndication services such as Television Programs of America and Independent Television Corporation during the 1950's. With Wrather-Alvarez Broadcasting Company in Tulsa, Oklahoma and in San Diego and Bakersfield, California, Jack and Helen owned or co-owned KOTV-TV in Tulsa; KERO-radio, KFMB-TV, and KFMB-radio in San Diego. Also owned was WNEW-radio in New York City, which had the world's largest radio audience at that time. KOTV-TV had been purchased from Cameron Television Corporation by General Television Company on July 13, 1952. Principle owners were listed as Helen Alvarez, Jack Wrather, and Jack's mother Mazie. The KFMB stations were purchased from Kennedy Broadcasting on January 22, 1953, with principle owners being Helen Alvarez and Jack Wrather.

Wrather is probably best known for several very popular, early 1950's television programs which he produced: *The Lone Ranger* (purchased on July 15, 1954), *Lassie* (purchased on June 18, 1956), and *Sergeant Preston of the Yukon* (purchased on October 1, 1956). These programs were standards among early syndication offerings and were syndicated to both television stations affiliated with the networks and to non-affiliated, independent stations. In many ways, Wrather's operations foreshadowed some of the most significant developments in the economic support structure of television for the next generation of that medium. Wrather produced seventy-eight episodes of *Sergeant Preston of the Yukon*, eight seasons of *The Lone Ranger*, and twenty years of *Lassie* for network television.

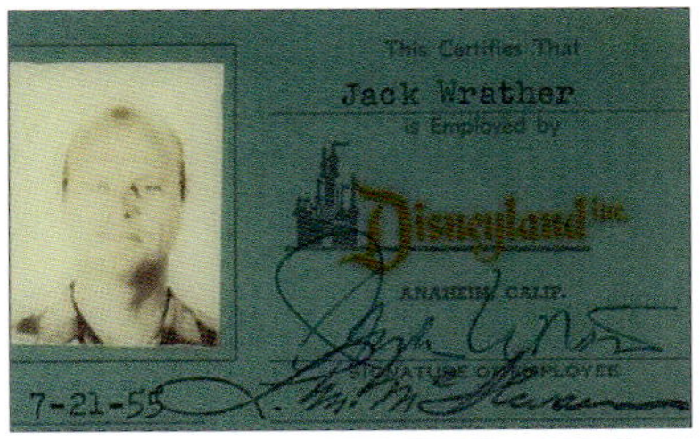

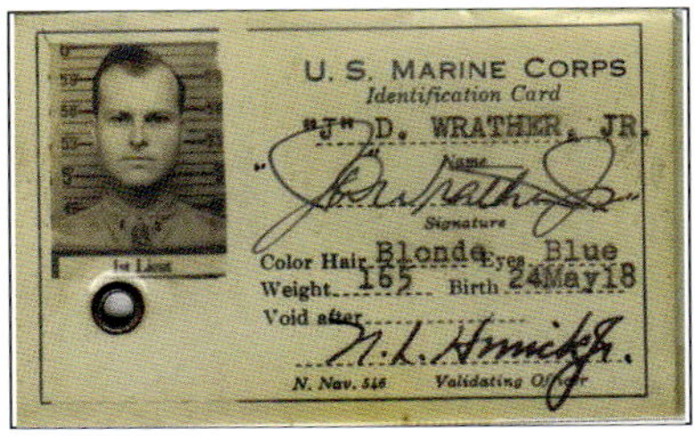

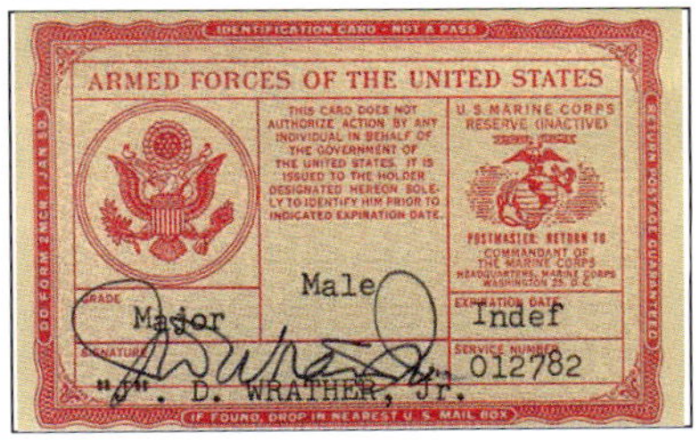

Jack Wrather's Disneyland and military ID cards & Marine Corp photograph.

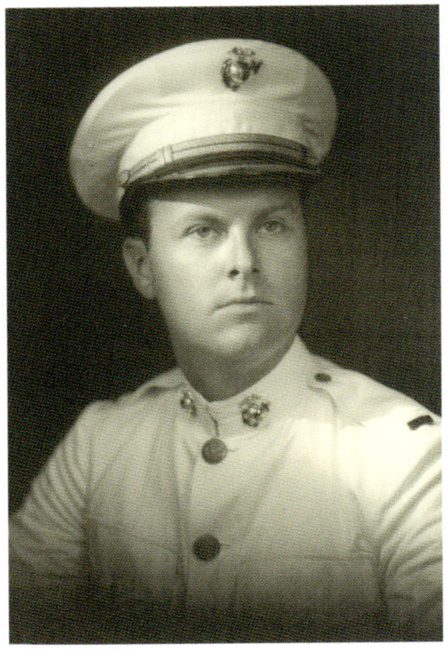

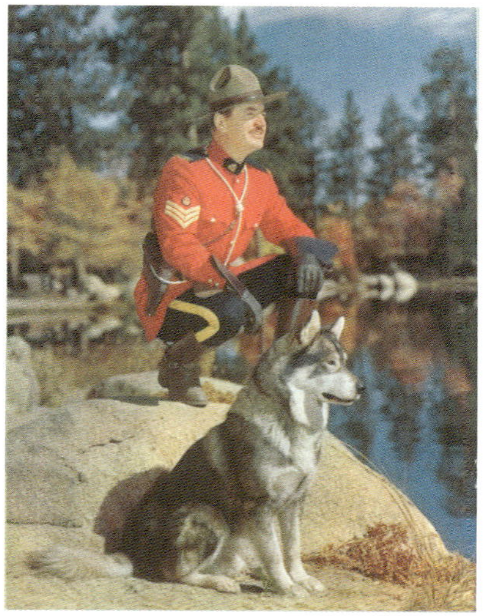

Sergeant Preston of the Yukon and The Lone Ranger.

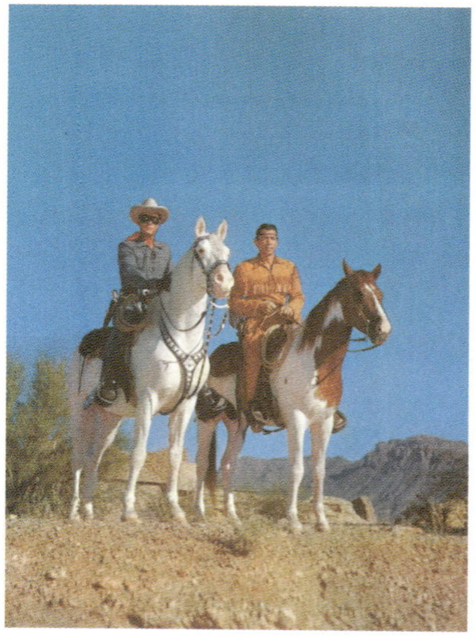

Like many of the programs for television's early years, *Sergeant Preston* had begun first as a radio series in 1947. George W. Trendle, who had also created *The Lone Ranger* radio series, created *Preston*. In 1954, Wrather bought the rights to *The Lone Ranger* from Trendle for $3-million. Wrather considered that purchase to have been an important part of American television history. Even after the passage of nearly a half century, the 221-episode, half-hour western series (licensed through the years to ABC, CBS, and NBC) remains in syndication to this date. As an interesting footnote: When Trendle sold *The Lone Ranger* to Wrather in 1954, he initially neglected to reveal that he personally owned the current Silver (the Lone Ranger's horse in that series) as well as the silver laden saddle and tack, those items not being included in the original $3-million prospective deal. Trendle demanded an additional $25,000 to close the deal and only then would he include the horse and saddle. Rumor has it that the businessmen at first planned to flip a coin to see if Wrather would or would not pay the extra money. Wrather suggested that instead they split the difference, and Trendle agreed. It was only then that Wrather received the ownership of the horse Silver and his saddle.

The next several decades saw Jack Wrather diversify into numerous other, exciting business ventures and avenues of opportunity. He became chairman of Muzak Inc., Independent Television Corporation, Television Programs of America, Inc., Stephens Marine Inc.; president and chairman of Wrather Corporation; and president of Wrather Television Productions, Wrather-Alvarez Broadcasting, Inc., Lassie, Inc., and Lone Ranger, Inc. He also became a director at Continental Airlines, TelePrompter Corporation, Capitol Records, Transcontinental Television Corporation, and Jerold Electronics Corporation. Wrather commented in 1956, "We're trying to blanket everything in the entertainment industry." He was also on the board of directors for Community Television of Southern California. In 1970, he was appointed by President Nixon to the National Petroleum Council and to the board of directors of the Corporation for Public Broadcasting in Washington, D.C.

A few of Wrather's public service activities included serving on the development board and on the executive committee of the Chancellor's Council of the University of Texas, the Board of Counselors for Performing Arts at the University of Southern California, working with the International Radio and Television Society and with the Academy of Motion Pictures Arts and Sciences. Wrather founded KCET-TV, Channel 28 in Los Angeles, an educational television station. He actively supported the Chamber of Commerce, Boys Town, the Menninger Clinic, and the Los Angeles Orphanage Guild. Wrather strongly supported Variety Club Charities (aiding members of the entertainment industry), and was a founding member of the Performing Arts Council of the Music Center.

In 1954, Jack Wrather and Helen Alvarez ventured into the hotel business, thus the origins of the Disneyland Hotel. Very early on, the Wrather-Alvarez partnership had begun to show signs of strain. Jack would be accused of "exploiting [the various] companies." Helen at times would refuse to agree to certain expenditures. In December of 1955, a meeting in Beverly Hills between Wrather and Alvarez became known as the "show down" meeting. At the May 4, 1956 meeting, Helen Alvarez was removed as Vice-President. A lawsuit was filed against Alvarez in San Diego in June of 1956. Another was entered against Alvarez in Dallas, Texas on December 10th of the following year; and the next day, a third lawsuit was filed against her in San Diego. A *Daily Variety* article on Monday, May 12, 1958, reported that "Wrather Buys Out Alvarez Interest." The result of years of disputes was the dissolution of all business relationships between Wrather and Alvarez. Beginning on September 26, 1958, the

Disneyland Hotel "officially" would be owned and operated by Wrather Hotels, Inc. and Helen Alvarez's involvement came to an end.

Jack Wrather increased his real estate holdings in 1960 with the purchase of the Balboa Bay Club in Newport Beach, California. In a letter to her son prior to the purchase, Jack's mother expressed her concerns that the resort had become "run down." On November 12, 1959, he replied: "In regard to the Balboa Bay Club, we are fully aware that it has not been operated correctly. In fact, one of our business principles is to try to buy basically good properties with big potential that for some reason the previous owners have not realized through lack of interest, bad management or other reasons." Later in that letter, Wrather invited his mother to enter into a partnership for the acquisition of that property. Within seven years, the Club had been expanded into a $15-million investment.

In June of 1961, the Wrather Corporation went public, offering 350,000 shares of common stock with Jack Wrather as President and Chairman of the Board. The Wrather Corporation had grown to include four major divisions: television and motion pictures, the Disneyland Hotel, the Muzak Corporation (the often satirized elevator music), and Stephen's Marine, Inc. The company was also involved in management services for various other marine based businesses.

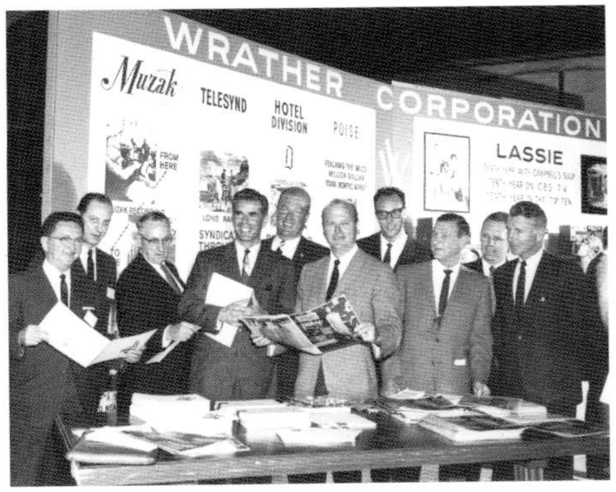

The Wrather business entities from a company shareholder function in 1964.

On January 24, 1961, Mr. A.C. Gilbert, the founder of the Erector Set Company, passed away requiring his family to sell stock to cover inheritance taxes. For $4-million, the Wrather Corporation acquired 144,000 shares of stock in the A. C. Gilbert Company, creator and manufacturer of the long popular toy. This purchase gave the Wrather Corporation a 52-percent share in the company, allowing Wrather to replace the Gilbert top executives with his own people. Due to dwindling profits (only $21,000 in the fiscal year); Wrather also brought in the firm of Product Design and Development Corporation to totally revamp the Erector system. The new management team immediately expanded the product line. Numerous new toys were created that it hoped to sell through television marketing. A $6-million order was placed by Sears Roebuck and subsequently cancelled when only too late, it was discovered that the antiquated Gilbert factory could not meet production demands.

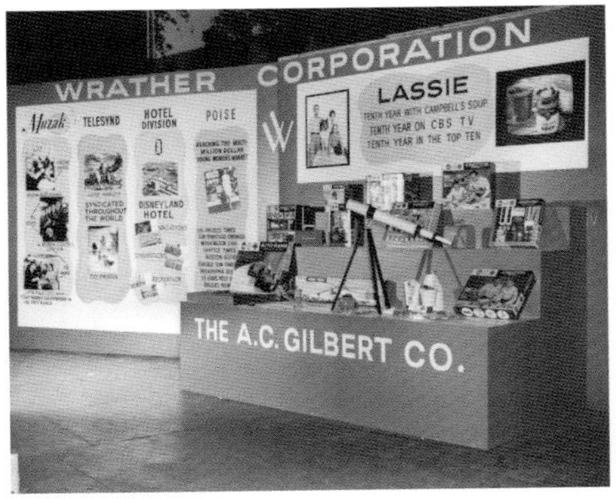

The purchase of the A. C. Gilbert Company turned out to be an unwise investment. Wrather Annual Reports for 1963, 1964, and 1965 reflected a combined three year net loss of $10.4-million due to the toy manufacturer. In an annual letter "To Our Stockholders," Jack Wrather wrote: "We have had a trying three year period in which, due to the unprofitable investment in The A. C. Gilbert Company, we reported net losses." On February 8, 1967 Wrather Corporation disposed of its investment in Gilbert and was forced to turn it over to his biggest creditor, Walter E. Hiller & Co., taking a loss of $11-million. Ownership of the Erector Set Company now passed into German hands. Almost twenty-years later, Bonita Granville Wrather would admit that "Jack was better at acquiring assets than at making money from them...."

On April 1, 1967, the Orange County Press Club honored Jack Wrather as "Headliner of the Year in Business." Held at the Santa Ana Elks Club, the event was emceed by Buddy Ebsen, popular television and movie star, who presented the award to Wrather. The citation, which accompanied the award, stated in part: "...for outstanding contribution to the economic well-being of the County and as the first to recognize and meet the need for hotels and meeting places for residents and visitors to Orange County." Further, it was noted that Wrather had changed the skyline of Orange County and had contributed greatly to the area's economy by making wise investments in the community. It was stated that Jack Wrather, from a business and industrial point of view, probably knew more about Orange County's past, present, and future than any other individual engaged in the commerce of that area. He was commended for his foresight and confidence for having risked $10-million in 1954 to build a hotel adjacent to an orange grove that Walt Disney was planning to turn into an amusement park, an extremely risky venture as predicted by so many at the time. By 1967, that "risky" venture had grown into the $30-million Disneyland Hotel.

In the 1960's, due largely to his business dealings in California, Jack became a close and trusted friend of one time film star Ronald Reagan and was instrumental in urging Reagan to run for political office. Wrather served as an advisor in Governor Reagan's "Kitchen Cabinet" and served as a member of Reagan's transition committee when Reagan was elected President of the United States in 1980. The Wrathers often socialized with Ronald and Nancy Reagan and together were involved in many charity and philanthropic endeavors.

The Wrathers with Ronald and Nancy Reagan on 4/19/82 at a White House state dinner.

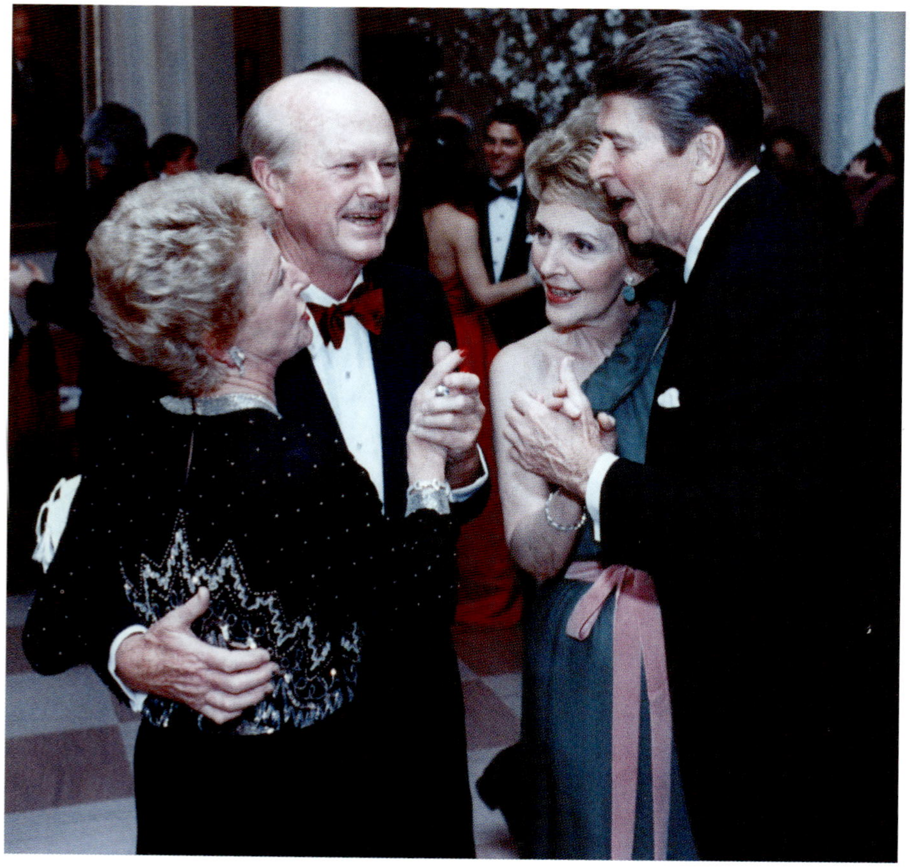

Photos courtesy of the Ronald Reagan

By the 1970's, the fortunes of the Wrather Corporation had begun to decline. Problems both in the nation's economy and unwise company investments compounded to create grave difficulties in the corporation's "bottom line." On December 31, 1971, Wrather disposed of Muzak through a trade for more shares of TelePrompter stock (already partly owned by Wrather). In 1972, a proposed plan for the complete liquidation of the Wrather company was offered to Disney. Negotiations failed when a "fair" purchase price could not be reached.

Yet another honor was bestowed upon Jack Wrather in 1975 when he received the Distinguished Alumnus Award from the University of Texas.

Inflation in the U.S. economy and high interest rates on loans created more financial difficulties for Wrather. To eliminate a troubling drain on the company, on October 15, 1980, TelePrompter was sold to Westinghouse Broadcasting for $61.6-million.

On September 1, 1980, Wrather Port Properties, Ltd. signed a sixty-six year lease for the rights to manage the *Queen Mary* and the adjoining properties in Long Beach, California. Berthed there since her final voyage on October 31, 1967, she had made 1,001 Atlantic crossings during her nautical career. Over $25-million was spent restoring the *Queen Mary*. In 1981, as a personal favor to his friend Howard Hughes, the World War II era *Spruce Goose* airplane was saved by Wrather from demolition and was given a new home next to the *Queen Mary*. The

Spruce Goose would remain there until 1992 when it was moved to Oregon and underwent extensive restoration. On June 6, 2001, the *Spruce Goose* (a.k.a. the *Flying Boat*) once again went on public display at the Evergreen Aviation Museum in McMinnville, Oregon.

In addition to the Disneyland Hotel, Wrather owned the Twin Lakes Lodge in Las Vegas, Nevada and the L'Horizon Hotel in Palm Springs, California. Jack Wrather never chose to utilize the option granted to him by Walt Disney in 1954 (which could have been quite profitable in later years) to use the "Disney" name on any other Wrather hotel properties in Southern California.

Considered one of the leading entrepreneurs of his time, Jack Wrather died in Los Angeles, California on November 12, 1984 at the age of sixty-six after a thirty-three month battle with cancer. On that day, the first telephone call received by Bonita was from the White House. With the Reagans, Bonita had a tearful conversation over the loss of her husband and their close friend.

Jack Wrather had been a member of the Methodist Church converting to Catholicism after meeting Bonita. His two marriages had presented him with four children. He was survived by his wife of thirty-seven years, Bonita Granville Wrather.

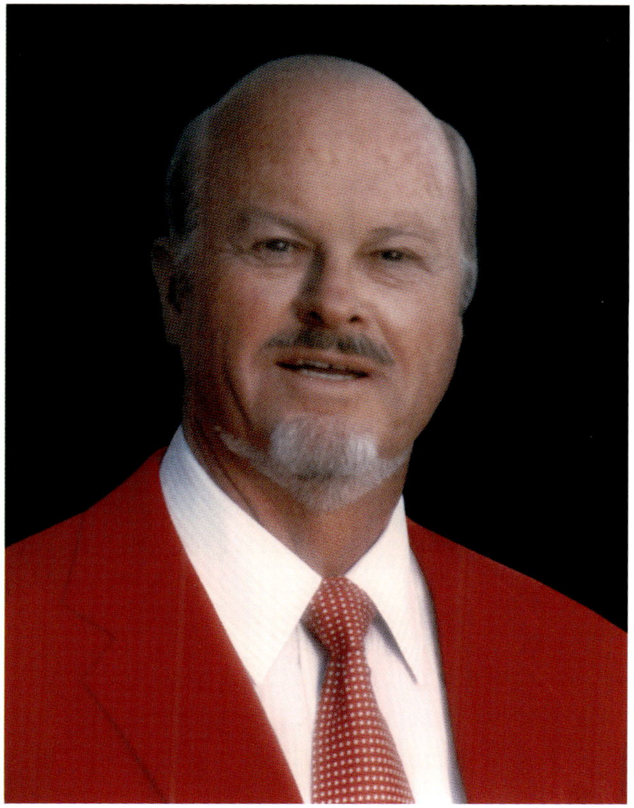

Jack Wrather - 1918-1984.

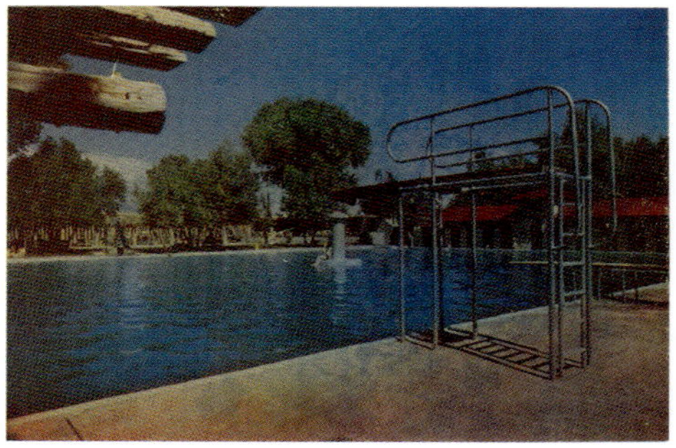

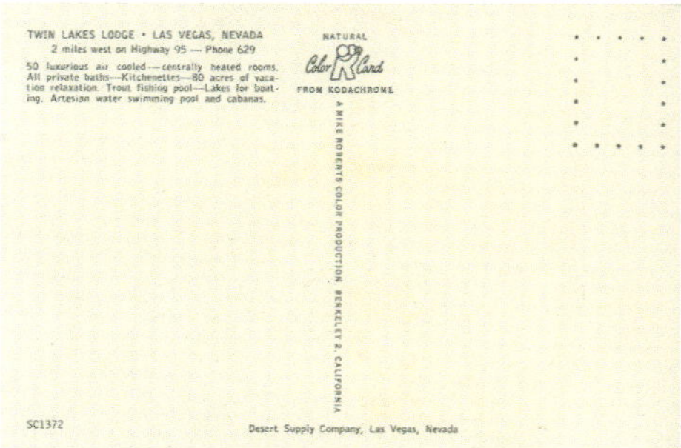

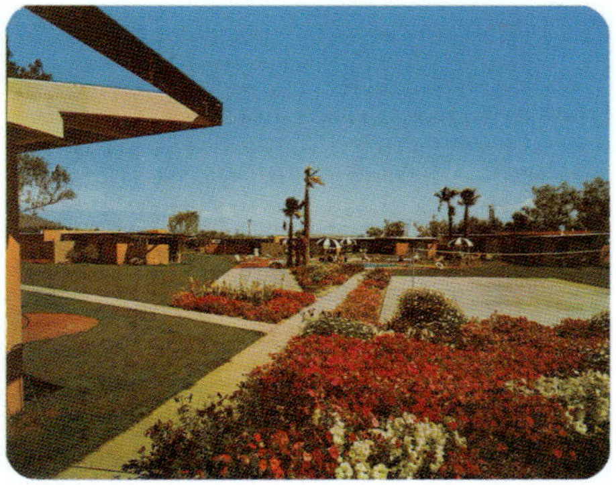

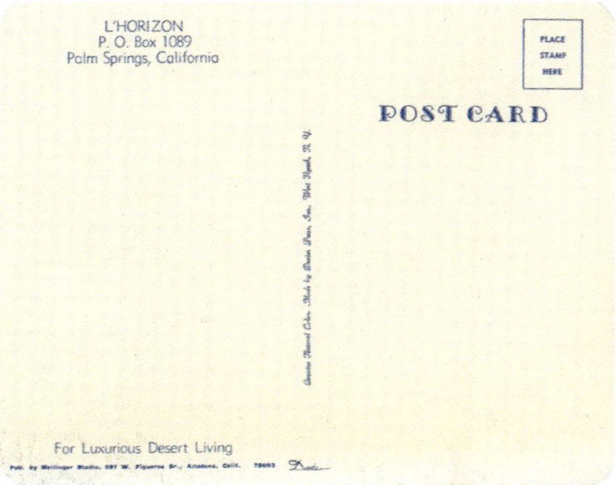

Twin Lakes & L'Horizon postcards.

BONITA GRANVILLE WRATHER

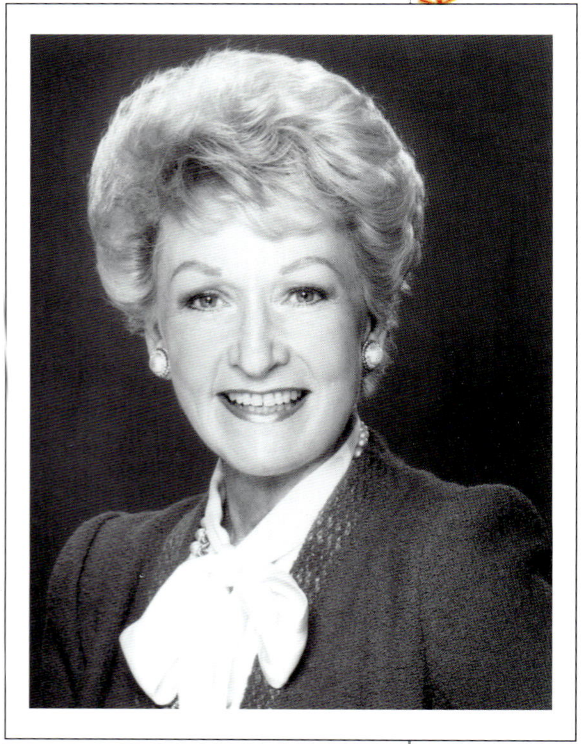
Bonita Granville Wrather.

Bonita Granville was born on February 2, 1923 in New York City into a show biz family. Her grandmother, Maria Brambilla, had been a prima ballerina in the Ballet Russe de Monte Carlo. Her grandfather, Francis Timponi, had conducted Milan's La Scala Opera. Rosina Timponi Granville was Bonita's mother. Her father, Bernard Granville, was a headliner in the *Ziegfeld Follies* and appeared in many other Broadway musicals. She first appeared on stage at the tender age of three and began making films when she was only nine.

The Depression would force the Granvilles to head west in an attempt to better the family's financial status. At the age of seven, Bonita moved with her family to California and began her film career. Her first films were *Westward Passage* (in which she played the daughter of the film's stars Ann Harding and Laurence Olivier) and *Silver Dollar*, both released in 1932. Those were followed with the role of Fanny Bridges as a child in the 1933 production of *Cavalcade* (winner of the Academy Award for Best Picture).

As a child actress, Bonita was often cast as a mean, spiteful, naughty little girl, such as in the film *These Three* (1936) in which she played a mischievous girl, spreading malicious lies about her teachers. Directed by William Wyler, produced by Samuel Goldwyn, and based upon Lillian Hellman's Broadway play *The Children's Hour*; the film starred such Hollywood heavyweights of that time as Merle Oberon, Miriam Hopkins, and Joel McCrea. For that portrayal at the age of thirteen, Bonita received a nomination for an Oscar as Best Supporting Actress (the first year that that award had been offered). She lost the award to actress Gale Sondergaard (famed for her villainous portrayals) for her performance in *Anthony Adverse*.

While Bonita worked at various studios during her motion picture career (including RKO, Fox, Paramount, and Metro-Goldwyn-Mayer), it would be at United Artists that she would find her greatest success in *These Three*. Concerning Bonita's abilities on screen, Leonard Maltin, in his book *Movie Encyclopedia*, states: "An energetic lass given to overacting, she generally played precocious, obnoxious brats, but gave a restrained, genuinely chilling performance as the mischievous Mary in *These Three*."

In *Maid of Salem* (1937), she acted with the famed Claudette Colbert and played the leader of a hysterical group of village girls who were the primary accusers in the Salem witch trials. By that year, Bonita was earning $500 a week as a supporting actress.

Soon, Bonita became Warner Brothers' resident child star, still being typecast as a nasty, little girl. Off screen, Bonita was the exact opposite of her movie persona. She was a kind, happy person, called "Bunny" by her friends (a nickname she had received from her father). She was also very intelligent and graduated from the studio high school at age sixteen. During her teen years, Hollywood tabloids and popular movie magazines related every aspect of her steady dating of child and teen star Jackie Cooper.

As a teen, Bonita occasionally played "nicer" girls. In 1939, she was selected for one of her more memorable roles when she starred as the title character in *Nancy Drew, Detective*. It was a film based upon the famous series of juvenile mystery novels. Warner Brothers attempted to extend this film into a series to rival that of MGM's successful *Andy Hardy* pictures; the planned series lasted through only three additional films.

In 1940, seventeen-year-old Bonita moved to MGM where she received mostly supporting roles in such major films as *The Mortal Storm* with James Stewart and *Escape* with Norma Shearer. Outside of MGM, she scored hits in the Alan Ladd film *The Glass Key* at Paramount and *Now Voyager* with Bette Davis at Warner Brothers. In the huge hit *Hitler's Children* in 1943, she played the blond, blue-eyed Aryan Nazi "ideal" of youth. This film was regarded as one of the best movies of that year. While *Hitler's Children* was a propaganda film that told of the horrors for young women living under the Nazi rule in Germany, it became more profitable for RKO than any of its previous pictures up to that time, even more profitable than RKO's earlier hits of *King Kong* and *Top Hat*.

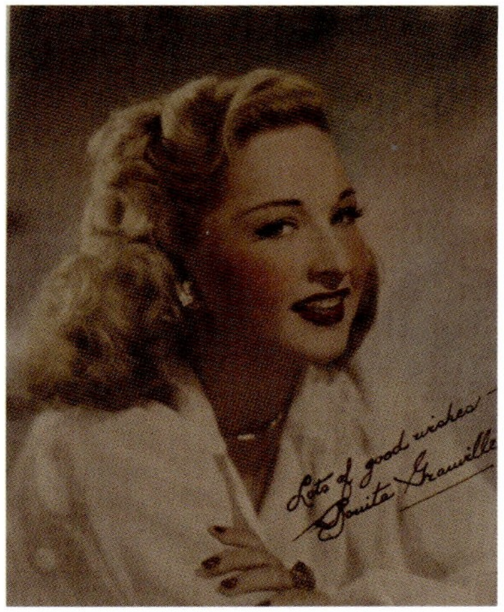

Bonita publicity photo.

In the late 1940's, Bonita's career took her to the smaller, poverty row studios such as Monogram, Allied Artists, and Eagle Lion Classics. She always seemed to manage to rise above whatever poor material she was offered. Now a young woman in her mid-twenties, she had had no problems making the sometimes-difficult transition from child star to adult star. During her screen career, Bonita Granville appeared in more than fifty-five motion pictures.

On February 5, 1947, Bonita Granville married Jack Wrather in the Catholic Church, giving up her career as an actress to become an executive in his huge business empire. She never had second thoughts about her choice to abandon an acting career. Decades later, she would reflect, "I decided that Jack was not the type of person...who would have a wife on [a film] location. He was a very strong man. And a jealous man, I'm happy to say. He wanted my time and my attention, and I gave it to him willingly and joyfully." Reflecting upon giving up her movie career, Bonita added, "I've never regretted anything."

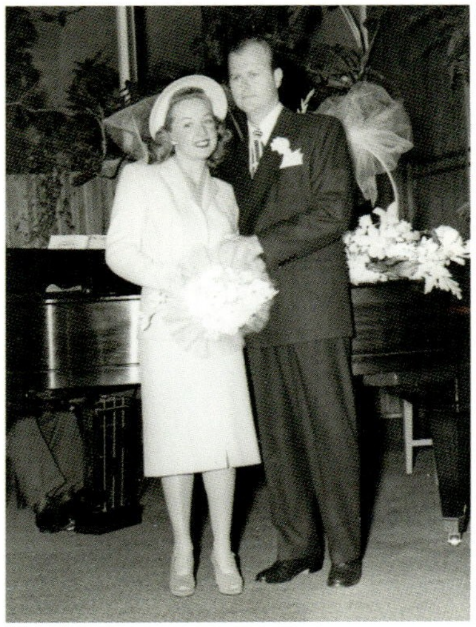

Wedding photo 1947 .

The Wrathers' Holmby Hills home had just a few reminders of her acting achievements. In Jack's den, there were two medium-size cases in which some of Bonita's movie photos were displayed. She had the cases built at Jack's request as a birthday gift.

Bonita did not leave show business entirely. In 1956, Jack Wrather purchased the television series *Lassie*, which she would produce while also producing *The Lone Ranger* series. In the late fifties and early sixties, she also resumed her acting career, this time on television. Bonita appeared in many dramatic productions, including *The United States Steel Hour*, *Climax*, *Studio One*, and *Playhouse 90*. She continued to help in the production of *Lassie* until 1972 when the show entered into syndication. Wisely, the Wrathers had retained all syndication rights to their television productions. Bonita was credited with having discovered Jon Provost, the child actor who played Timmy in the *Lassie* television series. Later, Bonita co-produced the 1978 film *The Magic of Lassie*, starring James Stewart, Alice Faye, and of course Lassie.

In 1972, President Nixon appointed Bonita as a member of the Board of Trustees of the John F. Kennedy Center for the Performing Arts in Washington, D.C.

In her later years, Bonita and her husband Jack were very active socially. They belonged to a very close circle of friends that included President Ronald Reagan and First Lady Nancy Davis Reagan (both former Hollywood actors). The Wrathers donated thousands of dollars to Reagan political causes and were very influential in the President's decision-making process.

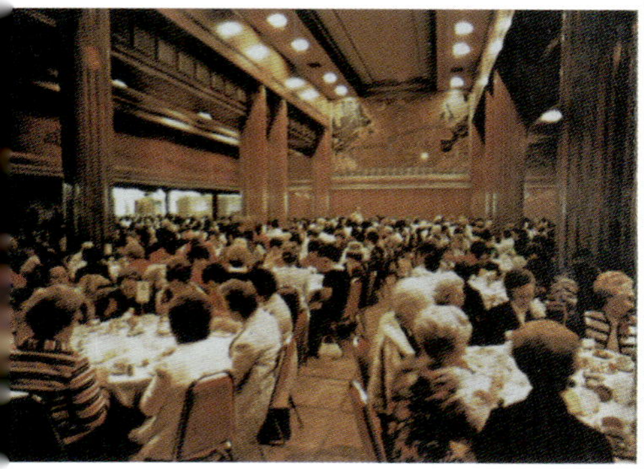

Queen Mary interior.

In 1981 and 1982, Bonita and her son-in-law Milton Schwartz played an active part in renovating the docked luxury liner *Queen Mary*. The efforts restored many sections of the ship to their original art-deco splendor. They obtained original period styled sofas, tables, and chairs to recreate an atmosphere more authentic to the ship's glory days. The *Queen* once again would gleam as before with fifty-six different varieties of woods, onyx fireplaces, silver and brass railings, and etched and leaded glass panels. After her maiden voyage in 1936, the ocean liner had provided luxurious travel across the Atlantic for such celebrities as Winston Churchill, Bob Hope, and Clark Gable. In 1951, Walt Disney had traveled on the *Queen Mary* to attend the world premiere of *Alice in Wonderland* in London. The ship's renovation was a part of the Wrather's $25-million renovation plan in Long Beach.

Ever interested in the arts, Bonita had been a founding member of the Los Angeles Music Center. In 1986, Bonita was selected as the fifth Chairman of the Board of Trustees of the American Film Institute, an organization famous for its work in preserving and restoring American films, serving in that position until her death. She was honored for her service to the American Film Institute with the dedication of the Bonita Granville Wrather Gallery in the Warners Communications building.

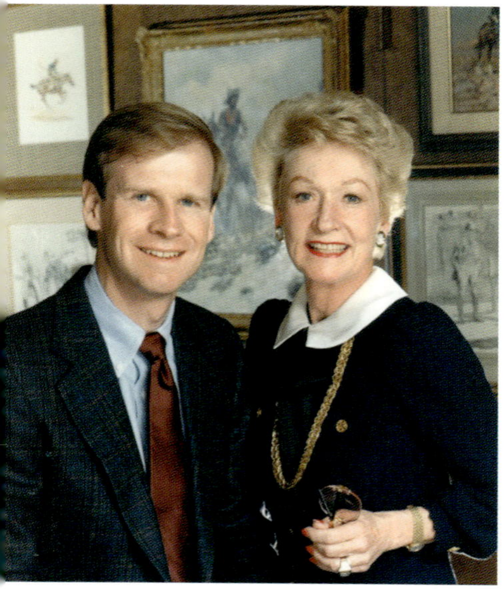

Bonita and son Christopher Wrather.

Only two weeks after the death of her husband in 1984, Bonita (a member of the board since 1968) assumed the chairmanship of the Wrather Corporation. While only five-feet-tall, she received the respect and dedication of members of the corporation. Along with her 32-year-old son Chris (CEO), she set about reorganizing the company that Jack built. The company's shares were valued at only $11-million, but there was over $112-million in long-term debts. Losing millions of dollars per year, the corporation had posted a profit only once since 1979. Pressures were great upon her to liquidate the company immediately. She chose to carefully plot a course for the company's future. Asked her first reactions to assuming leadership of the firm, Bonita replied: "Fear. Fear in capital letters."

Each morning before eight o'clock, she would drive herself to the office, never having liked the pretentiousness of a chauffeur. She seldom left the office before seven o'clock in the evening. As had been her habit for years, Bonita carried business files back and forth between office and home in a wicker basket. In a February 1986 interview, she reflected, "I love coming into the office in the morning. I don't like ladies' lunches. I don't want to get a facial or have my hair done every day. My life has always been going to lunch with the fellas."

The company's film library of *The Lone Ranger*, *Lassie*, and *Sergeant Preston of the Yukon* episodes was sold to Southbrook Entertainment for $10-million, taking the Wrather company out of the entertainment business for the first time since 1946. Now out of the oil industry and radio broadcasting, the Wrather Corporation was basically the Disneyland Hotel and the *Queen Mary* (with a handful of other minor holdings). By the end of Bonita's first year in control, the company's debts had been reduced by 25-percent and the company had realized a profit in its third quarter of $8-million.

As a 1973 *Business Week* article had predicted, "Ironically, it was the most successful venture--the hotel--that did the company in. Though it managed to carry Wrather through many storms, it recently had to borrow $24-million to add a convention center and marina. And the resulting heavy debt costs chopped the hotel's earnings...by well over half. Management then wanted to build more rooms to help pay off the new facilities, but the debt precluded raising the necessary funds." Even Bonita's efforts, while beginning to turn the company around, could not delay the liquidation of the Wrather Corporation at the end of 1987.

Unlike many other child stars, who frequently suffer at least one unsuccessful marriage, Bonita was married to only one husband for thirty-seven years until Jack Wrather passed away in 1984. A lifelong member of the Catholic Church, Bonita Granville Wrather passed away in Santa Monica on October 11, 1988 due to cancer at the age of sixty-five. She was laid to rest next to Jack at Holy Cross Cemetery in Culver City, California, close to the grave of Ava Gardner. At her death, Bonita left behind a very full and rewarding life and an on-screen legacy that will last for generations to come.

Bonita's memory also lives on in Anaheim. Two locations at the Disneyland Hotel were named to honor her: Granville's Steak House Restaurant and the Bonita Tower.

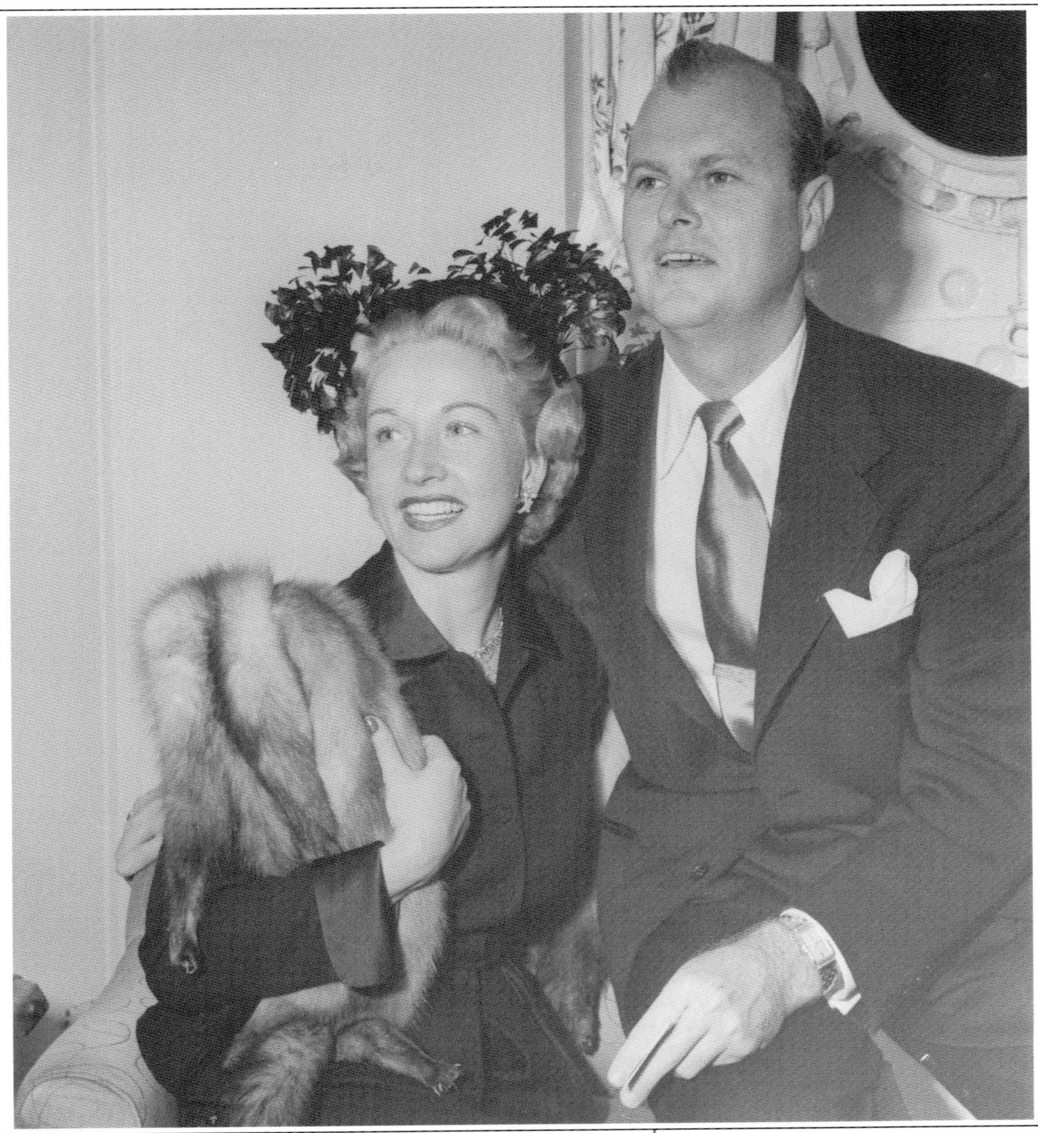

Jack and Bonita Wrather in 1949.

THE DISNEYLAND HOTEL 1954-1959

Hotel brochures from the 1950's.

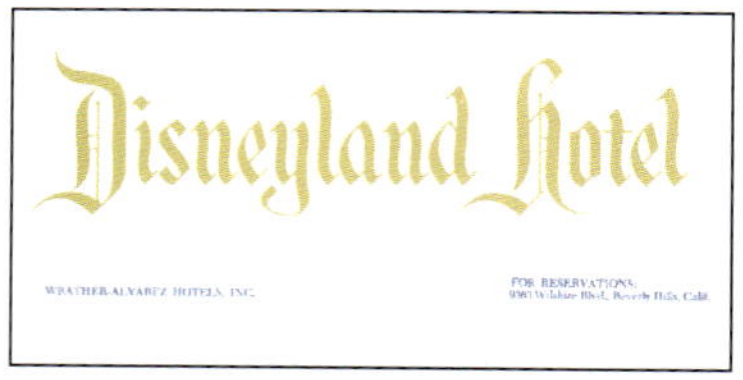

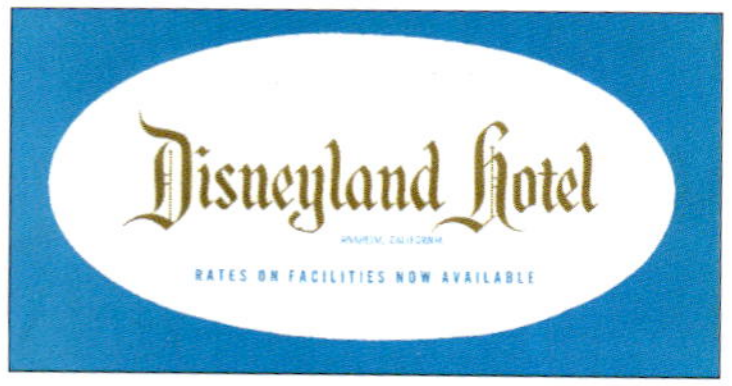

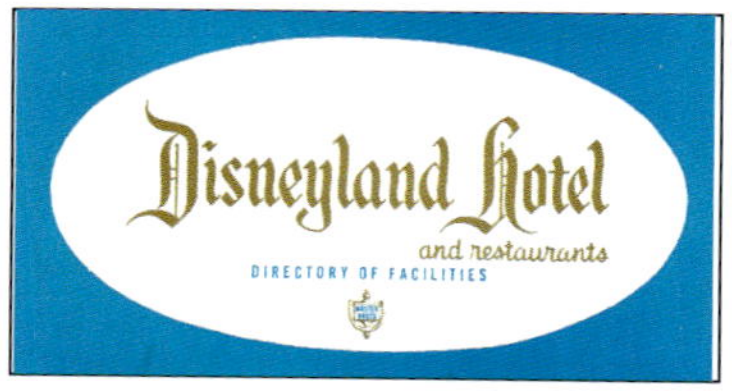

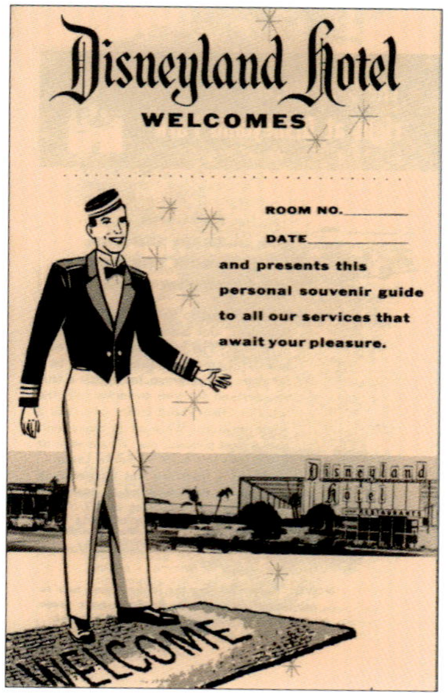

Walt Disney was convinced that, for the complete success of his theme park, an up-scale hotel would need to be built right next to his Park. That was especially true if he hoped to lure guests who would have to travel long distances.

During the spring of 1954, Walt Disney approached Texas oil wildcatter and television pioneer Jack Wrather with the possibility of his building accommodations for the many guests that Walt believed would flock to his innovative "Theme Park," then under construction in Anaheim, California. Since the imagineering and the building of

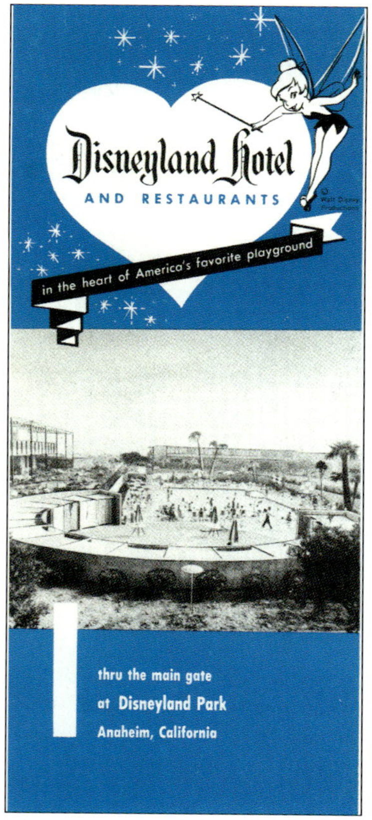

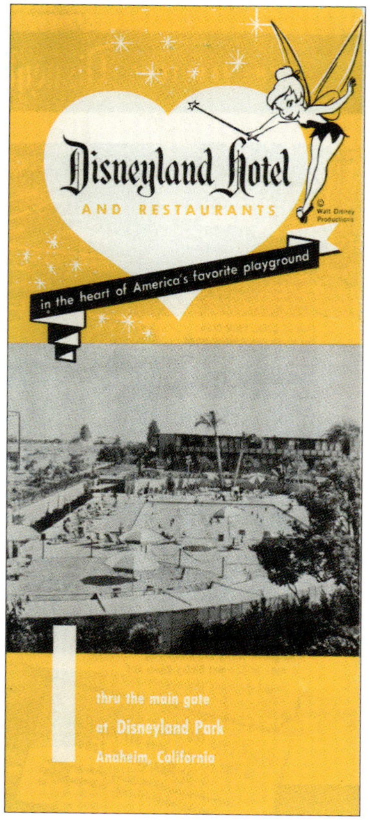

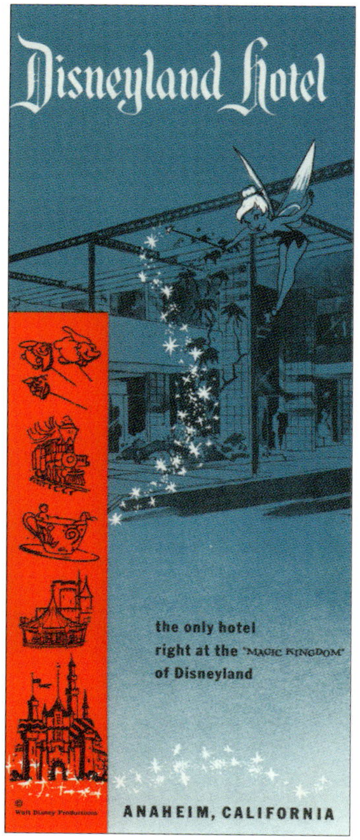

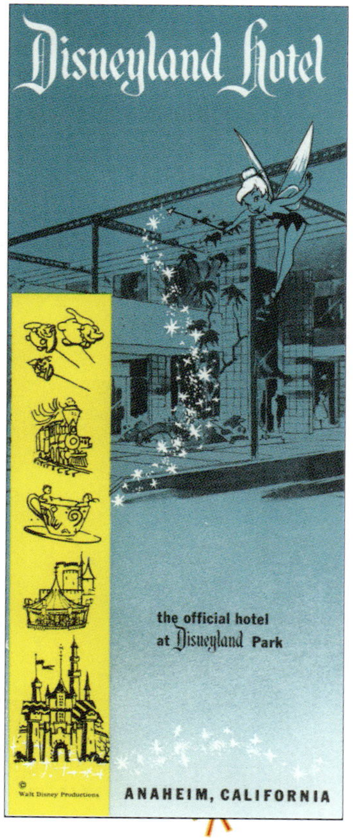

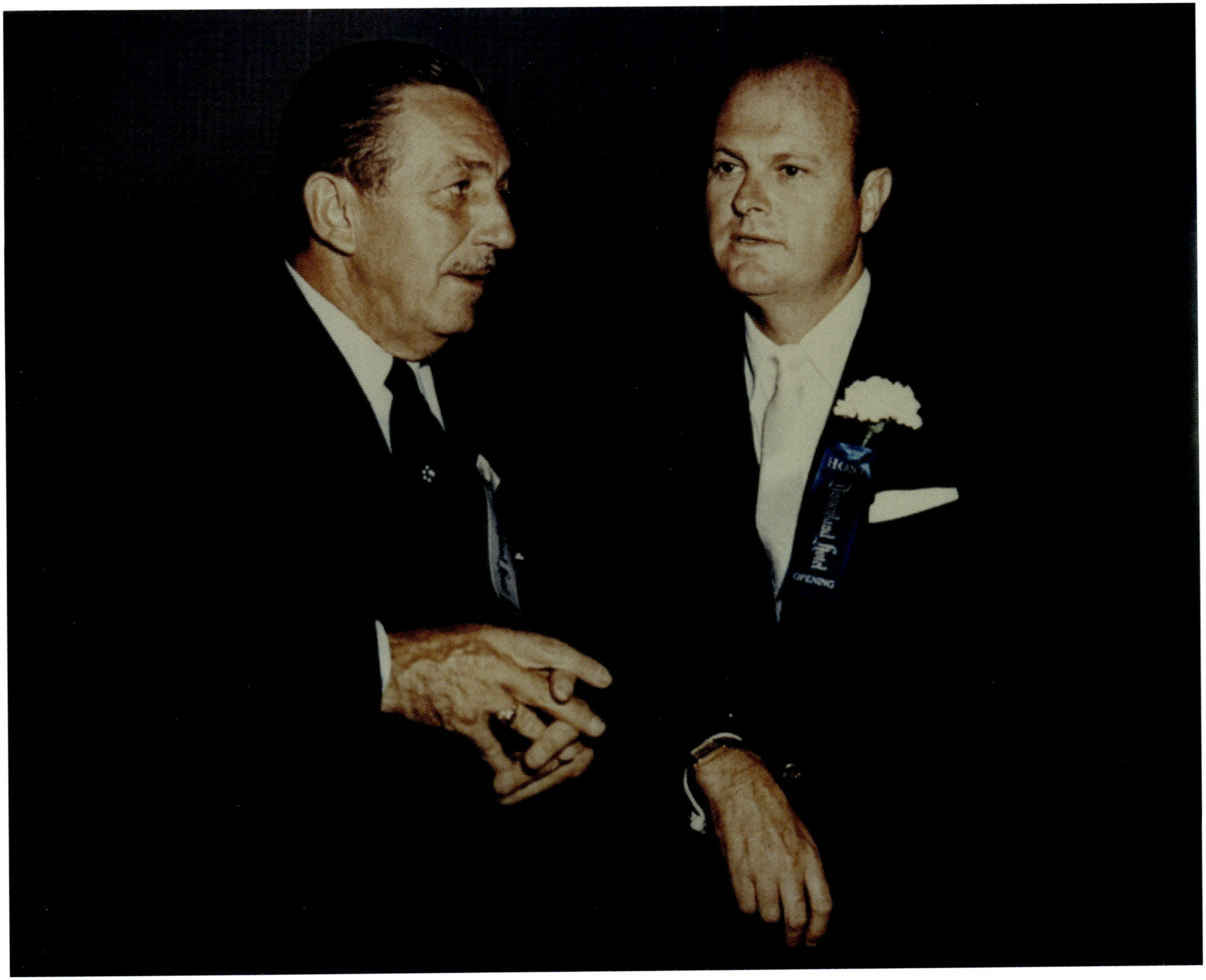

Walt Disney and Jack Wrather at the Disneyland Hotel's opening day celebration.

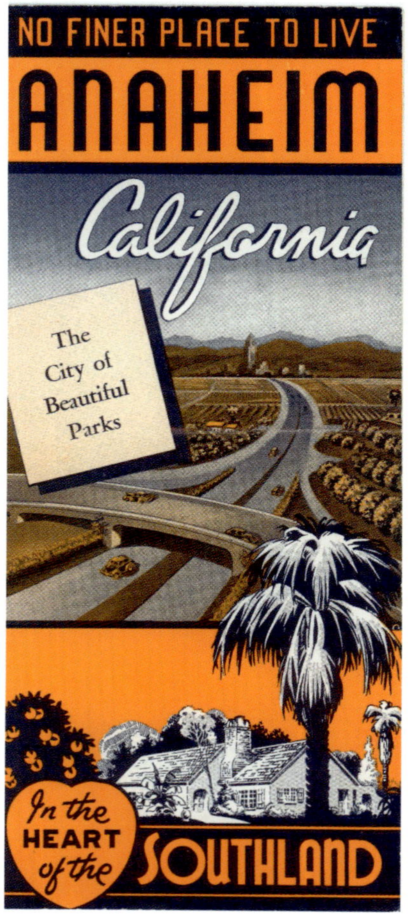

Anaheim brochure.

PEREIRA & LUCKMAN

planning architecture engineering

los angeles new york

Disneyland were taking nearly every penny he had, Walt approached his long-time friend, hoping that Jack would be willing to take such a huge risk. Wrather was the producer of popular early 1950's television programs and was flush with cash due to their success and from his other business concerns. Originally, Walt had approached Hilton executives and executives of other well-known hotel chains, hoping to convince them to finance the construction of a first-class hotel next to Disneyland. The general consensus was that such a venture was too much of a gamble. No one was certain that what was quickly becoming known as "Disney's folly" would be successful.

At the start of the 1950's, Anaheim was a little-known community, largely comprised of orange groves with a population of 14,556. Its police officers were expected to supply their own cars when on duty. The city jail was known as "the worst jail north of Tijuana," having only two cells. In 1947, an acre of land had sold for $2,750; by 1954, that price had risen to an average of $6,000 an acre. By 1954, the entire city had only two motels and five small hotels, providing a mere eighty-seven guest rooms. Seemingly unnoticed, Anaheim was becoming a "boom town," annexing thousands of acres annually and doubling its population every three years.

Walt invited Wrather for a visit to Anaheim, giving him the excuse that he wanted Jack's advice concerning the Park. As the two men toured the Disneyland construction site, it became apparent that Walt wanted much more than advice; Walt actually had something quite different in mind, money...money to be invested in a new hotel. Wrather admitted at the time that he was somewhat skeptical about building a large hotel in such a small community (approximately 30,000) and next to an experimental and yet unfinished theme park. His doubts were further increased by the fact that the risky venture had already been turned down by more than one major hotel chain. His first answer to such a proposition was "No," but Walt was persistent. Jack Wrather spent several days with Walt Disney, looking into the area's potential for expansion. Legend has it that Walt had tears in his eyes while describing his dream of Disneyland and the necessity for a new hotel. With a sense of adventure, Wrather became convinced that the idea just might be a success. With Walt showing such emotion for and dedication to his project, how could Wrather have resisted?

With an agreement to help Walt having been reached, one of the first discussions between the two friends was where the hotel should be located. Wrather first talked of locating the hotel near the entrance to Disneyland. Disagreeing, Walt said, "Jack, our guests aren't going to be thinking about a hotel when they begin their visit to Disneyland. They'll start looking for a room when they leave the park. The best place to build your hotel is near the Disneyland exit." Wrather agreed with Walt's logic and leased 60-acres of Disney owned land on the west side of West Street directly across from the Disneyland exit. There he built what was to become known as the "Official Hotel of the Magic Kingdom." Walt had also sweetened the deal by offering Wrather a 99-year lease on that land and the exclusive rights for the use of the "Disney" name for any future hotels that Wrather might build in Southern California.

On December 27, 1954, the architectural firm of Pereira and Luckman of Los Angeles was retained to design the Disneyland Hotel. A year and a half earlier that same firm had been fired by Walt Disney due to creative differences over the design for the master plan of the Disney park. [The partners had been architecture students together at the University of Illinois at the beginning of the Great Depression. Lack of jobs in their chosen field caused them to spend decades in other pursuits. Luckman worked his way up in the soap industry, finally becoming the head of Lever Brothers. Pereira spent many years renovating theatres before he became a set designer in Hollywood. In 1949, he received the Oscar for his photographic techniques utilized in Cecil B. DeMille's *Reap the Wild Wind*. Pereira returned to architecture in 1949. The firm of Pereira & Luckman was formed in 1950 with a mere ten employees. Due to the company's tremendous success by 1955, it then employed more than 400 persons...with more than $500-million in projects under construction. During their brief partnership (which ended in 1958), they collaborated on such well known projects as the NASA Space Center at Cape Canaveral, Florida and in California on the CBS Television City Studio and the Los Angeles International Airport.]

On January 18, 1955, the planned development was revealed when a Disneyland representative applied to City Planning Engineer, R.W. Mungall to reclassify the zoning in the area [of the proposed Hotel property] from rural-agricultural (R-A) to commercial (C-2) to permit a general commercial center.

On January 25, 1955, the first plans for the Hotel were presented to Jack Wrather. On that same date, Wrather's application for a $650,000 loan was approved to cover beginning construction costs. Contractors Harold M. Hodges and Byron E. Vandegrift (each with independent offices but combining their resources and talents for this joint venture) were retained to build the Hotel. [In 1951, Byron Vandegrift had constructed the Wrathers' home on Delfern Drive in Holmby Hills.] On July 22nd, Wrather would secure another loan for the Hotel in the amount of $1.25-million at 10-percent interest. The projected cost for the first phase of the Disneyland Hotel's development was set at $3-million.

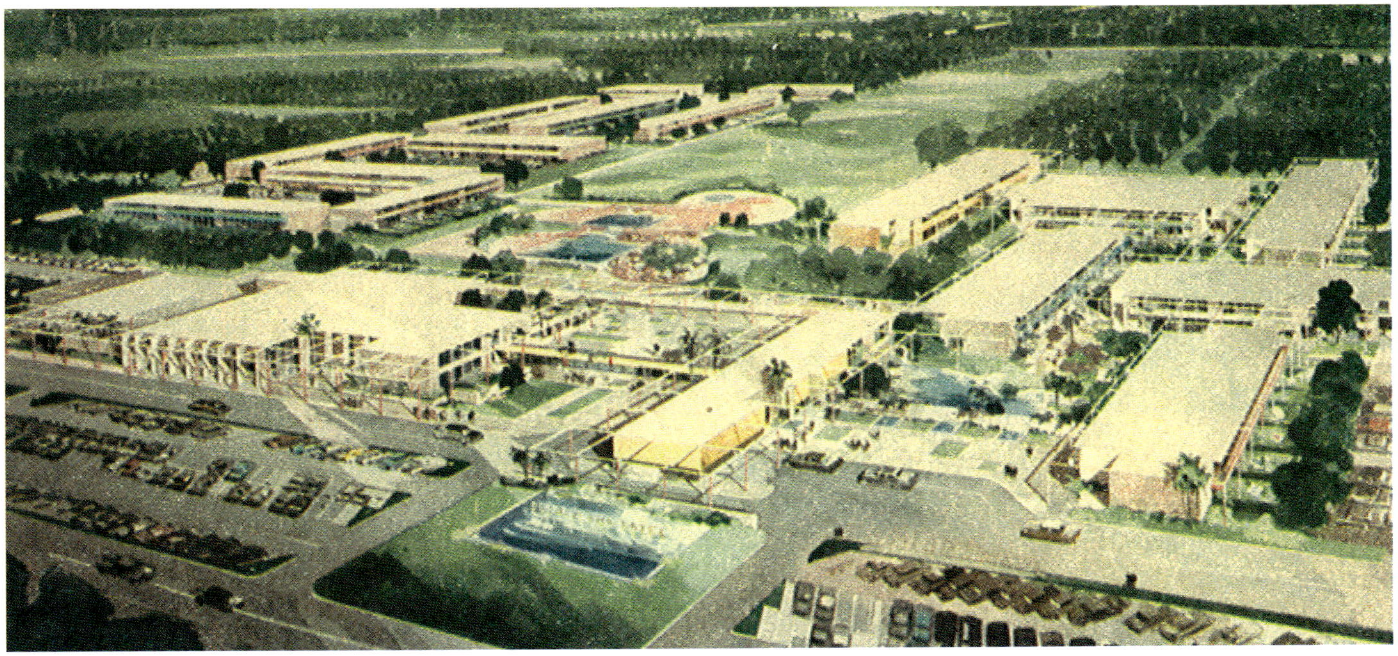

Artist concept of the Disneyland Hotel 1955. The structure would combine the luxury of a resort hotel with the convenience of a motor hotel.

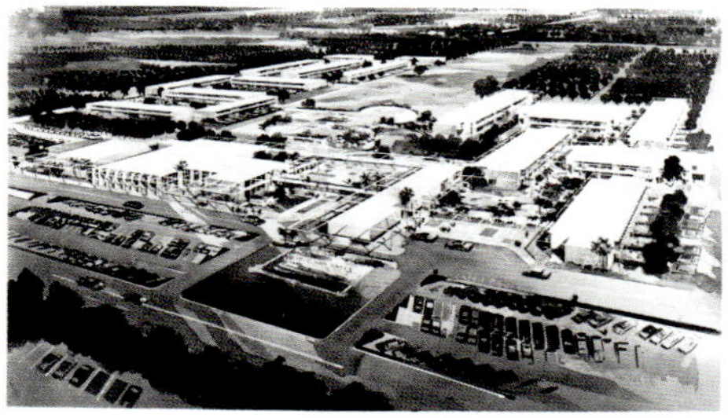

Plans for Slated Major Hotel Development Told

Plans for construction of what it was stated will be "the largest hotel and motor hotel" built in California since before World War II and representing in its entirety expenditure of more than $10,000,000 was announced yesterday by Disneyland, Inc.

It will contain 500 rooms and will be built by a group headed by Los Angeles and Texas Industrialist Jack Wrather on a site adjacent to Walt Disney's $14,000,000 Disneyland project at Anaheim.

Also stated was that associ-

EXTENSIVE HOTEL

Continued from Ninth Page

pected to visit Disneyland annually.

It is being planned and designed by the architectural and engineering firm of Pereira & Luckman.

The Disneyland Hotel will adjoin the 160-acre Disneyland project near the Santa Ana Freeway, it was disclosed.

Description

Description of the hotel project also stated the following:

It will have color TV in each room and it will have a swimming pool, a children's playground, a nursery, golf course and a wide range of other recreational facilities.

It will also include several restaurants with a total seating capacity of 1250, cocktail lounges and bars seating 500, along with a shopping service to service hotel residents and also residents of the area and visitors to Disneyland Park.

Busses will run from the hotel to Disneyland on a five-minute schedule, Wrather revealed, as part of the hotel operation, although the hotel itself will be situated immediately adjacent to the Disneyland entrance.

Wrather now owns and operates Palm Springs' L'Horizon and Las Vegas' Twin Lakes Lodge, described as highly successful hotel properties.

Construction is slated to begin immediately on the new project and one section, approximately 200 rooms, is expected to be ready for operation and occupancy at the time of the formal opening of Disneyland, scheduled for midsummer, 1955, it was announced.

From the Los Angeles Times, January 23, 1955.

On Friday, March 18, 1955 at 11:15 A.M., near the Edison high power lines at the southeast section of the property, Jack Wrather, Bonita Granville Wrather, and Anaheim's Mayor Charles Pearson, using a gold-plated, three-handled shovel, officiated at the groundbreaking ceremonies for the Disneyland Hotel. The ceremonies were held in the midst of busy workmen who had already begun laying the foundation for the Hotel. Among the thirty guests attending the event were Roy Disney (brother of Walt Disney) and C. V. Wood (formerly of SRI and now Disneyland, Inc.'s vice-president and general manager), representing the Disney's at the ceremonies, architect William Pereira, representing his architectural firm which was in charge of the design of the Hotel (Charles Luckman RSVP'd due to a vacation in Europe) and Harold Hodges and Byron Vandegrift the contractors in charge of construction on the Hotel. Also present were Herbert Perry, the President of the Anaheim Chamber of Commerce, members of the Anaheim City Council, and leaders of the area's businesses and civic organizations. At the ceremony's end, Mayor Pearson presented the gold-plated shovel to Jack Wrather as a souvenir of that special day's events. Helen Alvarez was invited but did not attend for reasons unknown.

Break Ground For New Hotel At Disneyland

Groundbreaking ceremonies for the new $10,000.000 Disneyland hotel and Motor hotel to be erected by the organization headed by Jack Wrather of Los Angeles and Mrs. Helen Alvarez of San Diego were held Friday on the 30-acre site in Anaheim adjoining the new Disneyland Park.

Mayor Charles Pearson, Herbert Perry, president of the Anaheim Chamber of Commerce, members of the Anaheim city council, and civic and business leaders of Anaheim joined in the ceremony.

C. V. Wood, Jr. vice-president and general manager of Disneyland, Inc.. represented Walt Disney at the ceremony. William Pereira, of the architectural engineering and designing firm of Pereira & Luckman, who are designing the structure, represented the architects.

Mrs. Jack Wrather (actress Bonita Granville) assisted Mayor Pearson in turning the first shovelful of dirt. Mayor Pearson then presented Wrather with the gold-plated shovel used in the ceremony as a souvenir of the occasion.

Following the ceremony the group, some 30 in all, moved to the Water Wheel restaurant in Anaheim for an official luncheon at which Clyde Cromer, chairman of the industrial committee of the Anaheim C. of C., acted as master of ceremonies, and Mayor Pearson welcomed the new enterprise to the community.

GROUND BROKEN FOR NEW DISNEYLAND HOTEL

Some 30 civic leaders of Anaheim turned out yesterday for the ground-breaking ceremonies of the new $10,000,000 Disneyland Hotel and Motor Hotel to be constructed on a 30-acre site adjoining the new Disneyland Park.

The hotel is to be erected by an organization headed by Jack Wrather, Los Angeles, and Mrs. Helen Alvarez, San Diego, who also are the owners of San Diego's television station KFMB-TV. Mrs. Wrather, who is Bonita Granville of the screen, assisted in turning the first shovelful of earth.

Among those on hand were Mayor Charles Pearson, Anaheim; Herbert Perry, president of the Anaheim Chamber of Commerce, members of the Anaheim City Council and other civic and business leaders.

Anaheim newspaper articles detailing the Hotel's groundbreaking. Four newspaper representatives were present: Anaheim Bulletin, Santa Ana Register, Long Beach Press Telegram and the Los Angeles Times.

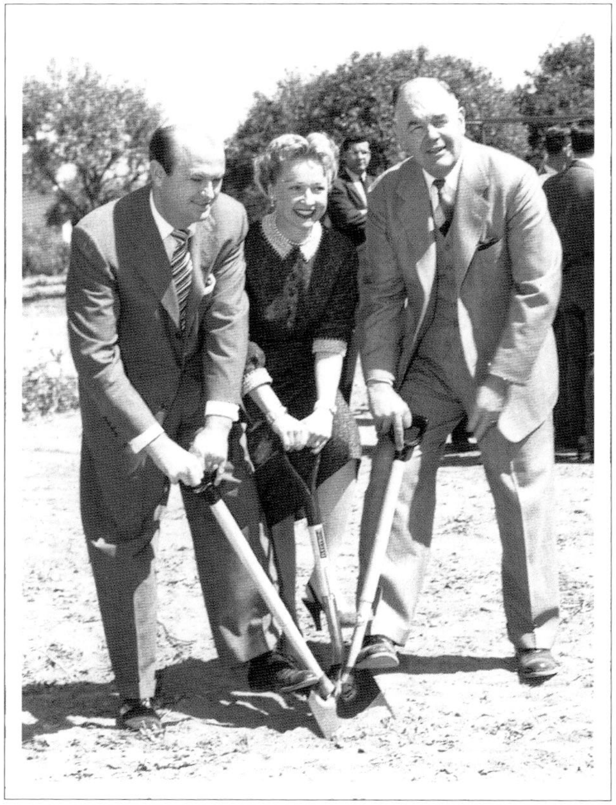

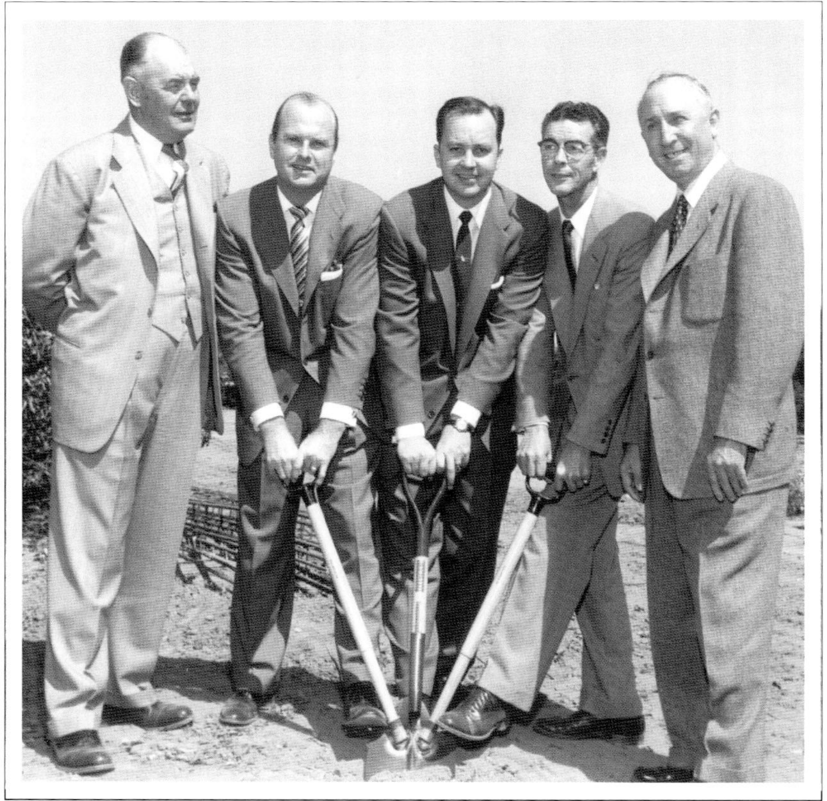

Groundbreaking photographs with Anaheim Mayor Charles Pearson, Jack Wrather and Bonita Wrather. Roy Disney is present on the far right of the second photograph.

Following the groundbreaking, (scheduled at 12:00 noon) the assembled guests attended a luncheon, held at Anaheim's Water Wheel Restaurant located at 7842 S. Euclid, Anaheim. Herb Perry opened the meeting welcoming the Disneyland Hotel on behalf of the Chamber of Commerce. He then introduced Clyde Cromer, the chairman

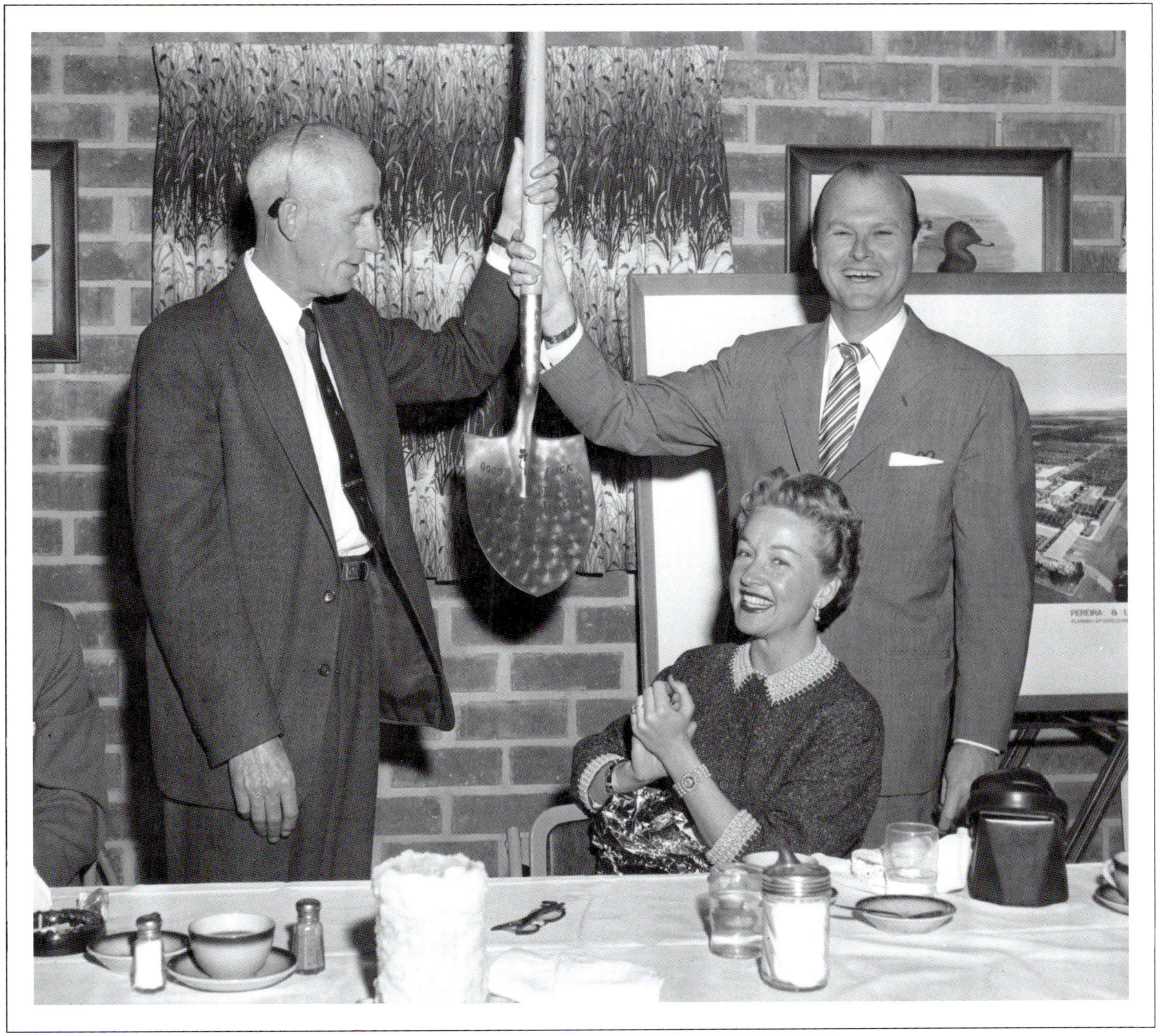

Jack and Bonita with Clyde Cromer at the post-groundbreak luncheon.

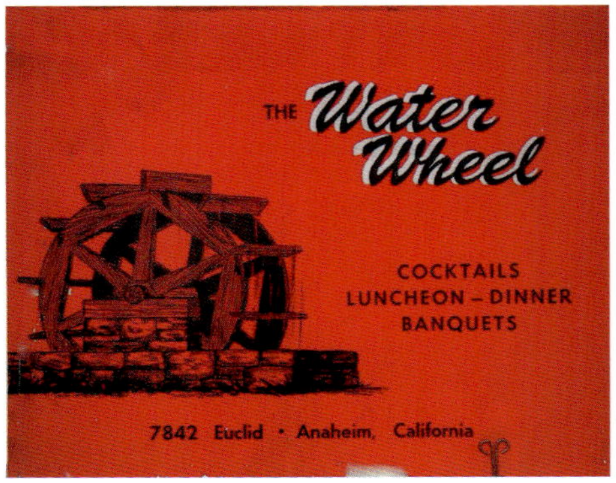

Water Wheel menu circa 1955.

of the Chamber of Commerce's industrial committee, who officiated as master of ceremonies. Mayor Pearson then followed introducing Anaheim's city officials. During the luncheon, Wrather, with the aid of an artist's rendering, explained the organization's plans for the construction and operation of the Hotel. Wrather also announced that at least 40 large companies had contacted him about holding annual conventions at the Hotel.

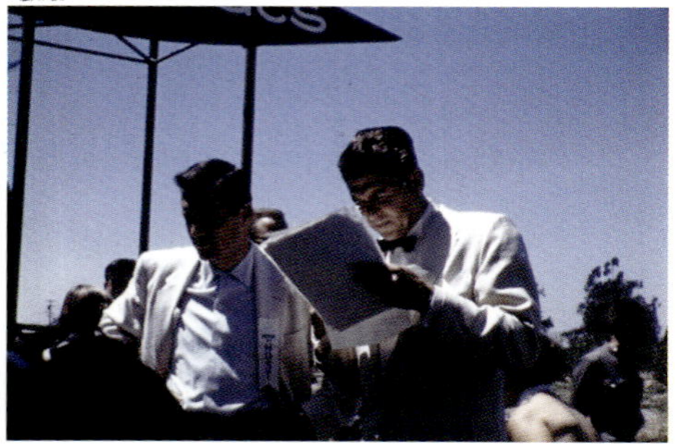

Ronald Reagan preparing to interview Jack and Bonita Wrather.

Around the time of the groundbreaking, Wrather received a "Projection Report" from the consulting firm of Harris, Kerr, Forster and Company. It was estimated conservatively that the Disneyland Hotel would have a $450,000 net profit after the first year. Wrather commented, "It certainly makes me feel good." It had been expected that the signing of the lease agreement for the 60-acres of Disney property would occur on March 25th. Due to delays, the lease would not be approved until April 12th, nearly a month after the groundbreaking.

Dateline Disneyland, the Park's Grand Opening, was a live, 90-minute, ABC broadcast at 4:30 p.m. Pacific time on Sunday, July 17, 1955. Jack and Bonita Wrather were interviewed by their friend, actor Ronald Reagan (near the short lived Phantom Boats attraction). The Hotel was briefly mentioned, but the interview seemed to get sidetracked onto Walt's new Park and how all of it could not be seen in only one short day. As the interview neared its conclusion, Bonita told Reagan that he "and Nancy have got to bring the kids and come out and stay with us [at the Hotel]." He agreed and dismissed the Wrathers so that they could enjoy a boat ride. With the Wrathers walking off camera, Reagan suddenly realized that he had forgotten part of the planned plug for the Hotel; and he quickly added, "You know, this is a good chance to tell the people that's a $10-million hotel with swimming pool and everything. Then you can take two or three days [to see the Park]."

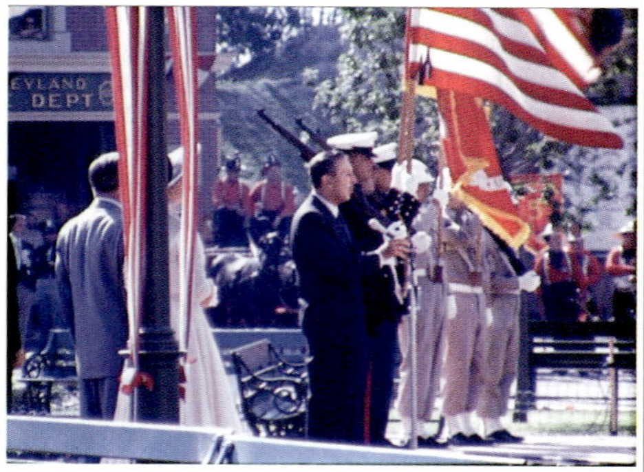

Walt Disney dedicating Disneyland.

No matter how disjointed that interview may have seemed, Jack Wrather must have been extremely pleased with even that short plug of his yet unopened hotel. It has been estimated that over ninety-million viewers were tuned in that day (approximately 54-percent of the total population of the country). That had to be the best free 60-second advertisement that Jack Wrather would ever receive for one of his business enterprises.

Although Disneyland's Grand Opening may have been somewhat chaotic with nearly thirty-thousand people storming the gates (or climbing the fences), that event did prove two important facts: the influence of television upon the viewers and the over-whelming drawing power of Disneyland. Cars were lined up bumper-to-bumper for over seven miles on the Santa Ana Freeway. Jack Wrather's earlier skepticism was about to be proven groundless.

On its opening day, Disneyland was far from being ready. Some buildings bore coats of wet paint. A number of the rides and attractions, originally planned for that day, would have to wait until later that year to make their debut. The Disneyland Hotel was still several months away from being ready to open to the public. The first Park souvenir booklet, *The Story of Disneyland*, contained only artists' paintings and line-drawings. Near the end of that first booklet, under a heading "Hotel Accommodations," was an aerial view painting of the original design of the Disneyland Hotel. The following is the 1955 version of what might have been:

"On a beautiful 30-acre site [the other acreage was still orange groves] opposite the main EXIT of Disneyland Park is the Disneyland Hotel. This distinctive 650-room resort Hotel and Motor Hotel offers every type of accom-

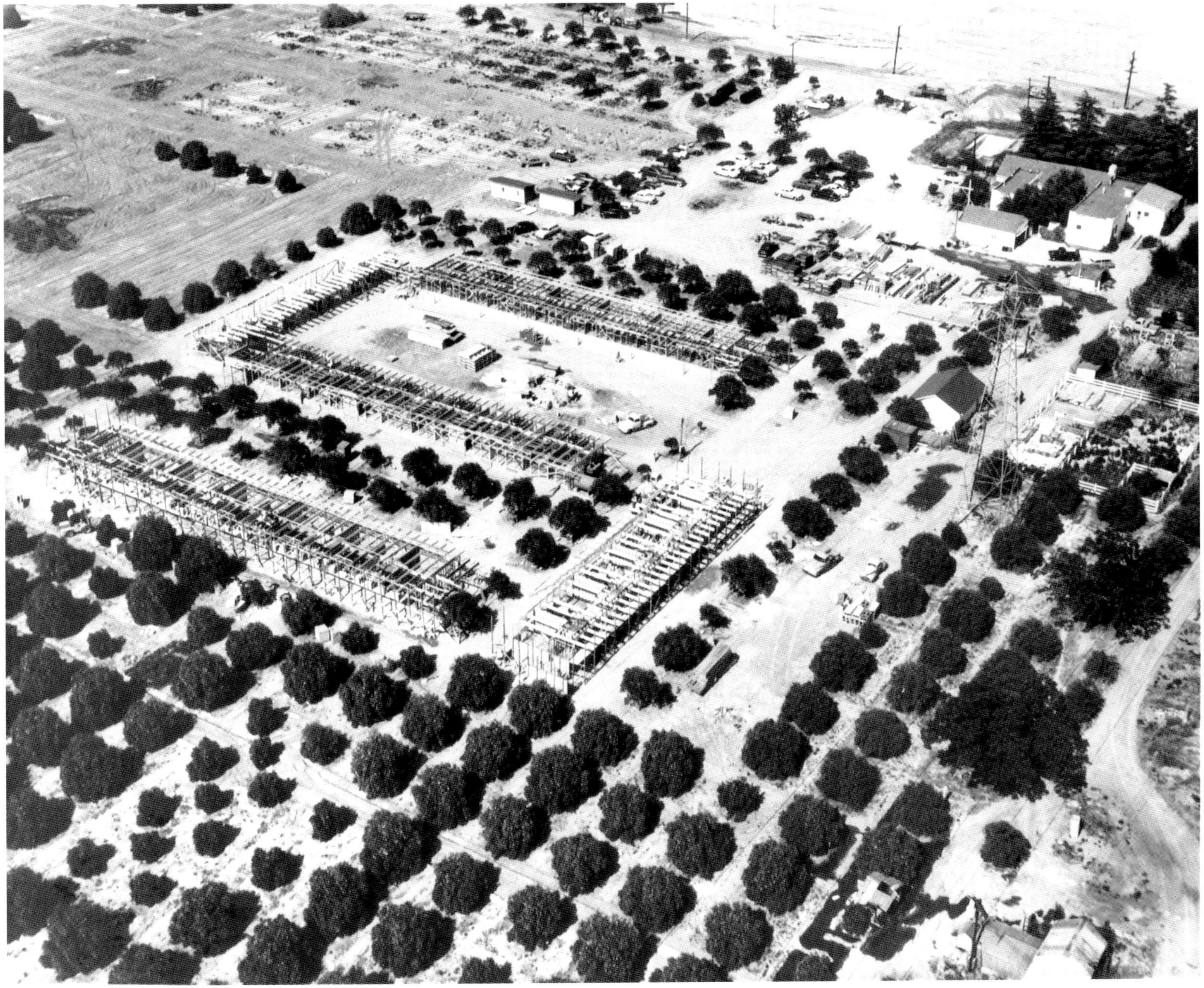

Construction underway on the initial five guest room structures at the Disneyland Hotel. Just to the left of the power pole was the spot where the groundbreaking ceremony had taken place.

modation from comfortable motel units to luxurious garden apartments. Among the many unique features are the economical dormitories for organized youth groups and nurseries for the care of small children. Recreation facilities include three swimming pools, tennis courts, and a nine-hole golf course. Four excellent restaurants with a

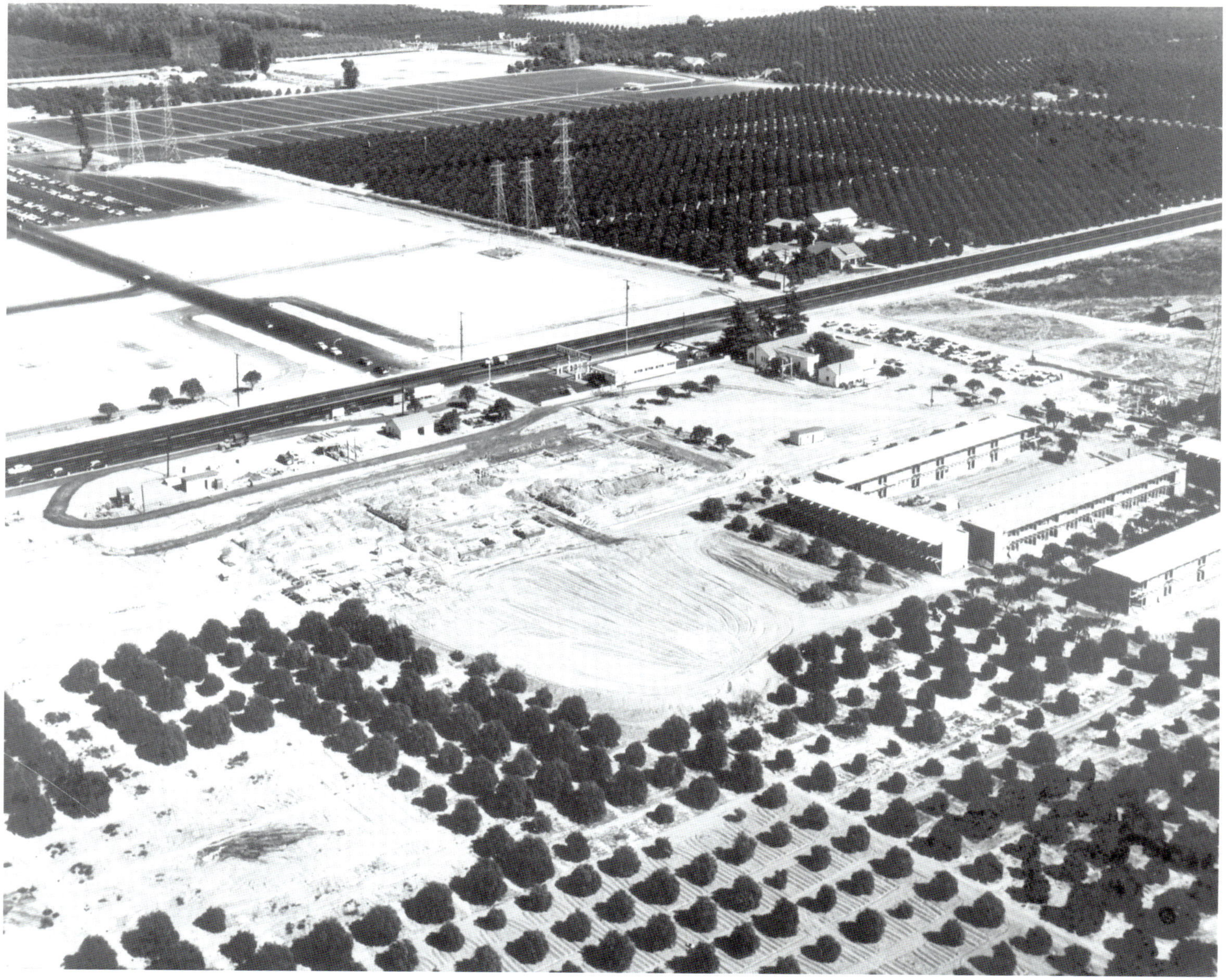

Construction is near completion on the initial five guest room structures. Construction is now underway on the Administration Building, restaurants, shops and the pool. At lower left, ground has also been broken for the additional guest room structures in the northeast section of the property. The building in the upper right would house the Little Gourmet Restaurant until the Gourmet Restaurant opened.

combination capacity of 1,250 persons serve superb food and beverages to suit every budget. The official opening is planned for late November. Limited accommodations available approximately the middle of August."

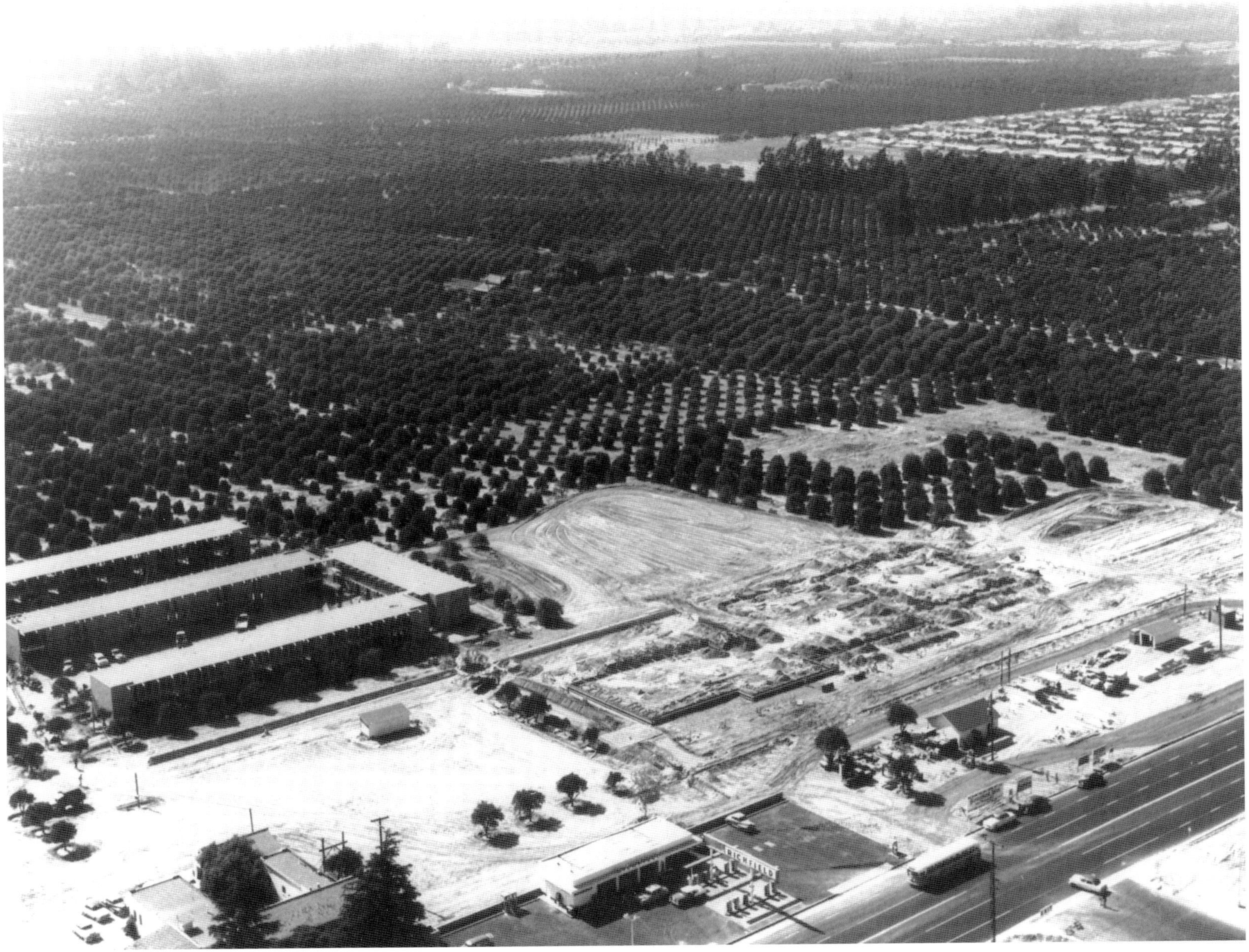

A reverse view from the previous picture. Note the Richfield Service Station in the lower center of the picture. Large, hand painted signs in lower right (near the bus) announce the impending opening of the Disneyland Hotel.

While Wrather had predicted that his "little motel in the middle of the orange grove" would open in September, the Disneyland Hotel opened on October 5, 1955; nearly three months after Disneyland's live televised Grand Opening. On its very first night of operation, the Disneyland Hotel had only seven guest rooms completed while the eighth guest room was being utilized as the registration office. The remainder of the rooms were rapidly finished and made available for guests. Built on the southeast portion of the leased Disney property, the first guests registered at a hotel having only 104 guest rooms located in five two-story complexes. These were the South Garden rooms, later to be known as the Oriental Gardens. It became Orange County's first major hotel, and was the first major resort to be built in Southern California since the early 1940's. The Hotel was to be a "year around resort" (not a common thing in 1955). The official operator was Wrather-Alvarez Hotels, Inc.

First 100 Units of Hotel Ready at Disneyland

The first 100 units of the new $10,000,000 Disneyland Hotel and Motor Hotel, now under construction on a 30-acre site in Anaheim adjoining the new Disneyland Park opened to the public yesterday, it was announced by Jack Wrather, president of Wrather-Alvarez Hotels, Inc., owners and builders of the distinctive 650-room project.

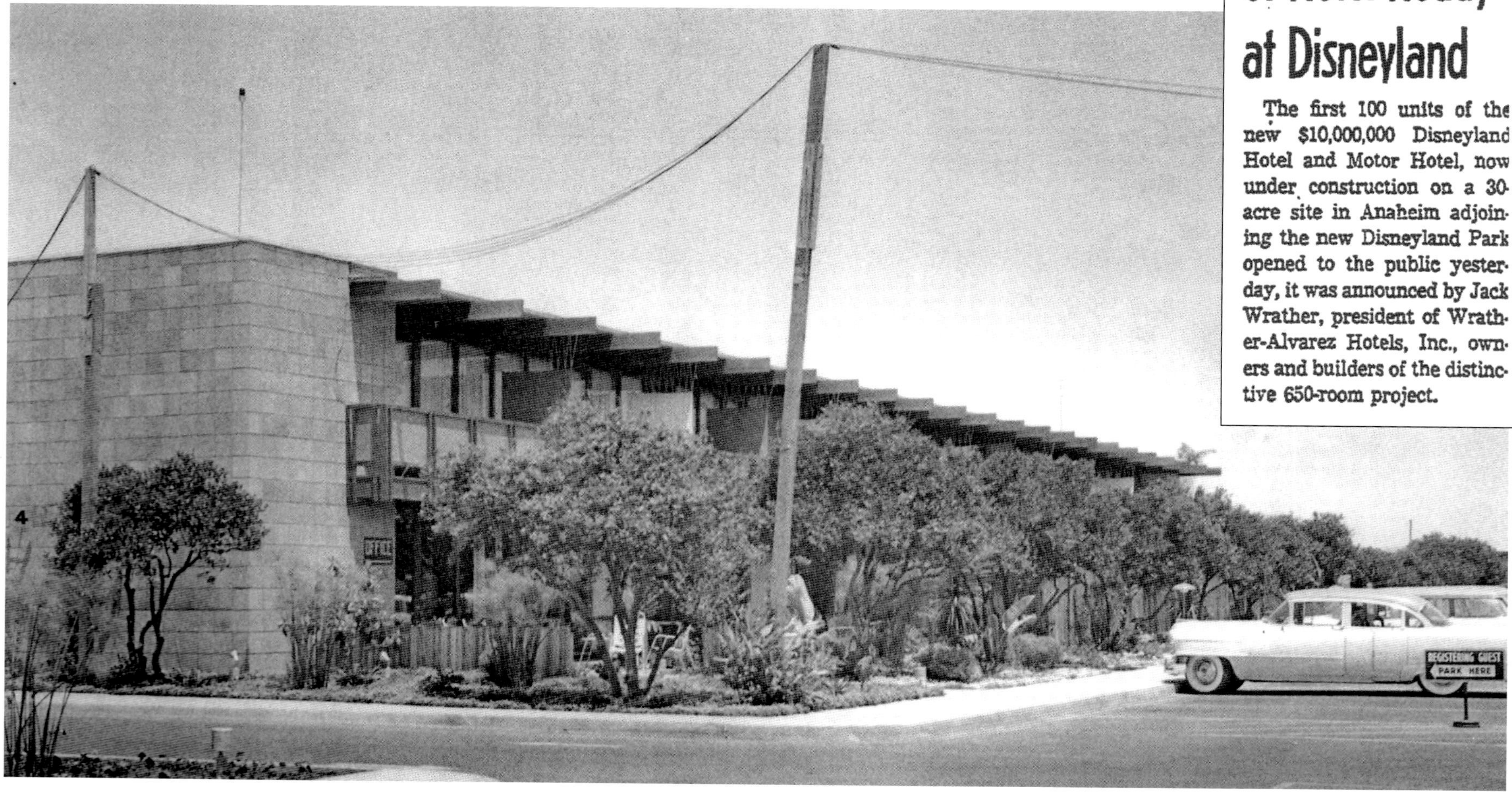

Parking for registering guests with the first office located in what would later become a guest room. Note the "Office" sign on the wall to the left, just below the balcony.

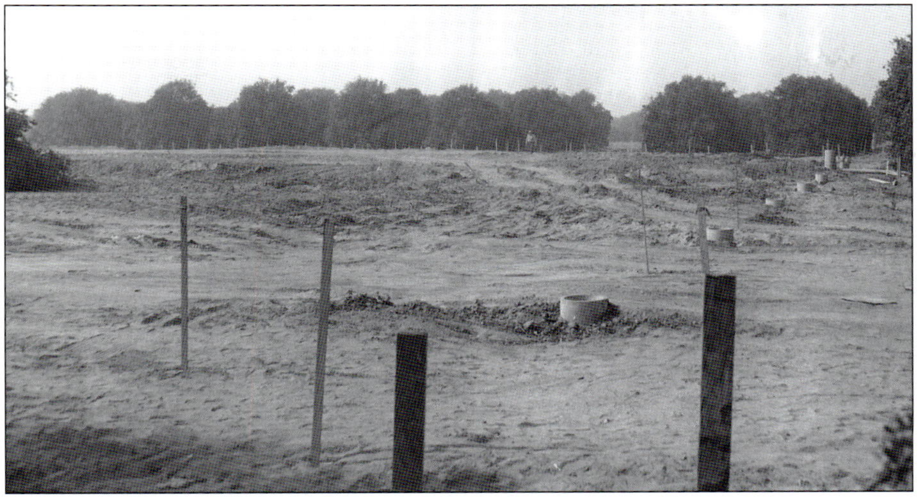

Ground cleared for North Garden rooms. Photo taken 11-9-55.

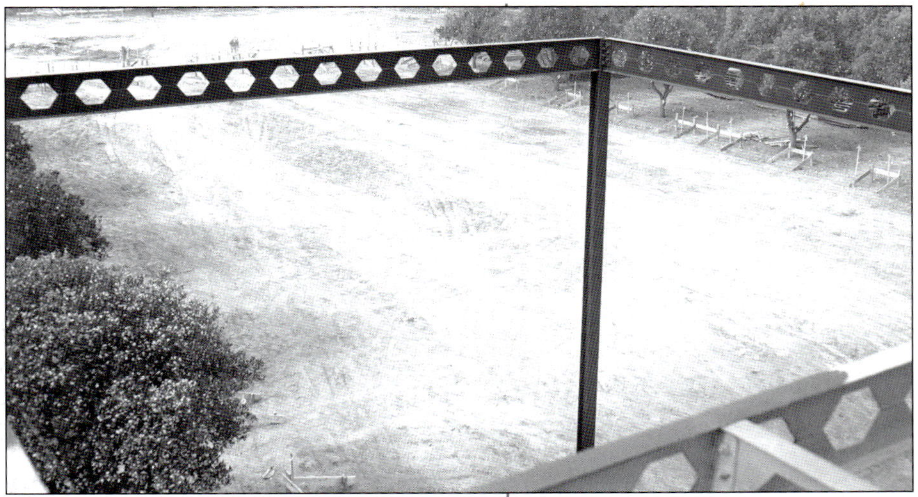

Further ground cleared for North Garden rooms. Photo taken 11-20-55.

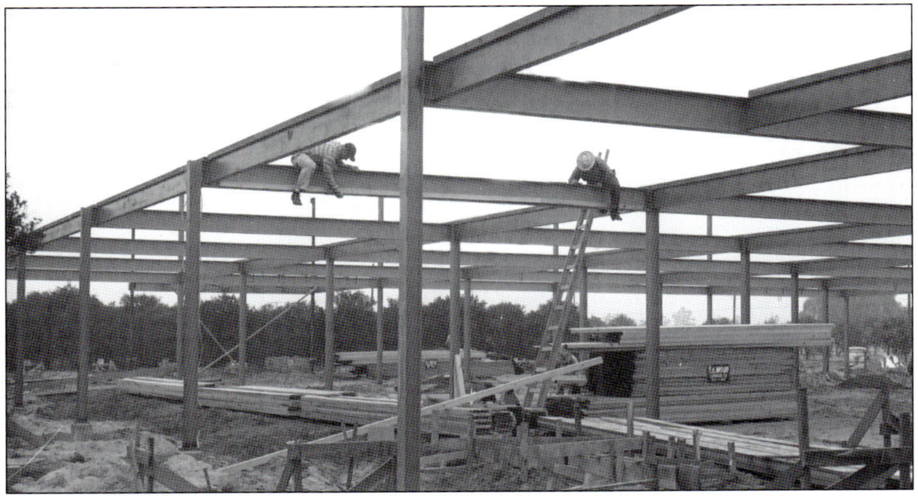

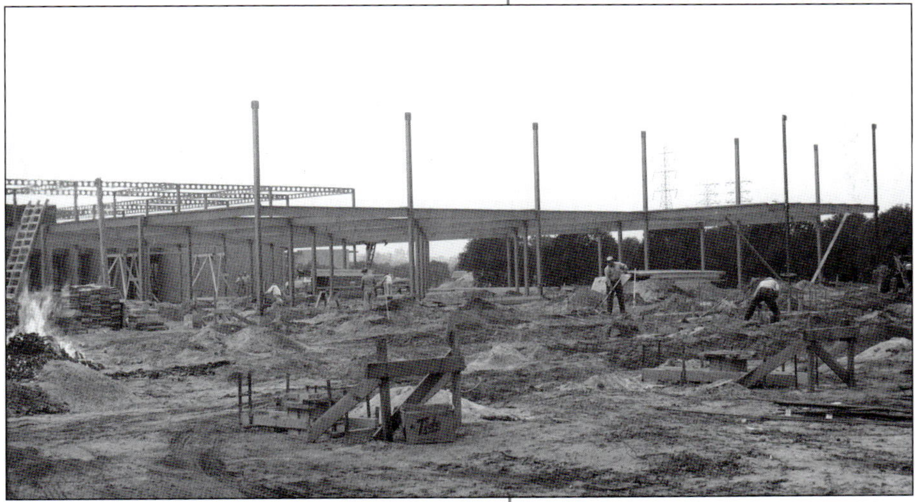

Construction of North Garden rooms & Administration Building. Photos taken 12-1-55.

The first guests to register were Mr. and Mrs. Robert Arnone of Inglewood, California. The number of available rooms quickly proved to be insufficient for the unexpected demand, and ninety-six more units of the same type were added the following year in June on the property's northeast section. Built again by Hodges and Vandegrift Construction Company, this new addition was called the North Garden rooms, later renamed the Garden Villas.

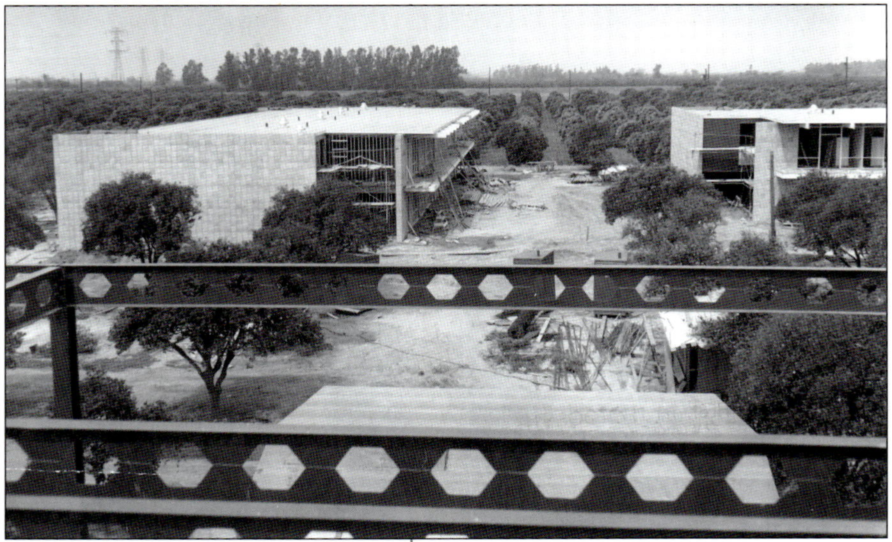

More development is completed. Photo taken 3-5-56.

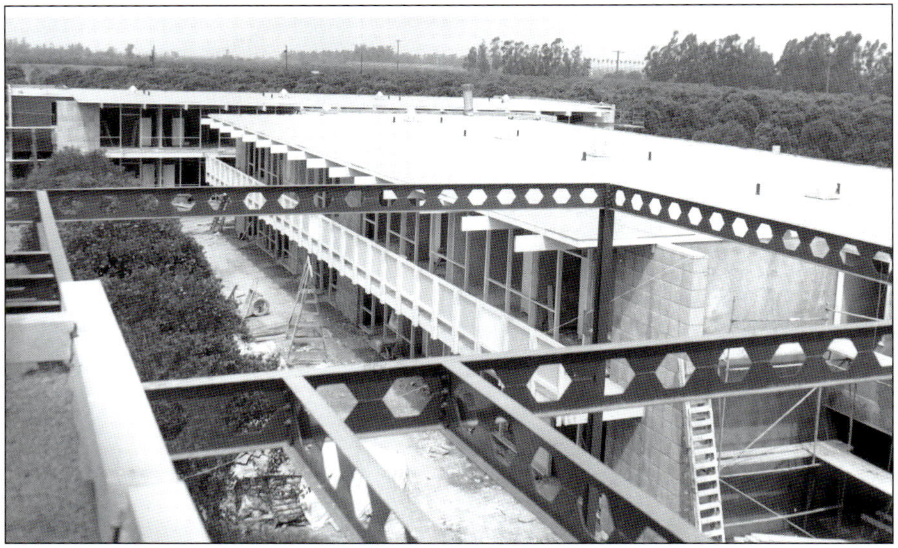

Nearing completion on North Garden rooms. Photo taken 5-4-56.

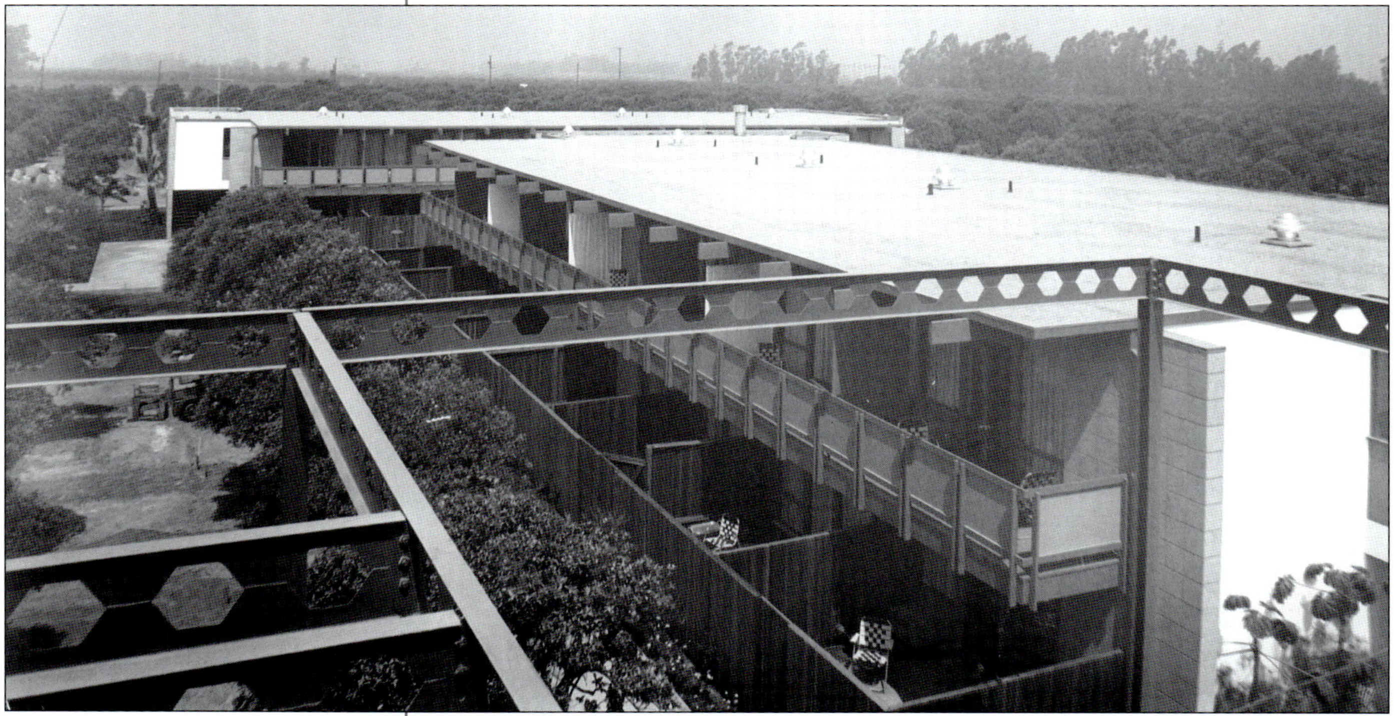

Six months after construction began; the North Garden rooms are completed.

During the first year, room rates ranged from $9 for a standard room to $22 for deluxe quarters. It was advertised that the majority of the rooms would accommodate four people. A major selling point was that children under twelve years of age stayed free. For an additional adult, there was a $3 charge. Each room on the first floor had its own private patio; second floor units had their own private balconies. At that time, less than half of the acreage that had been leased from Walt was planned for the Hotel's development. The Hotel's telephone number at its opening was KEystone 5-8171, and the official address was 1441 West Street.

For its first three months of operation, Disneyland charged $1 for an adult admission and from 10-cents to 35-cents for each attraction/ride ticket. On October 11, 1955, Disneyland introduced the "Ticket Book" which covered admission and contained eight ride tickets ("A," "B," and "C" tickets) at the price of $2.50.

At the same time construction had begun on the ninety-six additional garden rooms, construction was also under way on the Administration Building complex, which would house a lobby, restaurants, shops, and meeting rooms. This complex was built by the Ryan Construction Company of Los Angeles. In a converted ranch house that had been one of the original Disneyland park administration buildings, the Little Gourmet restaurant was opened on the southeast corner of the Hotel's property and had a seating capacity of five-hundred diners. The house had been re-designed into a restaurant by C. Tony Pereira.

The original Hotel design called for 300 motel and hotel rooms, suites, and garden apartments. Included were plans for three swimming pools, tennis courts, a golf course, cocktail lounges, and four restaurants. The original blueprints designated a total of ten buildings in the South Garden or Oriental Garden section. Only five of those buildings were actually ever built.

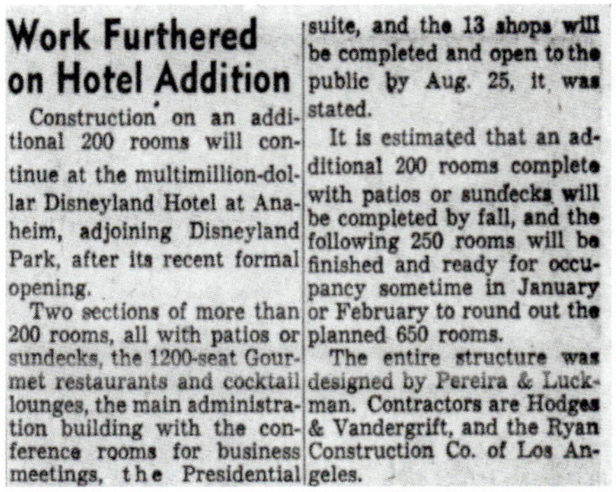

Work Furthered on Hotel Addition

Construction on an additional 200 rooms will continue at the multimillion-dollar Disneyland Hotel at Anaheim, adjoining Disneyland Park, after its recent formal opening.

Two sections of more than 200 rooms, all with patios or sundecks, the 1200-seat Gourmet restaurants and cocktail lounges, the main administration building with the conference rooms for business meetings, the Presidential suite, and the 13 shops will be completed and open to the public by Aug. 25, it was stated.

It is estimated that an additional 200 rooms complete with patios or sundecks will be completed by fall, and the following 250 rooms will be finished and ready for occupancy sometime in January or February to round out the planned 650 rooms.

The entire structure was designed by Pereira & Luckman. Contractors are Hodges & Vandergrift, and the Ryan Construction Co. of Los Angeles.

August 1956 newspaper article.

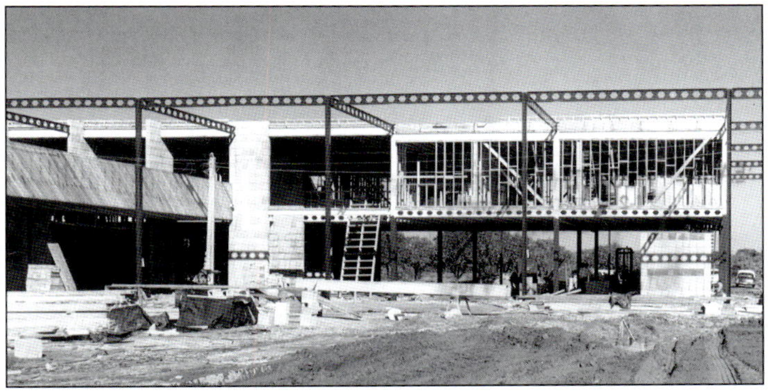

Construction underway on the Administration Building. Photo taken 2-1-56.

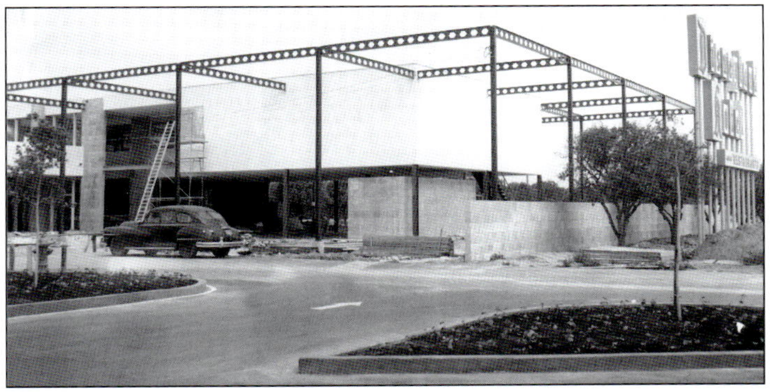

Further construction on the Administration Building. Photo taken 5-4-56.

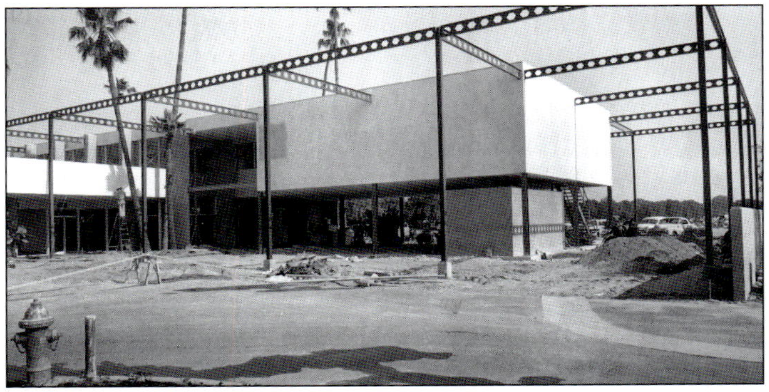

Further construction on the Administration Building. Photo taken 6-1-56.

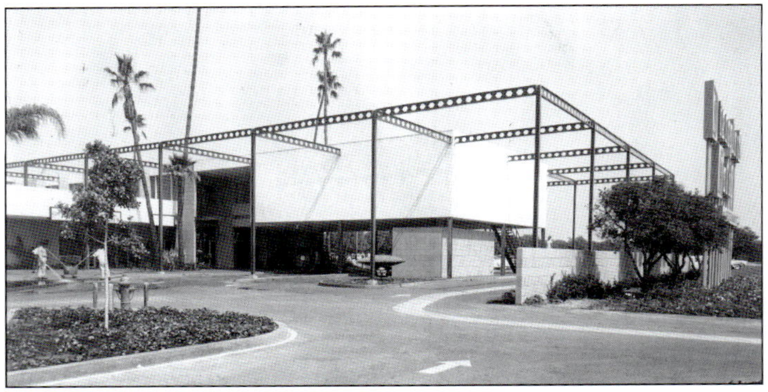

Construction near completion on the Administration Building.

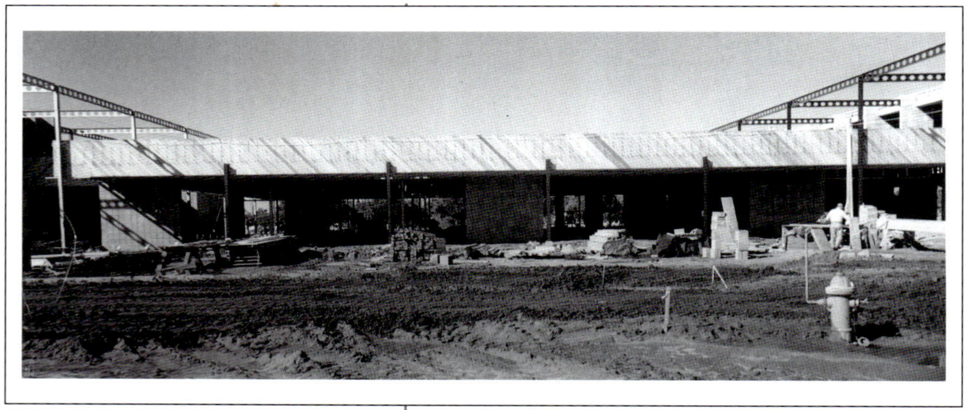

Construction underway on the Administration Building complex shops and restaurants. Photo taken 2-1-56.

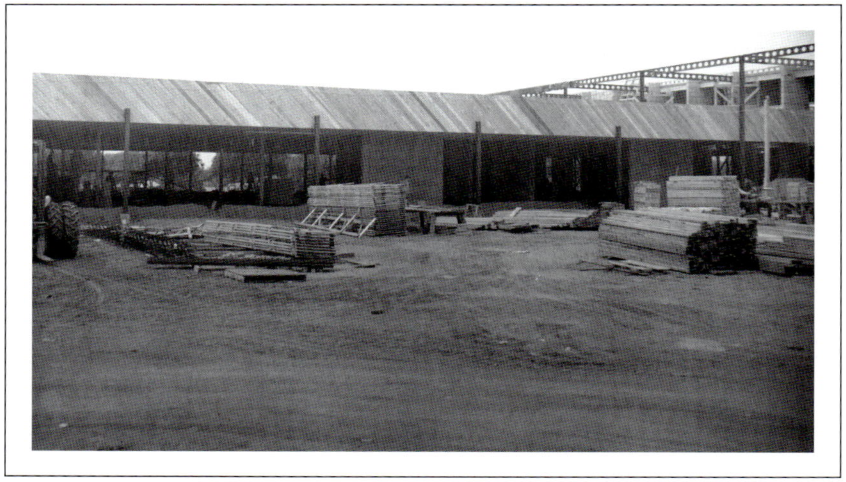

Further construction on the Administration Building complex shops and restaurants. Photo taken 2-10-56.

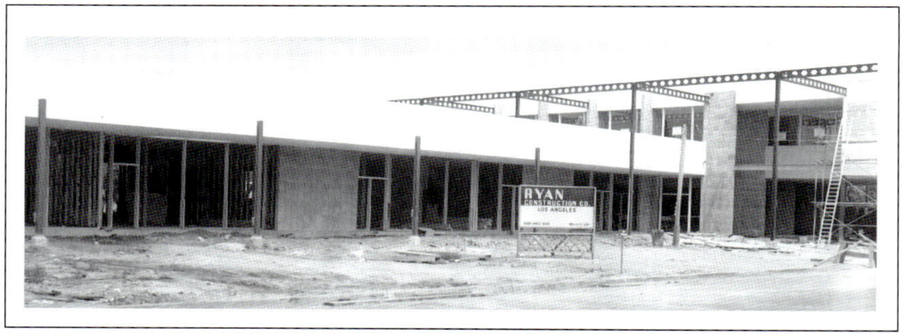

Further construction on the Administration Building complex shops and restaurants. Photo taken 5-4-56.

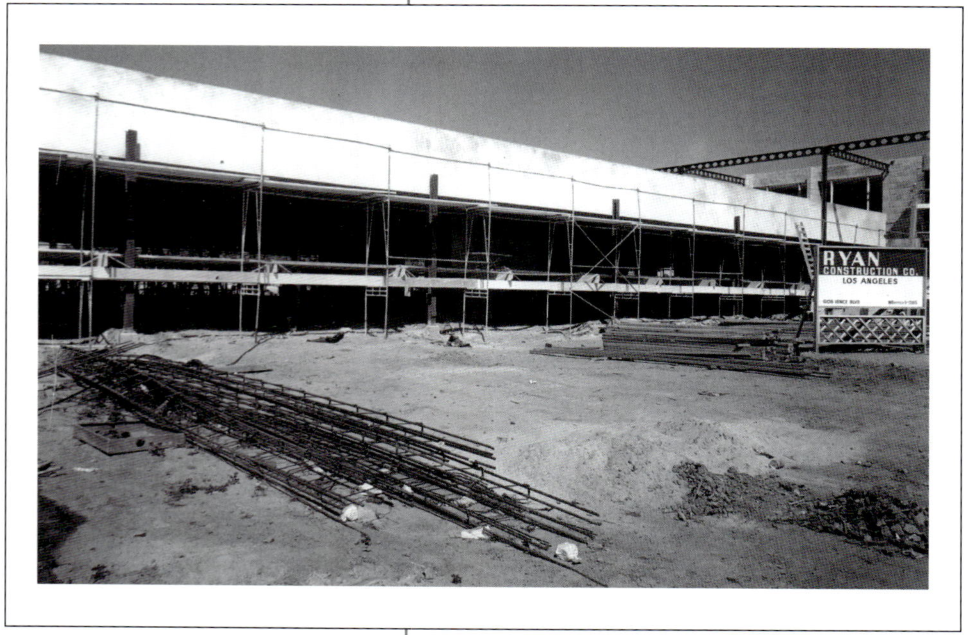

Further construction on the Administration Building complex shops and restaurants. Photo taken 4-5-56.

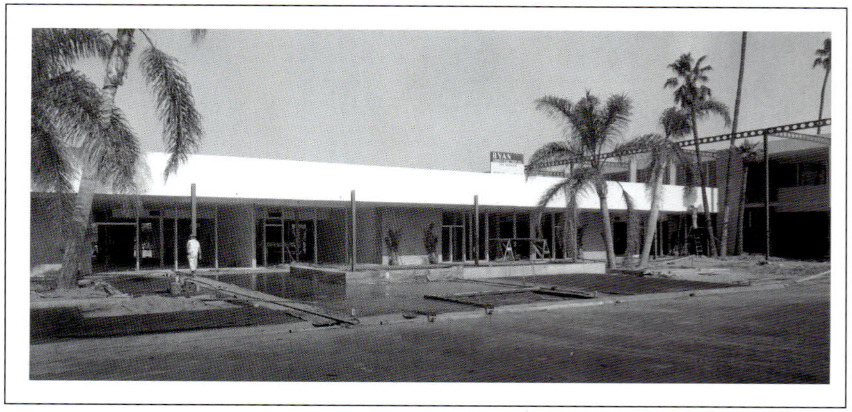

Construction near completion on the Administration Building complex shops and restaurants. Photo taken 6-1-56.

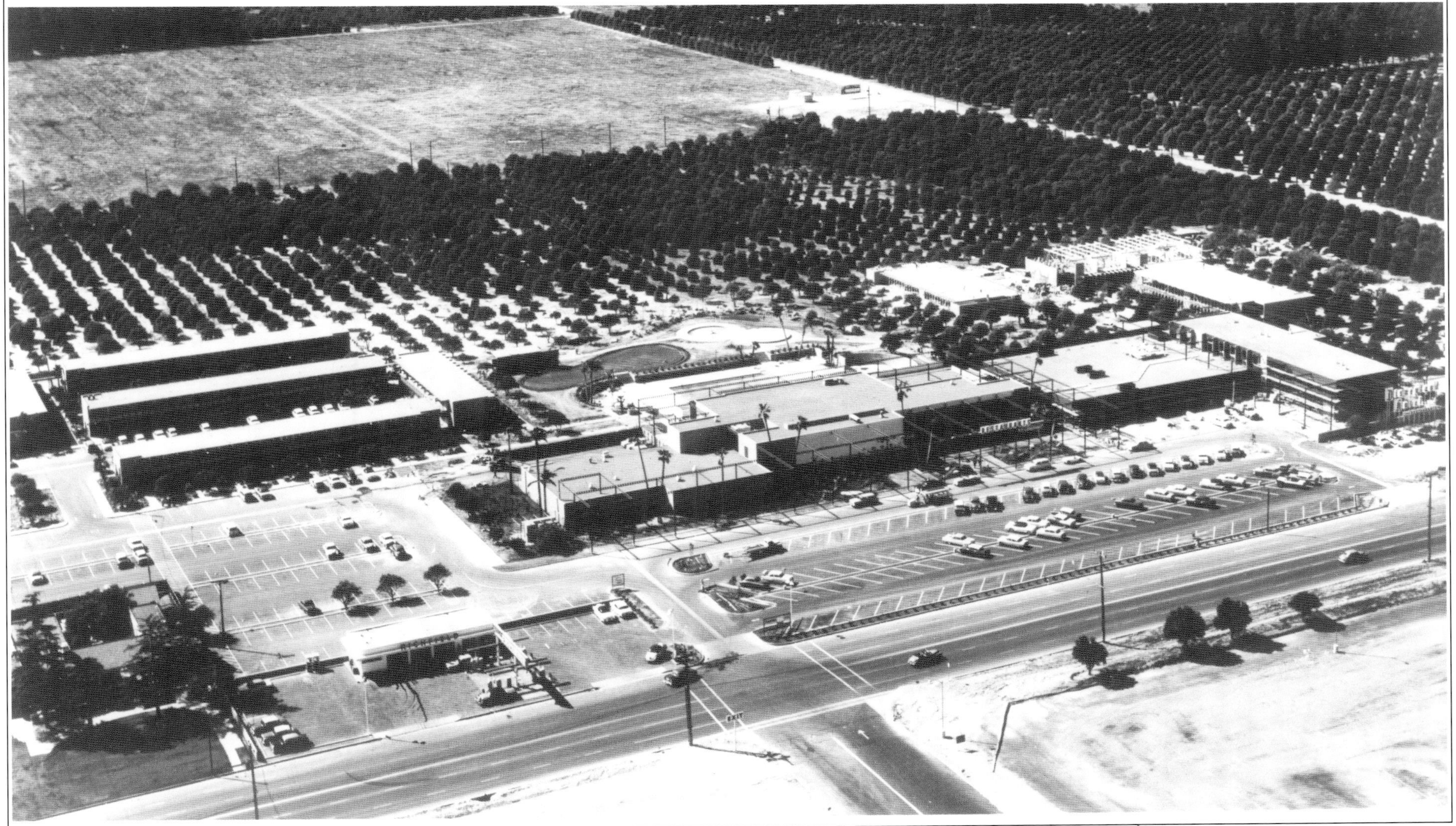

An aerial view March 16, 1956.

Ever after the Grand Opening of Disneyland, Walt Disney referred to that day as "Black Sunday." Too few drinking fountains (due to a plumbers strike), over crowding due to 20,000 gate crashers (either with counterfeit tickets or by fence climbing), a gas leak in Fantasyland, ladies' high heels sticking in the recently poured asphalt of Main Street, and mostly bad press reviews the next day did not seem to bode well for Disneyland's future. One newspaper reporter had earlier predicted that Disneyland would be a "Hollywood Spectacular--a spectacular failure." The very next day Walt and his staff began correcting the problems, improving those things that had worked well, and planning for the future of Disneyland.

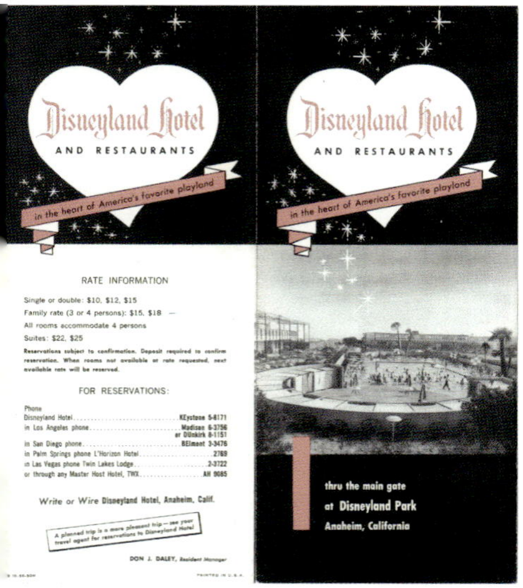

1956 Hotel brochure with rates.

Guests arriving at the Park in 1956 were greeted by such additions as the Main Street Omnibus, Tomorrowland's the Bathroom of Tomorrow exhibit and the Astro-Jets, the Skyway, and the adventures to be found on Tom Sawyer's Island. Also that year, the "D" ticket was added to the Park's ticket books.

Almost from the beginning, it was possible for guests at Disneyland to make direct reservations for the Disneyland Hotel while still in the Park. Rooms could be booked at the Hills Brothers Coffee House on Town Square and at the Carefree Corner at the opposite end of Main Street.

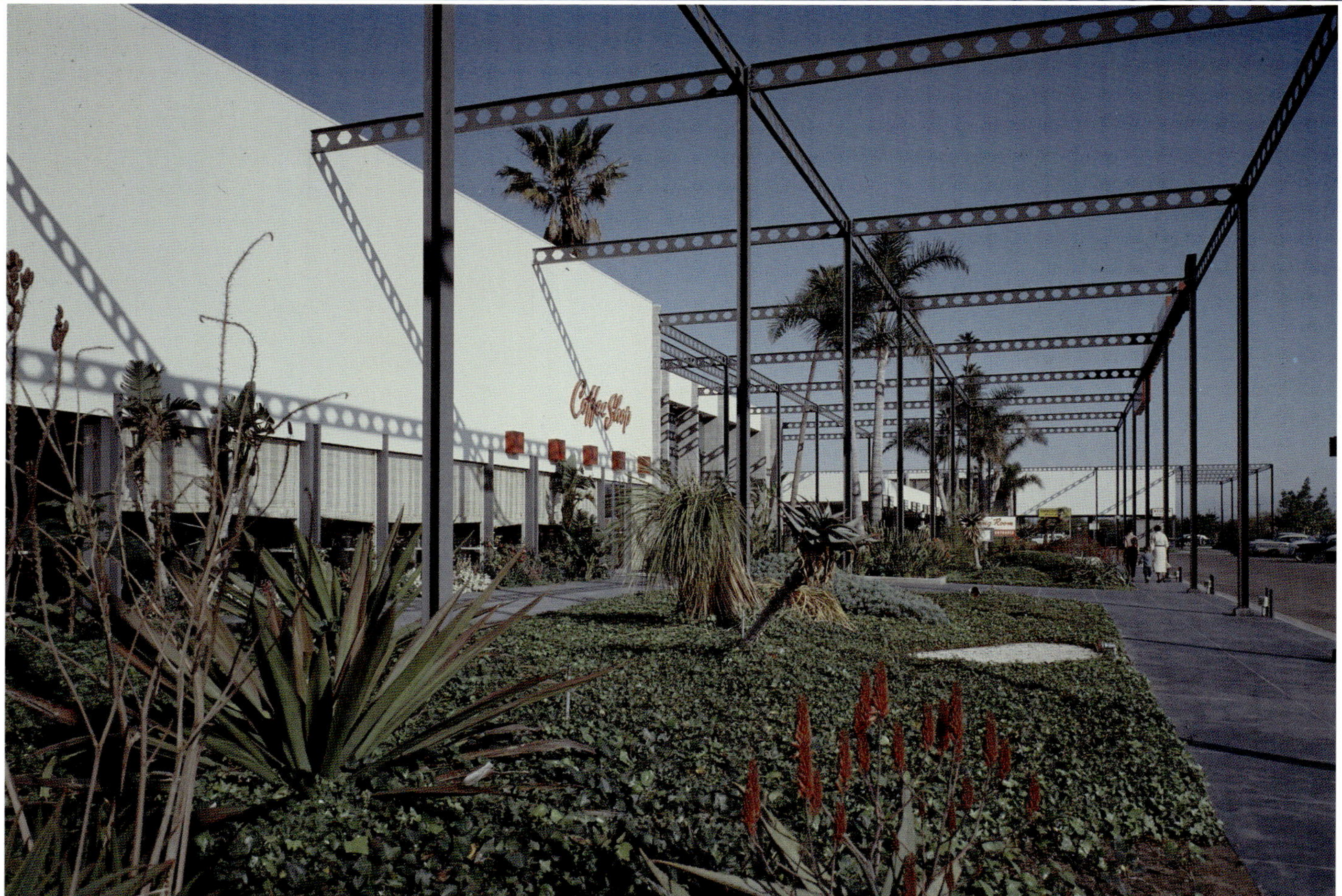

Exterior of newly opened Coffee Shop and Hotel Restaurants by Gourmet 1956.

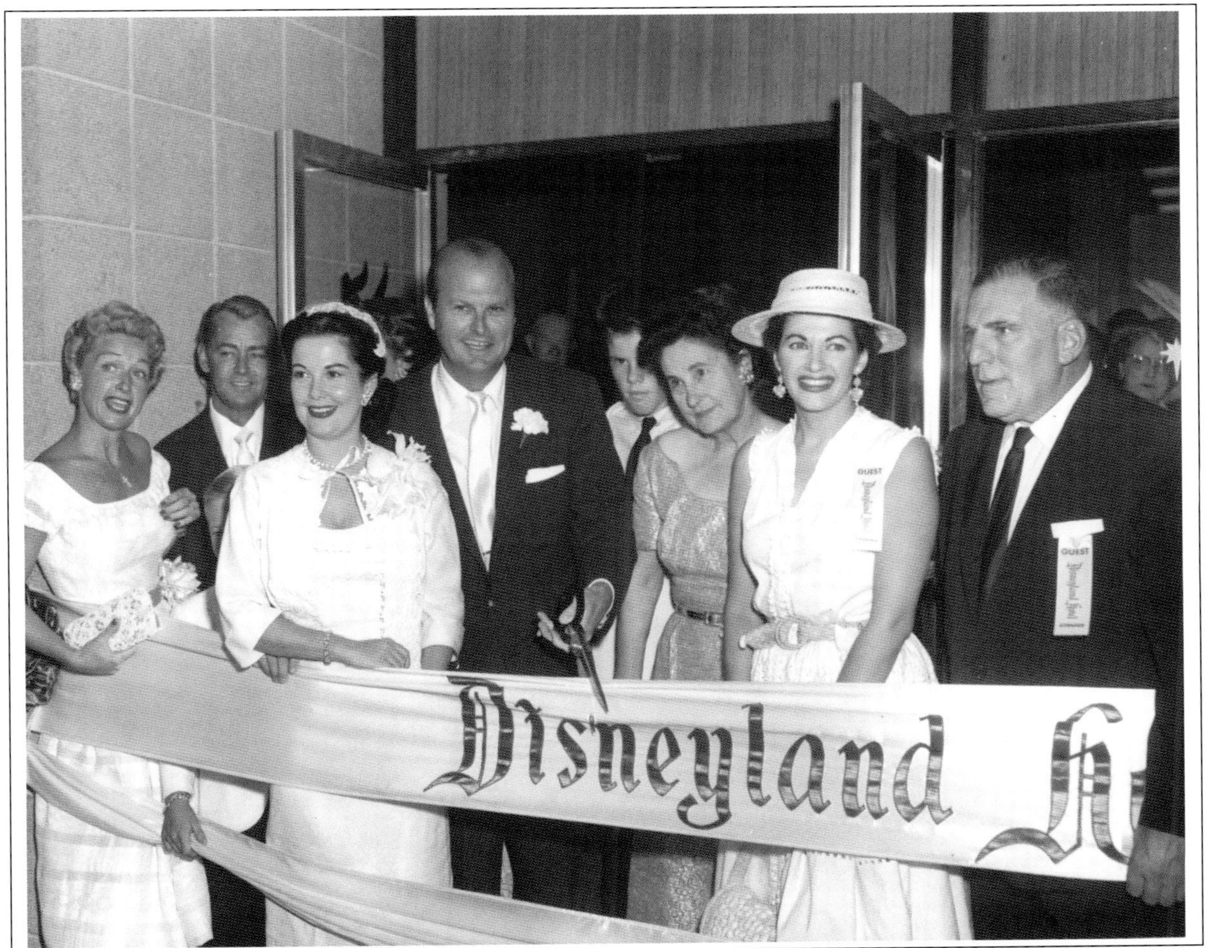

Jack Wrather and Helen Alvarez cutting the ribbon at the official opening of the Disneyland Hotel. Also pictured are Bonita Granville, Alan Ladd, Mazie Wrather, Yvonne De Carlo and William Bendix.

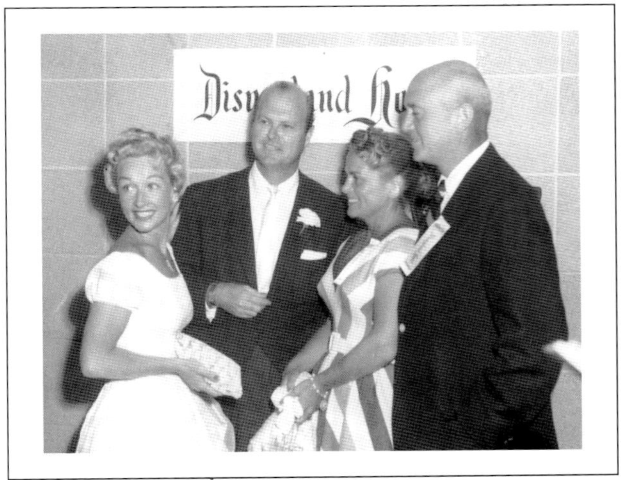

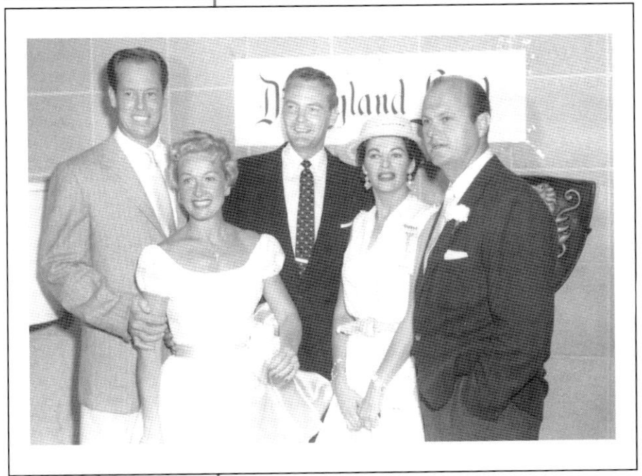

Jack and Bonita with celebrity guests at the Hotel's opening day.

The new Disneyland Hotel Restaurants by Gourmet was opened on February 15, 1956 replacing the Little Gourmet. The facility included a coffee shop (seating one hundred), a cocktail lounge, and a dining room which could comfortably accommodate up to a thousand guests. Through large picture windows, views from the main dining room overlooked the landscaped pool area (illuminated at night) and the foliage of orange groves beyond. The coffee shop opened at 11 a.m., had a special children's menu, and baby food was available for those making special arrangements. Breakfast was served beginning at 7:30 a.m. in the restaurant.

On the second floor above the Gourmet was located a banquet area that could serve parties ranging from twenty-five to five-hundred. On October 28, 1956, Disneyland Cast Members would hold their Halloween Masquerade Ball in the banquet room. Within a few years, this area had been expanded and could be divided into four different meeting rooms. By the early 1960's, it had become known as the Magnolia Room.

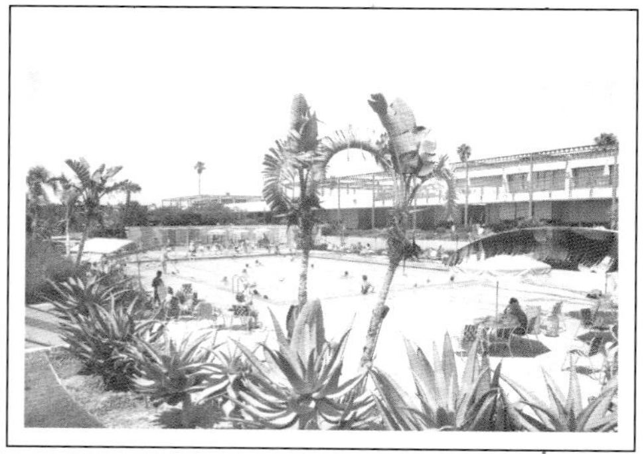

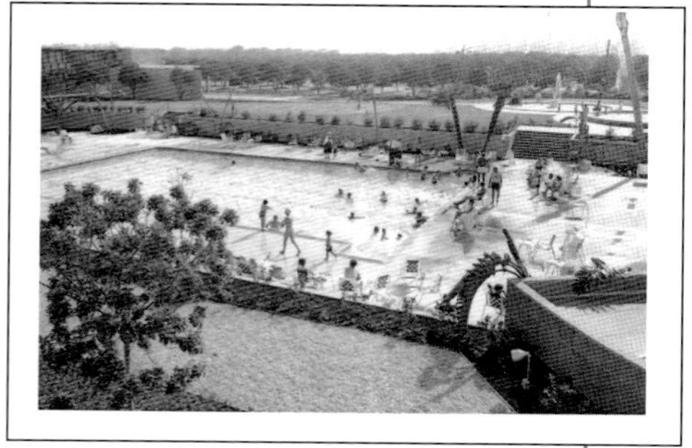

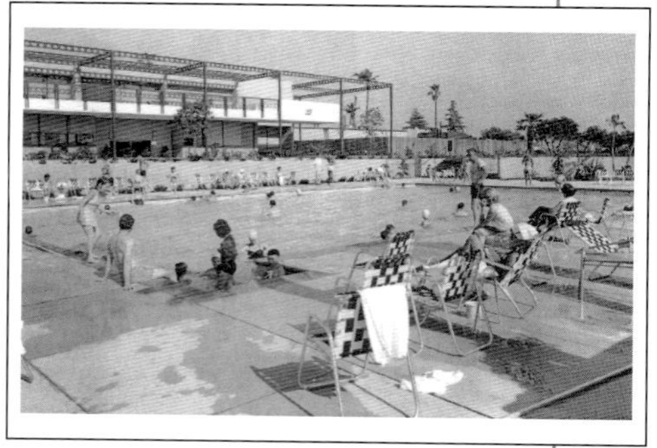

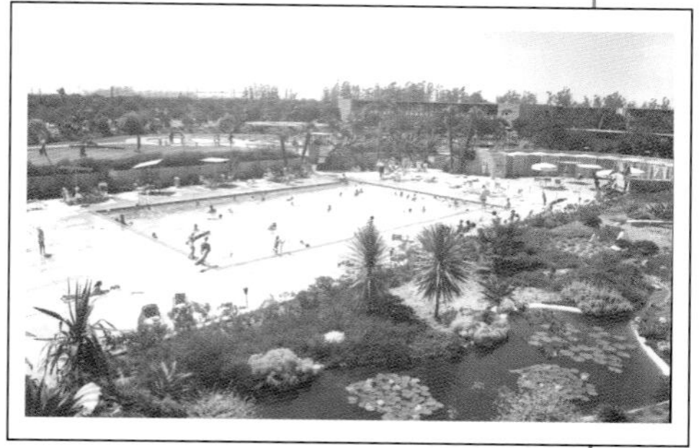

The Coral Swim Club with lush, tropical landscaping.

The first summer of operation would be an important indicator as to just how successful the Disneyland Hotel would become. In a June 11, 1956 letter to a business associate, Jack Wrather wrote, "...for the first 8 days of June the hotel has averaged 96% occupancy with 6 full days, 1 of 97% and 1 of 73%." Concerning income, he continued, "Through June 8th this month our rental rceipts [*sic*] are $9,521.00 as against $6,895.00 during the same period in May." Jack had to be pleased with such results.

On July 3rd, Wrather wrote to the same friend and relayed the following: "The Disneyland Hotel room rentals for the month of June totaled $43,849.00 as against May rentals of $31,057.00. During the month of June the average number of rooms open was 121. At this time there are 165 rooms open with the remaining 35 to open by July 15th." Concerning the Gourmet, he wrote, "The restaurant grossed $130,239 in June, a 30-day month, as against $106,686 in May, a 31-day month." Due to the overwhelming popularity of Disneyland across

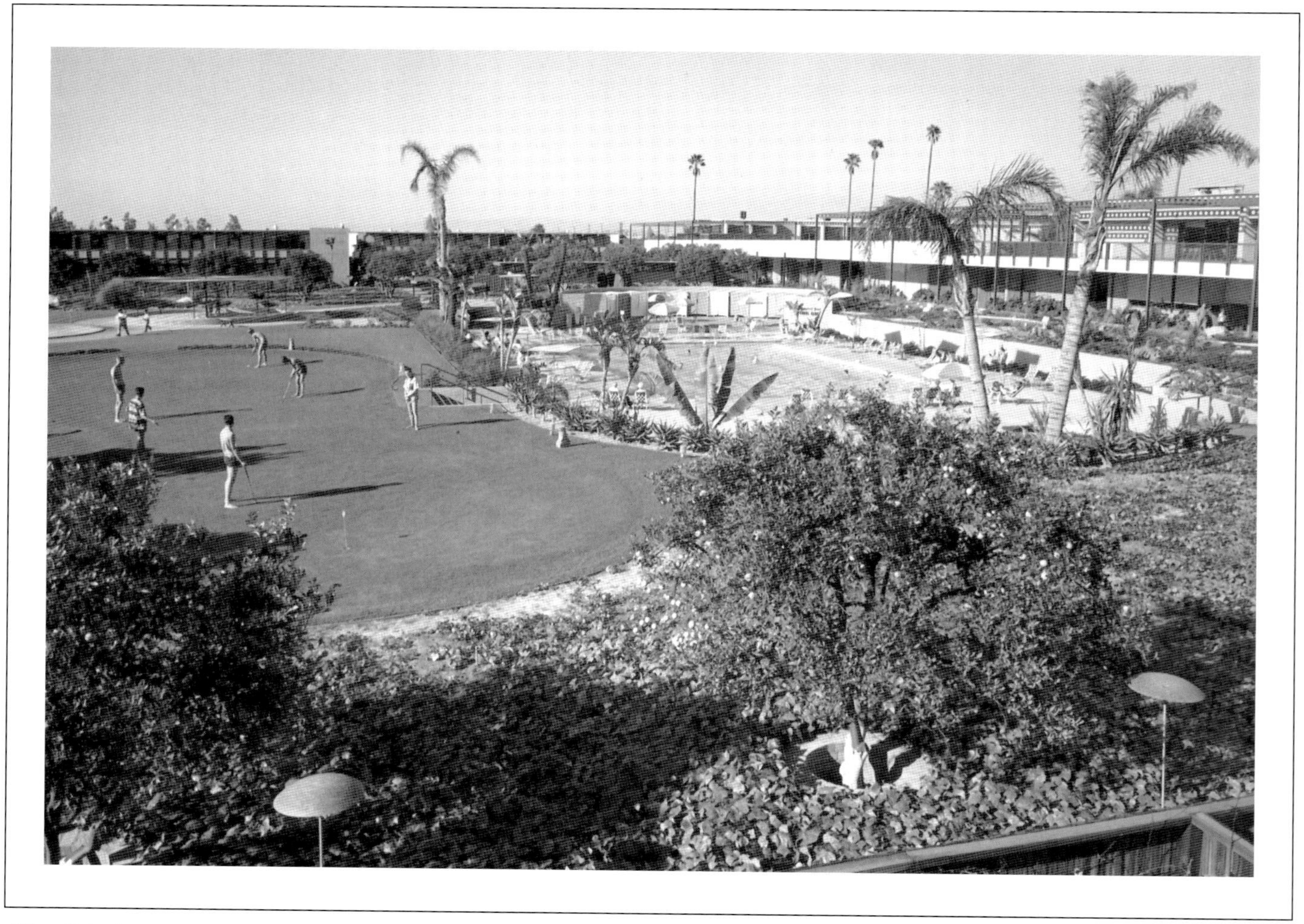

The 18 hole putting green and Olympic-size swimming pool.

the street, the Hotel was forced to turn customers away. Jack wrote, "During the month of June, the hotel has had to turn down about 300 requests for reservations, and has turned away from 20 to 100 rooms per night at the hotel. During the month of June there was only 1 night when we were not 100% occupied and that was June 3rd."

The opening of the Administration Building and the "official" grand opening for the Hotel took place on August 25, 1956. This was a star studded celebration that resembled a Hollywood movie premiere. Celebrities in attendance included Walt Disney, Art Linkletter, William Bendix, Alan Ladd, Sue Carroll, Yvonne DeCarlo, and Jeanne Crain. In attendance were as many as three-hundred enthusiasts, observing the ribbon cutting then taking a grand tour of the facilities. On the second floor of the main building was to be found the new, luxurious Presidential Suite. It came complete with foyer and living room, two large bedrooms, and two full baths with dressing rooms.

With the opening of this new addition, now running along West Street was to be found (in order from north to south) the Administration Building and lobby, the Patio Arcade (shopping center), the Lounge, the Gourmet, and the Coffee Shop. Behind this complex of buildings to the west were the pools and the two-story guest rooms.

In the Patio Arcade, in 1956, were to be found the Magic Land Toy Shop and the Disneyland Hotel Drugs. Both of those establishments were managed by Taylor and Hume, who also operated Merlin's Magic Shop over on Main Street, U.S.A. Also present were Wayne's (florist) and the Hawaiian Shop. On the mezzanine of the lobby were located Jade Barbers and de Cannis for Beauty. Hotel literature from the time boasted of seventeen stores and shops.

By November of 1956, (with the before mentioned ninety-six new rooms added), there were now 204 guest rooms and suites at the Disneyland Hotel accommodating up to eight-hundred guests. As an added attraction, each garden patio had its own orange tree, a reminder of what the original property had been only a few short years earlier. This had been a part of the original plans when the grounds were being cleared to build the Hotel. With the number of guest rooms now almost doubled, some room rates were slightly changed. First floor rooms were increased in price to between $11 and $22. Second floor rooms were priced slightly lower at between $9 and $20.

An additional amenity at that time was the Coral Swim Club which included a huge 45-foot by 75-foot completely tiled, year around swimming pool heated to 75-degrees. Food and refreshments were served poolside. Wading pools for children of all ages, fountains, sandlots, and a cabana area were also featured. The pools were surrounded by lounge furniture for guests' relaxation and so they might acquire a Southern California tan. The pools were conveniently situated directly in the middle between the guest rooms and the new Administration Building-restaurant complex. One-day laundry and dry cleaning services were provided, and a physician and nurse were on call. The Hotel boasted of four conference rooms for business meetings or conventions, an 18-hole putting green, shuffleboard courts, and a fully equipped children's playground.

Early on, guests were able to register for rooms from their cars or they could go into the lobby for a more traditional method of registration. The unique drive-in registration desk was located at the main entrance to the new Administration Building. This new system allowed guests to quickly register and then drive directly to their room without ever leaving the comfort of their automobile...no need to drag the luggage and the children into the lobby. There were parking spaces for one-thousand cars, and parking was free in 1956. Limousine and bus services were

The
Disneyland Hotel

Cordially Invites

to be guests at the official
Opening ceremonies and events
to be held on
Saturday, August 25th
Nineteen hundred and fifty-six
at the Hotel

Cocktails 5 p.m. Dinner and Dancing 8 p.m.
R. S. V. P.
Informal Resort Wear

Invitation to Opening Day ceremonies above. Jack Wrather with Hotel Manager Don J. Daley below.

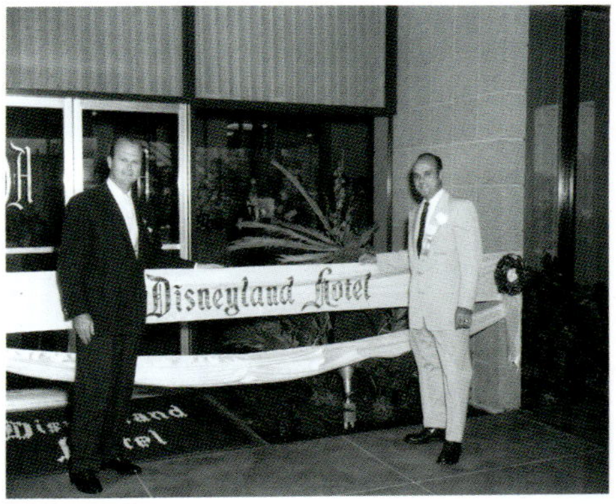

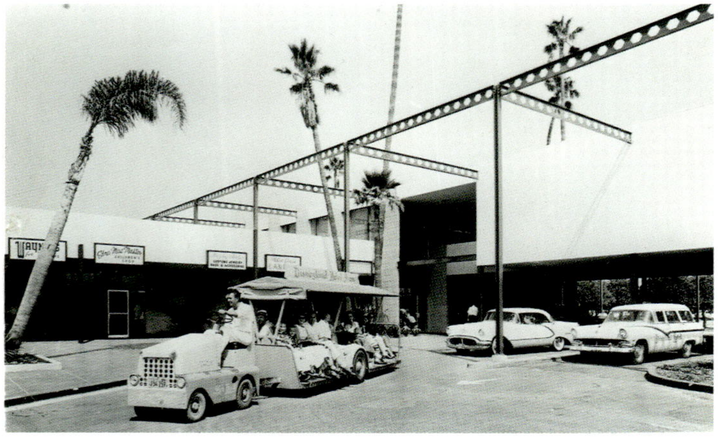

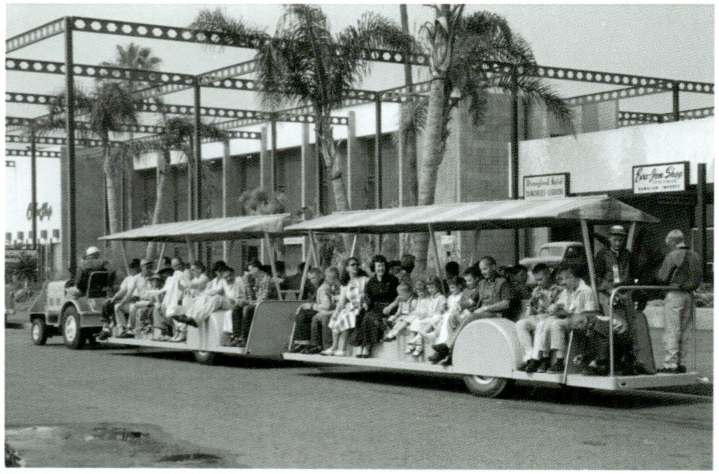

The Hotel tram bringing guests to and from the Park. The station wagon to the right was also used to transport guests to and from the Park. These automobiles mostly carried VIP guests.

additionally available. Since the Hotel's opening nearly a year earlier, Richfield Oil (also the Disneyland sponsor of Autopia) offered full automotive care. [The Richfield Oil service station was located on West Street on Hotel property, just to the north of the ranch house that had been the original Gourmet restaurant.] Even in the 1950's, every room was equipped with a black and white television set and with air conditioning.

During these early years, the attendance at Disneyland was beyond the most optimistic expectations. Even Walt must have been amazed by the overwhelming success of his dream. In the first eight weeks of operation in 1955, Disneyland had been visited by one-million guests. It was on September 8th that Elsa Marques walked through the Park's gate to obtain that honor. Attendance had continued to run 50-percent above projections made by SRI. Guest spending was 30-percent above predictions. The City Council of Anaheim began reviewing plans for other motels, hotels, and restaurants. One such proposal was for a drive-in restaurant to be located just south of the Park. It had been submitted by F. Donald Nixon, the brother of the then vice-president in the Eisenhower administration. Disneyland had proven all the skeptics to be wrong, and was destined to bring major changes to what once had been a sleepy, orange grove community.

From its beginnings, the Disneyland Hotel was one of the outstanding showplaces of Orange County. Celebrities such as Jack Benny, James Stewart, Henry Fonda, the Reverend Billy Graham, and Cary Grant were often spotted at the Hotel. These and other celebrities enjoyed bringing their families for a stay at the Hotel and for a trip across the street to Walt's Park. Business people were also attracted to the Hotel, coming for luncheons, meetings, and conventions. The Disneyland Hotel quickly had become the place to see and "the place" to be seen.

The Disneyland Hotel was a forerunner in providing services for the younger members of the family. It was the first major hotel to openly welcome children. Each guest room was equipped to sleep at least four people so that children could stay with their parents. Two children under twelve years of age could stay at no additional cost. The Hotel's pamphlets emphasized the bathroom safety as being "ideal for the small fry." An infra-red heating lamp in the ceiling eliminated the possibility of burns from the more traditional wall mounted heater. All bathroom fixtures were built lower for the ease of children. To prevent young fingers from getting a nasty shock, the electrical outlet was located in the light fixture above the medicine cabinet. Finally, all glasses (not today's plastic "glasses") were stored inside the medicine cabinet.

Someone attending a convention at the Hotel might now consider bringing the entire family given those policies and the vast array of activities for the young at the Hotel (and of course, just across the street was Disneyland). To tempt planners of conventions, a brochure from that time declared: "There's nothing like it, the wives will love it, the youngsters will be thrilled, and morale and attendance are bound to hit a new high. Be a hero, have your next group functions at Disneyland Hotel."

In 1957, Anaheim held its "Centennial Celebration." There were nightly parades, attended by capacity crowds. For four nights, "Centurama" was presented (an hour-and-a-half drama of the history of the city with a cast of 1,200). President Eisenhower sent his greetings: "Now as you enter your second century, you face the future with confidence in a rising population and a diversified industry united by the strong spirit of cooperation displayed by your original settlers." By 1957, most of the residents of Anaheim had moved there since 1950. That same year, Disneyland opened the Sleeping Beauty Castle Walk-Through, Holidayland, the Viewliner train, and Monsanto House of the Future (designed by the Massachusetts Institute of Technology).

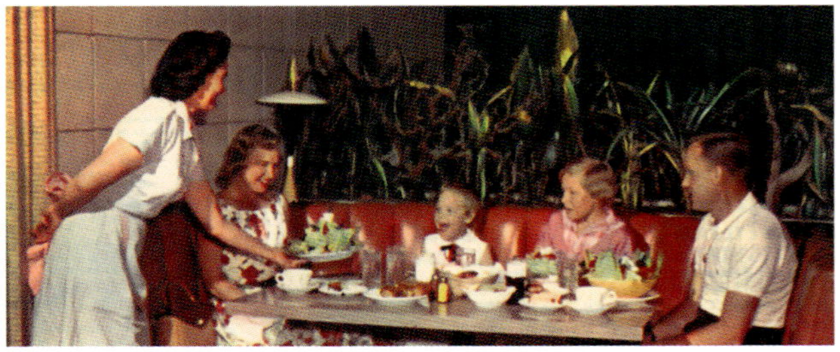

A 1950's family enjoying a meal at the Hotel's Coffee Shop. Look at the size of those salads!

Another form of entertainment was available at the Hotel. Every Thursday, fashion shows were provided in the Gourmet and in the Round-the-World Lounge. The lobby had a suspended fireplace and was described as "a setting of rare beauty and guest comforts." On the mezzanine level of the lobby were meeting rooms, accommodating from ten to one-hundred-fifty persons. Off the lobby were the Beauty Salon (the proprietor was Rique) and Jade Barbers. Some of the shops in the Patio Arcade were Latin Imports, Accessory Shop, Lee Wilson's Men's Shop, Eva Jon Hawaiian Shop, Children's Shop, and Magic Land Toy Shop.

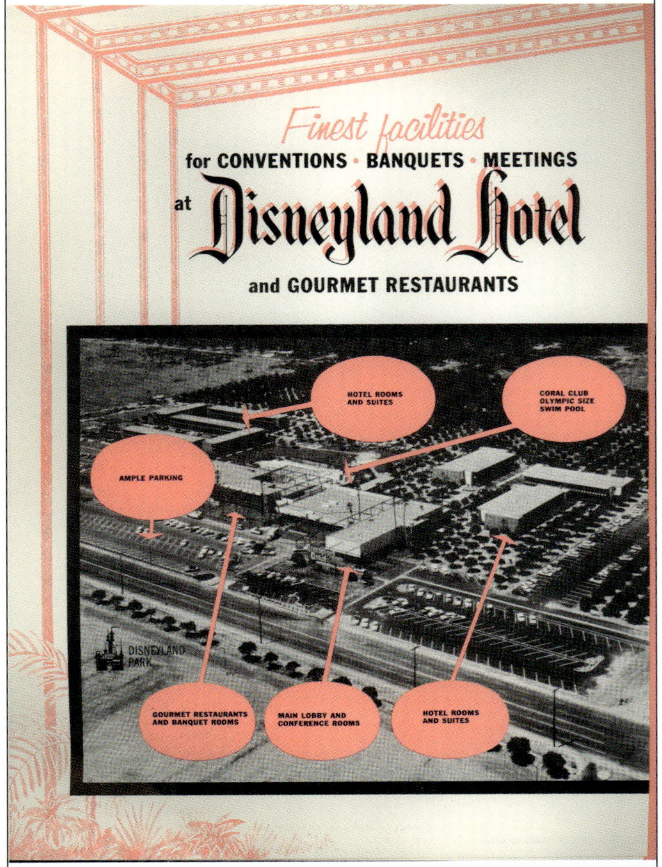

A 1950's Convention brochure.

The Disneyland Hotel was proclaimed as being "in the heart of America's favorite playground." Don J. Daley was the Resident Manager. Room rates in 1957 were advertised at $10 to $19 for singles and doubles. Family rates ranged from $15 to $18. Suites cost between $22 and $25. The Hotel's brochures boasted of an assortment of shops, air conditioned rooms, television in every room, pools of all sizes, restaurant and cocktail facilities. Tram service to Disneyland was available every five minutes or less frequently, transportation via a Disneyland station wagon. Playgrounds, childcare facilities, barber and beauty shops, doctor, nurse, and even dental facilities were available on the grounds. The brochures further emphasized a private sundeck or patio for every room. Best of all, the Disneyland Hotel was billed as being the only hotel right at the Magic Kingdom of Disneyland. In the late 1950's, the concept of "seasonal" and "non-seasonal" rates first appeared. It would typically cost a dollar or two more per night for a room during the holidays and summer months (defined then as late May through mid-September).

In May, the Wrather Corporation recorded in its Board minutes a "notice of completion" of the Disneyland Hotel. However, the following decades would witness continuous expansion.

By the end of 1957, Disneyland had welcomed its 10-millionth guest, Leigh Woolfenden on December 31st. As attendance grew, so did the attractions at the Park. The Grand Canyon Diorama, Alice in Wonderland, and the Sailing Ship Columbia were all added in 1958. From the original investment of $17-million, a total of $21.3-million had now been invested in the Park.

The well known Gourmet had restaurants in Beverly Hills, Hollywood and now, the

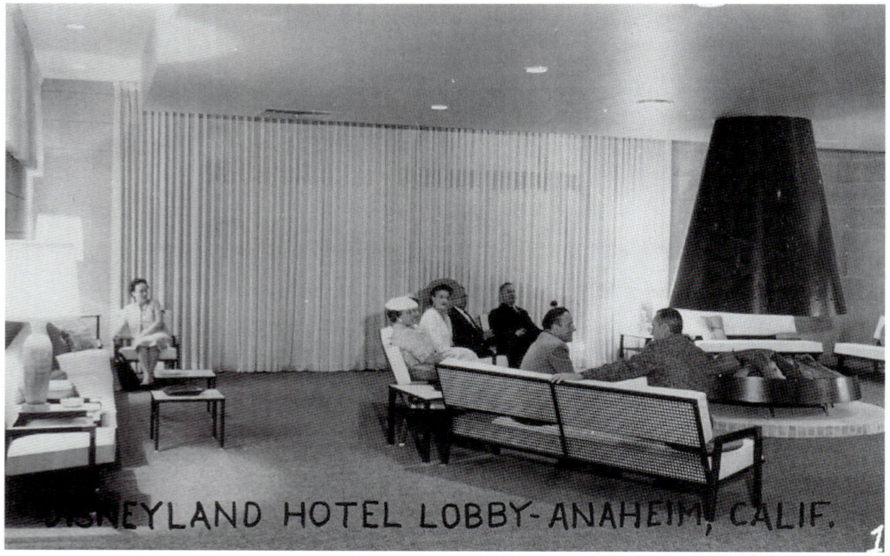

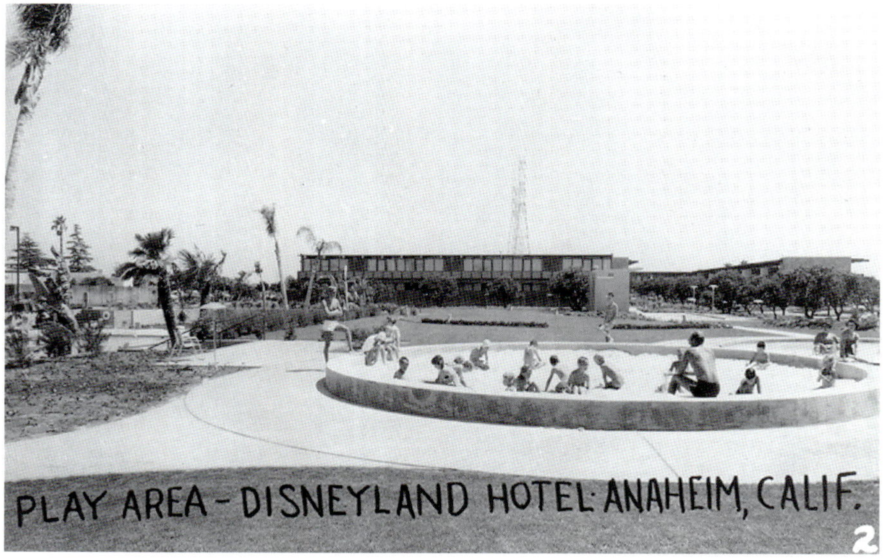

Two extremely rare, early postcards depicting the new hotel lobby and wading pool for small children. These postcards were actual pictures taken by hotel staff and given to guests. Stamped in the back were "Postcard", an area to write a note and addressee space.

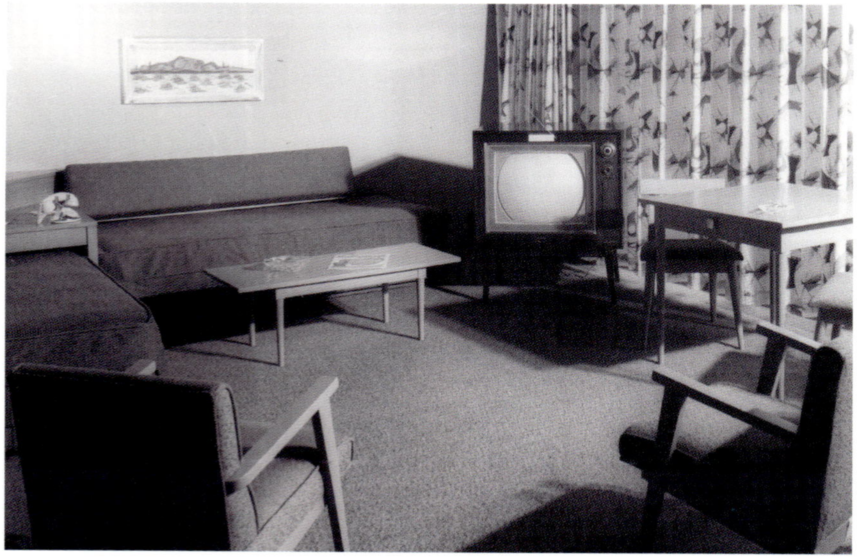

Interior photograph of a guest room from the 1950's. Each guest room had a television set which was unique for hotels at that time.

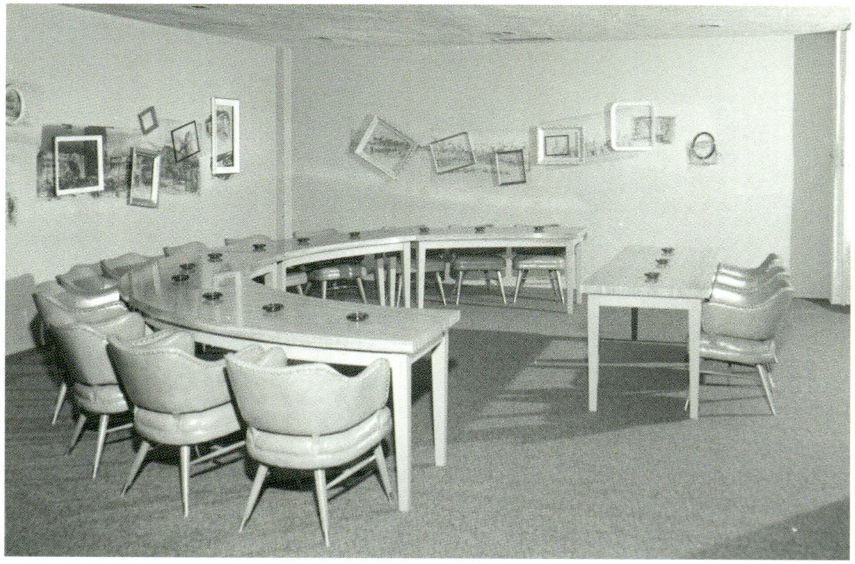

Interior photograph of one of the first conference rooms available at the Hotel. These meeting facilities featured acoustical ceilings, air conditioning, ample electrical outlets, built in audio systems, microphone and phono jacks and leather upholstered chairs.

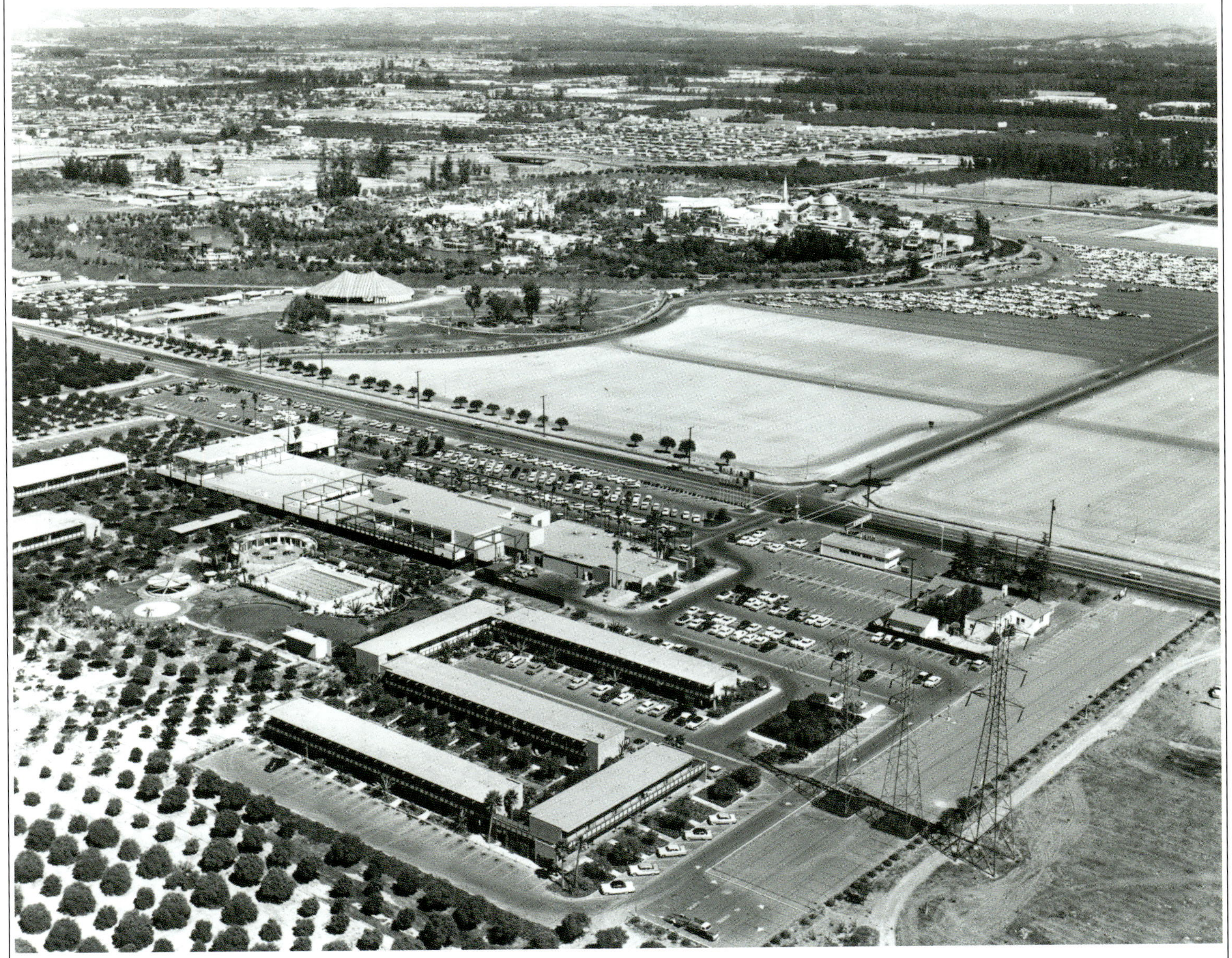

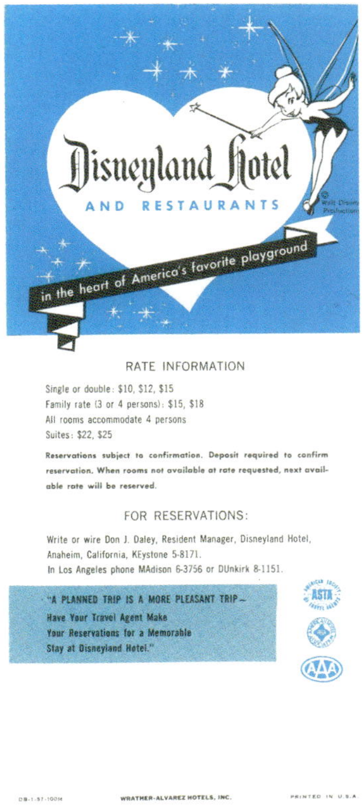

Disneyland Hotel
AND RESTAURANTS
in the heart of America's favorite playground

RATE INFORMATION

Single or double: $10, $12, $15
Family rate (3 or 4 persons): $15, $18
All rooms accommodate 4 persons
Suites: $22, $25

Reservations subject to confirmation. Deposit required to confirm reservation. When rooms not available at rate requested, next available rate will be reserved.

FOR RESERVATIONS:

Write or wire Don J. Daley, Resident Manager, Disneyland Hotel,
Anaheim, California, KEystone 5-8171.
In Los Angeles phone MAdison 6-3756 or DUnkirk 8-1151.

**"A PLANNED TRIP IS A MORE PLEASANT TRIP –
Have Your Travel Agent Make
Your Reservations for a Memorable
Stay at Disneyland Hotel."**

ASTA

AAA

DB-1-57-100M WRATHER-ALVAREZ HOTELS, INC. PRINTED IN U.S.A.

1957 Hotel rates.

An aerial photograph from 1957 showing Disneyland, the Disneyland Hotel and the surrounding area. The Little Gourmet Restaurant building is still in place but is now being used for storage only. The famous Disneyland Hotel sign had just been erected along West Street.

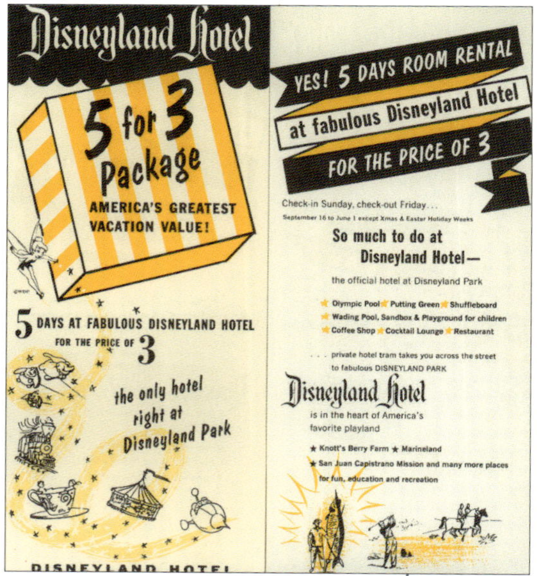

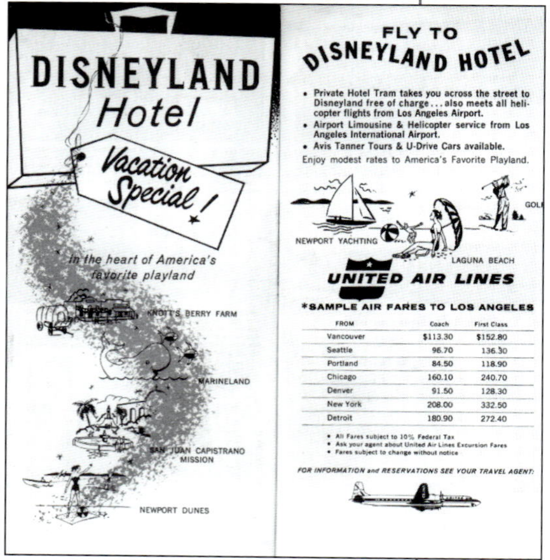

1950's package deal brochures. The Disneyland Hotel was a forerunner in offering these types of deals. This boosted room sales during non-peak times of the year.

Disneyland Hotel. On Sunday, April 20, 1958, at the Gourmet, a weary Park visitor or a Hotel guest would have enjoyed its relaxing atmosphere and a tasty meal. On that evening, the diner could have selected from five "Gourmet Dinner Specialties" such as Breast of Chicken on Broiled Ham with Wine Sauce and Almonds or Shrimp New Orleans en Casserole with Timbale of Rice for $3.25, or Broiled Tournedos of Steer Beef with Fresh Mushrooms for $3.95 (with salad, beverage, potato and vegetable included with each "Specialty" of the house). That evening's thirteen "Specials" included selections such as Broiled New Zealand Lobster Tail with Drawn Butter for $3.75, Spaghetti Neapolitan with Disneyland Garni for $2.20, or Roast Young Tom Turkey with Celery Dressing and Cranberry Sauce for $2.70 (with appetizer or soup, salad, vegetable, rolls and beverage served with each "Special" of the evening). The highest priced meal on that evening's menu was Planked Chateaubriand Bouquetiere (for two) for $11.00. A choice from a dozen "Desserts" ranged in price from 30-cents to 50-cents.

A Hotel brochure from 1958 described the shops in the Patio Arcade that were clustered next to the lobby: "In the main administration building, guests will find a wide variety of distinctive shops, offering gifts, clothing, cosmetics and sundries, cameras, film, handbags and jewelry, Hawaiian and Latin imports, toys, flowers and candy." The Disneyland Hotel Barber Shop was owned by Mr. Alberts.

Almost from the opening of the Hotel, special "package" plans were offered so as to lure guests to spend more time during the non-peak periods. In the late 1950's, the "5 for 3 Packages" appeared. Except for the Christmas and Easter holiday weeks or the summer season (June 2 to September 15), a family could stay for "5 days at fabulous Disneyland Hotel for the price of 3" days.

By 1959, over twenty-five motels had crowded around Disneyland, hoping to take advantage of the Park's spectacular drawing power. Because of the uncontrolled growth of motels, restaurants, and other such tourist facilities and because of the gaudy neon signs, the area around Disneyland had been dubbed "Glitter Gulch." By 1960, Anaheim had established itself as Orange County's largest city, with a population in excess of 100,000 (a 226-percent increase in just one decade). People were traveling from all areas of the world to visit the "Happiest Place on Earth." Anaheim had magically grown from a quiet, small agricultural community into a mecca of tourism, and the boom had only just begun.

In April of 1959, the 15-millionth guest passed through the turnstiles. As Walt had promised on opening day, the Park continued adding attractions. The Monorail (dedicated by Vice-President Richard M. Nixon and his family on June 14th), the Submarine Voyage, and the Matterhorn with its bobsleds, all opened in 1959. In June of that year, Disneyland added the "E-Ticket" to its ticket books. The total investment in the Park had grown to $30.9-million.

On the morning of May 18, 1959, Anaheim's first radio station went on the air. KEZY was to be found at 1190 on the AM dial; the call letters reflected the fact that its format was easy listening music. The station's offices were located on the main floor of the Administration Building of the Disneyland Hotel. As guests entered through the front doors, they could see a small, glass booth at the far south end of the lobby. That was KEZY's broadcast studio, located just across from the Patio Arcade shopping area's drug store.

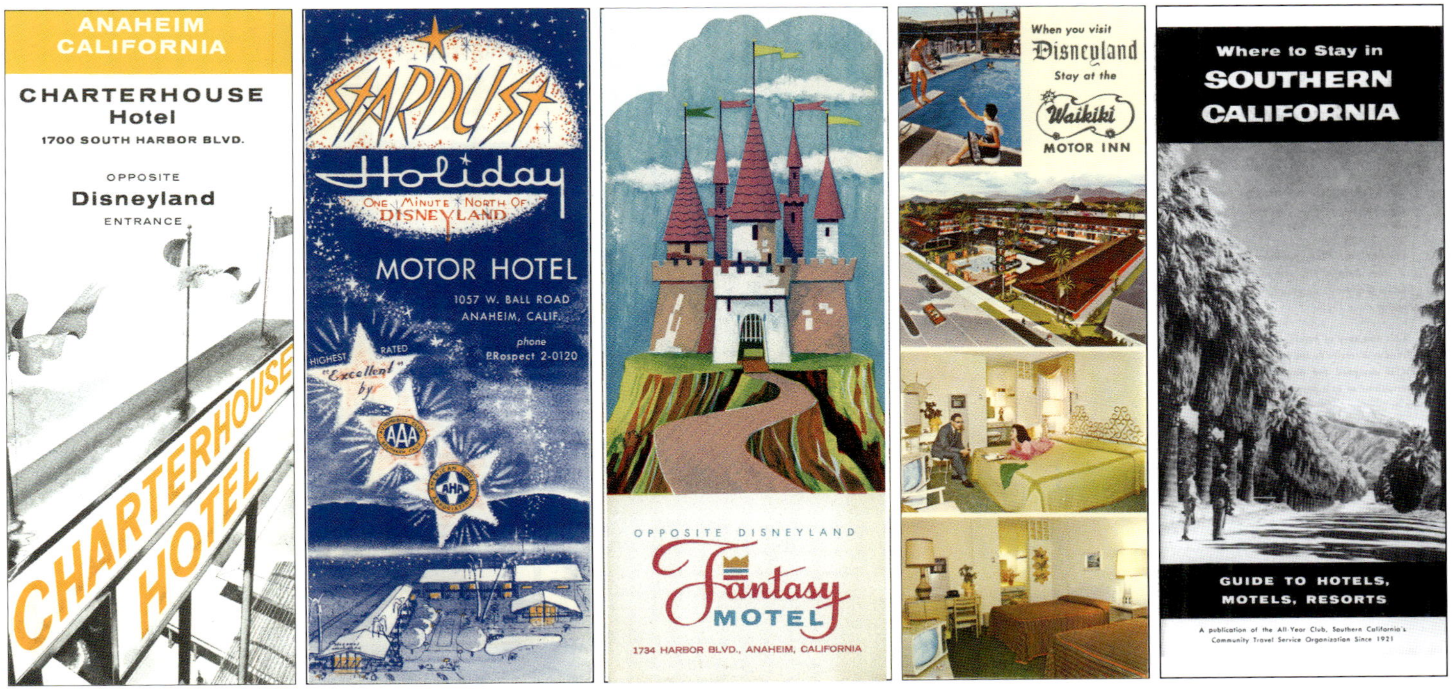

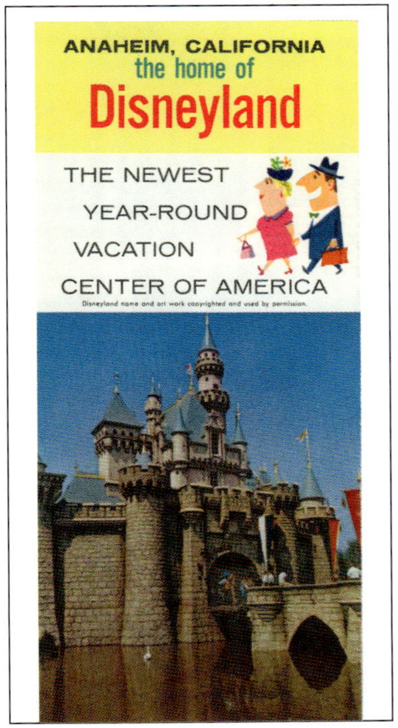

Anaheim area Hotel and Motel brochures. Most included their location as next to Disneyland on their brochure covers.

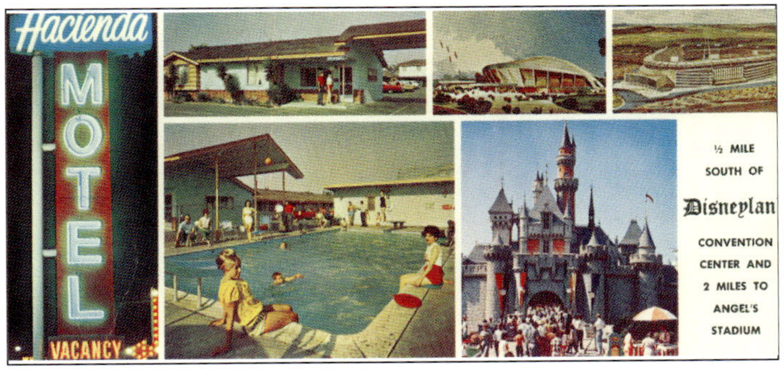

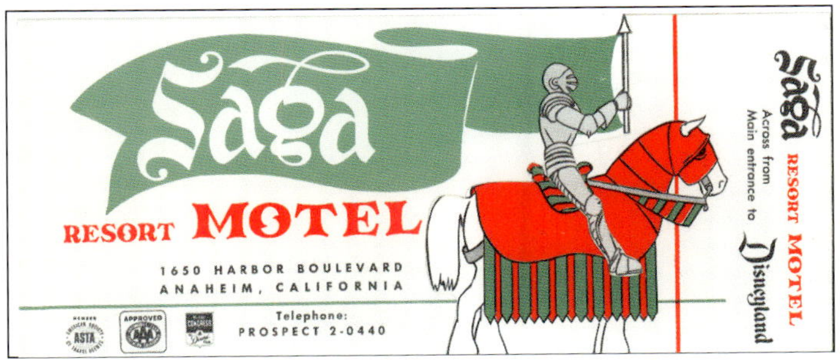

At exactly nine o'clock on that May morning, the first sound to be heard by listeners was the barking of television dog star Lassie. Nine-year-old Jon Provost, co-star of Lassie was one of a number of celebrities interviewed during the radio station's first day of broadcasting. Gene Barry, star of *Bat Masterson* and Richard Simmons, star of *Sgt. Preston* of *the Yukon* were also heard.

Cliff Gill was the 1000-watt station's first president and general manager. In 1966, KEZY increased its daytime power to 5000 watts. The radio station moved from its Disneyland Hotel location in 1969 into much larger facilities at 1190 East Ball Road. [Note that its new address was the same as its location on the dial.] Its programming was changed at that time to the more popular top-40 rock format, attracting a large, teenage audience.

In 1959, the Gourmet restaurant advertised "Luncheon from $1.25...Dinner from $2.35" and pro-

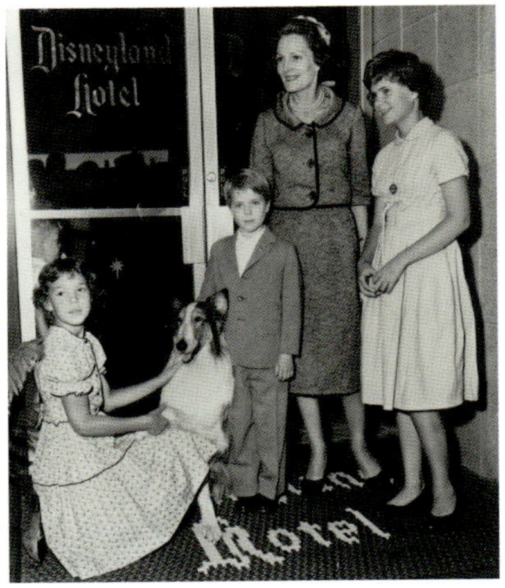

Pat Nixon and daughters with Jon Provost and Lassie.

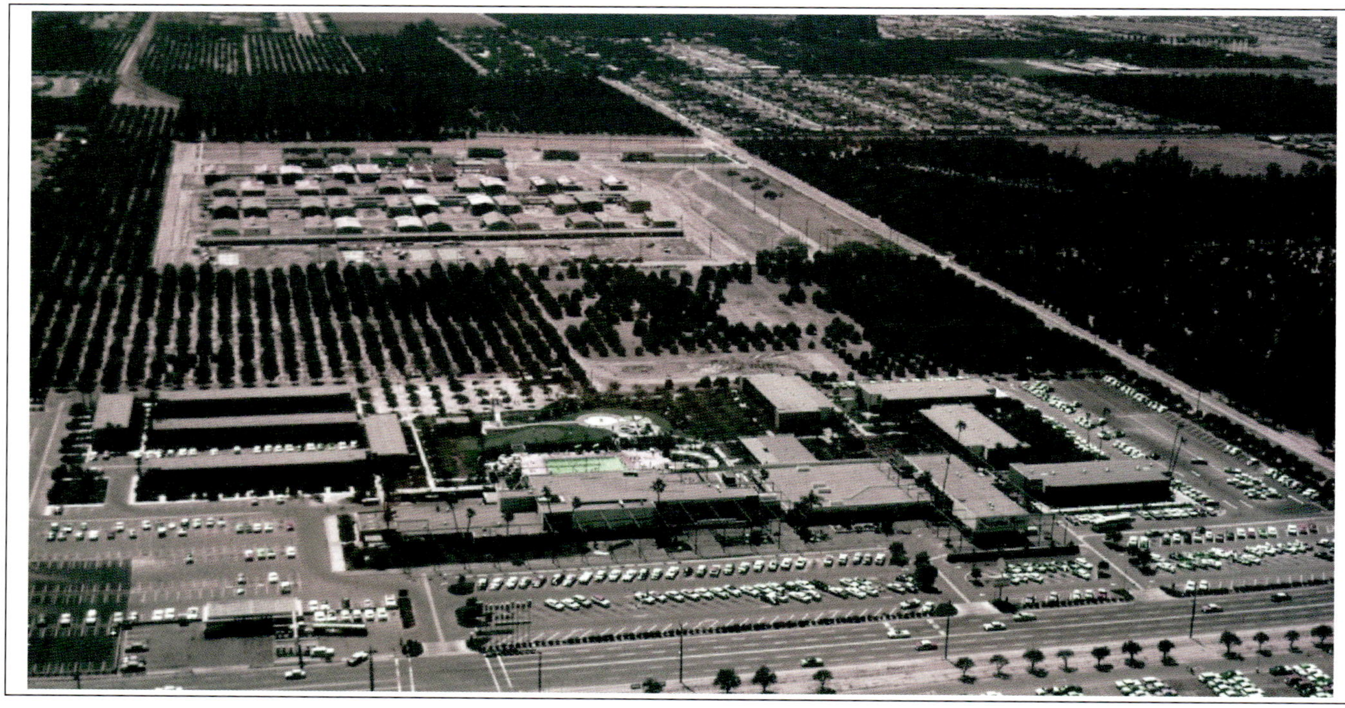

An aerial photograph from 1959 showingnthe Disneyland Hotel and the surrounding area. Large orange orchards are still prominent surrounding the Hotel and Park.

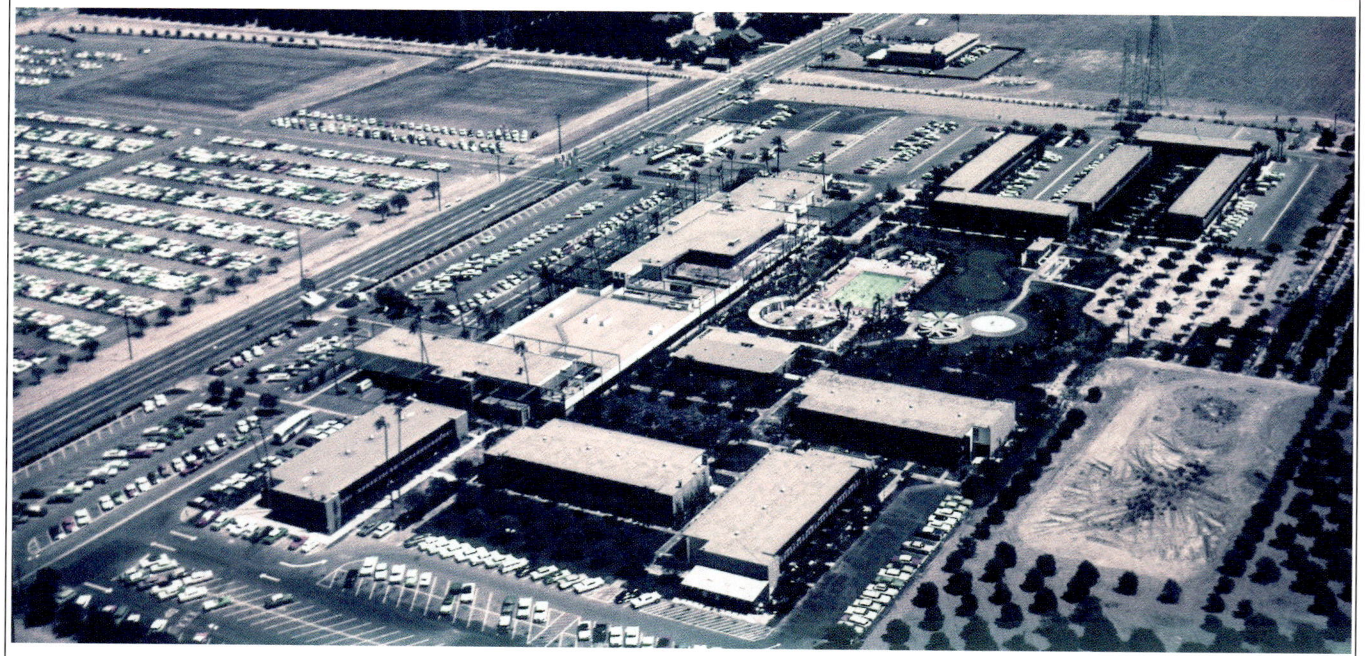

Close-up of the Hotel area. Note the area of fresh pavement in the upper middle where the Little Gourmet restaurant had previously been located. A fourth North Garden structure has now been added to the Hotel (lower left).

claimed "Enjoy Fine Food in Delightful Surroundings." From its beginnings at the Hotel, the Gourmet had offered breakfast, luncheon, dinner, and late night snacks. Another advertisement from the time proclaimed that "you'll find the most complete food service combination available under the Southland sun--formal restaurant, cocktail lounge--featuring nightly entertainment--and a briskly efficient Coffee Shop."

By July of 1959, a fourth Garden Room structure was added in the Northeast section of the property bringing the total to nine guest room structures (four in the Northeast and five in the South). No mention is made about additional available rooms in any of the brochures from this timeframe.

The Disneyland Hotel realized a $500,000 profit that year, and all indications led to the expectation that profits would increase with each succeeding year. On November 13th, Wrather wrote William L. Pereira, one of the Hotel's architects. In part Jack wrote, "Orange County certainly is living up to my feelings of 4 or 5 years ago, even though I was considered somewhat of a crackpot at the time, I guess, building a hotel in the middle of the orange groves!"

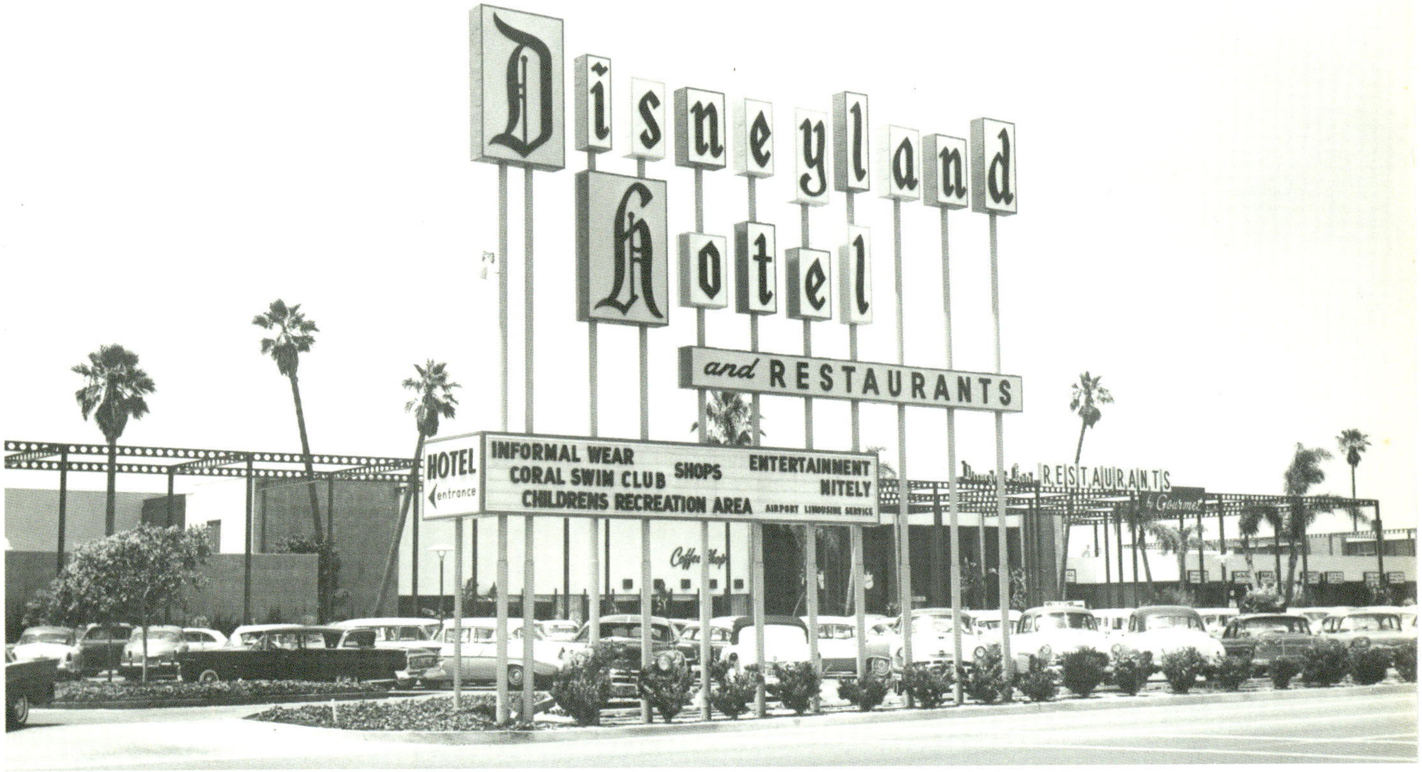

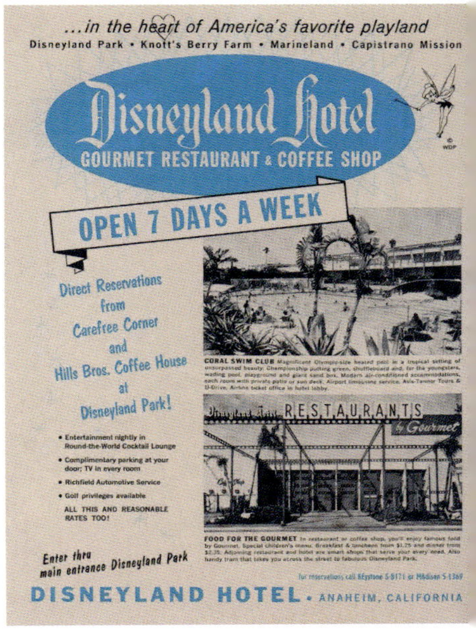

Gourmet Restaurant advertisement.

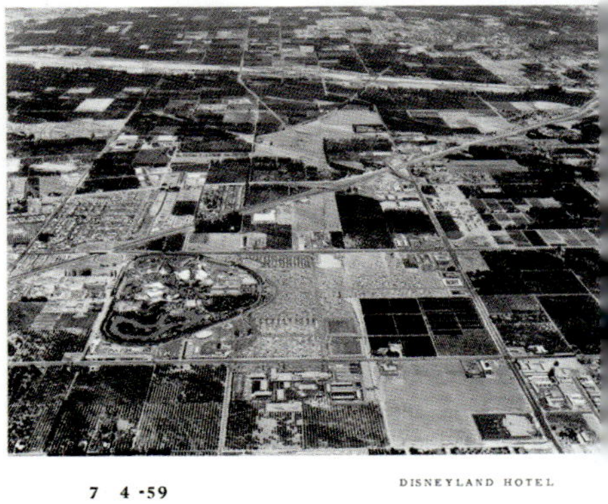

1959 aerial.

1960-1969

By 1960, Anaheim was the fastest growing city in the United States with a population of 104,184. An acre of land now could demand up to $20,000. Orange County had also become the fastest growing county in the nation. Disneyland guests for the first time could enjoy the Art of Animation exhibit, the Mine Train Through Nature's Wonderland, and Skull Rock and Pirates Cove in 1960. The 20-millionth guest entered the Park in April, and the total investment had climbed to $34.5-million.

The Hotel also continued to grow, having expanded to slightly more than 300 rooms. With room enough for 1,000 guests, the Disneyland Hotel was the largest hotel in Orange County. Rates for rooms in 1960 ranged from $10 to $26 a night during the off-season and from $16 to $29 in season, the holidays and the summer months.

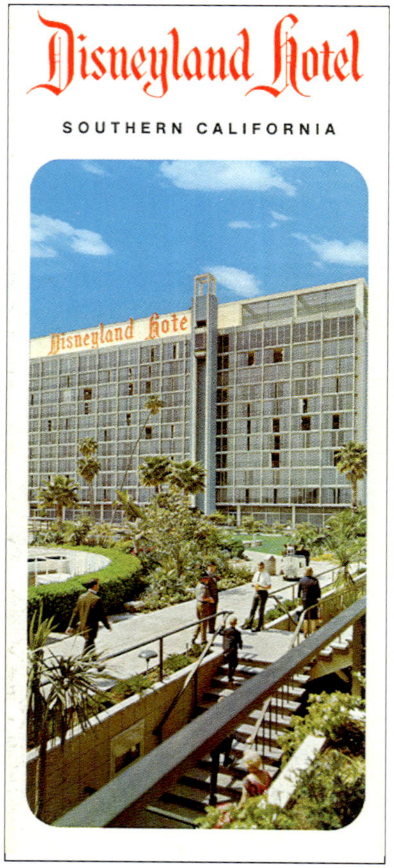

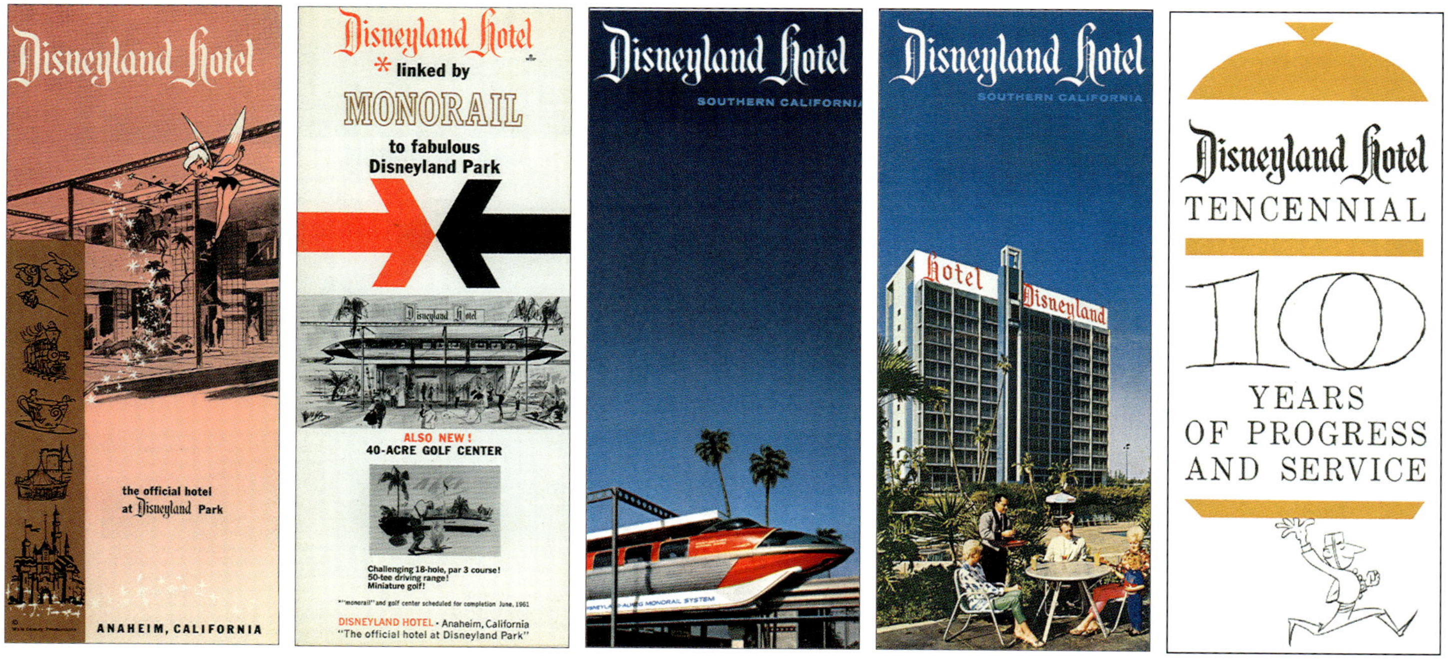

Hotel brochures from the 1960's.

A helicopter landing pad was built in 1960 (in the mid-block area next to the miniature golf course, across Cerritos Avenue just to the north of the Hotel) linking Los Angeles International Airport with Disneyland and the Disneyland Hotel. The new facility provided an efficient transportation link for both business people and tourists. Soon, Los Angeles Airways was operating an average of twelve flights per day to and from the airport in its twen-

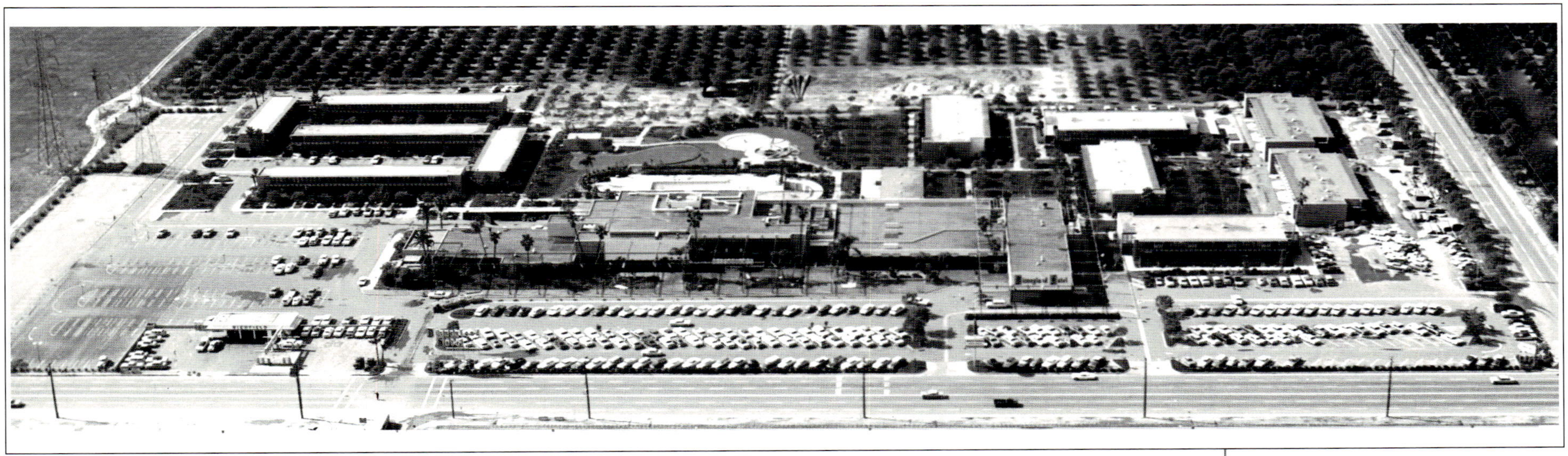

An aerial view from 1960 with the construction of the last two North Garden structures (upper right) well underway. These were the last of the two-story buildings ever constructed on the site. The Hotel would now advertise over 300 guest rooms and suites.

ty-eight passenger, turbo-jet copter liners. A one-way flight lasted approximately fifteen-minutes. [This air service had begun during the earliest days after the opening of the Park. The original landing site had been just off the Santa Ana Freeway on Harbor Boulevard, with tram service being provided to the Park and to the Hotel.] For the less adventurous, a limousine service provided eighteen daily round trips to the airport.

Walt Disney's interest in the Monorail, "the train of the future," went far beyond it being a mere amusement park attraction. Walt had long envisioned a rapid transit system operating in major U.S. cities. Dick Nunis, who worked his way up from a summer job at Disneyland in 1955 to become the president of Disneyland in 1980, stated "Walt saw the monorail as more than just an attraction; Walt saw it as a workable transportation system and as a possible answer to the inner-cities' transportation and environmental problems."

Since its opening in Disneyland in 1959, the monorail had already carried over 3-million passengers in safety and comfort. Still, its feasibility as public transportation needed to be tested in a real-life situation. In early 1960, Walt approached the City of Las Vegas and offered the proposition of constructing a public monorail system, running up and down the casino strip. It did not take city officials long to turn down the offer.

Walt was not deterred and had a solution to a working system. At a press conference later in 1960, Jack Wrather and Walt Disney announced plans for the extension of the Disneyland-Alweg Monorail System to link the Park to the Hotel. This addition to the monorail would provide Walt with a working model.

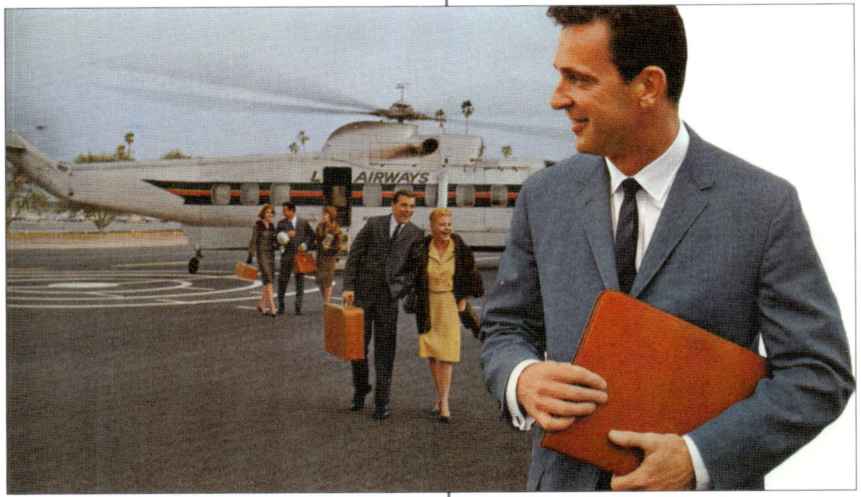

Guests arriving at the Hotel's Heliport from LAX.

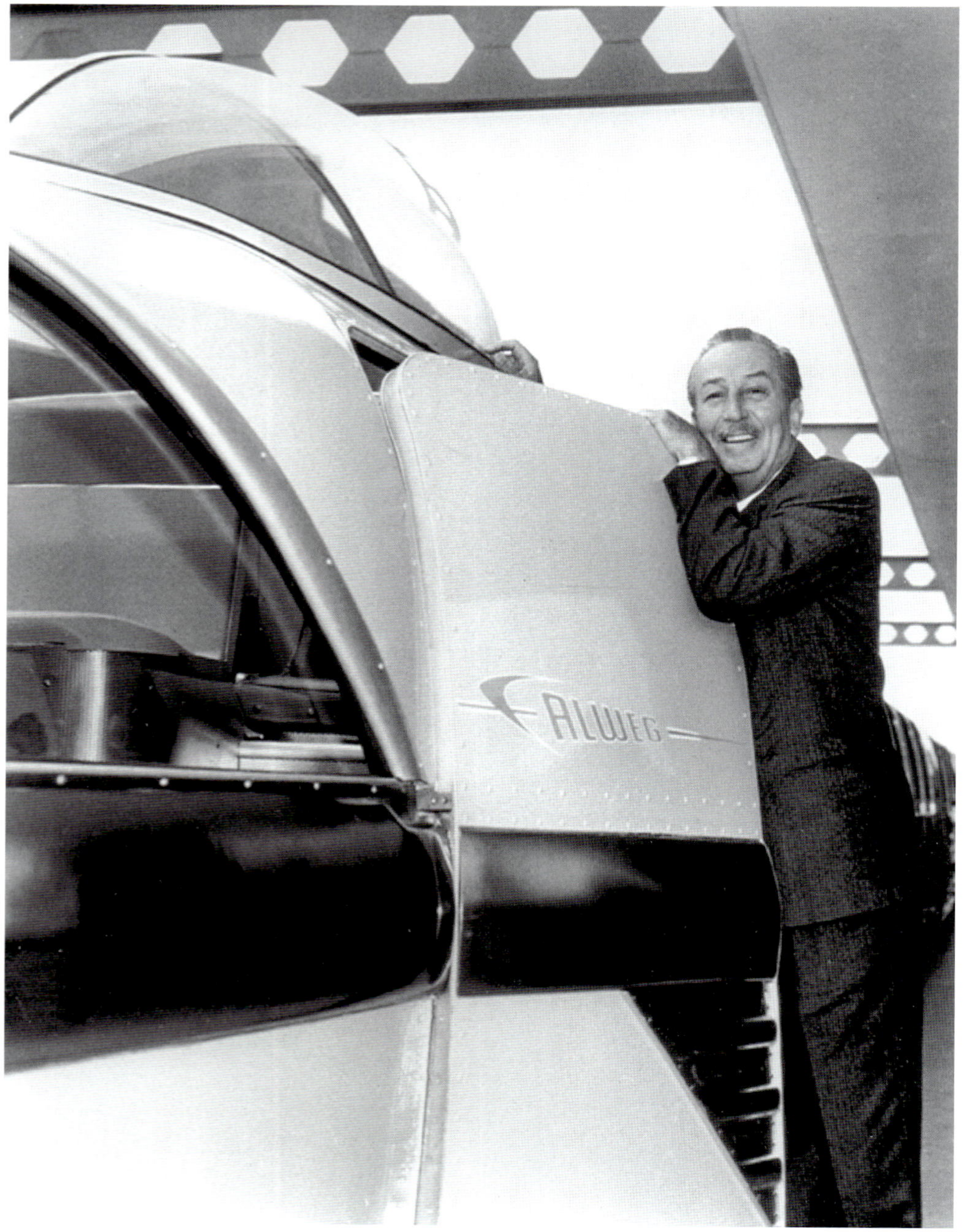

Walt's transportation of the future.

The Park's monorail was closed for construction on April 10, 1961. Disneyland also had to close Autopia to facilitate the installation of new pylons through its grounds. The original 8/10th of a mile track would be extended by 12,300 feet, making it nearly a two and a half mile round-trip journey between the Park to the Hotel. The cost of the extension was $1.9-million ($500,000 more than the original cost of the Monorail when it had been installed at Disneyland in June of 1959). The construction required more than 118,000 man-hours of labor, 10,760 tons of sand, 66,700 bags of cement, and 702 tons of steel. Over seven-hundred new pylons had to be added. New style Mark II trains were introduced for the extended monorail, including a new gold colored train. On May 25th, the press was given a preview of the project. The monorail, with its extension to the Disneyland Hotel, reopened to the public on June 11, 1961. Since that date, Walt's "Highway in the Sky" has provided smooth, swift and safe service for Hotel visitors.

With the addition of a third train and a fourth car added to each of the existing trains (now 112 feet long), up to 106 passengers could travel to and from the Disneyland Hotel on each train. The monorail traveled overhead at a height of between twelve and thirty feet above the ground. While the monorail operated at a top speed of 25 m.p.h. within the Park, across the straighter length of the Disneyland parking lot, it could reach a speed of 35 m.p.h. [With a longer stretch of straight track, the monorail could have cruised at 45 m.p.h.] When the monorail was installed in the Park in 1959, it had become the first regularly scheduled, daily operational monorail in the United States. Now with the extension to the Disneyland Hotel, it had become the first monorail to cross a public thoroughfare.

Surveys indicated that 99.6-percent of the passengers of the Disneyland monorail approved of its service. The success, the efficiency, and the feasibility of the monorail as mass transit were saluted by the addition of a monorail system to the 1962 Seattle World's Fair. That system is still in operation to this date. In 1986, the American Society of Mechanical Engineers would honor the Disneyland Monorail system by declaring it to be a "National Mechanical Engineering Landmark."

It was calculated that during the summer season "guests were pouring through the Main Gate [of Disneyland] at the average rate of 33 every minute." Many of those guests would ride the newly expanded monorail as an estimated 3-million people a year rode the "highway in the sky." The Wrather Corporation immediately understood the importance of its extension to the Hotel. In his 1961 annual report, Jack Wrather wrote: "Our already strong competitive advantage is significantly strengthened by this important addition [the monorail] to our facilities." The ease of traveling back and forth between the Hotel and the Park gave the Hotel a greater appeal over other hotels that had no direct connection to the Park. Many other riders disembarked at the Hotel just for a brief look and ended up spending a little money. The annual report further stated that "the monorail is improving the gross revenue of the Hotel, its shops and food facilities." At that time, the Hotel's 306 rooms were operating at 100-percent occupancy during the summer months and during other school-break periods.

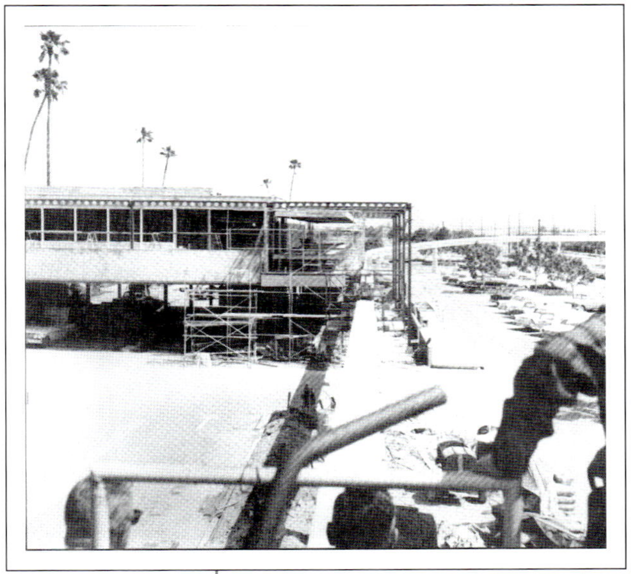

Construction of the Monorail Station at the Disneyland Hotel. The extended monorail would open at the Disneyland Hotel in June of 1961.

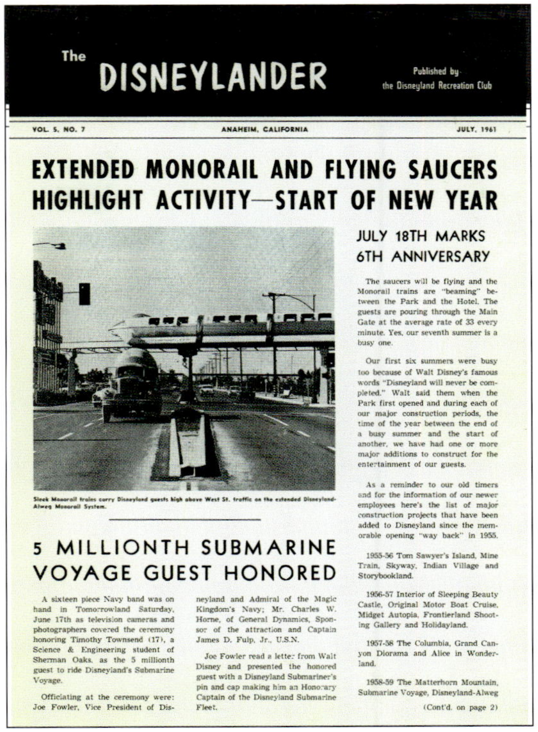

The DISNEYLANDER

Published by the Disneyland Recreation Club

VOL. 5, NO. 7 — ANAHEIM, CALIFORNIA — JULY, 1961

EXTENDED MONORAIL AND FLYING SAUCERS HIGHLIGHT ACTIVITY—START OF NEW YEAR

Sleek Monorail trains carry Disneyland guests high above West St. traffic on the extended Disneyland-Alweg Monorail System.

JULY 18TH MARKS 6TH ANNIVERSARY

The saucers will be flying and the Monorail trains are "beaming" between the Park and the Hotel. The guests are pouring through the Main Gate at the average rate of 33 every minute. Yes, our seventh summer is a busy one.

Our first six summers were busy too because of Walt Disney's famous words "Disneyland will never be completed." Walt said them when the Park first opened and during each of our major construction periods, the time of the year between the end of a busy summer and the start of another, we have had one or more major additions to construct for the entertainment of our guests.

As a reminder to our old timers and for the information of our newer employees here's the list of major construction projects that have been added to Disneyland since the memorable opening "way back" in 1955.

1955-56 Tom Sawyer's Island, Mine Train, Skyway, Indian Village and Storybookland.

1956-57 Interior of Sleeping Beauty Castle, Original Motor Boat Cruise, Midget Autopia, Frontierland Shooting Gallery and Holidayland.

1957-58 The Columbia, Grand Canyon Diorama and Alice in Wonderland.

1958-59 The Matterhorn Mountain, Submarine Voyage, Disneyland-Alweg

(Cont'd. on page 2)

5 MILLIONTH SUBMARINE VOYAGE GUEST HONORED

A sixteen piece Navy band was on hand in Tomorrowland Saturday, June 17th as television cameras and photographers covered the ceremony honoring Timothy Townsend (17), a Science & Engineering student of Sherman Oaks, as the 5 millionth guest to ride Disneyland's Submarine Voyage.

Officiating at the ceremony were: Joe Fowler, Vice President of Disneyland and Admiral of the Magic Kingdom's Navy; Mr. Charles W. Horne, of General Dynamics, Sponsor of the attraction and Captain James D. Fulp, Jr., U.S.N.

Joe Fowler read a letter from Walt Disney and presented the honored guest with a Disneyland Submariner's pin and cap making him an Honorary Captain of the Disneyland Submarine Fleet.

Disneylander employee newsletter announcing the extension of the monorail to the Disneyland Hotel.

In 1961, the Hotel comprised 16-percent of the Wrather Corporation's gross annual income. Based upon the strength of the Disneyland Hotel's operations, plans were already underway to expand all areas: rooms, restaurants, convention facilities, and recreation/entertainment. Two new Garden Room structures were added in the Northeast section of the property. The Hotel now had eleven guest accommodation structures (six in the Northeast section and five in the southern section of the property). Although these buildings were added, no mention is made in any brochure of additional, available rooms at the Disneyland Hotel at this time. It was still advertised that 300 rooms were available.

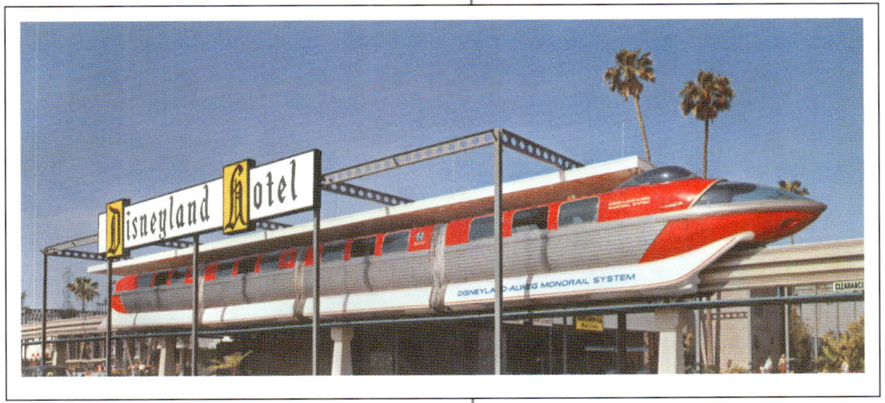

Tomorrows transportation system today-that's the Disneyland-Alweg Monorail-can speed you to tomorrow's resort hotel today.-that's the luxurious Disneyland Hotel. Within the beautifully landscaped grounds, you'll find every convenience, every luxury for complete leisure-time enjoyment.

Many new, major expansions were added to the Hotel in 1961. Included was a new golf complex (covering an area of 40-acres). It featured an 18-hole, par-three "pitch and putt" course (illuminated at night). Hole 17 was actually an island in the middle of a lake; there were seven other water holes along with sand traps galore. Ross Dixon was the course's original pro. There were also a 250-yard, 50-tee driving range and a miniature golf course with each of the individual holes themed after a different Disneyland attraction.

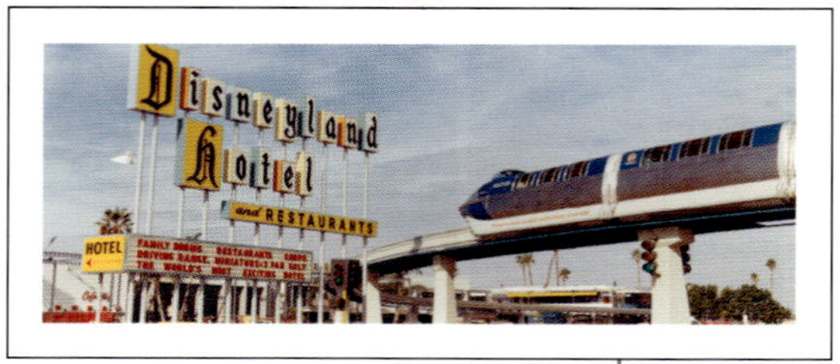

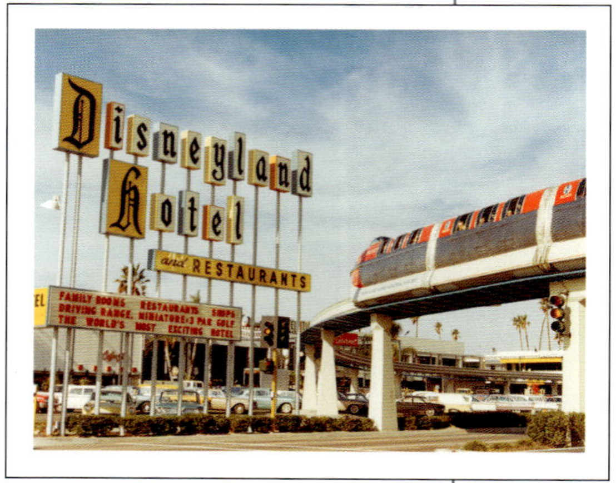

Sleek Monorail trains carry Disneyland guests high above West Street traffic on the extended Disneyland-Alweg Monorail System.

Officially named The Magic Kingdom Golf Course, the miniature course was located at 1125 West Cerritos. It was an 18-hole course also illuminated for night play. Disney Studios art director Al Applegate was construction coordinator. Disneyland provided the talents of Andy Anderson, Larry Smith, and Bud Washo. Hole one was dubbed "Main Street" and was a replica of the Santa Fe and Disneyland Railroad Station. The next three holes were themed after Fantasyland. The first of those three holes was simply named "Fantasyland," but nothing is known of its structure. The third hole was called "Sleeping Beauty's [*sic*] Castle" and was a miniature of the castle, its draw bridge, and its courtyard parapets, all set on a rock island. Hole four was the "Dwarf's Mine." The course's next four holes were themed after Tomorrowland. The fifth tee ("Matterhorn Bobsled" a course favorite by many) represented the Matterhorn's ticket office, the hole featured fairways to three separate greens, approached by means of two metal bridges to cross over the bobsled waterway. Holes six and seven were called "Tomorrowland" and "Moon Rocket."”Octopus' Lair," reminding players of the Submarine Voyage, was the eighth hole; and "Autopia" was the ninth. Hole ten was "Adventureland." The eleventh hole was the"Painted Desert" and consisted of rocks and simulated cacti. A replica of the fort's gate welcomed golfers to "Frontierland," the twelfth hole. Hole thirteen originally had been planned to be an Indian Village, but it finally became "Skull Rock." The fourteenth hole was "Tom Sawyer's Island" and was a reproduction of the Grist Mill on that island. "Monstro," the entrance to the Story Book Land adventure, was fifteen. The next hole was called "Mr. Smee" and was followed by "Alice in Wonderland." The final hole was "Mickey's Lagoon." In

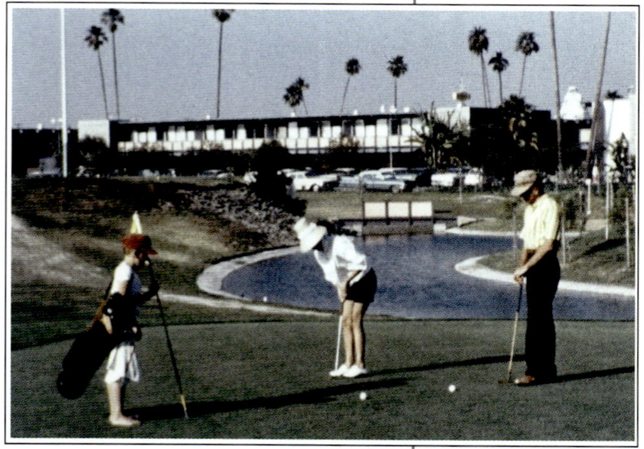

Golf facilities at the Hotel.

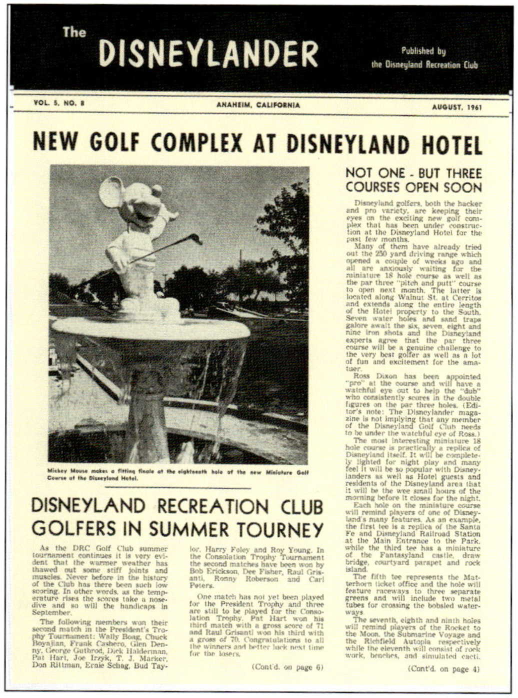

The DISNEYLANDER
Published by the Disneyland Recreation Club

VOL. 5, NO. 8 ANAHEIM, CALIFORNIA AUGUST, 1961

NEW GOLF COMPLEX AT DISNEYLAND HOTEL

Mickey Mouse makes a fitting finale at the eighteenth hole of the new Miniature Golf Course of the Disneyland Hotel.

NOT ONE - BUT THREE COURSES OPEN SOON

Disneyland golfers, both the hacker and pro variety, are keeping their eyes on the exciting new golf complex that has been under construction at the Disneyland Hotel for the past few months.

Many of them have already tried out the 250 yard driving range which opened a couple of weeks ago and all are anxiously waiting for the miniature 18 hole course as well as the par three "pitch and putt" course to open next month. The latter is located along Walnut St. at Cerritos and extends along the entire length of the Hotel property to the South. Seven water holes and sand traps galore await the six, seven, eight and nine iron shots and the Disneyland experts agree that the par three course will be a genuine challenge to the very best golfer as well as a lot of fun and excitement for the amatuer.

Ross Dixon has been appointed "pro" at the course and will have a watchful eye out to help the "dub" who consistently scores in the double figures on the par three holes. (Editor's note: The Disneylander magazine is not implying that any member of the Disneyland Golf Club needs to be under the watchful eye of Ross.)

The most interesting miniature 18 hole course is practically a replica of Disneyland itself. It will be completely lighted for night play and many feel it will be so popular with Disneylanders as well as Hotel guests and residents of the Disneyland area that it will be the wee small hours of the morning before it closes for the night.

Each hole on the miniature course will remind players of one of Disneyland's many features. As an example, the first tee is a replica of the Santa Fe and Disneyland Railroad Station at the Main Entrance to the Park, while the third tee has a miniature of the Fantasyland castle, draw bridge, courtyard parapet and rock island.

The fifth tee represents the Matterhorn ticket office and the hole will feature raceways to three separate greens and will include two metal tubes for crossing the bobsled waterways.

The seventh, eighth and ninth holes will remind players of the Rocket to the Moon, the Submarine Voyage and the Richfield Autopia respectively while the eleventh will consist of rock work, benches, and simulated cacti.

(Cont'd. on page 4)

DISNEYLAND RECREATION CLUB GOLFERS IN SUMMER TOURNEY

As the DRC Golf Club summer tournament continues it is very evident that the warmer weather has thawed out some stiff joints and muscles. Never before in the history of the Club has there been such low scoring. In other words, as the temperature rises the scores take a nose-dive and so will the handicaps in September.

The following members won their second match in the President's Trophy Tournament: Wally Boag, Chuck Boyajian, Frank Cashero, Glen Denny, George Guthrod, Dick Halderman, Pat Hart, Joe Irzyk, T. J. Marker, Don Rittman, Ernie Schag, Bud Taylor, Harry Foley and Roy Young. In the Consolation Trophy Tournament the second matches have been won by Bob Erickson, Dee Fisher, Raul Grisanti, Ronny Roberson and Carl Peters.

One match has not yet been played for the President Trophy and three are still to be played for the Consolation Trophy. Pat Hart won his third match with a gross score of 71 and Raul Grisanti won his third with a gross of 70. Congratulations to all the winners and better luck next time for the losers.

(Cont'd. on page 6)

Disneylander golf complex announcement.

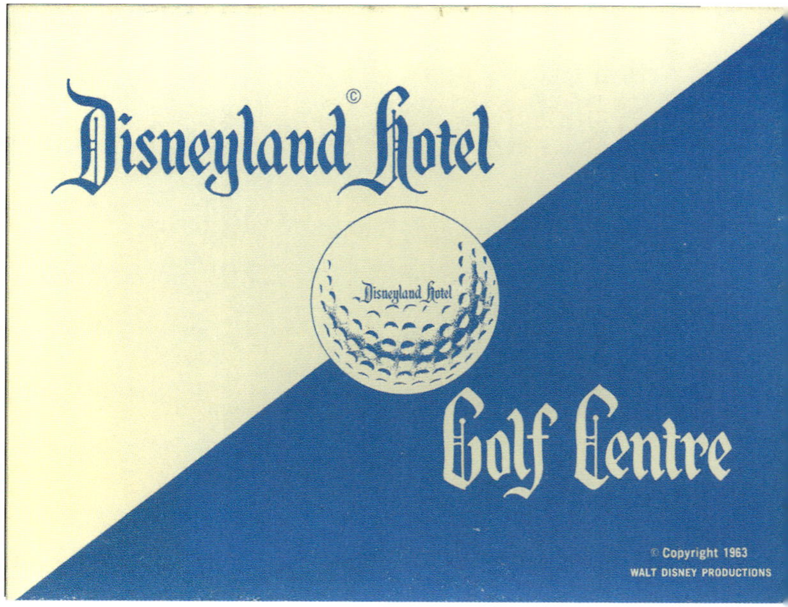

Golf ball box Disneyland Hotel.

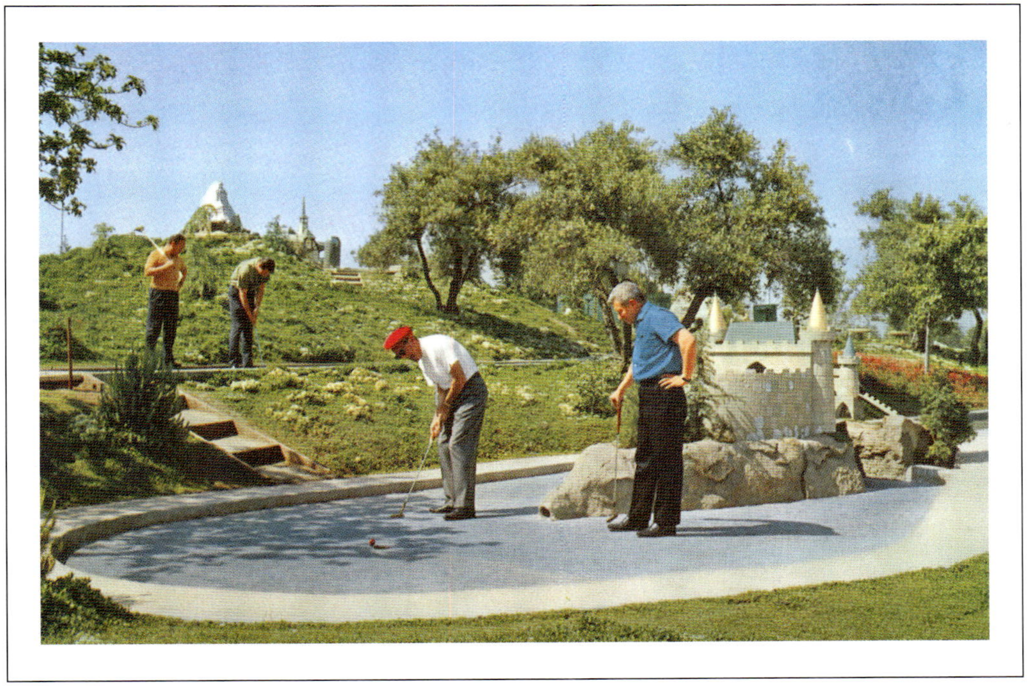

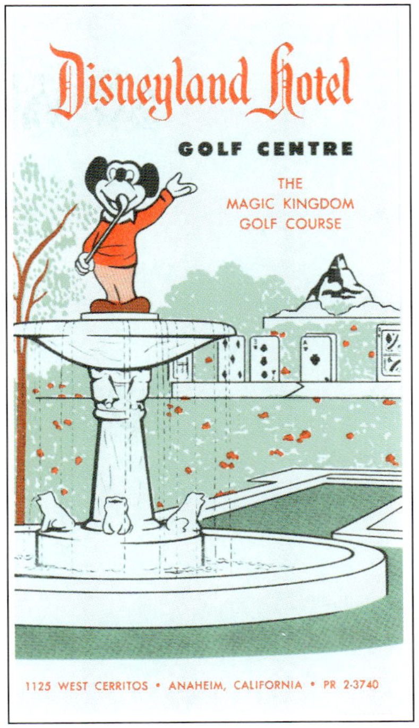

Mini golf course and 1961 scorecard. The third tee, Sleeping Beauty's Castle and fifth tee, Matterhorn Bobsleds are visible in this photograph.

the center of that green was a large fountain. On top was a sculpture of Mickey Mouse, holding a golf club. Originally, Mickey was a grayish white; he was later painted in bright colors.

[The par-three golf course was built on the acreage to the west that in the 1970's would be developed into the marina and its adjoining tower buildings. On the southeast corner of Cerritos Avenue and West Street, across from the Hotel, was one of the Hotel's parking lots. Just to the north of that parking lot was located the miniature golf course. The driving range was situated to the north of the miniature golf course.]

Disneyland added the Snow White Grotto, the Flying Saucers, and the Babes in Toyland exhibit in 1961. On April 19, 1961, Dr. Glenn C. Franklin became the Park's 25-millionth guest. The Park had now risen to a $37-million investment.

In 1961, the higher rate periods were "Vacation" (May 29 through September 15) and the "Christmas and Easter Holiday Periods." Rates at that time ranged from $16 to $29 for a single or double bedroom. Two connecting rooms (up to eight persons) cost between $41 and $51. "Off Season" rates were from $10 to $23 for a single or double, from $16 to $26 for "Family Rates" (three or four persons). Two adjoining rooms ranged from $29 to $45 (depending on the number of occupants: up to 4 people, 5 or 6 persons, 7 or 8 persons). At that time, most rooms were furnished with one double bed or two twin beds.

Built above the Hotel's shops near the main entrance on West Street, a 13,000 square foot convention and exhibition center was added. The convention hall became Orange County's first ballroom, the Embassy Room.

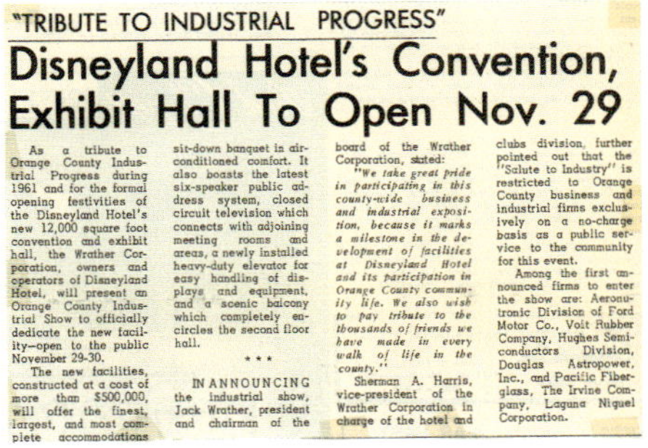

"TRIBUTE TO INDUSTRIAL PROGRESS"

Disneyland Hotel's Convention, Exhibit Hall To Open Nov. 29

As a tribute to Orange County Industrial Progress during 1961 and for the formal opening festivities of the Disneyland Hotel's new 12,000 square foot convention and exhibit hall, the Wrather Corporation, owners and operators of Disneyland Hotel, will present an Orange County Industrial Show to officially dedicate the new facility—open to the public November 29-30.

The new facilities, constructed at a cost of more than $500,000, will offer the finest, largest, and most complete accommodations sit-down banquet in air-conditioned comfort. It also boasts the latest six-speaker public address system, closed circuit television which connects with adjoining meeting rooms and areas, a newly installed heavy-duty elevator for easy handling of displays and equipment, and a scenic balcony which completely encircles the second floor hall.

* * *

IN ANNOUNCING the industrial show, Jack Wrather, president and chairman of the board of the Wrather Corporation, stated:

"We take great pride in participating in this county-wide business and industrial exposition, because it marks a milestone in the development of facilities at Disneyland Hotel and its participation in Orange County community life. We also wish to pay tribute to the thousands of friends we have made in every walk of life in the county."

Sherman A. Harris, vice-president of the Wrather Corporation in charge of the hotel and clubs division, further pointed out that the "Salute to Industry" is restricted to Orange County business and industrial firms exclusively on a no-charge basis as a public service to the community for this event.

Among the first announced firms to enter the show are: Aeronutronic Division of Ford Motor Co., Voit Rubber Company, Hughes Semiconductors Division, Douglas Astropower, Inc., and Pacific Fiberglass, The Irvine Company, Laguna Niguel Corporation.

Newspaper clipping November, 1961.

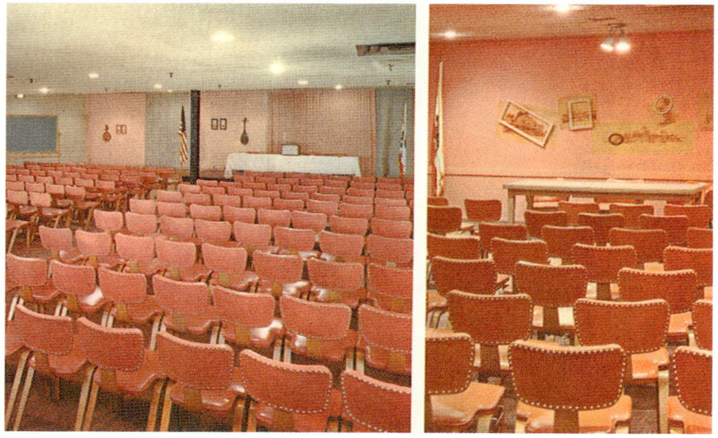

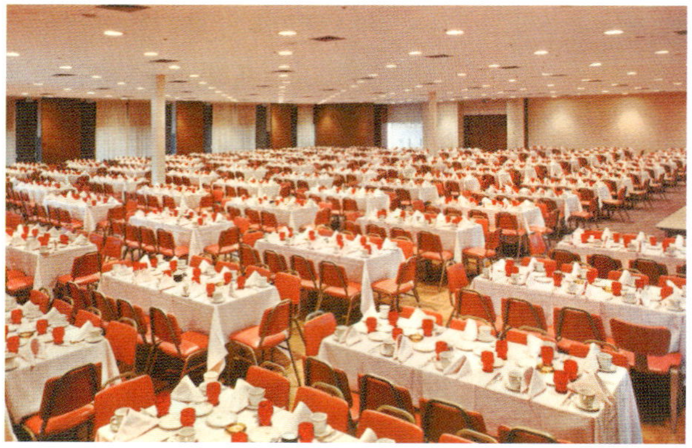

Embassy Room and interior convention facilities..

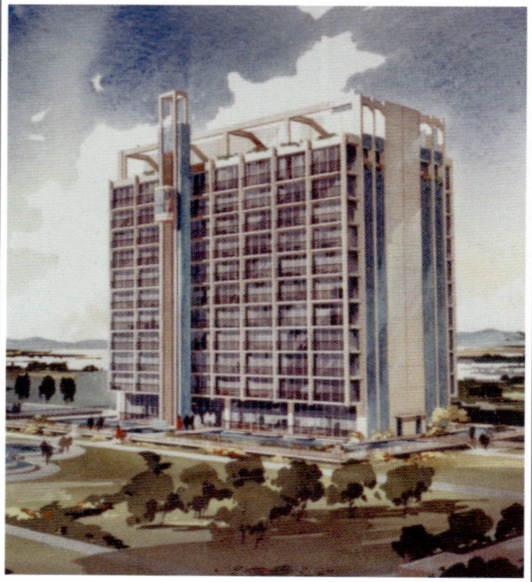

Artist concept of the new Tower Building.

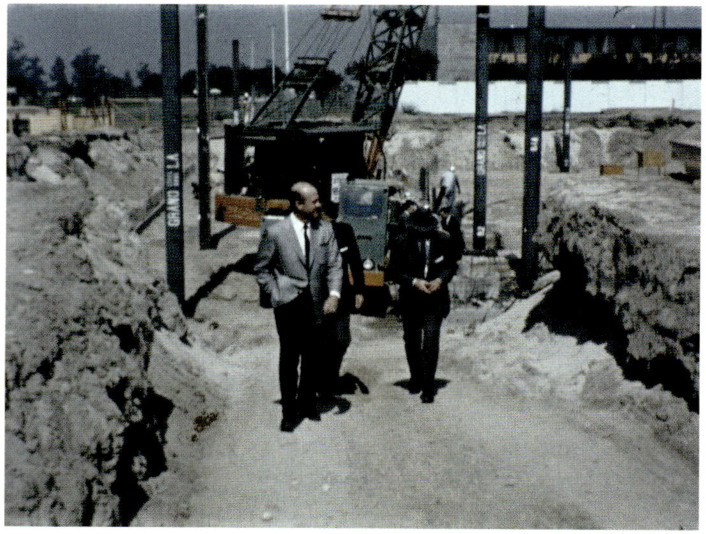

Jack Wrather at the Tower Building during official ground breaking celebration.

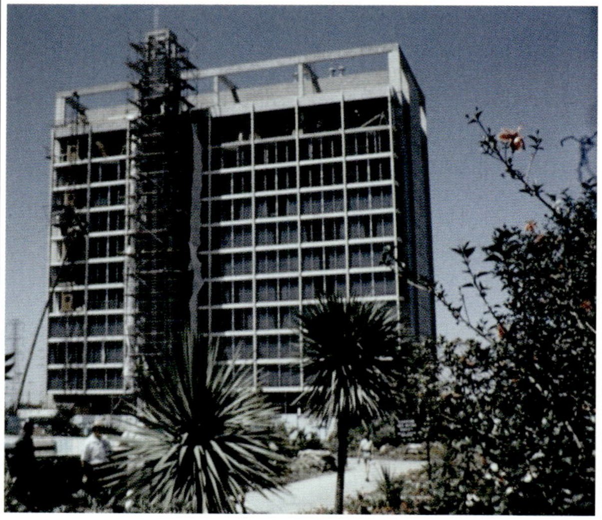

Further construction of new Tower Building.

[The original banquet hall (just to the south of the Embassy Room) would be redesigned and named the Magnolia Room.] It was able to accommodate more than 1,400 guests in a theatre seating formation and 1,200 guests for a banquet. Its "official" opening took place on November 28, 1961.

While the city had been changing dramatically since 1955, the Anaheim skyline also was about to undergo a major change in 1961 when the concept of "building up" replaced the concept of "building out." The Disneyland

Hotel was adding an eleven-story, high-rise tower. At formal ceremonies held in October of 1961, ground officially had been broken for the beginning of construction on the new Tower building. [Designed by Weber and Nicholson of Los Angeles and erected by C. L. Peck contractors and engineers, these two firms would oversee the expansion of the Disneyland Hotel for most of the next two decades.] The impressive Tower would be comprised of vertical pre-cast white concrete, inset with charcoal-tinted solar glass windows. The structure would be accented with horizontal wrought-iron railing across the balconies of each floor. At the time of its completion, the Tower would become Orange County's tallest building and also become the nation's tallest building constructed utilizing the post tension, lift slab method. The new Tower was to be construct-

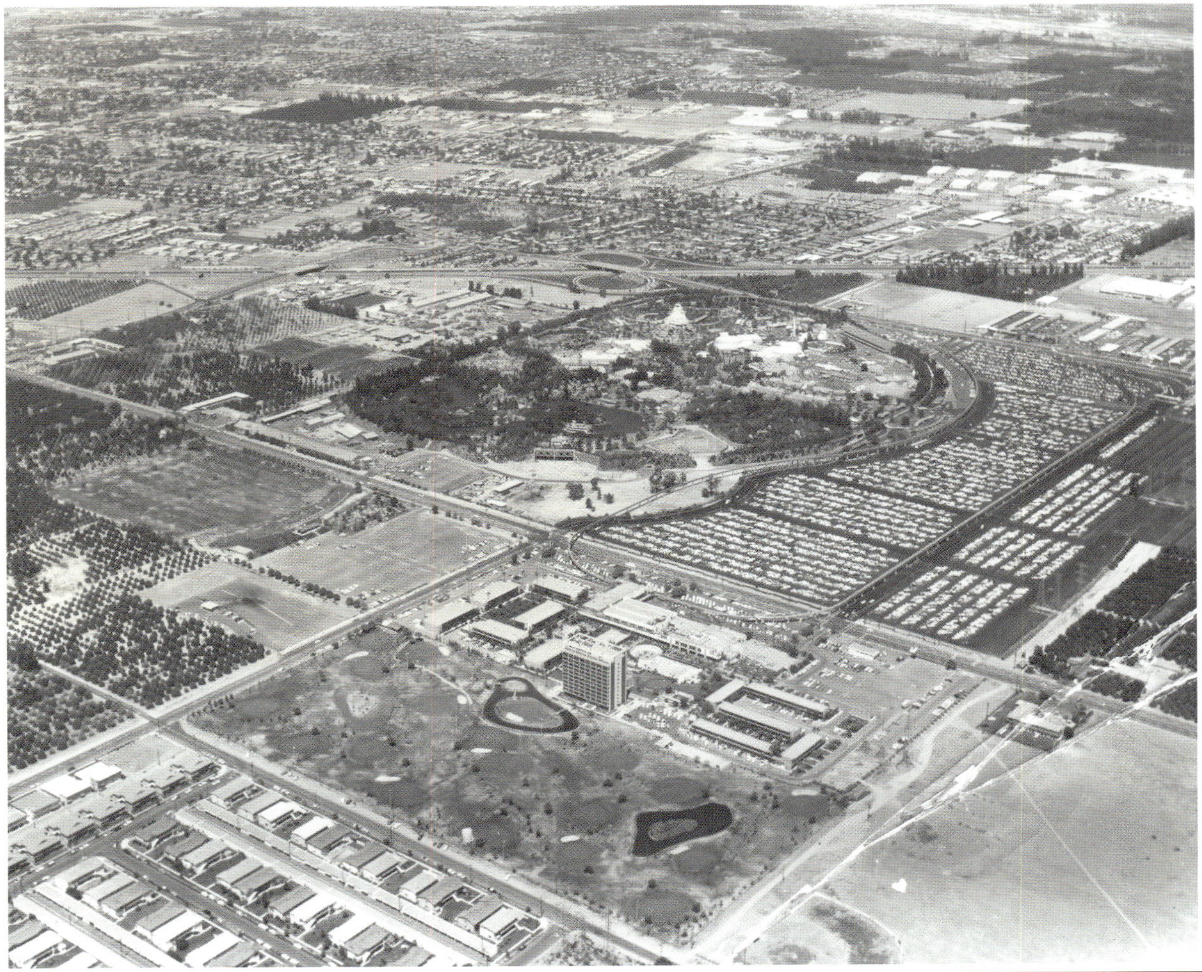

An aerial view of Disneyland and the Disneyland Hotel from July, 1963. At left center is the Hotel's Heliport and Mini- Golf facilities.

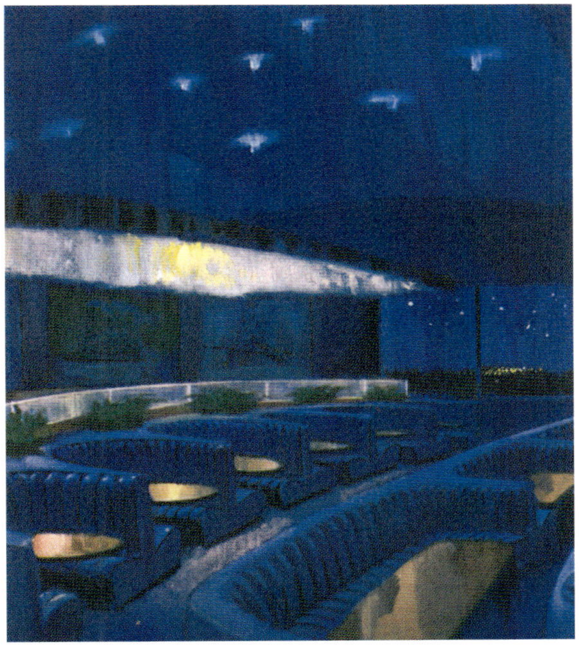

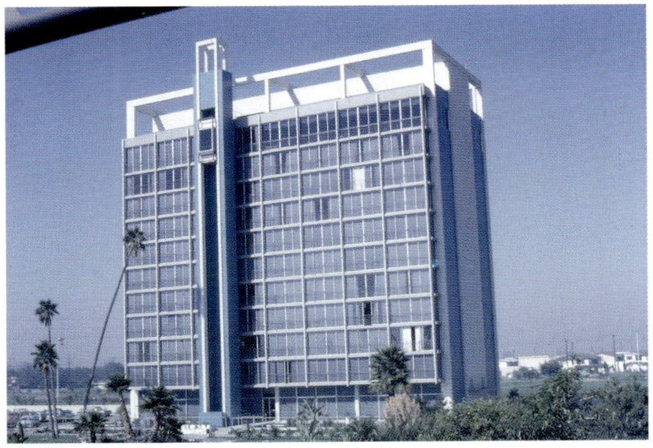

New Tower Building-Disneyland Hotel's new 11 story Tower Building is now completed and open. A glass elevator traveling outside the building takes visitors to the "Top-of-the-Park" a triple tiered cocktail lounge on the 11th floor. Eight conference rooms are on the ground floor.

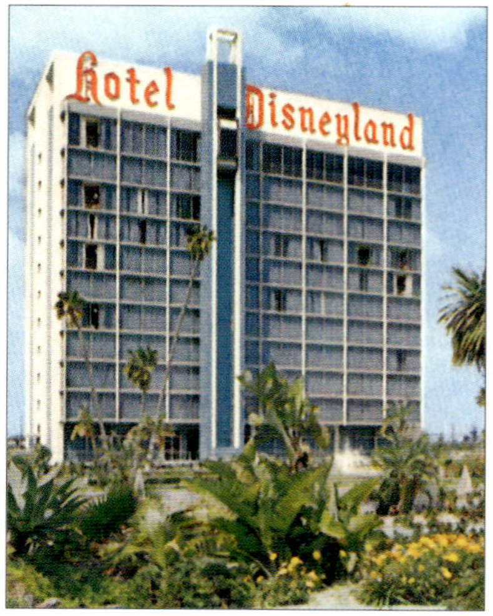

Orange County's tallest building at the time. It's now the north half of the Adenture Tower.

ed in the center of the 60-acre complex. While the 118 foot Tower would become the tallest building in Orange County, Disneyland's Matterhorn Mountain remained the tallest man-made structure at 146-1/2 feet.

The new Tower building opened in September, 1962. Surrounding the base of the Tower was a Japanese garden reflecting pool. A promenade, cantilevered over the pool, encircled the ground floor, with access into the building being by means of six bridges. On the ground floor were eight new conference rooms. When completed, this addition added 150 new guest rooms to the Hotel complex. The new rooms were advertised as providing "deluxe living accommodations of more than 500 square feet each." The Tower boasted a rooftop Presidential Suite, consisting of 2,000 square feet of space. A penthouse was also located on the roof. [The new Tower would later be named the Sierra Tower, and in 1966 would be re-designated the North Sierra Tower when the Sierra Tower Annex was added.] One of the earliest guests at the new Tower was French singer/actor Maurice Chevalier, who only recently had completed work on Disney's new live-action adventure feature *In Search of the Castaways* (1962).

On the east facade of the Tower was another exciting innovation, an external glass elevator, one of only a handful constructed at the time in this country. [During the 1970's, many brochures from and articles about the Hotel referred to it as the "Looking Glass" elevator.] Its designer, architect Kurt Weber, recalled that the spectacular glass elevator offered a dramatic view of the growing community of Anaheim. It also whisked guests to the luxurious Top-of-the-Park Lounge. The three-tiered lounge featured breathtaking, panoramic views of the Hotel's grounds, the Park, and vast vistas of Orange County through its tinted glass windows. Perhaps the most impressive of the views was that of Disneyland at night. Decorated in various shades of blue, the Lounge offered alcoholic beverages and nightly entertainment.

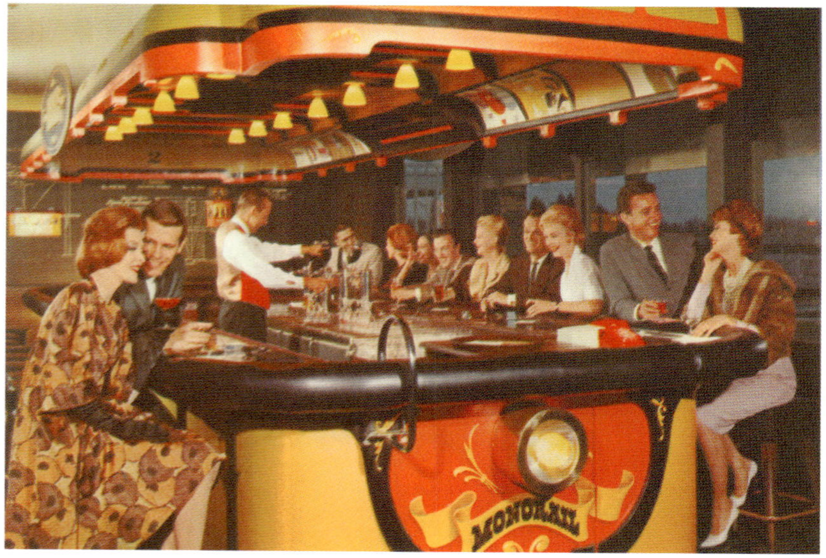

The Monorail Lounge with its wonderful view of arriving and departing trains.

A few years later, that elevator shaft would cause a slight problem when it was decided to place a large Hotel name-sign on the top of the Tower. Only three sections of the Tower were on the south side of the elevator, and five sections were on the north side. It was impossible to fit the one-story high "Disneyland" sign on the south end of the Tower. Until the Annex was completed in 1966, the sign would read: "Hotel Disneyland." The Hotel's vice-president during that time was Frank Bret, a native of Czechoslovakia. Due to the backward sign, he was forced to suffer much good natured ribbing. Frequently he heard, "Your sign's backward. Can't you read English yet after all this time in the States?"

Located next to the monorail station on the second floor level, the Monorail Lounge was constructed in 1961. Its decor was planned to give the impression of the interior of a railway passenger car. The Monorail Lounge provided a spectacular, panoramic view of the Disneyland-Alweg trains as they pulled into and left the Hotel's station. This total project (including the Tower) was completed by September of 1962, less than a year after ground breaking.

In 1962, in Adventureland, the Elephants' Bathing Pool was added to the Jungle Cruise and the Swiss Family Treehouse made its debut. The population of Anaheim had grown to slightly over 125,000.

In just a little over six years of operation, the Disneyland Hotel had hosted over one-million guests.

A tourist magazine ad of the time included this limerick: "A traveling gourmet from the east... / Was searching for somewhere to feast... / He was not satisfied / 'Til he finally spied... / The Gourmet Restaurant / The Greatest! to say the least!" Next door to the Gourmet was nightly entertainment in the Round-the-World Lounge.

The Hotel's 1962 room rates ranged from $17 for a room with twin beds to $53 for two deluxe and medium adjoining rooms during vacation and holiday seasons; $10 to $47 during off-season. There were new rates for the Tower building. A twin bedded room was priced from $24 vacation rate up to $35 for a room with two double beds. Off-season, tower rooms were priced from $20 to $26. Rooms were provided with music, news, and tourist information by means of the Hotel's own radio station KEZY. For the first time in the Hotel's history, annual sales of guest rooms topped the $2-million mark (during its 1962-1963 fiscal year).

Around that time, plans were formulated that over a period of years could increase the number of guest rooms from the present 450 to 1,000. The first stage would include 180 rooms in two-story Garden Room type structures. These were to be located on the southwest side of the Tower and on land adjacent to the 18-hole Golf Course, with some being clustered around the course's lake at hole 17. As with the original Garden Rooms to the east of the Tower, each new room would have its own private balcony or lanai. A sub-tropical landscape would surround these new units. To be included in this construction were several two and three bedroom suites, each with a spacious living room, a powder room, and a bar. [This is the site were the Bonita Tower would be erected in 1978.]

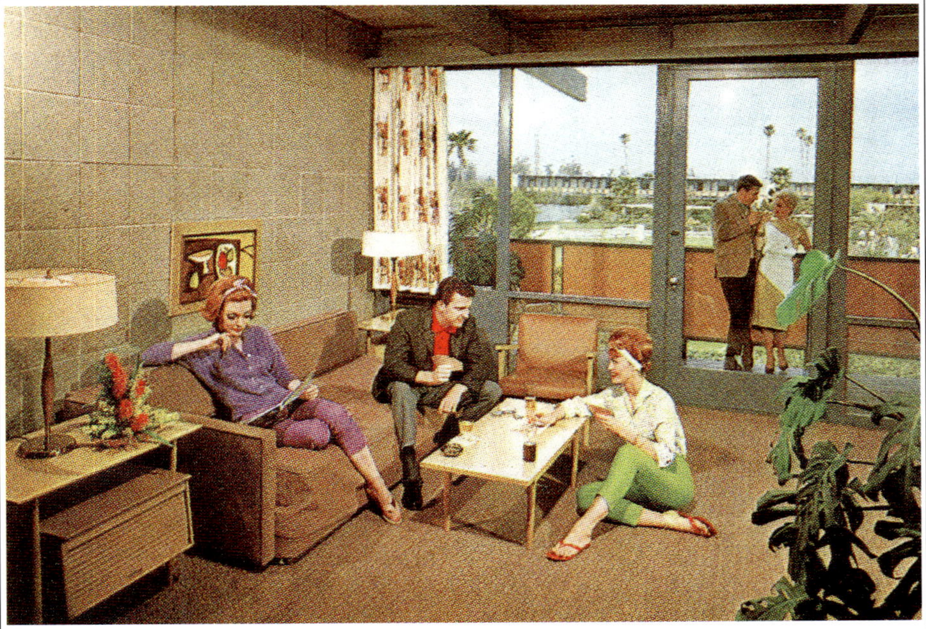

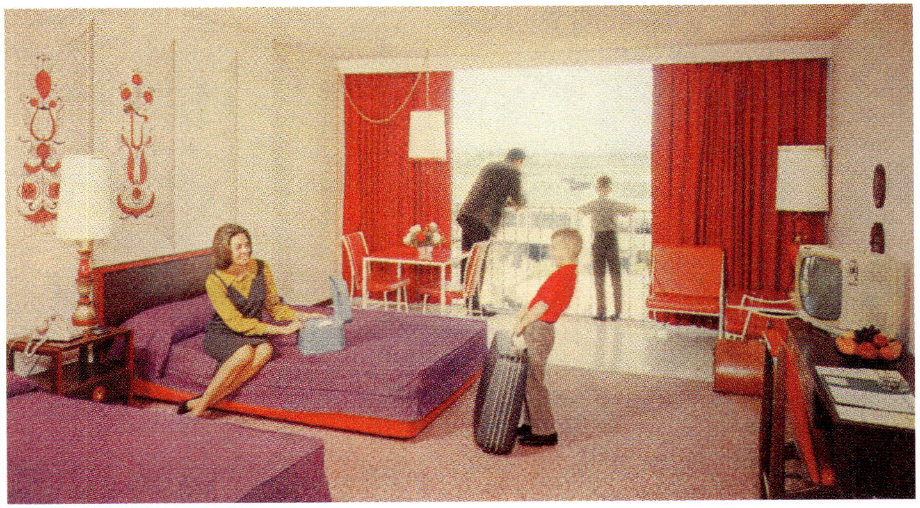

Inside guest rooms 1960's.

In a later second phase of expansion, 200 additional rooms would be built on the northwest side of the Tower around the Golf Course and in the same two-story style. [On this land, the Marina Tower would open in 1970.] A large shopping complex was envisioned (which would later become the Plaza Building). The third portion of the plan would include a second eleven-story tower, connected to the one recently opened. It was planned for the new tower to include a 300 car subterranean parking garage.

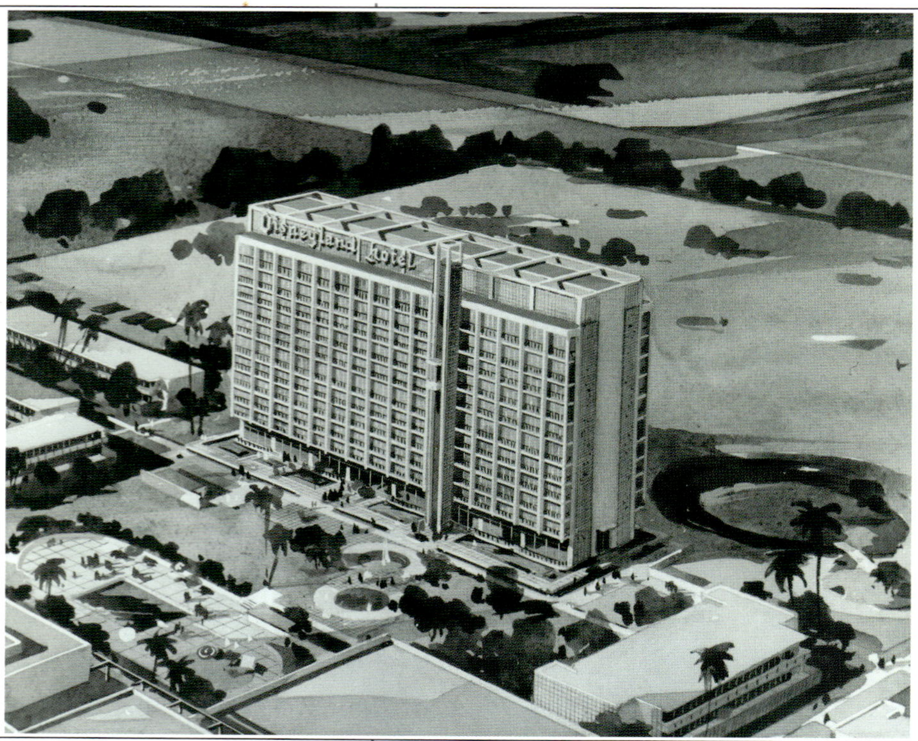

In 1966-The Disneyland Hotel would continue to grow. A twin 11-story tower suite would bring total rooms to over 600.

Of this development plan, Jack Wrather stated that "in view of the rapid growth in the Anaheim area, it is quite possible that the addition to the present multi-story building would precede those of the other phase developments." As it would turn out, that is exactly what happened. Of the various elements in this proposed expansion, only the tower addition and the new shopping building would be completed. The additional Garden Rooms to the west and the underground parking facility would never be built.

With the opening of the Enchanted Tiki Room, a new era of theme park attractions (utilizing Disney's revolutionary Audio-Animatronics system) was inaugurated at Disneyland in 1963. New Orleans Square was dedicated, the first new "land" since the Park's opening. In November of that year, another major event took place as Walt Disney and a very select group of close confidants began scouting a swampy area of central Florida called the Reedy Creek Basin.

Orange County celebrated its 75th anniversary in 1964. At a press conference held at the Disneyland Hotel, the announcement was made that Major League Baseball was coming to Anaheim. Gene Autry had been awarded the major league baseball franchise for the Los Angeles Angels at baseball's winter meetings in 1960. The Angels would continue to play in Los Angeles at Dodger Stadium until their new 43,204 seat Anaheim stadium was constructed in approximately two years. The first official game would be played in the new $15.8-million stadium against the Chicago White Sox on April 19, 1966. During their first year in Anaheim, the Angels would lead the American League in attendance, attracting over one-million fans.

That same year, the Below Deck Museum was added to the Sailing Ship Columbia and the African Veld and Safari was added to the Jungle Cruise in Disneyland. By the summer of 1964, Disney, using dummy companies, had spent $5-million to acquire 27,400-acres (forty-three square miles of land) in central Florida for the yet secret "Project X."

With the addition of the Tower building two years earlier, the Disneyland Hotel had over 450 rooms and had become a $15-million investment. By 1964, during vacation and holiday season, room rates were $17 for a single room, $53 for an adjoining deluxe room with a medium room, and $30 for a deluxe room alone. Winter rates were advertised from $10 for a single small room to $49 for an adjoining deluxe with a medium room. The Tower rooms were priced from $24 to $35 during peak season and $20 to $28 during off-season. Peak season was now being defined as June 1 to September 15, December 11 to January 3, and April 9 to April 24. The Hotel's pretax net income had increased by 44-percent over the previous year. However, a research firm's independent analysis had concluded that the Hotel would need to nearly double its present number of rooms within the next few years to remain profitable.

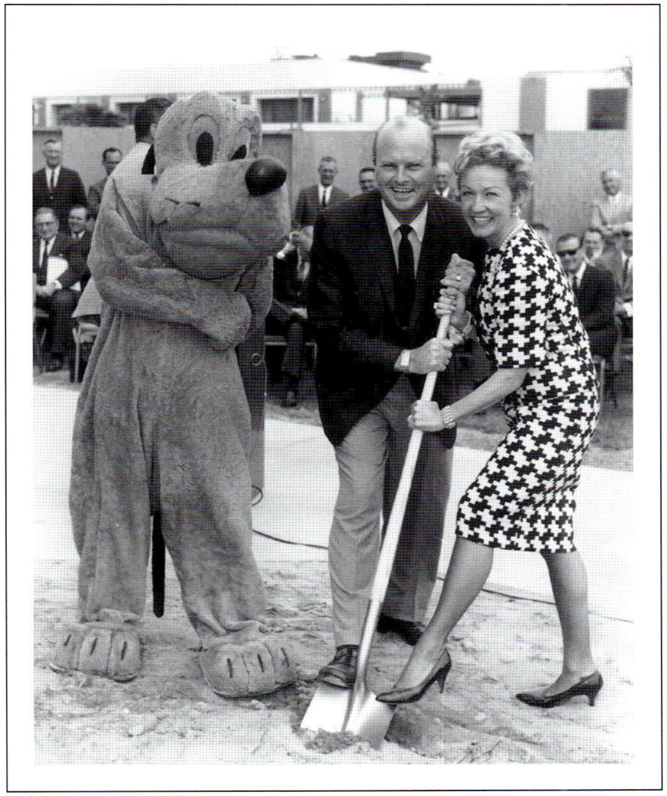

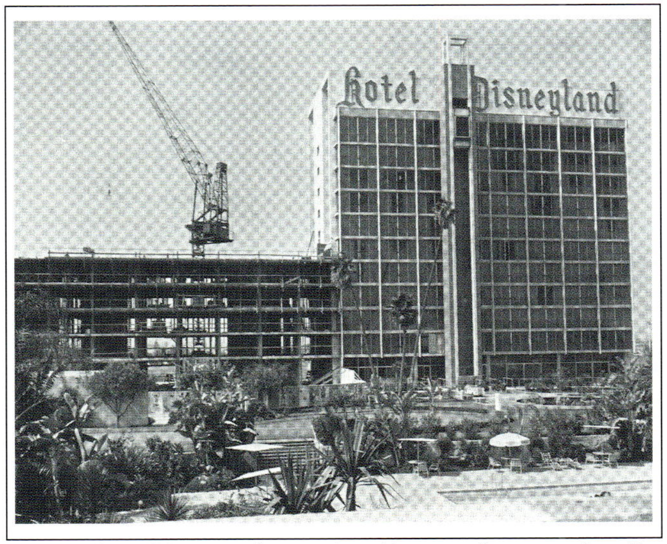

Groundbreaking and construction underway for the Tower Annex.

After a highly praised two year run at the New York World's Fair (1964-1965) in the State of Illinois pavilion, Great Moments with Mr. Lincoln was moved to the Opera House on Main Street, U.S.A. in 1965. Robert Moses, director of the World's Fair, had approached Walt Disney about taking over the operation of the fairgrounds after its closing and turning it into "Disneyland East," but Walt was not interested. Mary Adams became the Park's 50-millionth guest on August 12th. To date, $53-million had been invested in Walt's dream.

1965 saw both the Disneyland Hotel and Disneyland celebrating their "Tencennials," 10-years of successful operations. At a summer groundbreaking ceremony, the Hotel announced plans for the Tower Annex, an expansion to the existing tower, which would expand the Hotel to 616 guest rooms. This was but one part of the Hotel's major new $5.5-million expansion plan.

Summer 1965 saw the debut of The Disneyland Hotel Check-In magazine. This magazine was free to Hotel guests (a copy was placed in each guest room) and featured articles on Hotel shops and services, human interest stories, local places of interest, schedule of events at the Hotel and Disneyland, and showcased celebrities or VIP's who had stayed at the Disneyland Hotel. The magazine was published six times a year and ran until 1974.

The lobby on West Street was in the process of being remodeled. When finished the following year, it would be dominated by huge rectangular glass chandeliers, hanging

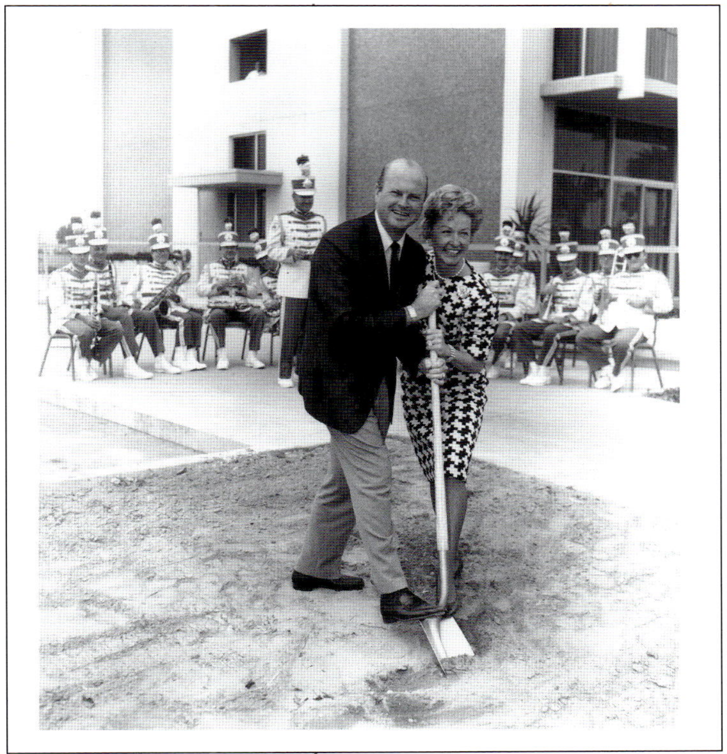

Bonita and Jack Wrather turn the first spade of dirt in groundbreaking for the Tower Annex.

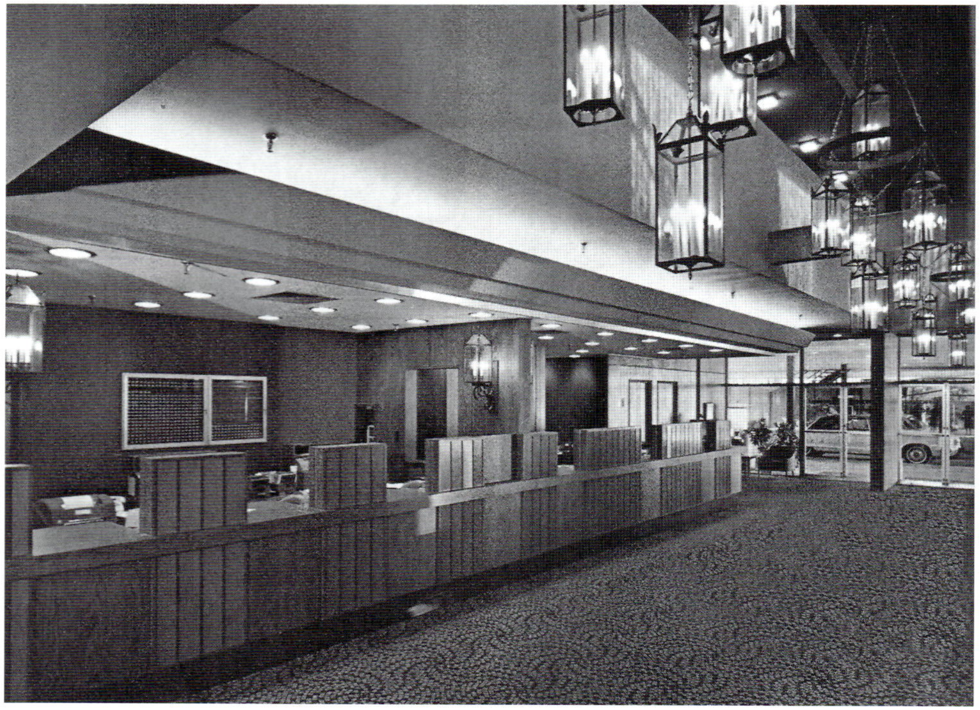

The newly redecorated Hotel Lobby.

in clusters. New furniture and a larger registration desk (paneled in brown wood) greeted Hotel guests. New thick wall-to-wall carpeting was in a bright mosaic pattern. This redecoration was by Albert Parvin and Company, who was also remodeling all 306 Garden Rooms. The Driver-Eddy Company repainted the rooms in "sunny hues." The refurbishing of the guest rooms would be completed for the summer of 1966 at a cost of $400,000.

The newly remodeled lobby also boasted new technology in the first Concord Interwrite system to be installed in a hotel in the United States. Five machines were installed at various locations throughout the Hotel...one at the front desk, one in the engineer's office, one in the executive housekeeper's office, and two more at housekeeping stations in other buildings. By writing directly onto a paper tape, the message was electronically reproduced almost immediately at any one of the various locations in the Hotel complex. If needed, messages also could be resent to another station. No time would be lost in lengthy telephone conversations or by waiting for pages to be answered or call-backs to be made. If clarification were needed, a "Talk" button could be pushed to put one into direct voice contact with the sender. The Hotel's General Manager Frank Bret called the new system "an unqualified success" and stated that it is "clear, easy to use and dependable--underline dependable." This new system fit well into the management style of the Hotel. For years, at the bottom of all "Inter-Office Communication" forms had been printed: "VERBAL MESSAGES CAUSE MISUNDERSTANDINGS AND DELAYS (PLEASE PUT IT IN WRITING)."

Mermaid hopefuls filled the Disneyland Hotel pool for several days during the summer. More than 100 young ladies attended try-outs to gain employment as "mermaids" in Disneyland's submarine lagoon. Swimming skills, ability to stay in the water for lengthy periods of time, and appearance were the main criteria focused upon by the judges.

On October 23, 1965, Services for the Blind, Inc. (a philanthropic organization) held a large dinner and dance at the Hotel to launch its annual fund-raising campaign. Pat Buttram (actor/comedian) emceed the evening's events. Several acts from Disneyland's Golden Horseshoe Revue and other professionals provided the entertainment for the large number of guests.

Disneyland Hotel Liquors (located in the Drugstore in the Arcade shopping area) provided alcoholic beverages to guests for private entertaining in their rooms. Simply by dialing number 169, a guest could order a quart of liquor of his choice. The price included napkins, bottle opener, ice, stir sticks, four souvenir glasses, and sales

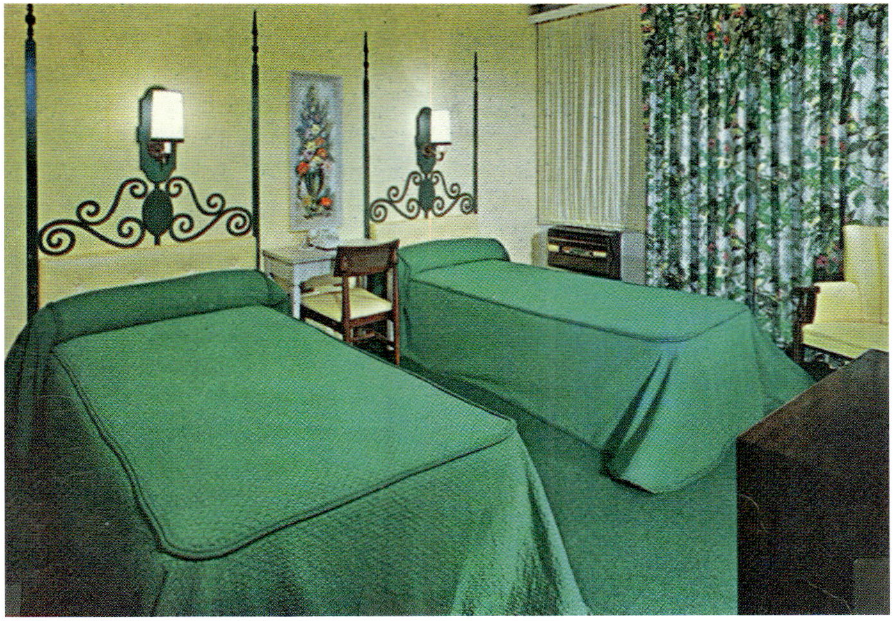

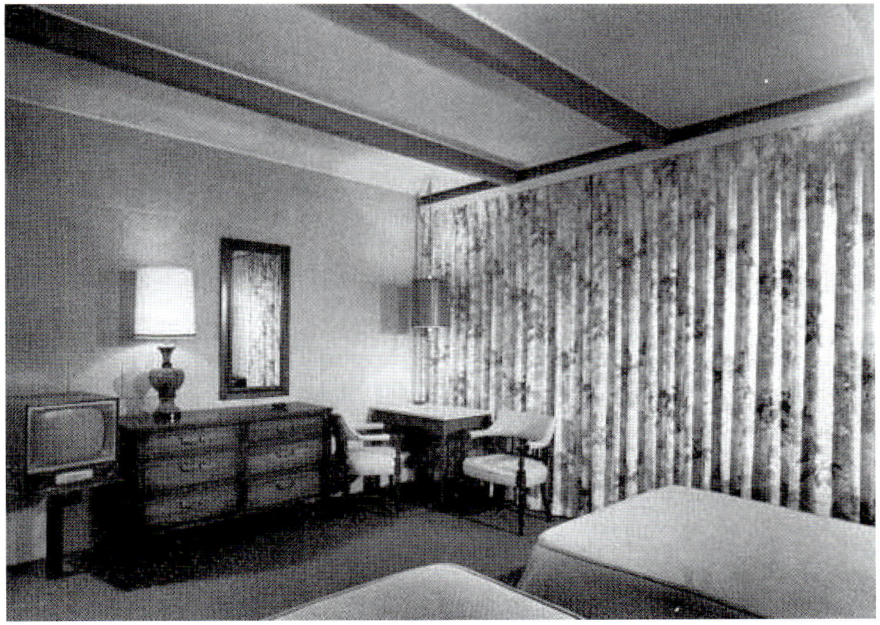

Newly refurbished guest rooms 1966.

tax. In 1965, the cost of a quart bottle was $8.00 for Smirnoff Vodka, $8.50 for Seagram's 7 Crown, $9.75 for Cutty Sark, or $11.00 for Jack Daniels. Party snack trays also could be ordered for an extra charge.

By the mid-1960's, the original Round-the-World Lounge had been replaced by the Por Que No? (Why Not?). Located near the Coffee Shop, the newly redecorated cocktail lounge provided nightly entertainment in the Latin style. By the end of the decade, the room was known simply as The Lounge or The Main Lounge.

During the year, the Hotel had hosted numerous celebrity guests. New York Yankee's slugger Mickey Mantle and his family enjoyed their accommodations, as did Albert Broccoli and his family (he being best known as the producer of the James Bond movies). The families of musicians Harry James (trumpet) [Betty Grable being his wife] and New Orleans' Pete Fountain (clarinet) also paid visits. Although only star of stand-up comedy and records at the time, Bob Newhart brought his family to the Disneyland Hotel (his television sit-com career still

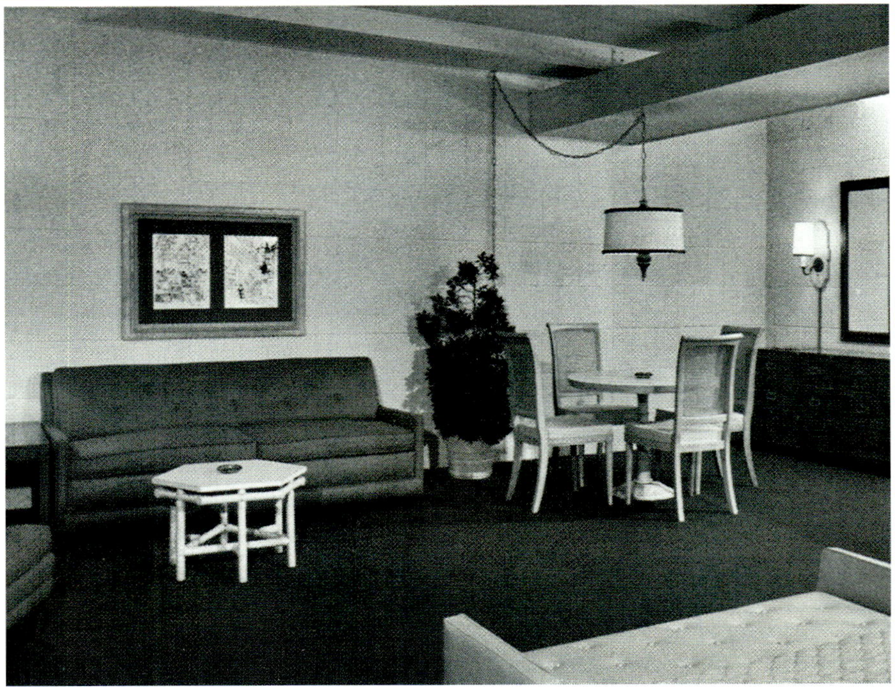

being a thing of the future). While jazz pianist Duke Ellington resided in a suite at the Hotel, he composed and arranged portions of the score for his new Broadway musical *Sugar City*.

Two more of Disney's creations for the New York World's Fair were added to Disneyland in 1966: the highly successful It's a Small World (sponsored by Pepsi-Cola and UNICEF at the Fair) and Primeval World Diorama (a portion of the Ford Motor Company's presentation at the Fair).

By 1966, Orange County had become the tourist hub of America, producing tourist income greater than any other county in the United States and more than the combined tourist income of all the other fifty-seven counties of California. During the first decade of the operation of Disneyland, nearly $275-million had been spent by guests inside the Park, and an additional $555-million has been spent by tourists for restaurants, motels, and other travel related services in the Anaheim area. Anaheim now had 125 hotels and motels (providing nearly 5,000 guest rooms) and a population of over 150,000. During those ten years, over 250 businesses had been started, providing an annual payroll of $190-million to over 33,000 area residents. In a little over a decade, this once tranquil area of orange groves had grown into a $944-million annual economy.

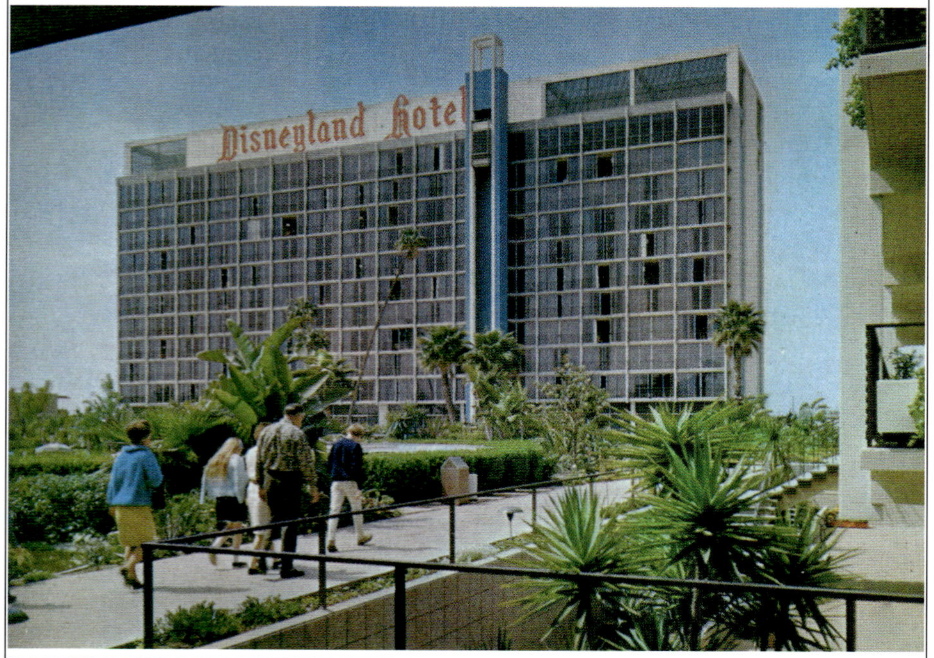

The new Tower Annex completed and fully opened for business 1966. The Hotel now boasted over 600 rooms and suites.

Sadly on December 15, 1966, Walt Disney, the man voted "Showman of the World" by his peers in the entertainment industry and a man who had been one of the most influential men in Anaheim's history, passed away. Walt had been a long time cigarette smoker and had developed lung cancer. It was reported that Jack and Bonita Wrather were devastated upon hearing the news of Walt's passing. Half of the two pioneers of tourism in Southern California was now gone. These two had plotted a course in the 1950's for the future of tourism and conventions in Orange County, thereby forever-changing Anaheim's destiny.

Over the years, Walt Disney had established a highly creative team of artisans, designers, and executives who were capable of carrying on with Walt's "Dreams" after his death and of making certain that his Opening Day promise that Disneyland would never be completed, would be honored. Likewise, Jack Wrather continued the expansion and enhancement of the Disneyland Hotel.

In January of 1966, Robert G. Seaman became manager of the Hotel. He expressed his pleasure concerning his new position by stating, "The thing that really strikes you about the Hotel is its happy atmosphere. I've never encountered anything quite like it anywhere, and I'm a career hotel man." During the early portion of that year, the Disneyland-Alweg Monorail was temporarily out of service due to the relocation of tracks within the Park to make room for the construction of new attractions that were being prepared for the summer season.

On June 1, 1966, the Disneyland Hotel saw the completion of the Tower Annex which added 160 guest rooms and suites to the Hotel. [The first seven floors were opened on June 1st; the remaining top four floors were opened on June 15th.] The Annex was actually a separately constructed building that was eventually connected upon its completion to the original Tower building to the north. A Hotel advertisement of the time proclaimed: "Discover the scientific marvels of soundproof airwalls, missile age communications [Muzak, television, and radio in every room]...blended with gracious conventional hospitality and experience!"

Hotel pamphlets of the time declared: "Disneyland Hotel in the center of all the fun." Rates in 1966 for what was billed as wintertime ranged from $15 for a queen-sized bed up to $30 for a deluxe room. During vacation times, the rates were $20 and $35 for the same rooms. The Tower now had a North and South designation, with the South side being the more expensive. The North side rates were priced from $20 for a queen-sized bed up to $28 for two double beds. The South side went for $22 to $30 for the same bed types. There could be as many as 2,400 daily guests at the Hotel. Each day, there would also be thousands more attending meetings, banquets, and other functions.

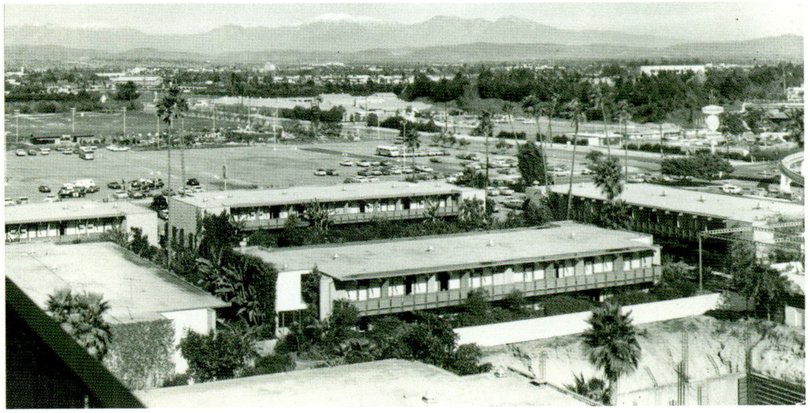
At lower right, the Plaza Building construction can be seen in its initial phase.

The *Los Angeles Times* of Tuesday, April 19, 1966, carried a full page color advertisement for the Hotel. The ad contained both photographs and a listing of the various types of accommodations and facilities to be found there. Heading the ad, in larger print, was the following: "NOW! The Southland's most fabulous FUN N' CONVENTION LAND, the Disneyland Hotel. Come! Explore and enjoy California's landmark of hospitality, this 60 acre all-in-one Hotel City!"

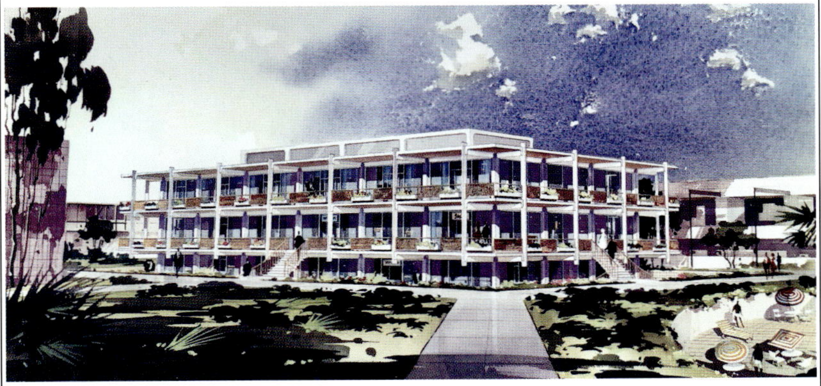
Artist concept of the Plaza Building.

Since the opening of its first four meeting rooms in 1956, the Disneyland Hotel continually had increased its conference business and steadily had expanded its meeting facilities. In only ten years, it now boasted twenty-seven meeting rooms and two banquet halls and ballrooms (the Embassy Room and the Magnolia Room). These conference rooms could accommodate a small meeting of fifteen people or a convention of two-thousand. A total of 23-thousand square feet of exhibition space was available. In just a period of several weeks of the coming year, the Hotel hosted the following groups: the American Association of Hospital Accountants' Educational Foundation, the American Petroleum Institute, the Boy Scouts of America, the California Association of Convention Bureaus, the California Association of Directors of Activities, the California School Nurses, the Christian Business and Professional Women's Council, the Christian Women's Clubs of America, the Credit Union National Association, the Sales and Marketing Executives International, the Society of Automotive Engineers, the Southern California Self-Service Laundry and Dry Cleaning Association, the Toastmasters International, the Travelodge Corporation, and the Western Radio and Television Conference.

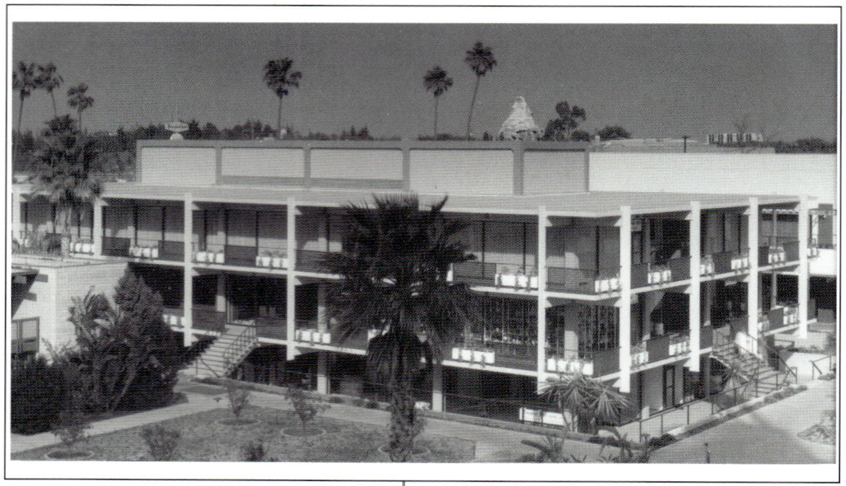

The Plaza Building with its distinctive shops, boutiques and offices.

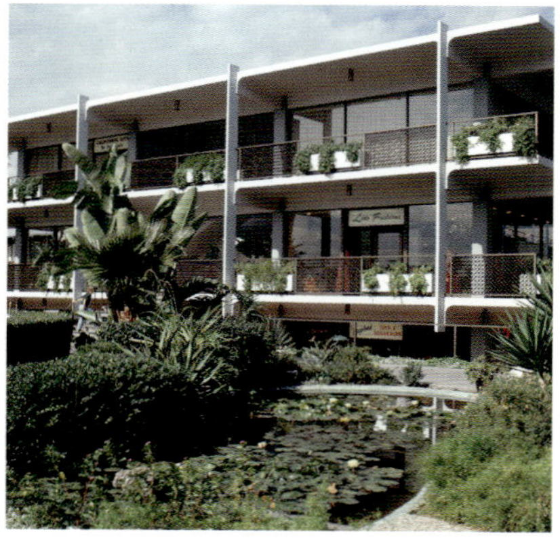

Just to the west of the lobby and shopping arcade, the new shopping Plaza Building opened on the Hotel's grounds in November of 1966. It was a three-story structure with offices on the upper level and shops and boutiques occupying the first two floors. Built of concrete and glass, it contained an elevator that served all three floors and individual air conditioning to each shop and office in the complex was provided. The architects were again Weber and Nicholson of Los Angeles, who also had designed the Sierra Tower. Once again, the contractor was C. L. Peck of Los Angeles. The leasing of shop space in the Plaza Building was handled by John Holmquist of Coldwell, Banker & Company of Newport Beach (at the time operating only in Arizona, California, and Nevada...years before it became a national presence).

This new structure was actually a sunken building, patrons having to descend a short flight of stairs to enter the shops on the first-floor level. A sunken garden landscaped that lower level, and red tile walkways led guests from shop to shop. It was described as having glass walls and graceful grillwork, gleaming in a lush garden setting. It was further described as resembling a necklace on green velvet, containing the beautiful and unusual in a score of smart, avant-garde specialty shops. Here one could buy aromatic tobaccos from Turkey, candles from Mexico, leathers from London, toys from the United States, Germany and Japan, and here one could select from fashions inspired in Paris, Rome, and on Carnaby Street. The Plaza also featured a beauty shop, a travel agency, and a dental facility. The sounds of tinkling fountains and of Muzak added to the calm atmosphere of the new shopping area.

The Plaza Building was not only a place of leisurely shopping for necessities (forgotten in the haste of packing back home) or for finding those unusual gifts and souvenirs. From the first days of its operation, the Plaza was also a place of entertainment and of the unexpected. A shopper might discover a Mariachi band playing outside Flavia (a specialized gift store that featured the paintings of wide-eyed children by the renowned Southern California artist whose name was to be found above the entrance to her shop). Turning a corner, one might be greeted by Native Americans performing age-old ceremonial dances in front of Treasure Trails (a shop filled with

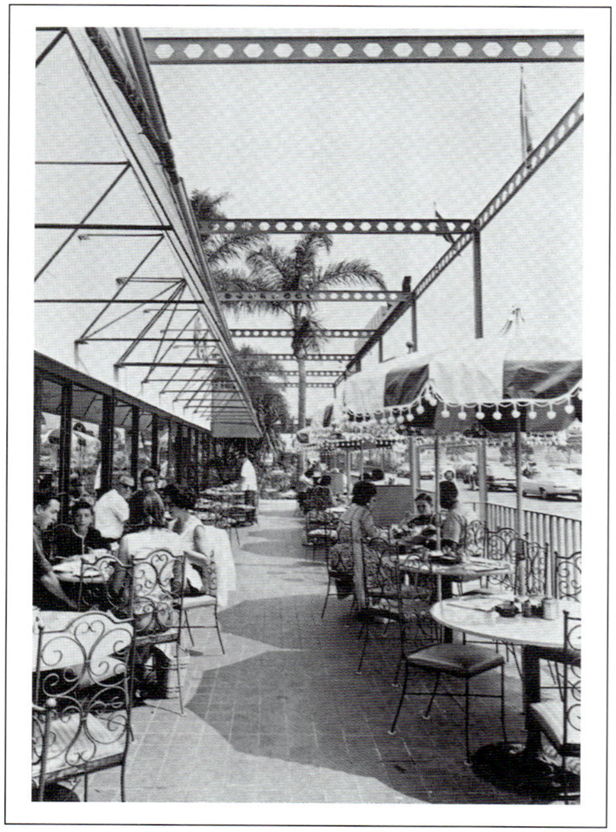

The Sidewalk Café.

authentic Indian dolls, crafts, and works of art). At another time at that same shop, one might be delighted by a young Navajo girl's demonstration of her skills of rug weaving. Only a few steps away one's dreams of the Pacific Islands could be realized at Waltah Clark's Hawaiian Shop. A former Hawaiian beach boy, Clark had established himself as an importer of fashions and accessories from his former home. The Yelland Galleries also held surprises for Plaza visitors.

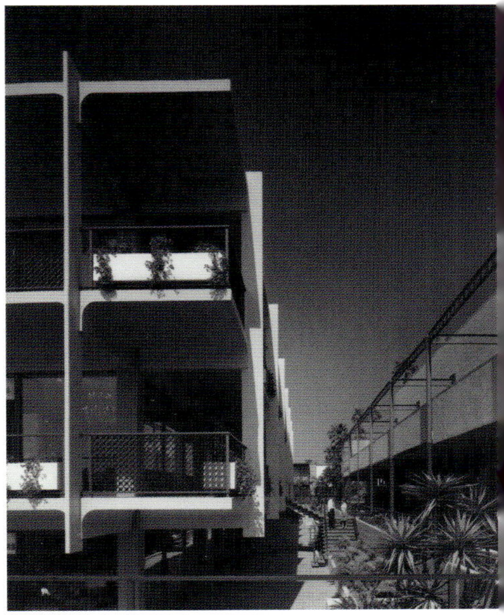

Plaza Building.

With the addition of the Plaza Building and with the pre-existing Arcade, the Hotel now had forty-thousand square feet of shopping area, occupied by nearly two dozen specialty stores. The Disneyland Hotel could now boast of having "the most complete hotel service and shopping center in the nation."

Both the Tower Annex and the Plaza Shopping Center were a part of the before mentioned $5.5-million Hotel Expansion Program. By itself, the Plaza Building had cost $1.25-million. As a part of this project, the lobby and the restaurants had been remodeled. Enlarged and redecorated (with a completely refurbished kitchen) at a cost of $250,000, the Coffee Shop now had a seating capacity for 245 patrons, either at the counter, at a table or in a booth. The menu selections ranged from sandwiches to complete meals. Beamed ceilings and planked walls gave its interior a warm, cozy atmosphere. For years the Coffee Shop had been one of Southern California's most popular eating places. Reopened in April of 1966, the Coffee Shop now boasted the adjoining Sidewalk Cafe. Patrons of the picturesque Cafe could enjoy their meals in the warm sunshine or under the shade of orange and yellow, striped umbrellas. Located along West Street, the Sidewalk Cafe provided diners with a view of the arriving and departing monorail. One could even enjoy a four o'clock tea at the Cafe.

To create an atmosphere of California's Spanish heritage, the Gourmet and its adjoining banquet rooms were redecorated in woods, wrought-iron, and grillwork. The new chairs and plush booths were covered in red leather. The unusual carpeting simulated planked flooring and large wrought-iron chandeliers illuminated the spacious dining room. Major renovations were additionally completed at the Round-the-World Lounge. Its new furnishing included big barrel-like chairs and king-size bar stools for the comfort of its patrons.

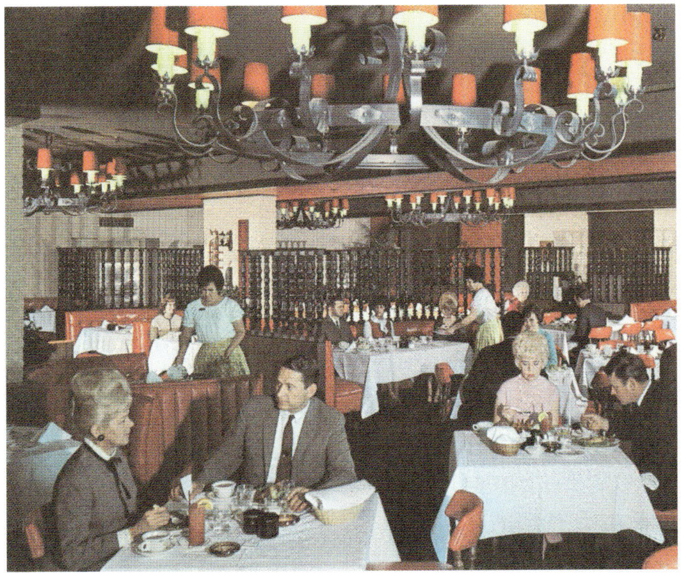

Redecorated Gourmet Restaurant.

A relatively new financial concept was creating major changes for the average consumer and within the tourist industry. The "credit card" was coming of age. For the first time, the Disneyland Hotel began accepting payment by means of other than cash or check. In 1966, the American Express Card became the first credit card to be accepted as payment of Hotel bills.

State politics were changing in 1966. California Governor Edmund "Pat" Brown was standing for re-election. The incumbent chief executive used the Hotel's Presidential Suite for a press conference and a meeting with his supporters. As he had passed through the Hotel lobby, one enthusiastic supporter had handed him a white carnation. Not many days afterward, the challenger Ronald Reagan (yet to hold a political office) utilized several of the facilities at the Hotel to hold news conferences, fund-raising dinners, and "get out the vote" rallies. The results of that

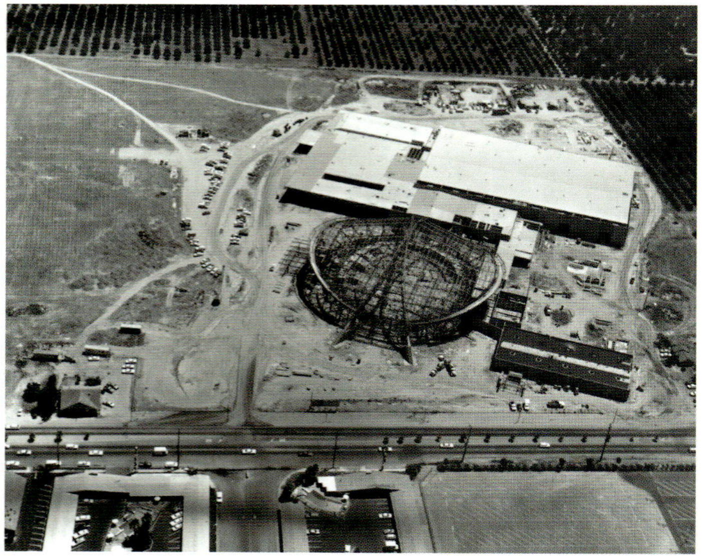

November's election would greatly alter the political landscape of California and the future of the nation.

As in all previous years, numerous celebrity guests could be spotted during their brief stays at the Hotel in 1966. Celebrating their seventeenth wedding anniversary at the Hotel were actress Greer Garson and husband Buddy Fogelson. She had only recently completed her work on *The Happiest Millionaire* (1967), the last live-action musical to have been supervised by Walt Disney. Two time Grammy winner, pianist Peter Nero also spent a pleasant time with his family at the Hotel and in the Park. Although of slightly lesser status, the eighth annual "best newspaper carries and circulation managers" winners from Ohio's *The Cleveland Press* enjoyed the many amenities that the Hotel provided during their stay. Sir David Trench (Governor of the British Crown Colony of Hong Kong) and his family spent some time in the Presidential Suite of the new Tower building.

For 1967, Walt had been planning Pirates of the Caribbean and a New Tomorrowland (which would include the PeopleMovers, Adventure Thru Inner Space, and the last of Walt's four New York World's Fair attractions to be added to Disneyland, General Electric's Carousel of Progress). That same year would see the 60-millionth Disneyland guest visit in March. By now, the Park had become a $95-million investment in growth and improvements. That summer, groundbreaking took place for a new Disney theme park and hotels complex in Florida.

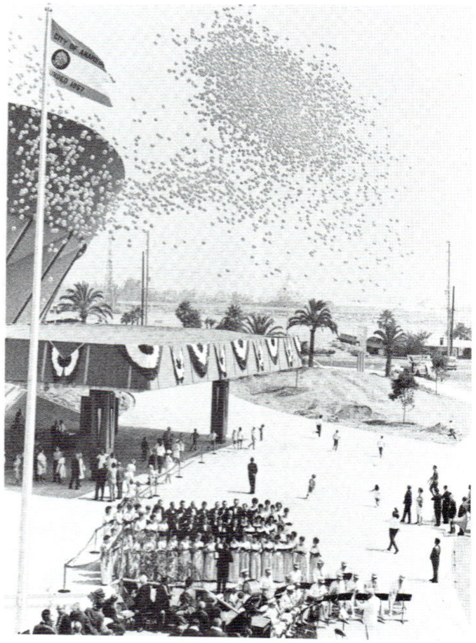

Anaheim Convention Center under construction (top) and opening day 1967 (bottom).

Still tourism in the Anaheim area was mainly seasonal (the summer months and holidays). To attract major hotel chains to the area and to stimulate off season business, the city (now with a population of 152,000) constructed the 9,100 seat Anaheim Convention Center, just to the south of Disneyland. Opening ceremonies on July 12, 1967, included the spectacular display of the "Dancing Waters." A few years later, this water show would find a permanent home at the Disneyland Hotel.

By now, the Disneyland Hotel had grown into a $20-million resort. "Vacation Rates" at the Hotel in 1967 covered the dates of March 17 through April 1, May 27 through September 9, and December 15 through January 1. Garden Rooms ranged from $20 (queen-size bed) to $35 (deluxe). Two connecting rooms (depending upon the number of occupants, up to nine persons) were priced from $48 to $61. Sierra Tower rooms cost between $24 and $34. Suites (a sitting room and either one or two bedrooms) were priced at $65 and $90. Covering the remainder of the year, "Winter Rates" were $5 less for Garden Rooms, $11 to $16 less for two connecting rooms, $4 less for the Sierra Tower, and $15 less for suites. Due to higher room rates, additional rooms available, and improved vacation and convention occupancy, the Hotel experienced its largest annual revenue growth in its twelve year history, up by 25.7-percent. At this time the Sierra Tower had yet to be named and was referred to in Hotel literature only as the "11 Story Tower."

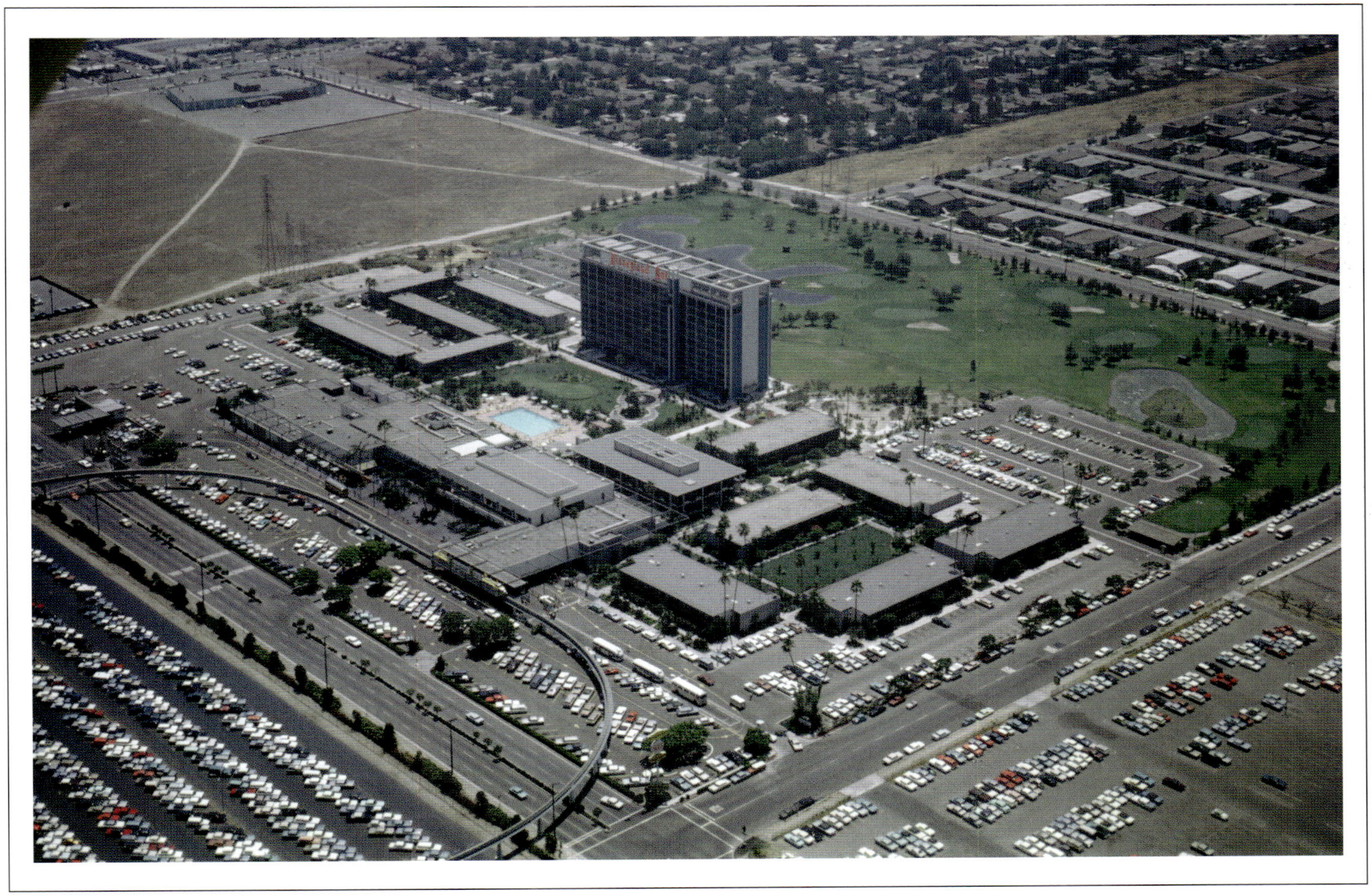

Beautiful 1967 aerial.

During the summer season, a number of well known persons were spotted by other Hotel guests. California's recently elected Governor Ronald Reagan (less than one year in office) spoke at the 14th National Institute on Crime and Delinquency. The topic of his key-note address was "The Threat of Crime to the Creative Society." Diners in the Gourmet restaurant might have seen United States Senator Thurston Morton (R., KY) or Rod Serling, creator of the popular *The Twilight Zone* television series, enjoying meals with their families in the Gourmet.

The Disneyland Hotel became the headquarters for the players and officials of the American League for the 28th Major League Baseball All-Star Game. The Hotel was utilized by many of the national sports writers covering the July 11, 1967 game at one-year-old Anaheim Stadium. John Hall, popular sports columnist for the *Los Angeles Times*, wrote: "Prior to the game, the Disneyland Hotel became a world's fair of sports. It was a happy madhouse." He added that the "Disneyland Hotel must have set a world's record for press conferences, receptions and parties on Monday and Monday night." For the average Hotel guests, the lobby, the restaurants, and the pool

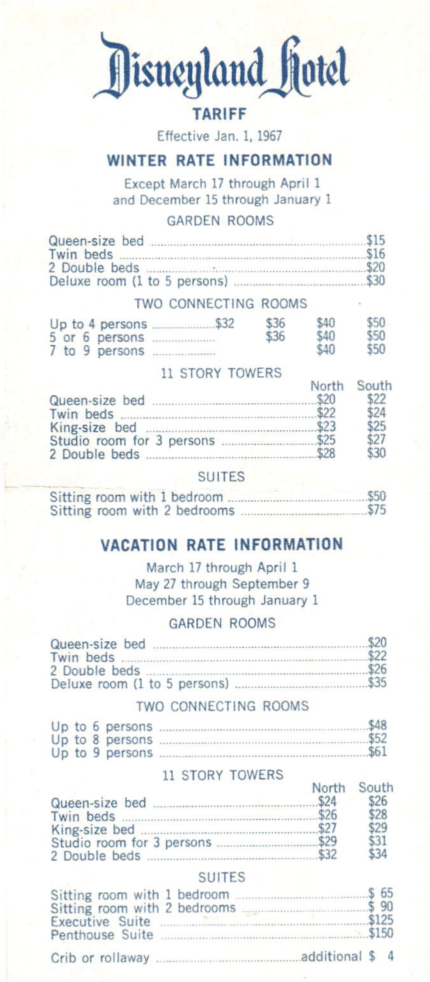

Disneyland Hotel

TARIFF

Effective Jan. 1, 1967

WINTER RATE INFORMATION

Except March 17 through April 1
and December 15 through January 1

GARDEN ROOMS

Queen-size bed	$15
Twin beds	$16
2 Double beds	$20
Deluxe room (1 to 5 persons)	$30

TWO CONNECTING ROOMS

Up to 4 persons	$32	$36	$40	$50
5 or 6 persons		$36	$40	$50
7 to 9 persons			$40	$50

11 STORY TOWERS

	North	South
Queen-size bed	$20	$22
Twin beds	$22	$24
King-size bed	$23	$25
Studio room for 3 persons	$25	$27
2 Double beds	$28	$30

SUITES

Sitting room with 1 bedroom	$50
Sitting room with 2 bedrooms	$75

VACATION RATE INFORMATION

March 17 through April 1
May 27 through September 9
December 15 through January 1

GARDEN ROOMS

Queen-size bed	$20
Twin beds	$22
2 Double beds	$26
Deluxe room (1 to 5 persons)	$35

TWO CONNECTING ROOMS

Up to 6 persons	$48
Up to 8 persons	$52
Up to 9 persons	$61

11 STORY TOWERS

	North	South
Queen-size bed	$24	$26
Twin beds	$26	$28
King-size bed	$27	$29
Studio room for 3 persons	$29	$31
2 Double beds	$32	$34

SUITES

Sitting room with 1 bedroom	$ 65
Sitting room with 2 bedrooms	$ 90
Executive Suite	$125
Penthouse Suite	$150
Crib or rollaway	additional $ 4

1967 rates.

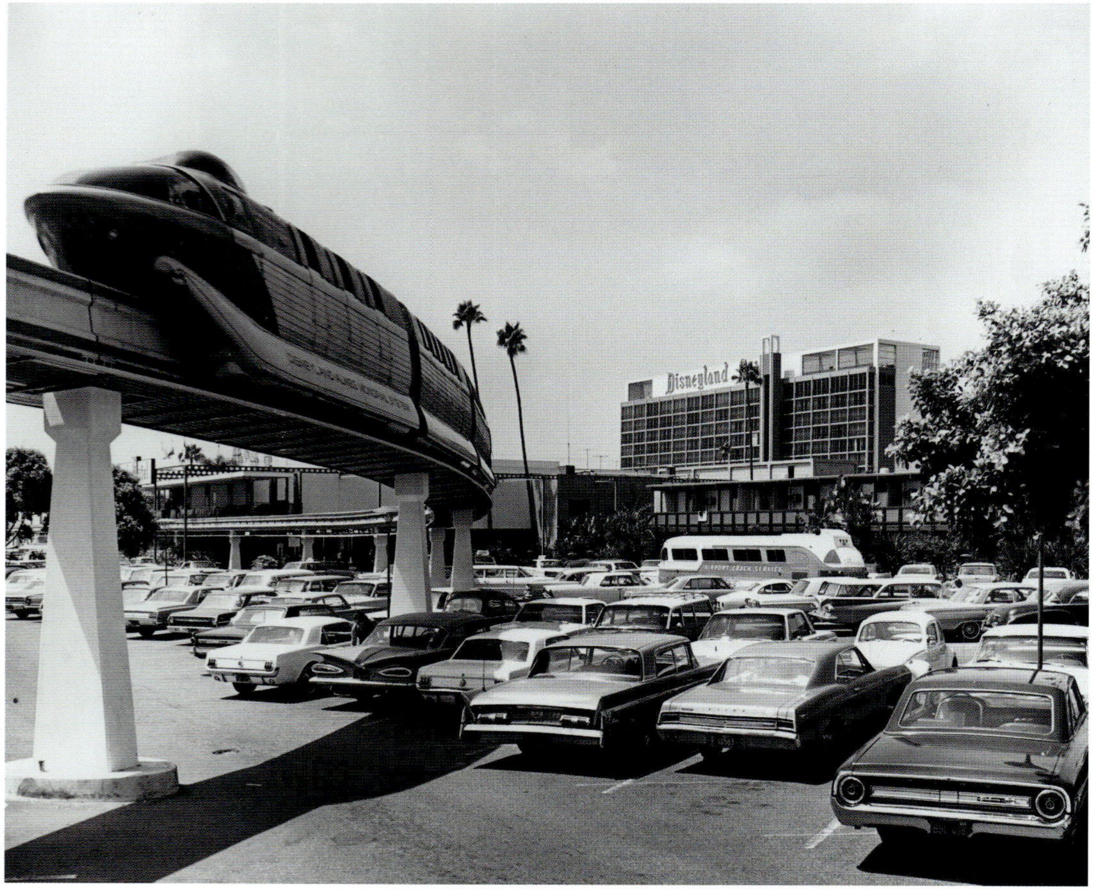

Monorail leaving Hotel station with 11-story Tower in background, 1967.

area became a wonderland for baseball fans and autograph seekers. A "standing room only" crowd of 46,309 were held spellbound by a fifteenth inning 2-1 win by the National League.

Near summer's end, Prince Ranier of Monaco and children (Prince Albert and Princess Caroline) stayed in the Presidential Suite. The Hotel's staff was disappointed that former actress Princess Grace (Kelly) was "indisposed" and unable to accompany her family. Upon his departure, Prince Ranier raved, "Wonderful! A wonderful, enchanting place. I've got to come back." While not royalty, the A. H. Richards family of New York City stayed at the Disneyland Hotel at approximately the same time. The following letter of thanks was later sent to the Hotel: "May I commend you for the beautiful park-like grounds you maintain surrounding the Disneyland Hotel? The abundance of flowers, orange trees (how wise of you to keep when the hotel was built!), the palm trees and semi-tropical plants add greatly to the pleasure of staying with you."

As 1967 counted down its last weeks, the Hotel continued to host well known guests. The Presidential Suite was once again occupied by Governor Ronald Reagan. A short time later, that Suite was home-away-from-home for Edna Francis Disney (wife of Walt's brother Roy), Roy E. Disney (her son), his wife, and their four children (Abagail, Roy, Susan, and Timothy). Other special guests included the 1930's child actress Shirley Temple, western stars Roy Rogers and Dale Evans, comedian Jimmy Durante, and H. Soeager, the manager of Copenhagen's Tivoli Gardens.

At Disneyland in 1968, no major attractions were added but what Park officials referred to as a project to "polish" the Magic Kingdom brought the total investment now to $100-million. That year Cast Members welcomed the 77-millionth guest. By June of 1968, the monorail had carried 22-million passengers, the vast majority of whom had been transported between the Park and the Disneyland Hotel.

Early that year, the Hotel hosted *Peanuts* comic strip artist Charles Schultz and his family. Pierre Salinger (former press secretary to President Kennedy) attended the convention of the California Democratic Council. Also present for that event was civil rights leader Martin Luther King. The press conference that King held in one of the Hotel's suites was one of his last major public appearances before his assassination in Memphis, Tennessee on April 4th.

The quadrennial presidential election brought extra excitement to the Disneyland Hotel in 1968. In September, Republican presidential candidate and former Vice-President Richard Nixon was scheduled to appear at a campaign rally at the Anaheim Convention Center. Nixon selected the Disneyland Hotel as the location for a major press conference and for a one-night stay for his wife, himself, his huge campaign staff of eighty (not to mention the forty Secret Service personnel) and over eighty members of the press all staying at the Hotel. Over the entrance to the Sierra Tower was hung a banner reading "Disneyland Hotel WELCOMES MR. NIXON." This short political visit required 140 rooms to be set aside. The entire eleventh floor of the Tower was reserved for the Nixon's and his staff...and it was "off limits" to all except those cleared through the Secret Service. Hotel staff members with limited access to that floor were required to wear security badges at all times. Suites in the Tower were turned into offices. Pat and Richard Nixon occupied the Presidential Suite. During their stay, the Nixon's ate all of their meals in their rooms. The Hotel was required to add extra staff to the kitchens, and the Secret Service supervised the preparation of all meals before being delivered to the candidate.

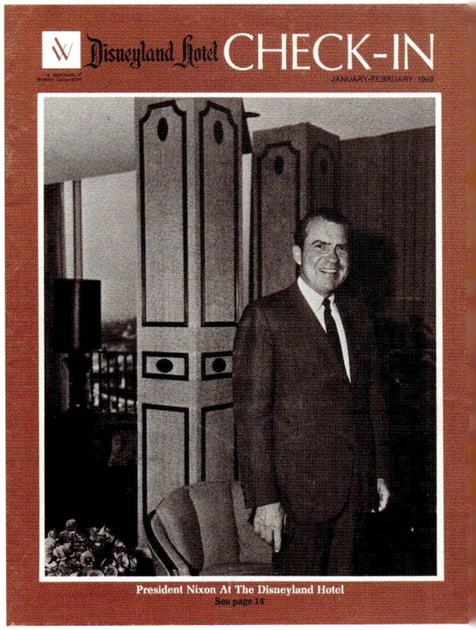

Richard Nixon at the Disneyland Hotel

For that very brief visit, the telephone company had labored for one week to install for Nixon and the press twenty-five long distance lines, ten direct outside lines, eight teletype lines, and four portable phone booths. All that equipment was utilized for a period of less than 24-hours. The Embassy Room became the headquarters for the numerous members of the media following Nixon.

As quickly as he had arrived, Nixon was gone. The Hotel later received this note from him: "Sirs: This is just to tell you how much I appreciated the fine accommodations you arranged during our visit to Anaheim last month. We greatly enjoyed the friendly cooperation of your excellent staff, and the special touches of hospitality certainly made us feel very much at home."

Shortly after his election that November, Nixon and his family once again visited Disneyland (where in 1959 they had dedicated the monorail). That 1968 visit would be his last trip to the Park.

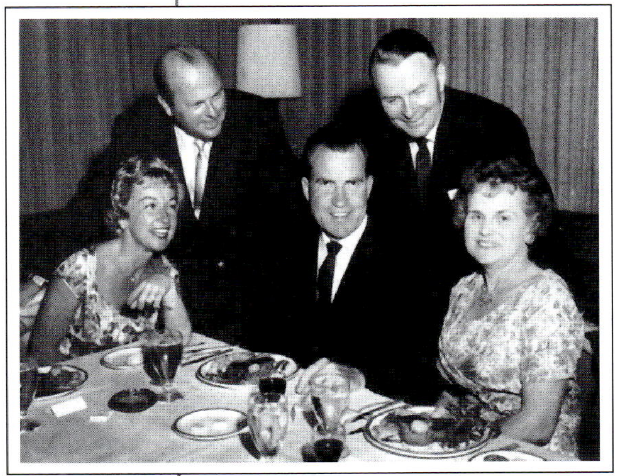
Jack and Bonita with Richard Nixon and Mr. and Mrs. Dick Richards.

Ronald Reagan (one of the television emcees on the opening day of Disneyland) stayed again at the Hotel in late 1968. He delivered the welcoming speech to the 31st Annual Conference of Secretaries of State of the United States in the Embassy Room.

Anaheim's 54th Halloween Parade was attended by over 250,000 celebrants. The Disneyland Hotel's float was called "Gypsy Magic." It consisted of four sections: a fortune teller and her crystal ball, gypsy musicians and dancers (who performed for the entire two mile parade route), a witch and her boiling cauldron, and a gypsy cart being pulled by a huge, white horse (constructed, not live). The Hotel's float was honored with the Mayor's Award for unique design.

Early in 1968, Jack Wrather announced the largest expansion of the Disneyland Hotel in its history. The project would be implemented over a period of years in at least three major stages. In fact, some of the

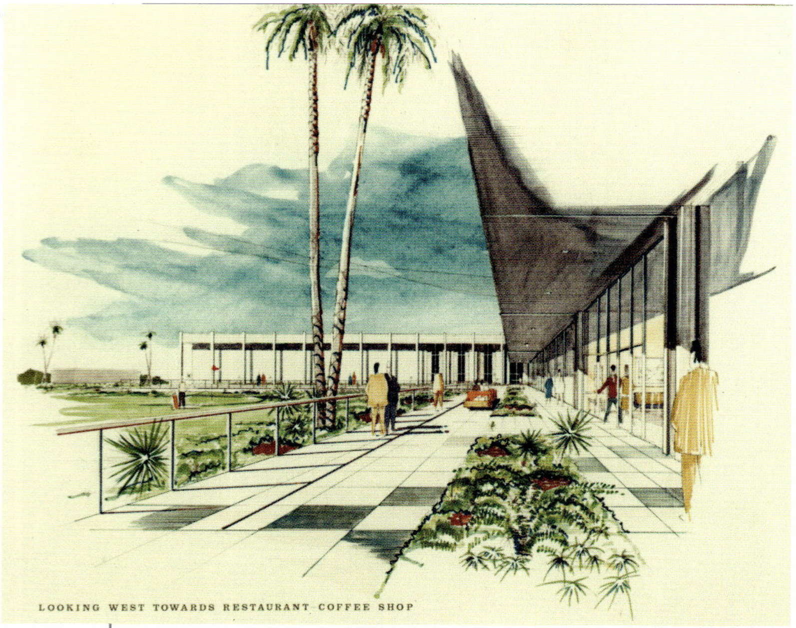

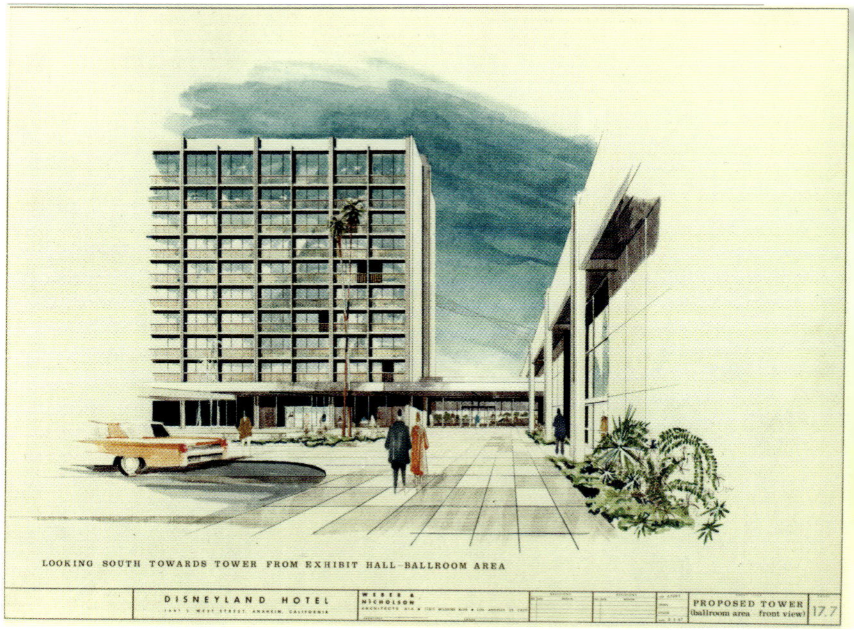

Artist concept sketches 1968.

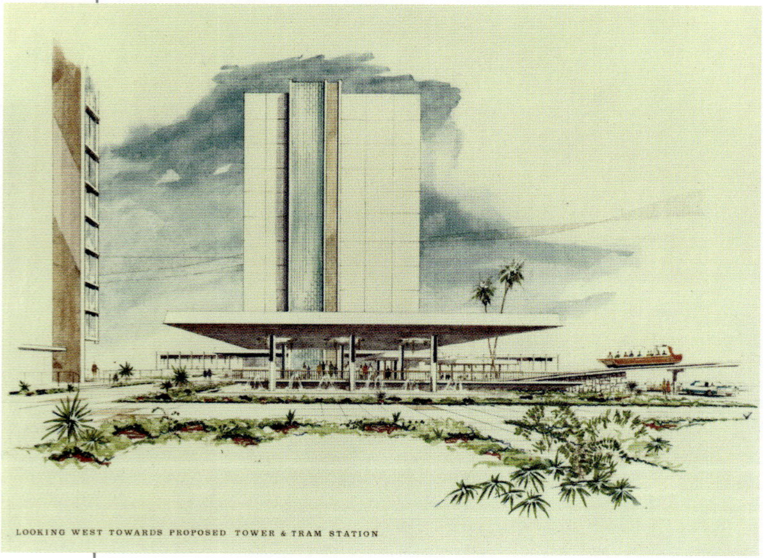

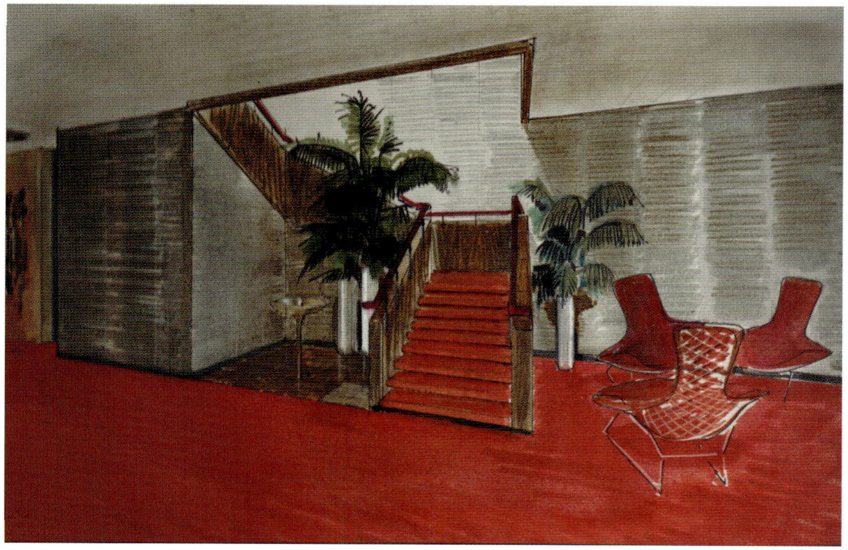

planned additions would not be completed until as late as 1983. Two of the first construction projects would add new Towers (the Marina and the Bonita) to the Hotel complex. It was projected that by the latter part of the 1970's, the Hotel would have nearly 1,500 guest rooms which would make it the largest hotel west of Chicago. The

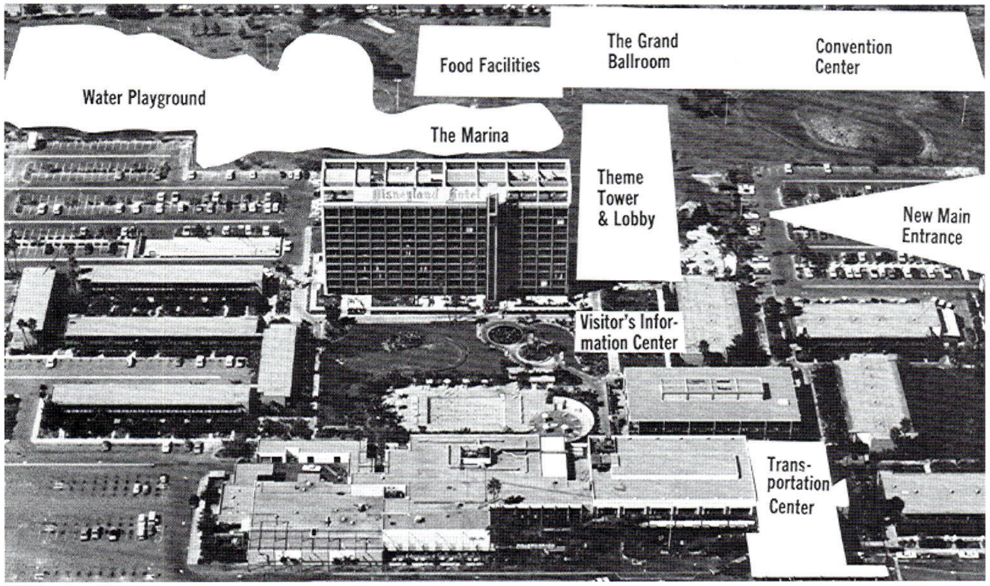

An aerial view with inserts of proposed new additions to the Hotel grounds 1968.

final stage of the expansion was to add a huge, state-of-the-art, all-purpose convention center to the property. All of this new construction would spread across the entire property bordered by West Street on the east, Walnut Street on the west, and Cerritos Avenue to the north. It would cover slightly more than half of the 60-acres originally leased from Walt Disney back in 1954. The remainder of the leased property lay north of Cerritos (occupied by a parking lot, the miniature golf course, the driving range, and the heliport).

At the announcement, Jack Wrather commented that the "Disneyland Hotel will become a complete city of recreation--an attraction in itself." He added that the "range of entertainment will be unusually wide and the environment unique." The plans called for Cerritos Avenue to be widened and for the Hotel's lobby to be shifted there from West Street (where it had been since near the Hotel's opening over a decade before). Plans were unveiled for additional restaurants and many new recreational and entertainment facilities. Many of the pre-existing facilities would be updated and expanded during this spectacular project. In July of 1968, ground was broken for the first phase of this expansion, a new 11-story tower building and a 3.5-acre marina area. It had been predicted that the new tower would be fully operational by November of 1969; various delays would prevent the meeting of that deadline.

Near the year's end, the Hotel hosted opera star Maria Callas, comedian Jonathan Winters (appearing at a benefit for American Indians), singer Andy Williams (attending a fund raiser), and the First Lady of California Nancy Reagan (speaking at a Republican Party function).

During the holiday season, actor Henry Fonda stayed at the Hotel while he was the narrator of *A Christmas Carol* at the Park. Motion picture star Cary Grant and his daughter also were guests. He later wrote: "My little daughter Jennifer, her nurse Mrs. O'Connell, and I are extremely grateful to you and your cheerful, well-trained staff at Disneyland Hotel for making our stay so comfortable. My child was delighted with everything and, if only for the constant joy I found in watching her, I'm deeply obligated to you and everyone I had the pleasure of meeting there." Grant ended his letter: "Visiting Disneyland while staying at your hotel is an unforgettable experience that all parents and children should be fortunate enough to enjoy; and if you know of any way I could spread that good word please call upon me."

In his year-end message to guests, general manager Frank Bret heralded the planned growth of the Hotel by writing, "When Walt Disney opened Disneyland, he said it would never be completed.... Here at the Disneyland Hotel we are of like mind. We are continually looking for new and exciting ways to entertain our guests and to

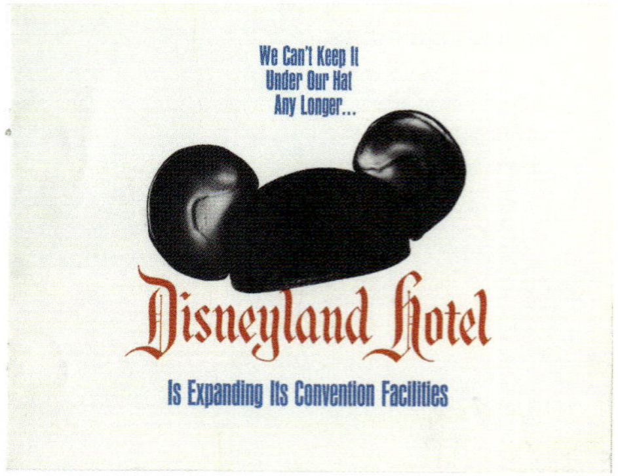

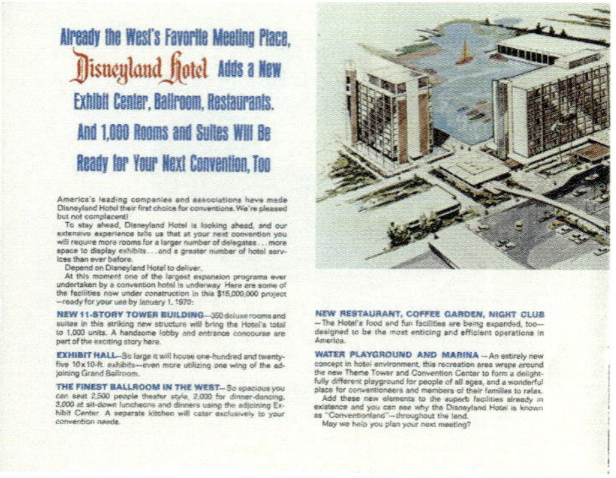

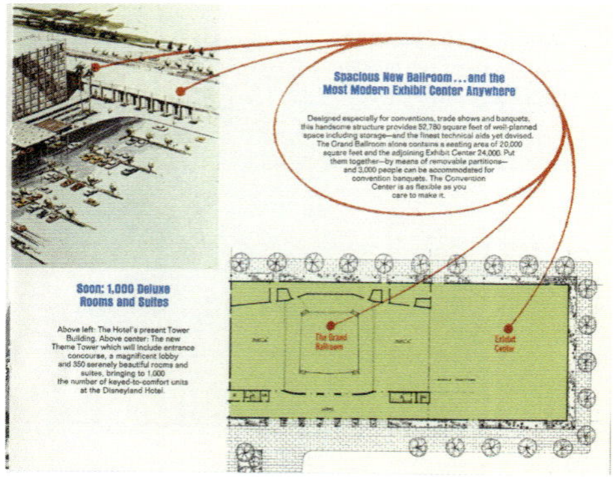

1968 new facilities brochure.

make their stay here enjoyable in every way." Bret went on to detail some aspects of the new projects that had been announced earlier by Wrather.

In 1969, the Haunted Mansion (the last attraction to have been begun under the supervision of Walt Disney) was added to the Park. The 85-millionth guest was welcomed in August to the now $126-million investment.

In the spring, Dick Van Dyke spent some time at the Hotel while acting in Disney's newest live-action comedy *Never a Dull Moment* (1968). The summer season saw Julie Andrews making yet another of her annual visits to the Hotel and Park. [Her first such experience had been when she had been personally escorted by Walt Disney during the production of *Mary Poppins* (1964).] Also during that summer, actress Anne Baxter and her children spent a weekend at the Hotel.

The previous summer of 1968 had been an unusually dry one. The weather forecast for January 18, 1969, called for "light showers." What followed were nine straight days of rain. On Friday, February 21st, the rains began again. During this period, 21-inches of rain fell (an eighty-seven year record). The average annual rain fall for the area was only 9.8-inches. Three-hundred Marines sandbagged for three days. Business at both Disneyland and the Disneyland Hotel were adversely affected.

On August 1, 1968, Jack Wrather purchased Gourmet Restaurants, Inc. (which operated the Disneyland Hotel's primary restaurants since opening day). In 1969 on West Street, the Hotel's Gourmet restaurant was renamed the California Dining Room (which would be redesigned and renovated in June of 1972 and closed in 1978). The restaurant provided a "special souvenir menu" for children; after orders had been placed, it could be turned into a Mickey Mouse mask.

The Crown and Pillow Pub (a lounge with a distinctive old English atmosphere) was opened in 1968, adjoining the Oak Room restaurant. Artifacts (both original and reproduced) from 19th Century England covered the walls. One could see an 1845 regimental bugle and a British Navy officer's dress hat with feather plumes and gold braid. From the early 1800's, an "Inn Keeper" sign (hand-painted on clay substances--now a lost art form) and a map of the County of Cornwell decorated another wall. True to tradition, the pub included a stand-up bar. Bartender Marcus Fetherston added greatly to the pub's English character since he originally hailed from London and spoke with a distinct Cockney accent. He previously had worked in the Oak Room. On-tap were imported English beers with the "specialty of the house" being Watney's Lager, imported from London. Domestic beers and mixed drinks were also available and pretzel bowls were kept full at all times.

Patrons of the Lounge in 1969 were entertained by something more than just music. A large, silver machine had taken its place behind the bar. Its many gauges, tubes, and valves became a center of interest and curiosity. Built in Milan, Italy, especially for the Hotel, it was more than just a coffee pot. Its right spout dispensed Espresso Coffee. Its left spout provided aromatic Cappuccino. Its product was also available for order in the Lounge Restaurant and the Oak Room. A new policy now provided almost continuous musical entertainment in the Hotel's various lounges and bars (expect on Sundays) from five o'clock in the afternoon until one o'clock in the morning.

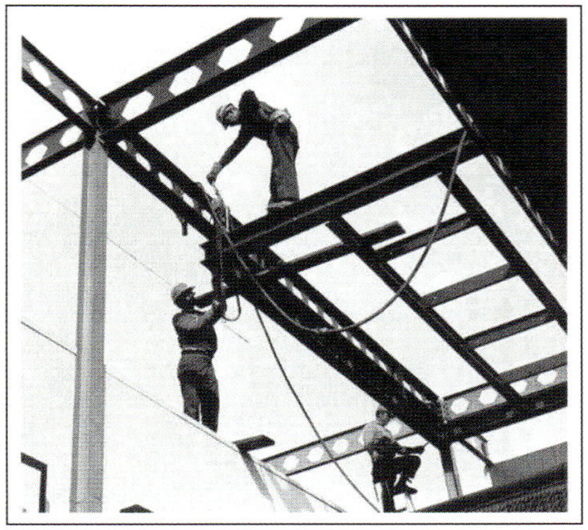

Monorail Station enlargement 1969.

By April of 1969, the Hotel's monorail station had been enlarged to accommodate bigger and better monorail trains. An extra car had been added to each train (now five cars and a total length of 137 feet). The interiors had been redesigned for more convenient seating arrangements. Seats were padded with foam rubber. Better views were provided through the new panoramic windows and more aerodynamic bodies were built upon super-soft air suspension. The new monorail trains provided capacity for more passengers, thereby creating shorter wait times at the Hotel's monorail station. The Monorail Bar was redecorated with wall murals depicting the history of railroading.

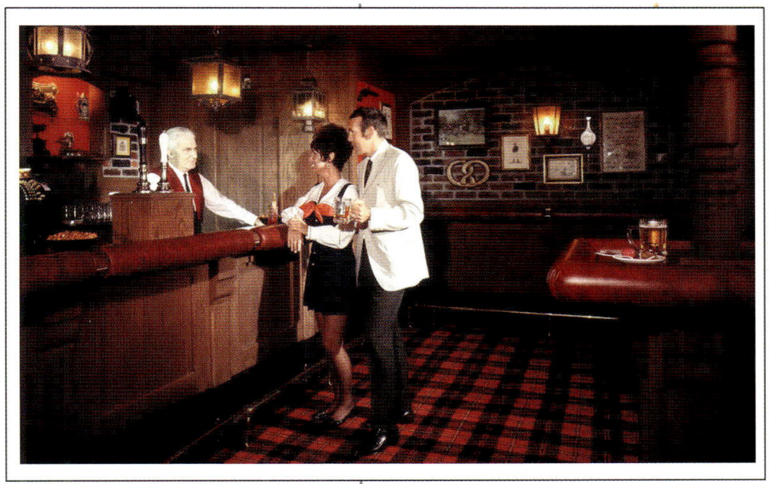

The Crown and Pillow Pub.

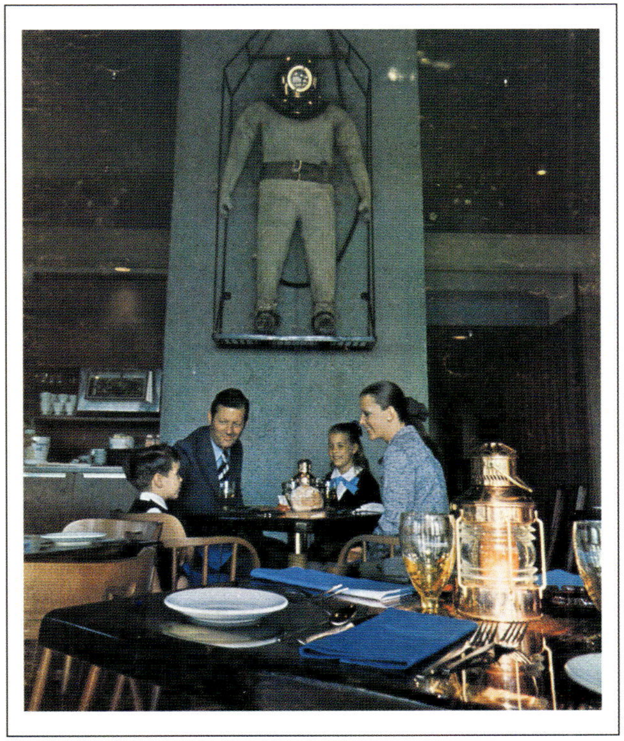

The Shipyard Inn with its distinctive nautical interior.

In 1969, to the west side of the Sierra Tower, the Shipyard Inn restaurant was under construction. It would specialize in gourmet seafood dining. Upon being seated, guests would be presented with a large , colorful, porthole - shaped menu. Appetizers included bisque filled with lobster chunks or a garden salad of mixed greens, cucumber, sprouts, and tiny shrimp. Before the entree, patrons cleansed their palates with a lemon sherbet intermezzo. Specialties of the restaurant would include French bouillabaisse, Dungeness crab claws, clams on the half shell, and a fish-of-the-day (sea bass, Red Snapper, or sole, depending upon availability). The menu also offered fresh Maine Lobster, Crabmeat Cannelloni,

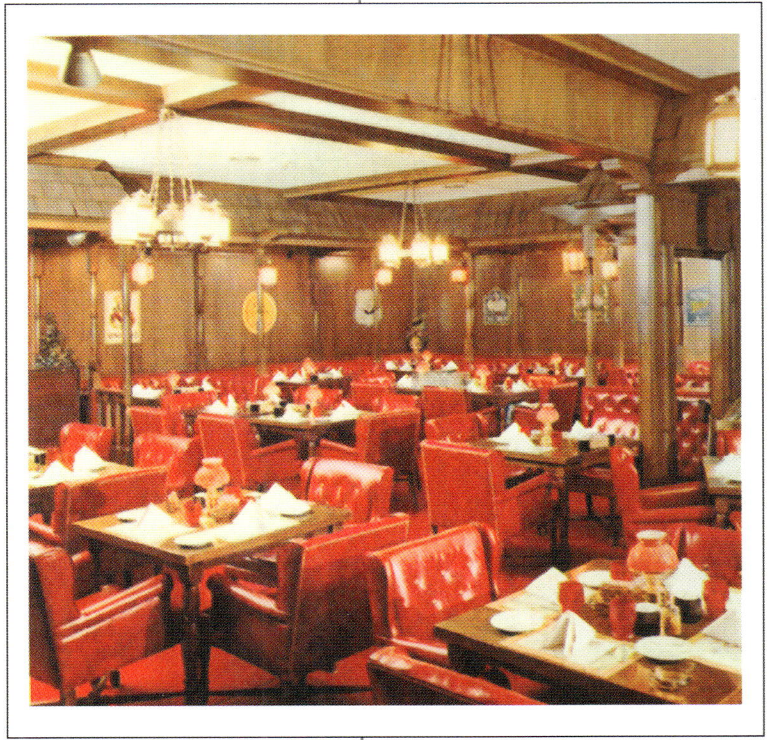

The Oak Room-a private gentleman's club.

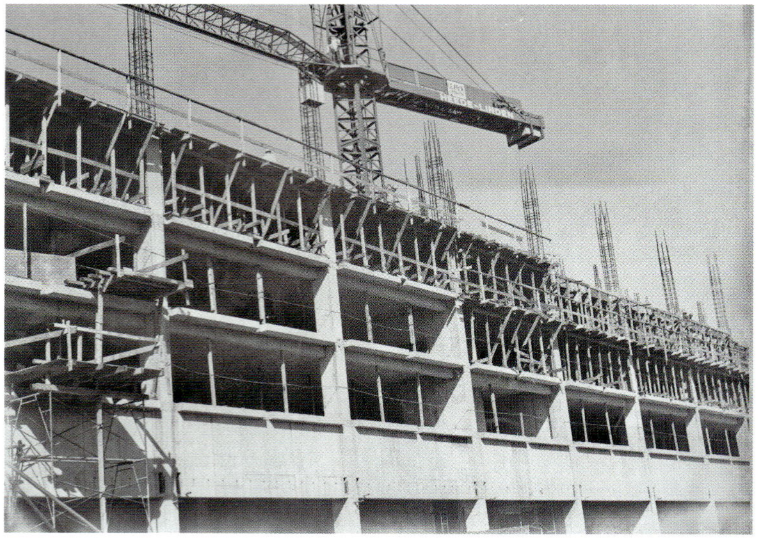

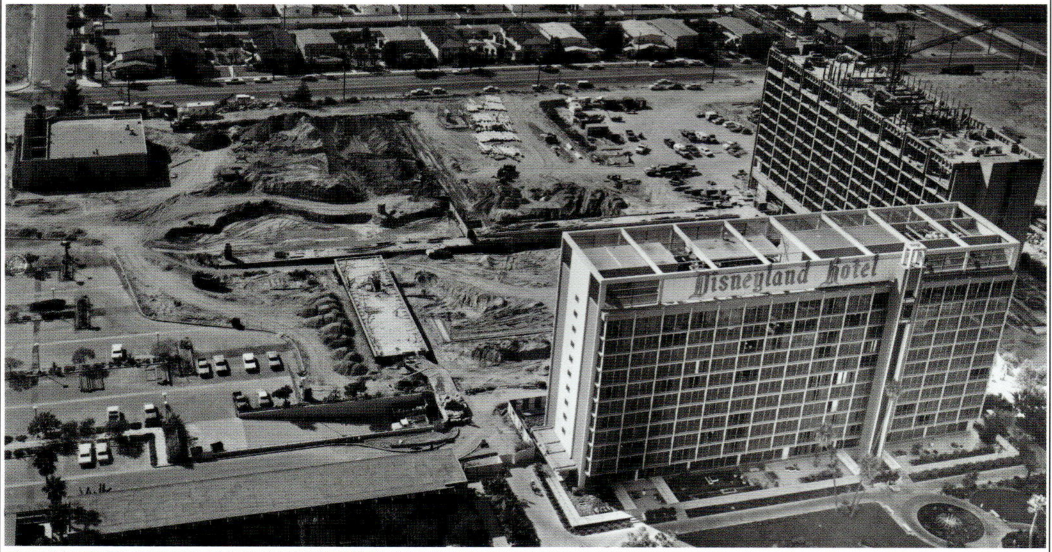

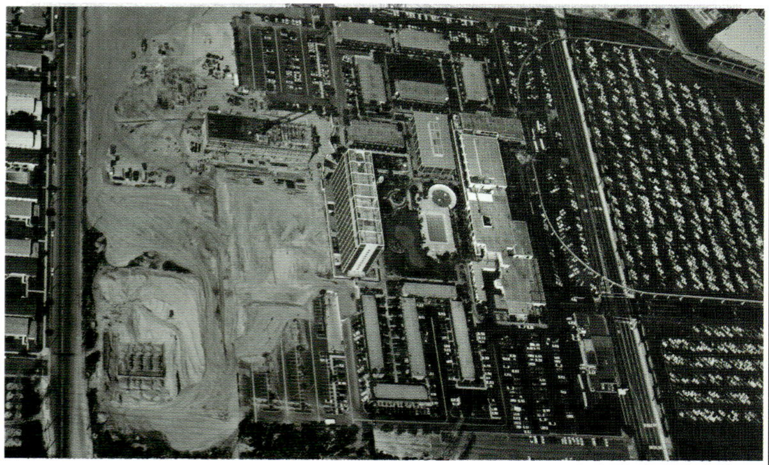

Marina Tower construction 1969.

and Stuffed Scampi Lorenzo. Bibs would be provided to guests for the "safe" enjoyment of their seafood treats. Decorated in a nautical theme, the Shipyard Inn tables were designed from ship hatch covers, bordered with thick ship cable ropes. On the wall hung a deep sea diving suit.

Described as having a "salty seaside atmosphere" (located downstairs at water level) was the Sailmaker's Den lounge. The later addition of an outside deck would provide patrons with a grand view of the marina area. As with the decor, drinks had a definite nautical theme. For years, Fredrick de Marseille, dressed in sailor's garb, strolled between the restaurant area upstairs and the lounge, singing lively sea chanteys. An order of a "Load Line" allowed the guest to keep the special souvenir glass.

Donald J. Spilger and Zoltan Kovaks of Fred Schmid Associates, Los Angeles were the designers of the food service areas. The architectural firm had again been Weber and Nicholson of Los Angeles. [The Shipyard Inn and the Sailmaker's Den would continue operations until being closed on January 3, 1999. They would be replaced by Hook's Pointe Restaurant and Wine Cellar on April 8, 1999.]

A flight from Los Angeles International Airport to the Hotel's heliport lasted a mere fifteen minutes, with twenty-six round trip flights scheduled each day. In September of 1969, thirteen-year-old David Swartwood (accompanied by his parents) of Parma, Ohio became the one-millionth passenger on Los Angeles Airways' Disneyland Hotel shuttle service. Upon landing, he was welcomed by officials of the Hotel, Disneyland, and L.A. Airways. Mickey Mouse, Pluto, and Goofy also greeted the Swartwood family. As with every Disney celebration, special gifts were presented. Even before this milestone, the Disneyland Hotel Heliport long had ranked as the busiest in the world. In 1968 alone, it had handled 78,857 passengers.

Frank L. Bret had been hired in 1960 as general manager of the Disneyland Hotel and was promoted a year later to vice-president of the Wrather Corporation. In October of 1969, Bret was honored by being elected president of the California State Hotel and Motel Association, during its annual convention held in Palm Springs. Bret had been active in that organization since 1949. Later in 1970, Bret would be elected president of the Anaheim Visitors and Convention Bureau and would be appointed a board member of the California Hotel and Motel Association. He also served as a director of the American Hotel and Motel Association and the Southern California Visitors Council.

For three days in late 1969, the Disneyland Hotel played host to men from outer space, two Russian cosmonauts and one United States astronaut. Major General Georgiy Beregovoy and civilian scientist Konstantin Feoktistov. They were escorted on their brief visit by U.S. Commander Eugene Cernan and his wife. The spacemen were able to visit the Park, giving those two Russians a pleasure that ten years earlier had been denied to Soviet Premier Nikita Khrushchev due to overwhelming security concerns. Back in 1959, Walt Disney had been extremely disappointed by that cancelled visit. He had planned to line up all of the submarines in Tomorrowland and then boast to the Premier that Disneyland had one of the largest navies in the world. In 1969, the cosmonauts admitted that their brief stay in Anaheim was the "most exciting" part of their tour of this country. They were most pleased by the baskets of fresh fruit provided in their suites (fresh fruit being a scarcity in the Soviet Union).

By Christmas, the new tower building was partially opened to receive its first guests. The original plan had been to have the tower fully operational by then. Strikes by two construction unions would delay the official opening until mid-January. On December 25, 1969, with only a limited number of rooms available, the A. S. Briggs family (including their 12-year-old son) from San Francisco became the first to register at the new facility. Mrs. Briggs later stated: "We surely enjoyed our stay with you. The room was beautiful and comfortable; the service excellent and friendly. Never have we had such good food at a hotel dining room." Approving comments also expressed their delight for the Hotel's beautiful landscaping.

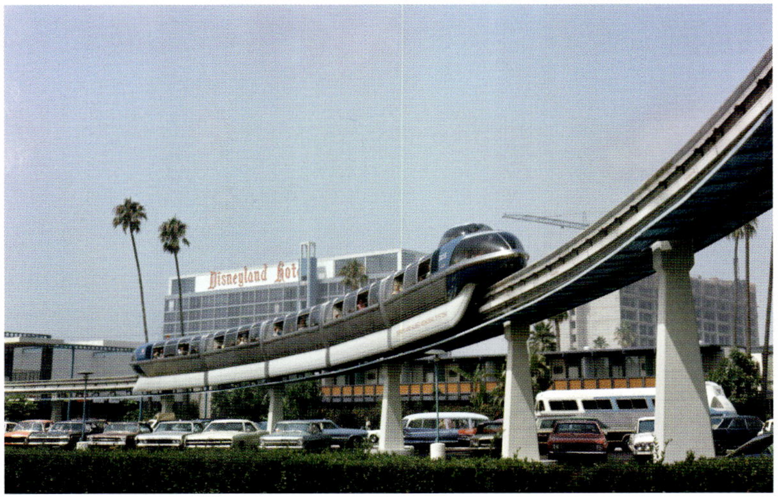

1969 showing construction on the latest Tower Building.

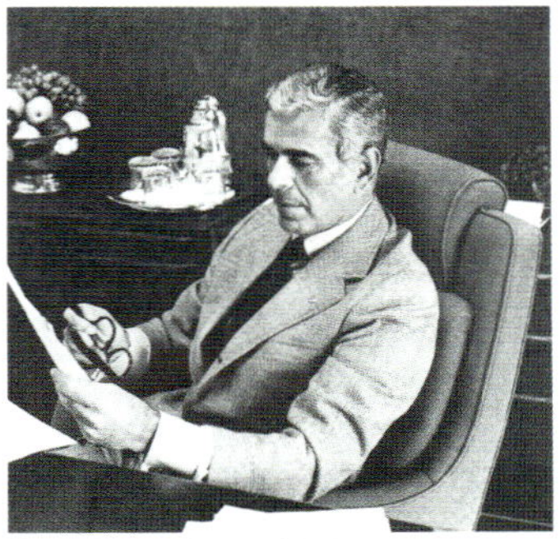

Frank L. Bret, general manager of the Disneyland Hotel, is active in industry affairs.

Frank L. Bret
Named to Important Posts

Disneyland Hotel

PLEASURE AND CONVENTION HEADQUARTERS IN SOUTHERN CALIFORNIA

- 616 deluxe rooms and suites. (1000 deluxe rooms and suites available November 1, 1969).
- Gourmet Restaurants.
- Popular priced Coffee Shops.
- 40-acre night lighted, 50-position driving range and 18 hole miniature golf course.
- Olympic size Swimming Pool.
- Merchandising Center with 25 exciting shops.
- Heliport on hotel grounds. 28-passenger turbojet with 76 daily flights to and from the Los Angeles International Airport.
- Direct hourly coach service between the Los Angeles, Orange County and Long Beach Airports and the Disneyland Hotel.
- Monorail - Highway in the Sky - from the hotel to the heart of the Magic Kingdom.
- 24 hr. baby-sitting service.
- All travel services in the lobby, including Avis and 6 major airlines.
- Tours arranged to studios and all southland pleasure spots.

AND FOR CONVENTIONS THAT CLICK

- 23,000 sq. ft. of exhibit space.
- 27 conference and meeting rooms to accommodate 15 or 1500 people.
- Outstanding banquet rooms.
- Free parking for 2000 cars.
- 60 sunny acres of the finest and most complete convention facilities . . . and an expert convention staff to help you to stage a most successful convention.

FOR INFORMATION CALL
(714) 535-8171
From Los Angeles
Call MAdison 5-1369

1969 Hotel information.

1970-1979

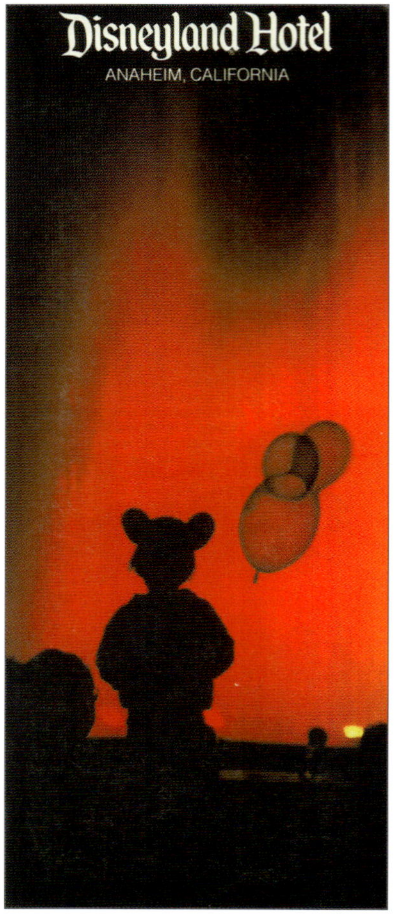

At 9:41 on the morning of September 19, 1970, Verda McFarlane of Riverside, California was honored as the first 10-millionth guest to visit Disneyland in a single year. The Park had by now hosted 95-million guests and had become a $128.5-million family experience. June 22 was memorable for the establishment of the Walt Disney Archives on the Studio lot in Burbank, created by its current director Dave Smith. Anaheim had become the fastest growing industrial area in the nation and had a population of 166,701. Land values in the area had increased ten-fold since the Park had opened.

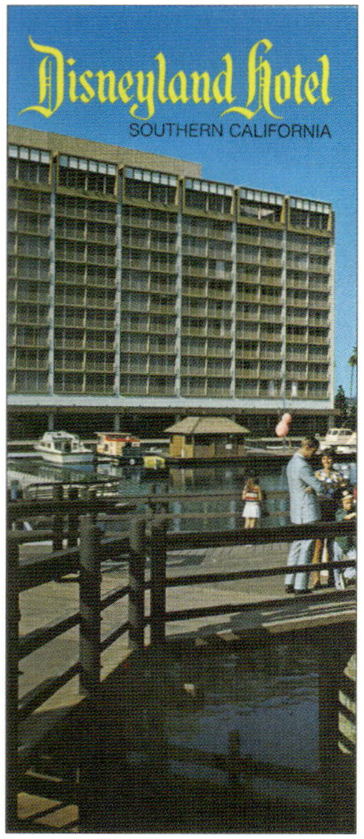

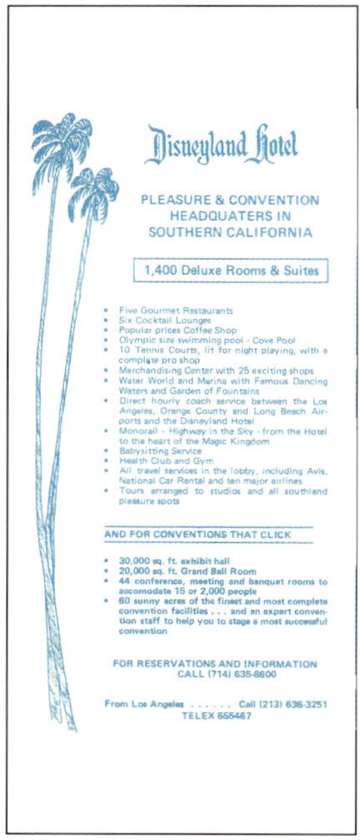

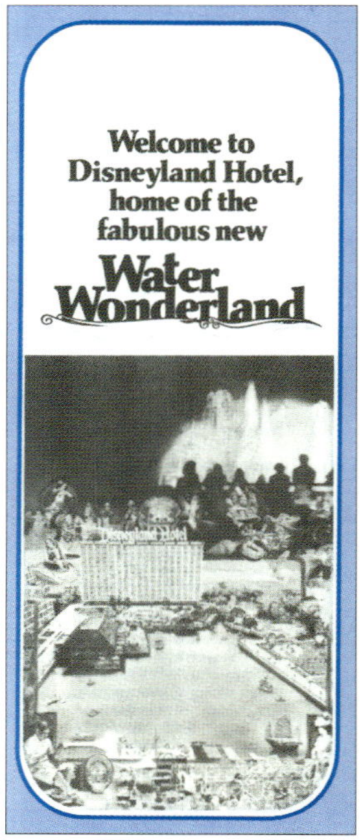

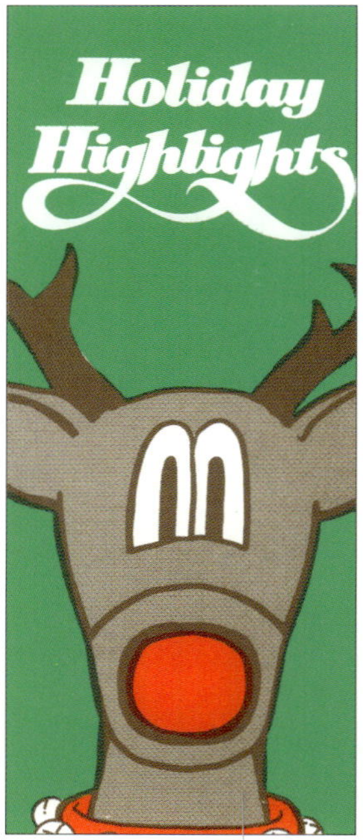

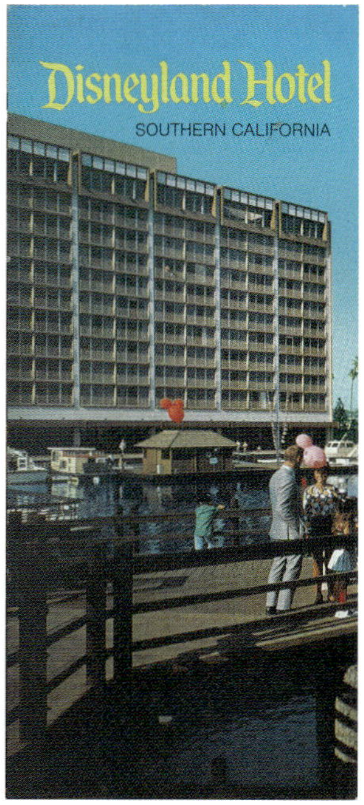

Hotel brochures from the 1970's.

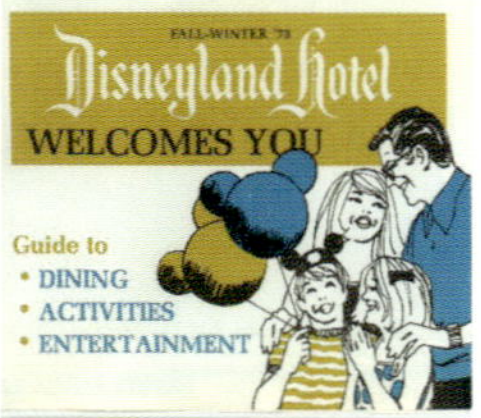

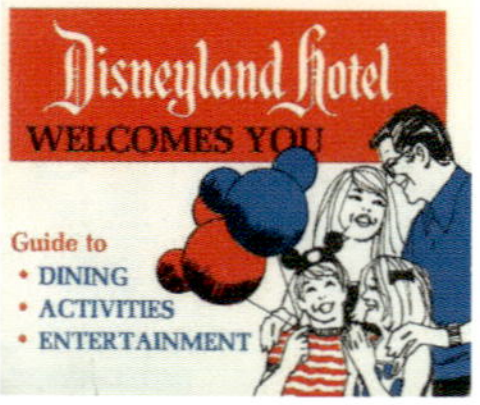

As the result of a $12-million expansion project, the Disneyland Hotel witnessed major changes and additions in 1970. An advertising slogan used at that time declared the Hotel to be "The World's Most Exciting Hotel."

The newly renovated Restaurant Row opened along West Street. The aim of Restaurant Row was to provide guests with an intimate, themed dining experience...a departure from the national trend at that time to larger hotel restaurants. The California Dining Room and the Coffee House restaurants continued their usual excellent service. The Country Kitchen (a family oriented restaurant) was added with its old-world decor and a buffet of Mediterranean cooking (renamed the Chef's Kitchen in the latter part of 1973). On Sundays, a Champagne Brunch was available with a bubbling punch fountain for children. The specialty was Eggs Benedict. Served from 11 a.m.

to 2 p.m., costs for adults (including one glass of champagne) was $2.95, and children under 12, $1.50. The Country Kitchen overlooked the Hotel's original pool, now named the Sierra Swimming Pool. The Oak Room (entered through a huge hand-carved wooden door) was finally opened to the public for dinner. Diners needed to be at least sixteen years of age and gentlemen were requested to wear jackets. Both dinner and dancing were provided in an English atmosphere until midnight. Established in the early-1960's, the Oak Room originally had been a private gentlemen's club. Although it was now open to the general public in the evenings, the private luncheons for "men only" still continued.

At the Plaza Building, Blum's of San Francisco (a cafe and candy store) was opened. Its menu featured a wide variety of sandwiches and ice cream treats. Joining the Shipyard Inn on the marina's wharf was Molly Malone's Fish Market, providing a fast service and take-out menu which featured seafood snacks, seafood cocktails, hot dogs, and soft drinks. The Hotel now offered its guests seven themed and varied dining experiences. Those were only minor changes found by Hotel guests visiting in 1970.

On January 15th, the 11-story, 319-room Marina Tower was officially opened. [Originally, this new building was to have been named the Cerritos Tower.] The Hotel now offered over 1,000 guest rooms. North side rooms of the new tower offered a spectacular view of the San Gabriel Mountains and snow

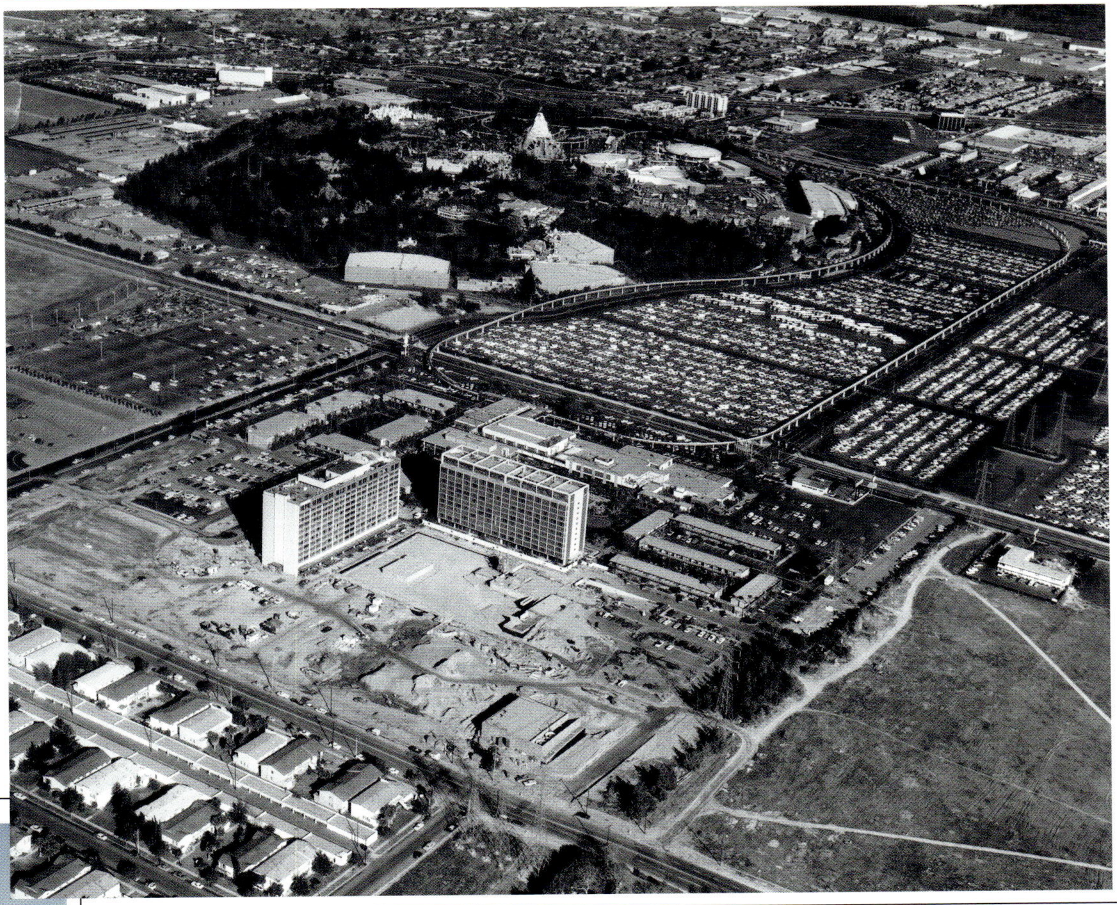

An aerial view from early 1970 with the new Marina Tower.

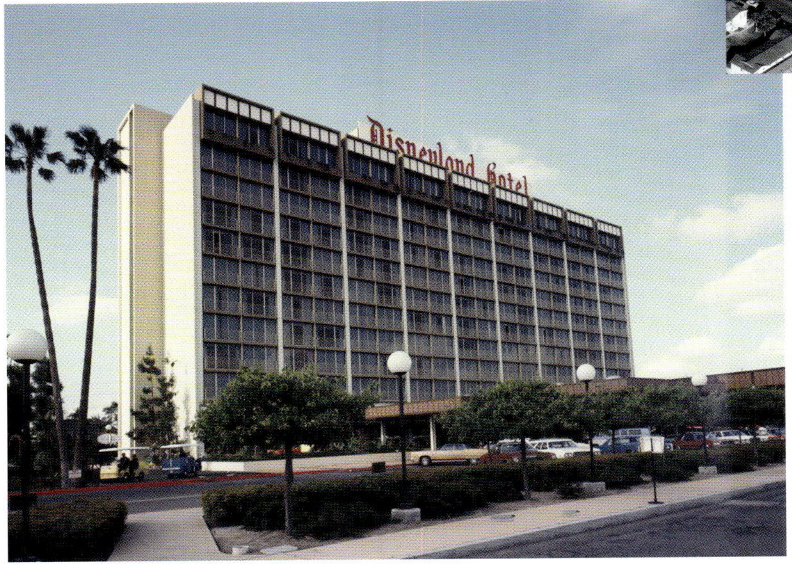

The Marina Tower building 1970. The Hotel now advertised over 1,000 guest rooms and suites.

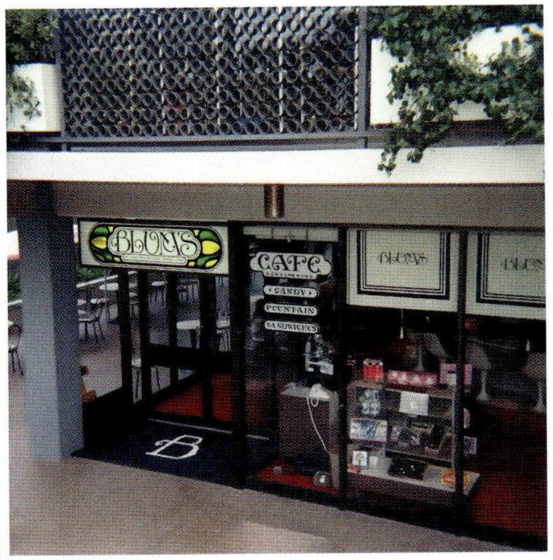

Blums in the Plaza Building.

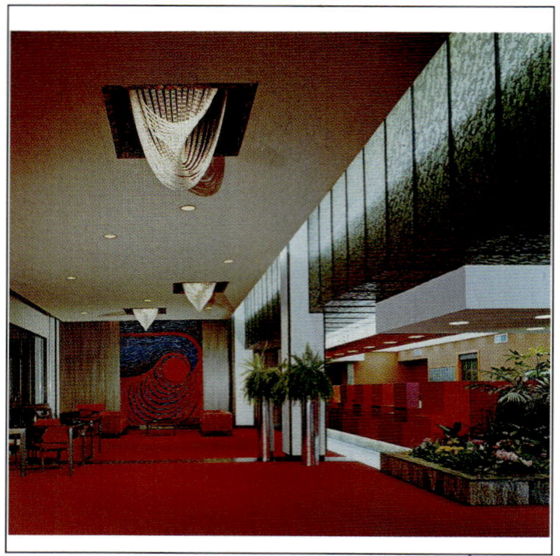

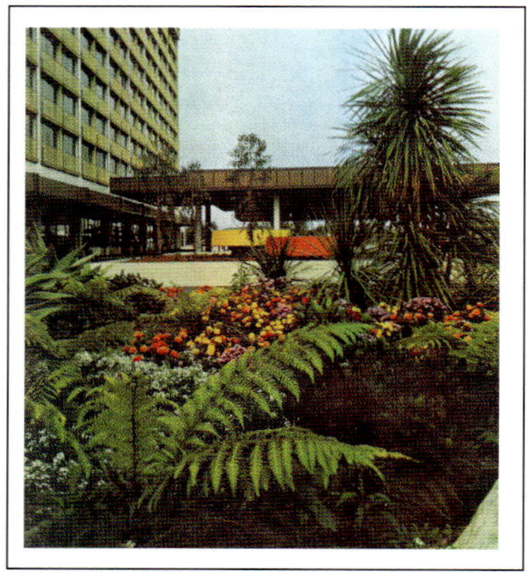

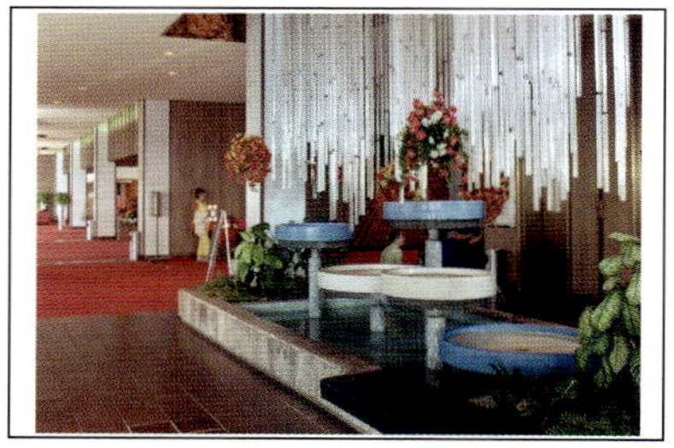

Marina Tower landscaping (top) and interior lobby (bottom).

capped Mount Baldy. Southern rooms overlooked the newly completed marina area. Due to the earlier strikes, it was not until March that the newly opened tower reached its full occupancy. Most of the first floor was a new registration lobby that changed the entrance of the Hotel from West Street to the north side of the property. The Hotel's official address had now become 1150 West Cerritos Avenue. A newly widened Cerritos included a center, landscaped median and a left-turn lane for ease of access to the Hotel's new parking area. Soon, parking at the hotel would no longer be free.

Upon approaching the Marina Tower's front doors, guests were greeted by bubbling fountains and a variety of flowers. Inside the 300-foot long by 70-foot wide lobby were sixteen check-in stations. Each station was computerized for faster service. [At the time, this was one of the largest hotel lobbies in the nation.] The lobby was decorated in bright colors, an abundance of plants, and large picture windows running its length. On the walls were hung seven huge, gaily colored tapestries. Their addition had been planned partly as a noise-deadening device. The largest of these tapestries was 10-feet wide and 18-feet high. Designed by John Gary Wallis of Los Angeles, their bright patterns were artistic impressions of California's natural scenery. Edward Fields, Incorporated (a New York carpet manufacturer) turned the original artwork into wall hangings. The technique of carpet production allowed the seven wool tapestries to have a three-dimensional quality.

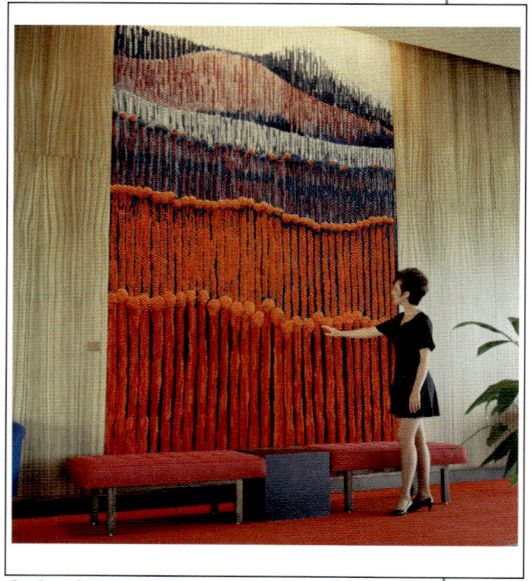

Colorful interior lobby and tapestries adorn the first floor of the Marina Tower.

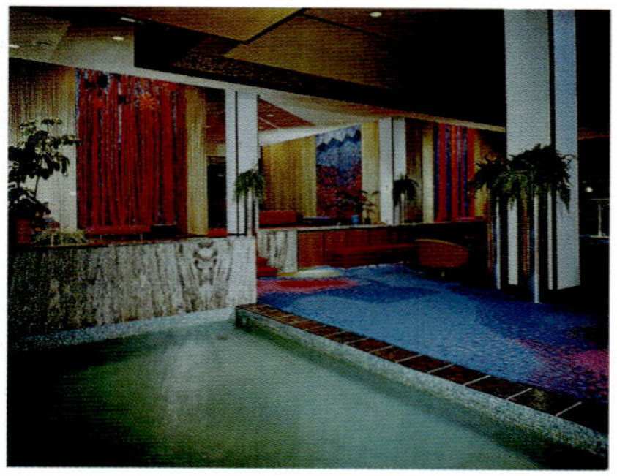

After registration, five high-speed elevators whisked guests to their rooms. Beyond the elevators, at the west end of the main floor, was the circular Palm Court Lounge. Slightly sunken below lobby level, the lounge was dominated by an immense, imported crystal chandelier. An outside waterfall flowed into the cocktail lounge, adding to its tranquil atmosphere. Views from the lounge overlooked the marina area. Also to be found in the new Tower was the Oak Room Health Spa (opened on January 12, 1970 on the B-level below the lobby). Entered through a massive black walnut door, the spa's changing, training, and work-out areas were finished in oak paneling.

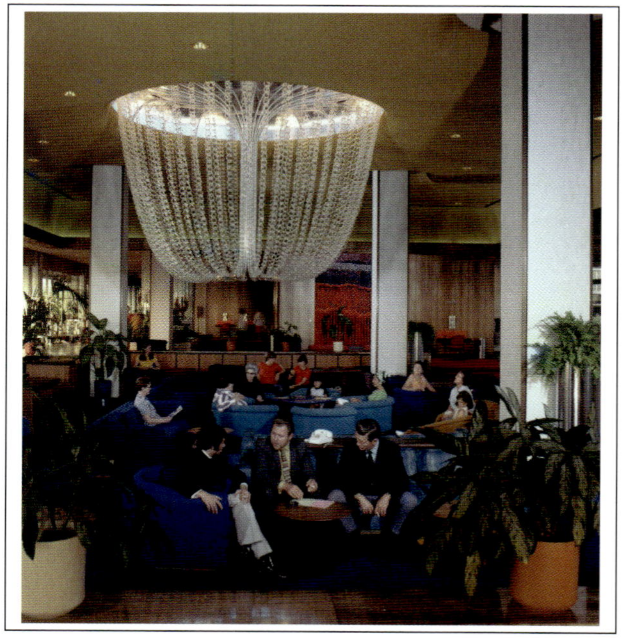

The Palm Court Lounge with its beautiful décor and crystal chandelier.

Wet areas had a decor of ceramic tile and Italian marble. The spa was opened to gentlemen only and provided a sauna, massages, a completely equipped exercise room, and a hydro-massage pool (with mineral treated water). The manager was Joe Kaributas who was an expert in physical therapy.

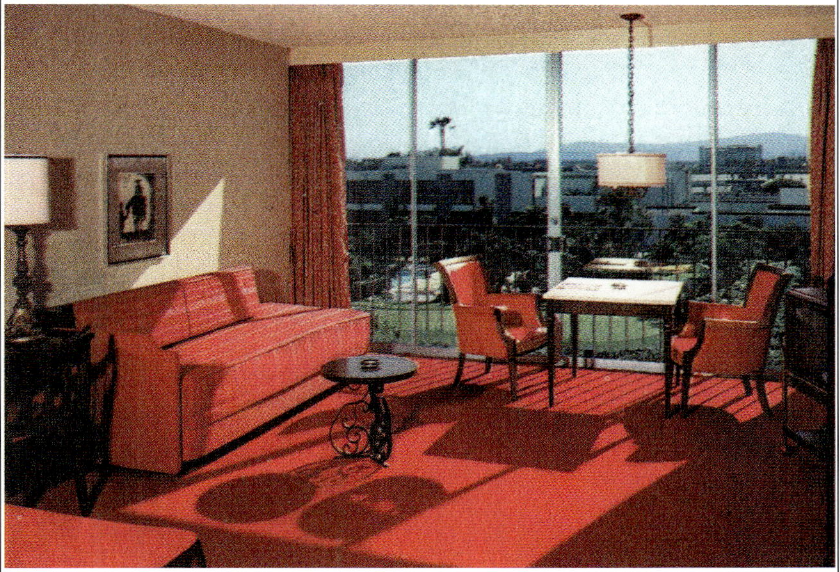

Guest rooms in the new Tower included over-size beds, color television, Muzak, and a sun balcony. Breakfast room service was almost instant. Precooked meals were delivered from the main kitchen to three dispensing kitchens located throughout the building. Using technology utilized in the airline industry, meals were carried in specially designed, insulated carts. At the appointed time, the pre-cooked Continental Breakfast or Hearty American Breakfast would be reheated in a microwave oven (a relatively new technology at that time). This system allowed delivery to guests' rooms in as little as 45-seconds, and up to 5-minutes during peak periods. The variety of evening entertainment at the Hotel could be enjoyed by parents since in-room babysitting service was available.

Inside guest room 1970's.

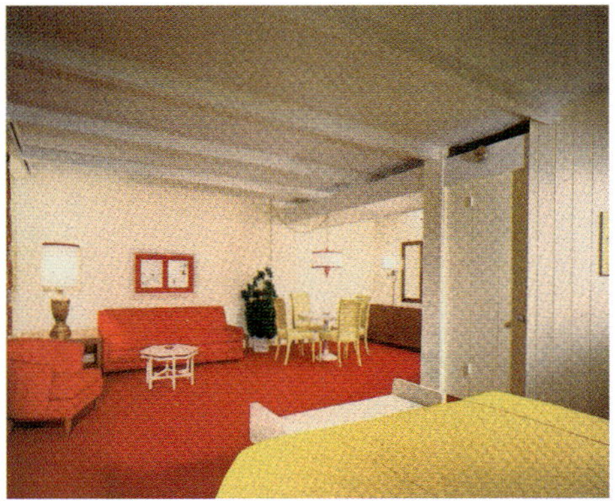

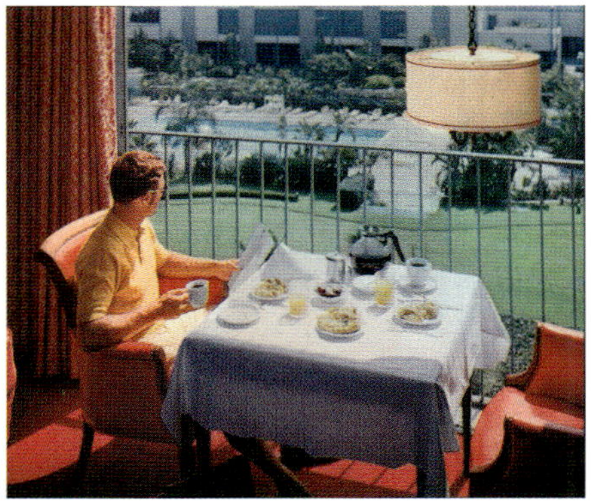

Advertised room rates for 1970 were as follows: Garden Rooms- Queen-size bed regular $16, vacation $22. Twin beds regular $18, vacation $24. Two double beds regular $22, vacation $28. Twin Towers-Queen-size bed regular $23-25, vacation $27-29. Twin beds regular $25-27, vacation $29-31. King-size bed regular $26-28, vacation $30-32. Studio room for three, regular $28-31, vacation $32-34. Two double beds regular $31-33, regular $35-37. Deluxe Suites-sitting room with one bedroom regular $55-60, vacation $70-75. Sitting room with two bedrooms regular $80-90, vacation $95-100. Sitting room with three bedrooms regular $100-110, vacation $120-125. Royal Suites –regular $125-175, vacation $125-175. Regular rates were in effect except March 20 through April 4, May 29 through September 5, December 19 through January 1 when Vacation Rates applied.

The first convention group to utilize the newly opened Marina Tower was the National Swimming Pool Institute. The annual convention began on January 26th. While its meetings were held at the Anaheim Convention Center just to the south, the Disneyland Hotel was designated as its official headquarters.

Development of this $12-million first stage of the Disneyland Hotel's expansion program had again been under the supervision of C. L. Peck Contractor-Engineer of Los Angeles.

Reopened early in 1970, the Sierra Tower's Top-of-the-Park cocktail lounge had been enlarged and redecorated at a cost of $65,000. The new furniture, carpeting, and decor were all in various tones of red. New, huge, wall hangings represented the lounge's views of the San Gabriel Mountains and of the new Water World area. The lounge had been expanded by eliminating the former lobby entrance. Patrons now exited the glass elevator directly into the lounge.

In late spring of 1970, Jack and Bonita Wrather dedicated a 3.5-acre World of Water marina (later to become

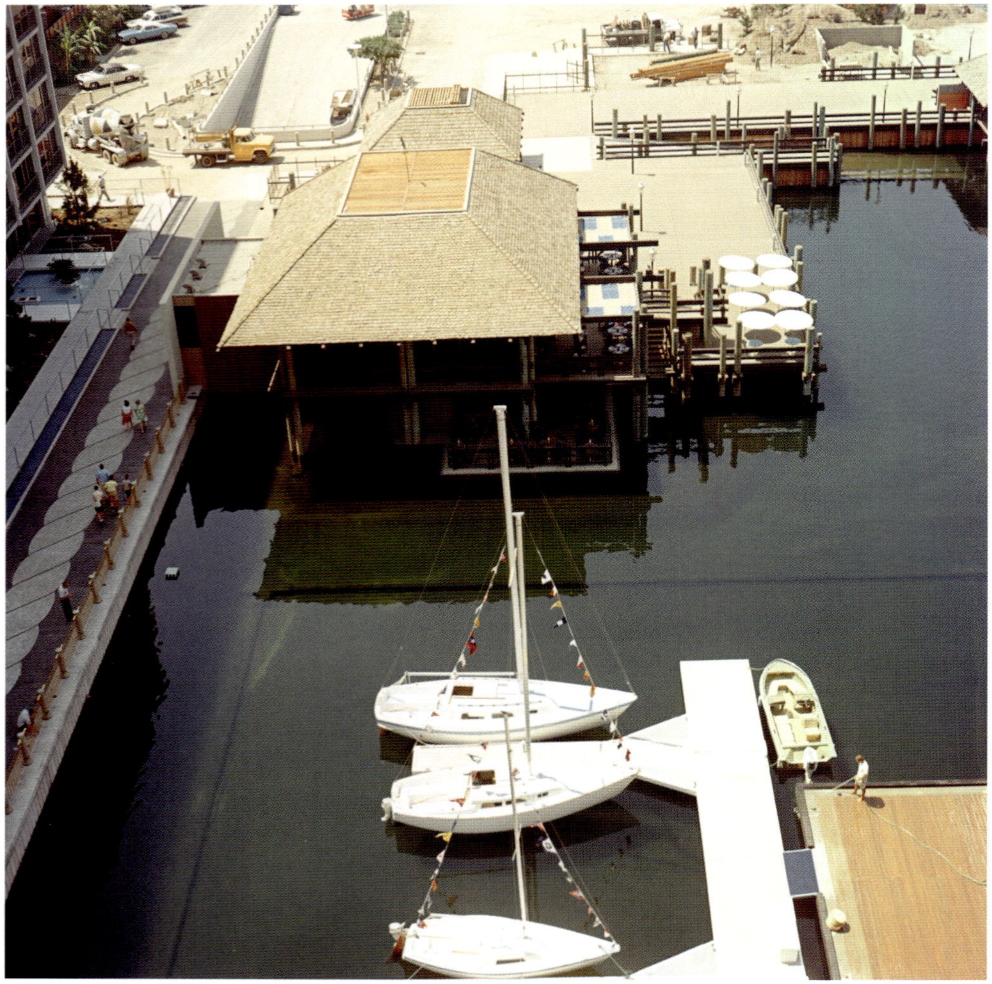

The new Marina with its display of boats and recreational vehicles.

Seaports of the Pacific), situated in the middle of an "L" formed by the Sierra Tower (to the east) and the Marina Tower (to the north). Concerning the concept for the marina, Jack Wrather stated, "We wanted something completely unique for the hotel, something unique for an inland hotel. We came up with a water area. Not a lake--other hotels have lakes--but a marina. Everything else then fit into the water theme." The marina held two million gallons of water, measuring 55-thousand square feet on the surface. Its filtration system processed 2,000 gallons per minute through a screening chamber. Constructed of cement and steel, the marina had a depth ranging from 4.5-feet to 8-feet. Underground service tunnels surrounded the marina and provided unseen staff access to the various facilities around the marina. Hotel officials predicted that the new water attraction would draw at least 3-million spectators, diners, and guests per year.

At the north end of the marina, guests were treated to a display of the latest designs in powerboats, cruisers, and sailboats, ranging in length from 6-feet to 40-feet. Even a fully furnished houseboat was docked for Hotel guests to inspect. More than fifteen watercraft were on permanent display, provided by the Bangor-Punta Corporation, a major U.S. manufacturer of leisure time crafts. A spokesman for the company stated that "the boat show was conceived to give visitors an opportunity to inspect boats and other leisure time products in a relaxed atmosphere with no high pressure salesman to bother them." During the evenings, a slide program presented the various water craft in their natural environment. Other leisure time equipment such as SCUBA gear, snow-mobiles, and camping needs were on display. An amazing display arrived near the end of the year...a Piper Cherokee, four-passenger, single engine aircraft. To get it to the marina, the plane had been flown from Florida to Long Beach. From there it was flown to the Disneyland Hotel and on that day, the access road to the west of the Hotel was closed and turned into a landing strip.

Along the borders of the marina were dining and liquid refreshments at Molly Malone's Fish Market, the Shipyard Inn, and the Sailmaker's Den. On the south side on the Wharf was the Game Room, which contained twenty coin-operated games "of all types." [Over the next few years, the Game Room would have various names, such as Video Adventure and Video Arcade. By 1985, this facility had been moved to the north end of the marina to the Dock area and occupied a room below the marina. It then was called the Atari Adventure and contained sixty-four electronic, state-of-the-art games.]

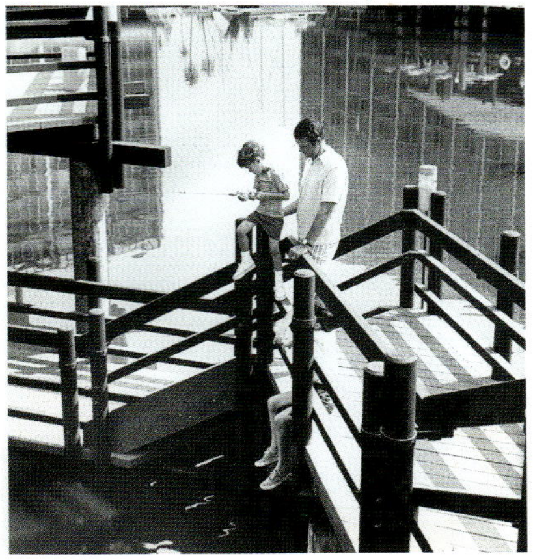

At a later date, two-passenger pedal boats were added to the marina. Available at the Dockmaster's office, use of the boats was free for the first few years. Later there would be a small rental charge (in 1973 it cost 75-cents for each fifteen minutes). A Hotel publication stated: "After you've seen the beautiful new marina and Wharf from land, take a ride in a pedal boat and see just how the ducks view it."

To the south and the southwest of the marina, new entertainment and recreational areas had been added. Running from east to west were to be found a fishing pool, an outdoor crescent-shaped amphitheater, a white sand beach and swimming pool, and a tropical tidal pool for wading.

Operated by Russ Cleary, the Fishing Pool/Stream was added in early August of 1970. It was themed with boulders and trees to recreate the environs of the Rockies and the High Sierra mountains. The pool was stocked with over 7,000 Rainbow trout, averaging 11-inches long and up to three pounds. At least twice a week, trout were trucked or flown from hatcheries in Apple Valley and Palm Springs, California or from as far away as Utah if the demand required. Refrigeration coils were installed in the pond so as to keep the water temperature below 70 degrees Fahrenheit (over that temperature and the trout could not survive for long). Hiding places were built in the pond to replicate nature and to give the trout a sporting chance from the fishermen above them. On the banks, "helpers" were provided to aid in baiting hooks and giving casting advice. Fishing was free and no license was required. Successful anglers could have their fish specially packed to take home at the end of the day or to be shipped home at a later date (at a cost of $1.00 for each fish landed and 25-cents extra if the fisherman desired to have the fish cleaned). Fishing derbies were held on weekends. A professional photographer was available to capture on film as a souvenir that special moment of excitement for any lucky angler. In a few short years, this fishing area would be closed due to construction for the third Hotel tower building.

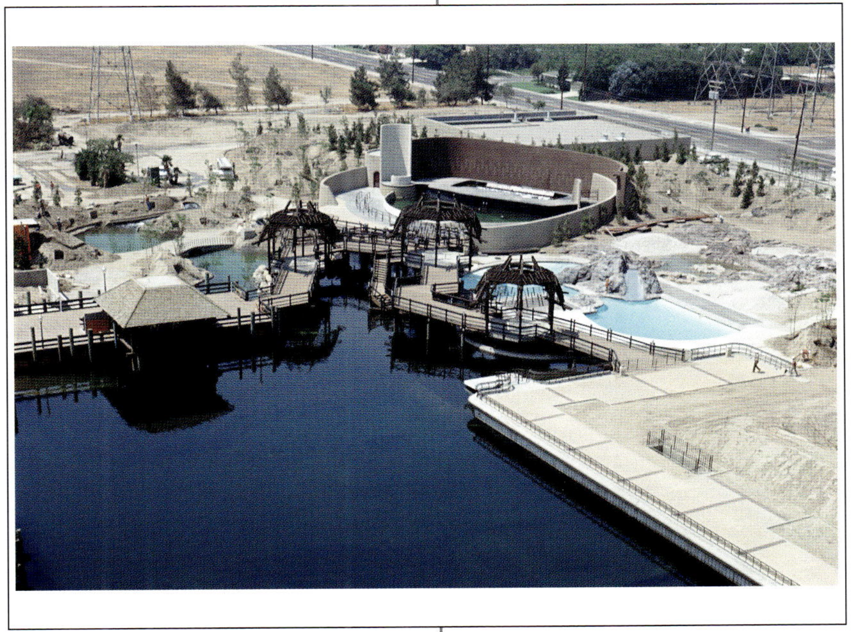

The southwest section of the new Marina.

In May, the Dancing Waters show had premiered at the outdoor, crescent shaped amphitheater to the southwest of the marina. The twenty-minute program was presented three times nightly at no charge to Hotel guests. Originally presented by Harold Steinman during the 1952 Industrial Exhibition in Germany, it was brought to the Hotel in 1970. During the show, multi-colored lighting effects (from 88 lamps) and music (from 154 speakers) were synchronized with 1,800 jets of dancing water, reaching heights between 15 and 150 feet. Nineteen motors were required to control the water. All this took place in front of the amphitheater's 18-foot high and 76-foot long back wall. The director of the show sat at a large console, resembling an organ, and operated over 200 switches and buttons. Mike Berkus (one of only nine people in the U.S. trained to play this show) was the Hotel's first director of

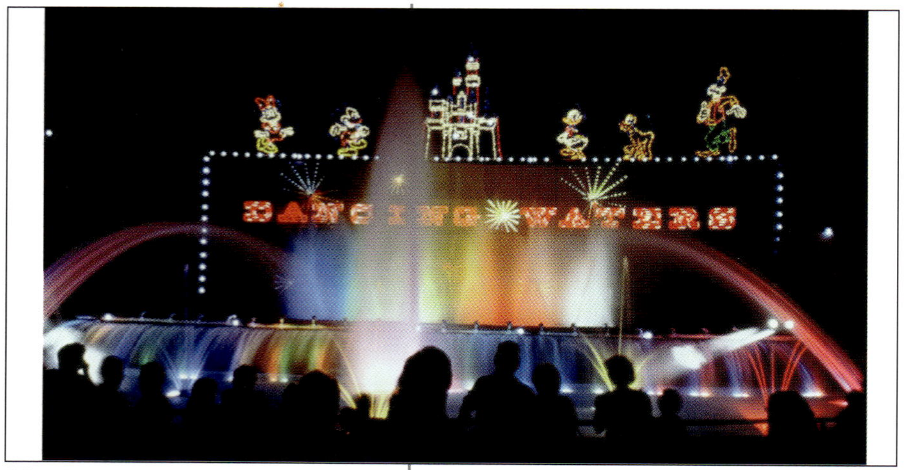

The Dancing Waters show.

the Dancing Waters. The program included music as varied as Judy Garland's "Over the Rainbow," the Mormon Tabernacle Choice's "Battle Hymn of the Republic," and lively Latin American music. While the program was changed frequently over the years, one selection was retained from the original presentation, "The German Waltz." Fireworks also added spectacle to the performances. Beginning in the late afternoon and in-between the several nightly performances of Dancing Waters, guests were entertained with images and shapes projected onto the 18-foot waterfall of the amphitheater, accompanied by Muzak. From eleven o'clock in the morning and throughout the daylight hours the Garden of Fountains filled the amphitheater. [In 1992, the Dancing Waters program would be retired. It was replaced with the Fantasy Waters Show--a water, lights and special effects display, accompanied by Disney music.]

The Cove (later called Papeete Beach) was a swimming pool that appeared to be a tropical lagoon with a beach of white sand (imported crystal silica), lined with palm trees. This 3,800 square foot pool was built on two levels. A rock formation in the center was both a waterfall and a slide from the upper to the lower level. Anthony, the world's largest pool builder constructed the pool. Next to the Cove was a tropical tidal pool. The Tidal Pool was a wading and splashing area for the younger set. The area had timing machines that created tides on cue. To achieve realistic rock formations for the pool, noted sculptor Greg La Chapelle spent months searching the California coastline from Laguna Beach to Santa Barbara to find interesting and unusual rock formations, many encrusted with ancient sea creatures. He would apply a plaster cast to an interesting formation and later reproduce the cast in concrete at the Hotel.

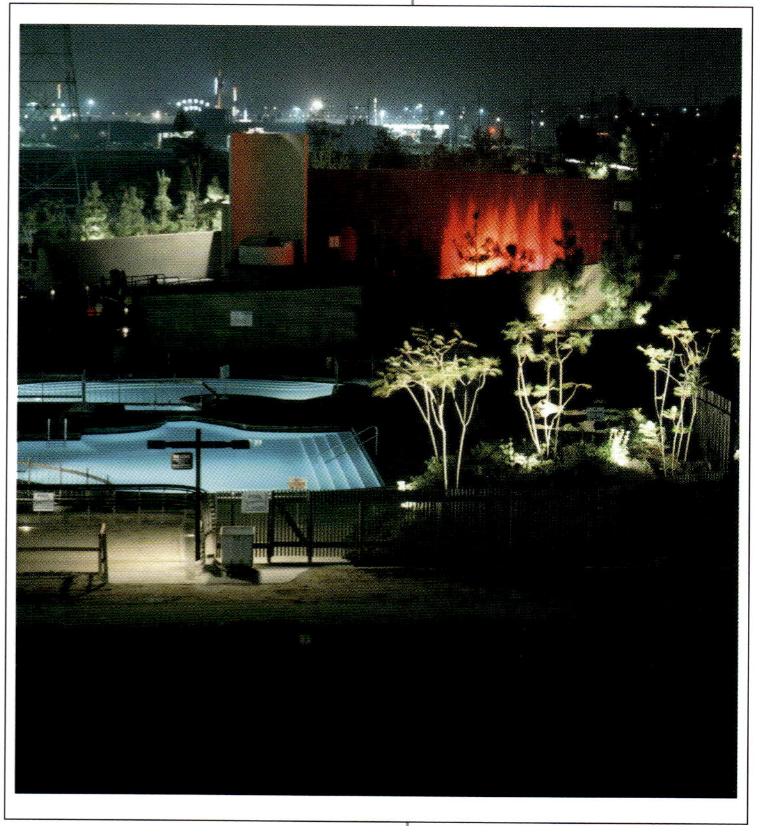

The Cove Pool with Dancing Waters.

Vacationland opened at 1343 South West Street on June 15, 1970 and was located north of the Hotel just past an area known as the "strawberry fields." Operated by the Hotel, it was a park for recreational vehicles of all sizes, including travel trailers, motor homes, pickup campers, and tent trailers. Full utility hookups were provided for all 280 parking spaces. Located on 10-acres, this beautifully landscaped area was the largest RV park in Orange County. It included a large recreation hall, housing a television area, a billiard room, a card playing area, and a lounge. A heated swimming pool, a playground for children, a facility with restrooms--showers--dressing rooms, and a coin operated laundry were also available to campers. The daily cost was $4.50 per vehicle for the non-peak season. During Christmas, Easter, and vacation season (from May 30 to September 7), the fee was $7.50. RV travel clubs were given special consideration in making reservations. Vacationland had been designed by Walters and Son of Newport Beach, California, specialist in recreational vehicle parks. [In 1981, the camp grounds added a tenting section with space for sixty tents. This new area quickly became popular with foreign students who either were traveling by bus or were hitchhiking across the country and spending nights at various camp sites. A covered picnic area with tables and grills was also added.]

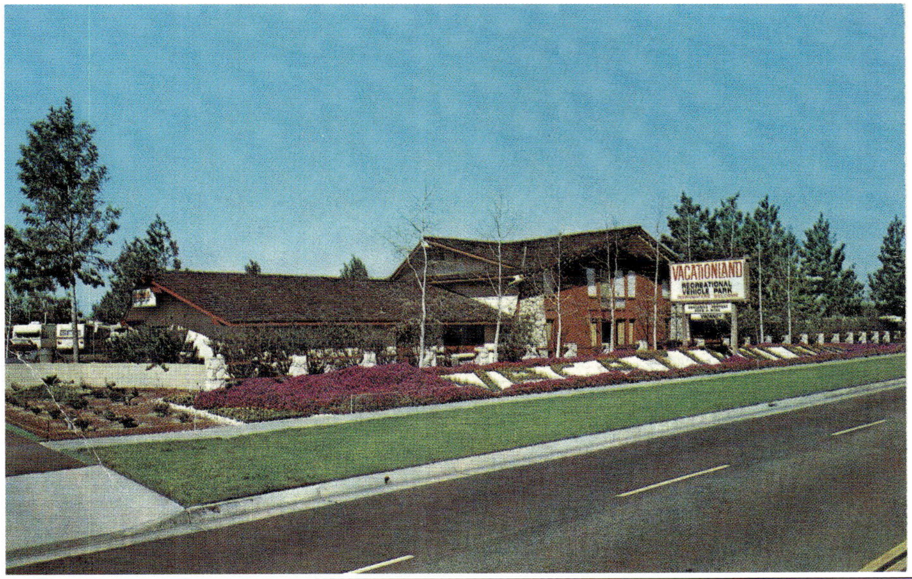

An artist concept of Vacationland.

In the latter part of 1970, the National Restaurant Association's Menu Idea Exchange Award was presented to the Oak Room's dessert menu as one of the top ten in the nation. Of particular interest to the judges were three menu items: seedless grapes in sour cream, cheese cake with fresh strawberry sauce, and macerated strawberries in champagne. Praised both for its selections and for its design, the dessert menu was printed on parchment paper, had burnished edges, and was mounted on a board. The menu had been designed by Ernest Furstner, the Hotel's food and beverage manager. The Hotel also won the Anaheim Beautiful Committee's award for "the best landscaping for a commercial business in Anaheim." At that time the Hotel's landscaping was under the direction of Mels Lindberg.

Due mainly to the opening of the Marina Tower and the opening of two new restaurants, the Disneyland Hotel experienced a 40-percent increase in revenue in 1970.

Shortly after presiding over the Grand Opening of Walt Disney World in Florida (a portion of Walt's last project) on October 1, 1971, Walt's older brother Roy O. Disney passed away on December 20, 1971. In Anaheim on Thursday, June 17th at 11:13 in the morning, Valerie Suldo (a 22-year-old payroll clerk from New Brunswick, New Jersey) became the 100-millionth guest to enter the "Happiest Place on Earth."

As 1971 began, the Disneyland Hotel complex included 936 guest rooms and suites, six restaurants, six cocktail lounges, twenty-four conference rooms, twenty-one shops, and numerous recreation and entertainment facilities.

After being totally remodeled and redecorated, the original Hotel Lobby was reopened as the Travelport. The building sported a new facade and in front was a fountain plaza, facing West Street. Travel services that previously had been located at different sites around the Hotel complex were now conveniently located in one central area. The new location also allowed for the expansion of those services. Here one could make airline reservations, book site-seeing tours, and arrange for bus, taxi, or rent-a-car services. Of the new facility, Hotel president Frank Bret stated: "Located as we are in the geographical, population and travel center of the county, we feel the Hotel is ideally suited to offer this service to our many visitors." The Travelport also continued to be the location where guests could board the monorail or could catch a tram to the Park. Tram service was also provided on the Hotel's property to shuttle guests to their rooms, the golf course, a restaurant, or the shopping area.

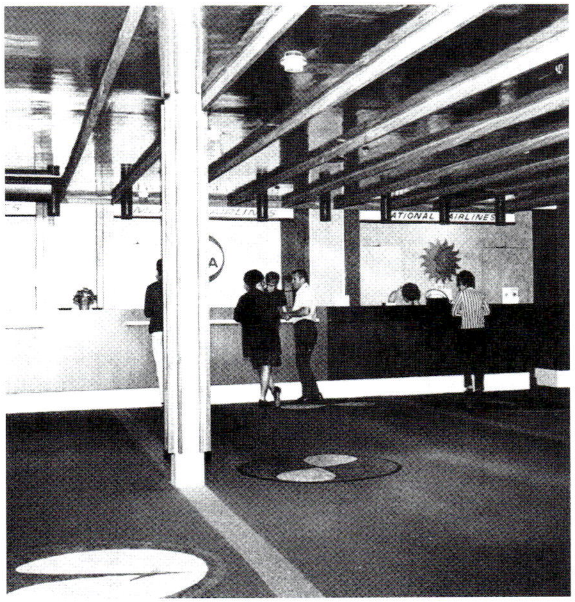
Interior reservation area of the Travelport.

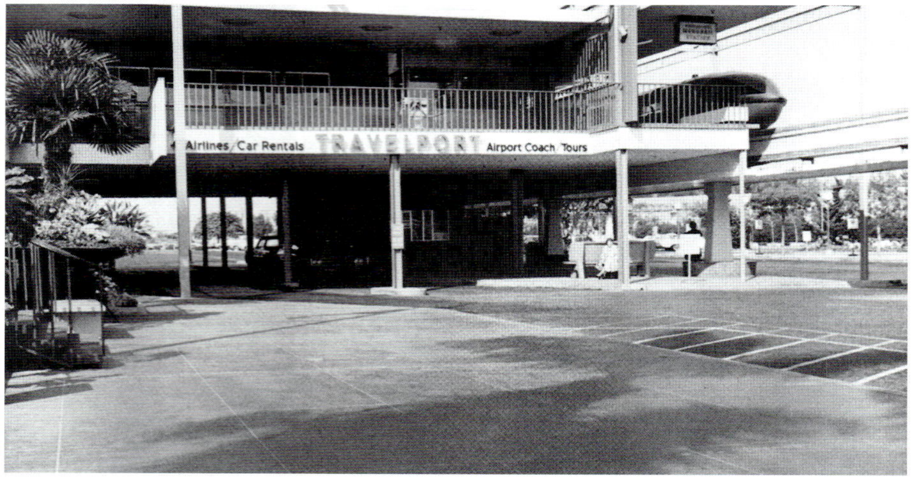

The Disneyland Hotel Travelport.

Early this year, dinner guests arriving in the lobby of the California Dining Room were greeted by a rather amazing sight. There stood a 70-inch tall, edible model of the Eiffel Tower. Made of sugar, flour, and egg whites, the tower's 1,500 individual pieces had been cemented together with caramelized sugar. Created by the Hotel's baker Paul Gauweiler, it had taken him twenty hours to complete.

In March of 1971, one of the giant propellers from the *Queen Mary* (permanently docked at Long Beach and operated by Wrather Hotels, Inc.) was added to the many other maritime artifacts displayed around Waterworld. Many years of encrusted barnacles had to be sandblasted before the prop could be refinished and installed by giant cranes on a concrete and steel pedestal. The 32-ton prop, cast of high tensile manganese bronze, measured 18-feet across. This prop from the *Queen Mary* was one of four that at one time had turned at 3,600 revolutions per hour at top speed.

Ground was broken in June for the Disneyland Hotel's Convention Center. Planned as the largest such hotel facility of its type in Southern California, the Center would rise on acreage at the northwest corner of the Hotel's main property and would be directly connected to the Marina Tower. This marked the beginning of the second phase of the massive expansion program announced by Jack Wrather in early 1968.

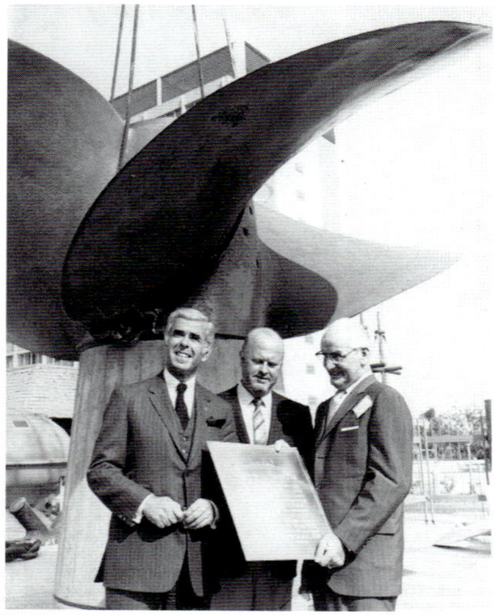

A propeller from the Queen Mary.

At 7:00 a.m. on June 24th, the Hotel inaugurated its own television network (a first in the nation). Transmitted on Channel Six, it provided daily information on activities, services, attractions, and entertainment available to Hotel guests. The studio was located in the top level of the Travelport. Live (with two cameras), taped, filmed, and slide programming could be presented. William Wyper, a twenty year veteran in the industry, was the station's first manager. He stated that "our planning and particular on-the-air programming makes the Disneyland Hotel system unique since the entire operation is designed solely with the guest in mind. This holds true even for the commercials, which provide a valuable service to the guest, helping him make the most of his valuable vacation time." The system was available for use by conventions and other meetings. During its earliest years, the Hotel's television network broadcast only in black and white.

In July of that year, the Shipyard Inn and the Sailmakers Den received the Institution Magazine's national award of special distinction. Cited for "excellence of planning in kitchen and serving areas," the Shipyard Inn was the only restaurant in the U.S. to receive that award. Ernest Furstner, the Hotel's director of food and beverage (who also had supervised the project when built only two years earlier) accepted the award at the annual banquet, held in Chicago. The Hotel also received awards from the National Restaurant Association where silver certificates were awarded to the Oak Room, to the Shipyard Inn, to the room service menus, and to the Hotel's wine and beverage list.

In late summer of 1971, the Hotel briefly hosted Vice President Spiro T. Agnew...and his Secret Service detail. Upon departure, he indicated that he had been "particularly impressed with the view of the Marina" from his eleventh floor suite. He also expressed his thanks to Hotel manager Jose Arias for the cordial treatment he had received from the Hotel staff. Agnew was in Anaheim as the keynote speaker at the International Chiefs of Police convention, held at the Anaheim Convention Center.

Near year's end, the Disneyland Hotel's Spirits and Gourmet Shoppe opened in the Arcade area next to the Travelport and at the foot of the stairs from the monorail station. Available were a hundred varieties of imported and domestic wines (ranging in price from $3 to $60) and twenty-two brands of domestic and imported beers, ales, lagers, pilsners, and stouts (including English, Japanese, German, Mexican, and Swiss). Gourmet delicacies such as quail eggs were to be found at the new store. The cheese section provided both imported and those from the Southern California area. Included was the tea and coffee corner. The gift section included Swiss, German and Italian carving knives, Swedish glassware, and Espresso machines. The world's largest selection of salt and pepper mills was to be found and the store boasted of one of the largest collections of cookbooks. Frequently, the Spirits and Gourmet Shoppe was called upon to aid Room Service in providing special items requested by Hotel guests.

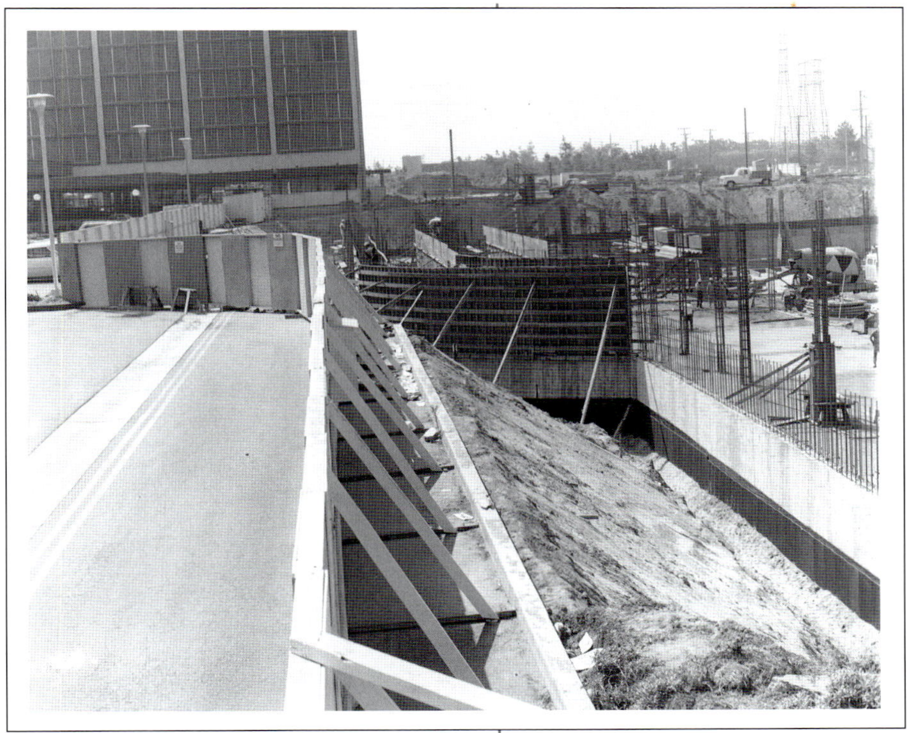

Convention Center construction shot.

Room rates in 1971 were designated as either being in the "Regular" or the "Vacation" periods, with the latter being March 20 to April 4, May 29 to September 5, and December 19 to January 1. Depending upon type of bed (queen-sized, twin beds, or two double beds), Garden Rooms ranged from $16 to $22 during Regular and $22 to $28 during Vacation dates. In Hotel brochures, the Sierra and the Marina were referred to as the Twin Towers. Again, depending upon bed type (queen, twins, doubles, or king); Tower rates for the off-season were from $23 to $33. The same rooms during "Vacation" time ranged from $27 to $37. Deluxe Suites (a sitting room with either one, two, or three bedrooms) went for between $55 to $110 and $70 to $125, depending upon the time of year. Royal Suites were available year around at $125 to $175. An additional $5 was charged for a crib or a roll-away bed.

In 1972, Bear Country was opened in March at a cost of $8-million. On June 17th, perhaps the most popular parade in Disneyland's history premiered, the Main Street Electrical Parade. By that time, Disneyland investments had grown to $136-million.

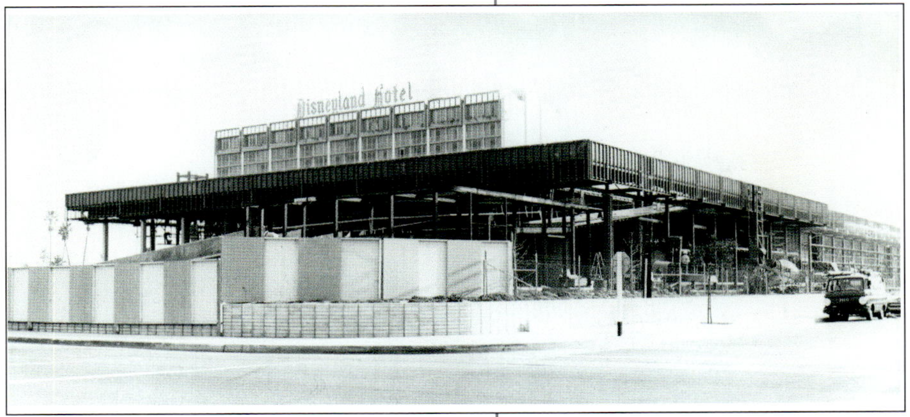

Convention Center construction shot.

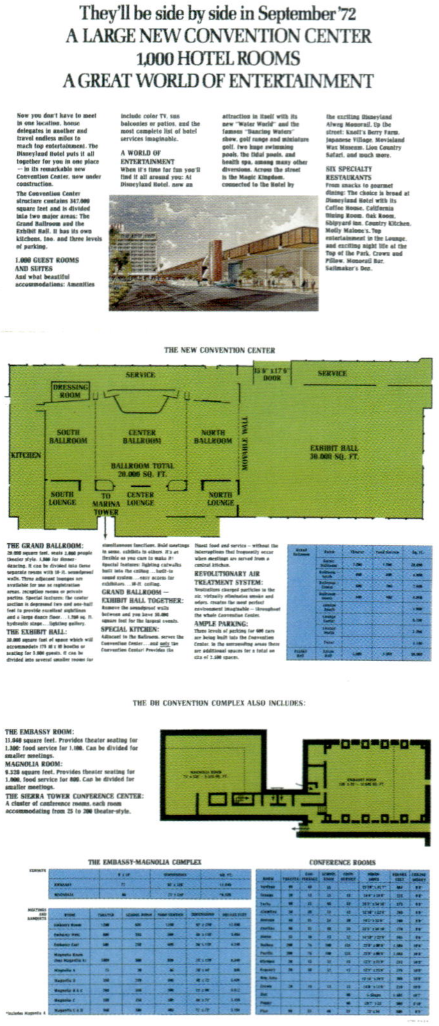

1970's Convention Center brochure.

Helicopter service to the Hotel had been suspended for a short time with service being restored early in 1972 with Golden West Airlines as the new provider. For the inaugural flight, a celebration was held, and guided tours were taken through the newly constructed terminal across Cerritos, north of the Hotel. On hand to greet guests was Hollis B. Roberts, the airline's board chairman. The shiny white copter was available for inspection. Huge 30-seat Sikorskys (with plush interiors) made twenty-eight daily flights between the Hotel and LAX. The new copter's travel time was 16-minutes. The first flight left Los Angeles at 6:10 a.m., and the last flight left the Hotel at 9:55 p.m. (with a 20-minute turn-around time at each end).

The very first employee of the Disneyland Hotel retired in July after seventeen years of service. Leeds Chesshir (64-years-old of Anaheim) had been the Hotel's credit manager. Recalling his first day on the job, he stated, "It was May 9th 1955. There was no Hotel then...just holes in an orange grove. The Hotel office was in an old ranch house building." Chesshir also recalled the beginnings of the Hotel's operation: "A few months after the Park opened in 1955, we opened the Hotel. We had 104 rooms. No, that's wrong. We had 103 rooms. We used one room for a lobby." A small sign in the parking lot merely stated, "Registering Guest Park Here." During his years at the Hotel, he had witnessed its evolution from a construction site into a resort offering 1,000 guest rooms.

For the second summer in a row, a six man team of the Disneyland Hotel's lifeguards won first place in the Great Canoe Race, held annually in the Submarine Lagoon across the street at Disneyland. They had competed against 145 other teams on a 5/8th of a mile course. Their winning time was 3:59.4 minutes.

The morning of July 28, 1972, seemed like so many other mornings in the Disneyland Hotel lobby. On the main floor, guests paid their bills, requested directions, chatted quietly while awaiting a companion to join them, or just enjoyed the warm, sunny atmosphere of the two-year old Marina lobby. Felix E. Welmaker (49-years-old carpet retailer from Midland, Texas) approached the main desk and began to register his family, having just arrived via helicopter at the Hotel heliport. Suddenly, the morning calm was broken by a roll of drums and a blare of trumpets. Across the length of the lobby strode Frank Bret, president of the Wrather Hotels, carrying a large bouquet of red and white roses and a magnum of champagne. "Welcome to the Disneyland Hotel," Bret greeted Welmaker. "As you signed the register, you became the five-millionth guest!" Instead of the room they had reserved, the family was escorted to a Marina Tower suite, compliments of the Hotel. There they discovered Disneyland ticket books, fresh flowers, bowls of fruit, and a variety of cheese snacks. For three years, the Welmakers had been planning for these two days that suddenly had turned into a grand adventure.

In September of 1972, the Disneyland Hotel added the $7.2-million Convention Center, which included the Exhibition Hall (30,000 square feet) and the Grand Ballroom (20,000 square feet). Constructed of steel and concrete, the Center contained a total of 347,000 square feet of floor space on five levels. The "topping-off" had taken place on August 9th, when the four main roof trusses (each weighing 15 tons and each measuring 120-feet) were lifted into place. It was the largest hotel meeting complex in the western United States. A Grand Opening Celebration for the new Center was held on November 9th, with Harry James and his Orchestra, the Disneyland Marching Band, and numerous Disneyland characters in attendance.

The Grand Ballroom could be divided into three smaller ballrooms, using 18-foot high double-soundproof, movable walls. Each of the smaller ballrooms would have its own hardwood dance floor and adjoining lounge area, able to be used as a registration or reception area. Decorated with a California poppy theme, the Ballroom's center piece was a 30-foot Italian crystal chandelier, suspended above the sunken 53-foot by 40-foot dance floor. In the foyer and lounges hung large poppy tapestries. The 1,200 square foot stage could be raised or lowered hydraulically in three sections, and was dominated by a beautiful Florentine curtain. Backstage were three fully equipped dressing rooms. On the mezzanine level were the lighting gallery and an audio-visual control room, allowing for the presentation of theatrical, film, and television programs. The Ballroom boasted a $220,000 sound system. It had been designed to accommodate 2,000 people for meetings or 1,800 for dining. For larger events, the Ballroom and Exhibit Hall could be united into one huge 50,000 square foot hall.

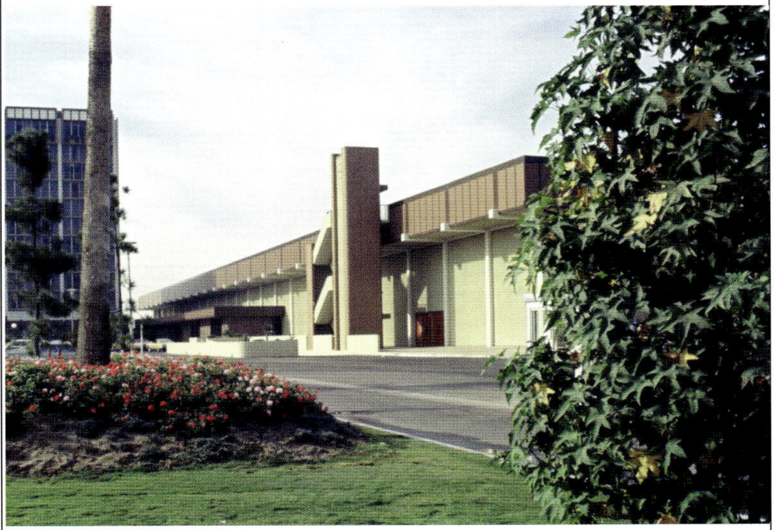

Exterior of new Convention Center facilities.

The Exhibit Hall could accommodate 175 display booths, a meeting of 3,000 people, or could be divided into a dozen smaller rooms. To avoid a barn-like atmosphere, the 18-foot ceiling and all walls were paneled and carried on the Ballroom's gold and orange poppy theme. The floor was of polished terrazzo. The entire Hall had only three support pillars, which were utilized to provide water, drainage, electricity, telephone outlets, and conduits for gas and compressed air. Large moving vans could enter directly into the Hall through a 17-foot high entrance.

The Center contained a stainless steel kitchen (next to the Ballroom), designed to service large groups rapidly or to serve several smaller groups at the same time. This was a "parallel, progressive kitchen" with ingredients started at one end and moved down the line during the preparation. Much of the kitchen's equipment was portable so as to be easily rearranged as needed. The pride of the Center's chefs was the largest rotary oven ever built. It could cook sixty 28-pound prime ribs at the same time, or it could hold 2,400 chicken breasts simultaneously. Three coffee machines each brewed 1,500 cups (the bags of grounds being so heavy that they were removed with a special winch). A conveyor belt allowed for the more rapid dishing of food. This kitchen provided food only for the Convention Center and not to other areas of the Hotel complex. Fred Schmidt Associates had planned the food service facility.

Inside the Grand Ballroom.

The Center's special air filtration system (designed to eliminate smoke and odors) was the first of its type to be installed by any hotel in the nation. A complete television facility for tape, film, and live programming was another unique feature of the newly opened Convention Center. This state-of-the-art, closed circuit television studio (located on the mezzanine) allowed activities at the Center to be viewed in any of the Hotel's other twenty-four conference rooms located outside the Center complex or in any of

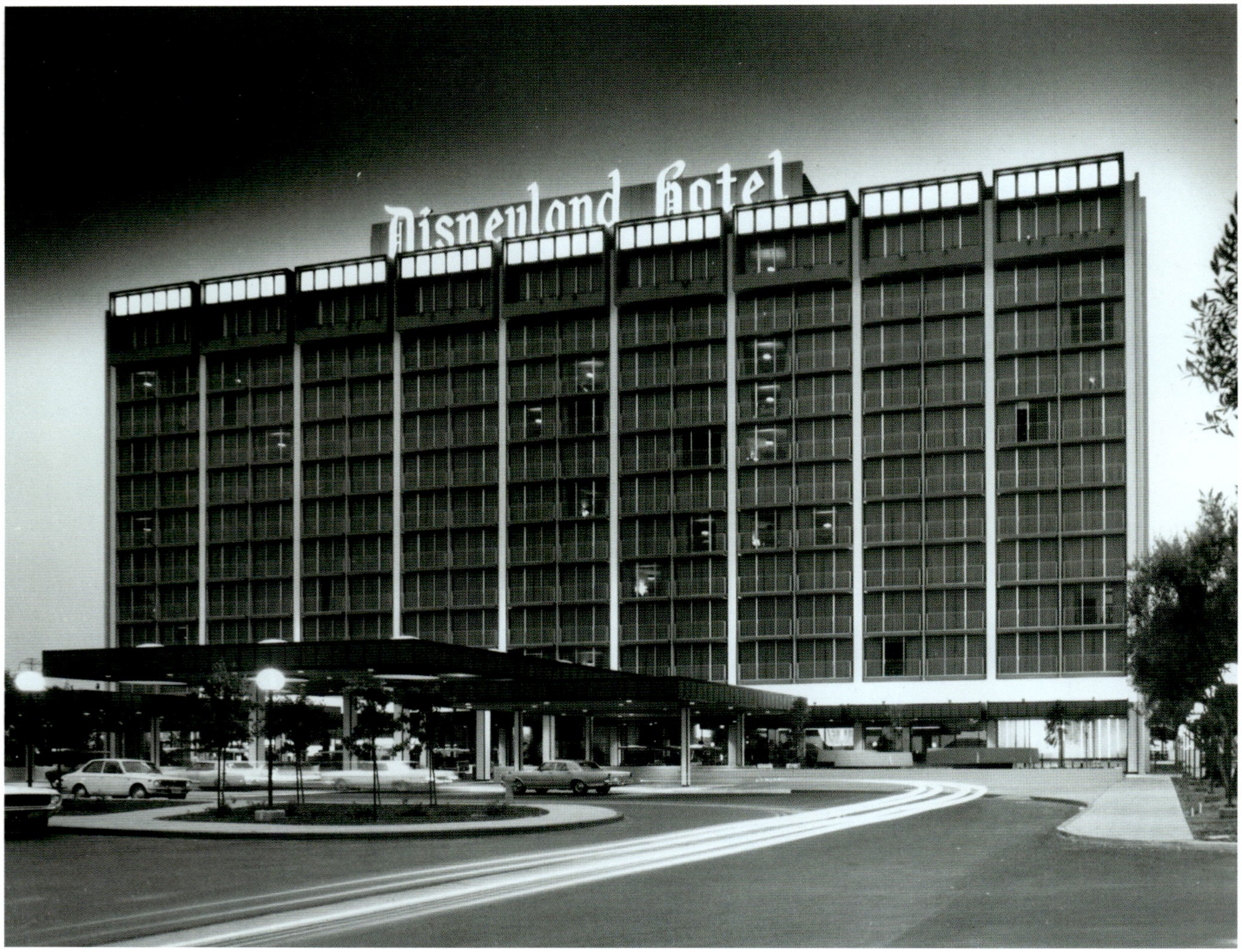

The Marina Tower.

the Hotel's 1,000 guest rooms. Special rooms for press conferences were also available. Two levels for parking were below the main floor, and another parking level was on the roof, providing space for 650 cars. Escalators and elevators accessed the main floor. The Disneyland Hotel now had a total parking capacity for 2,600 vehicles.

One of the first scheduled meetings in the new building was a party held by the Wrather Corporation in celebration of the beginning of the nineteenth season of its *Lassie* television series. The famous collie and her owner/trainer Rudd Weatherwax attended with several hundred other guests. The event was hosted by Jack and Bonita Wrather in the newly opened Grand Ballroom. A buffet dinner of American, Continental, Chinese, and South American dishes was served. In late August (before the official opening of the Center), a dealers preview for the 1973 Chevrolets was held at the convention facilities. Scheduled during it first few months of operation, were the conventions of the National Parks and Recreation Association, the Retired Officers Association, the League of California Cities, the California Veterinary Medical Association, and the Western Association of Fire Chiefs. The Grand Ballroom hosted one of its first formal affairs on Monday, September 25, with the 8th Annual Gourmet Dinner held by the Big Brothers of Orange Country. The black-tie stag was attended by 250 guests.

To see that each meeting and convention received the best service possible, the Disneyland Hotel had long ago established a system by which four of its personnel would be assigned to each client, and all four would follow the progress until the successful conclusion of that particular convention or meeting. The initial contact would have been made with a sales representative, responsible for reserving all guest rooms and for booking all needed meeting areas. Next, the catering manager would arrange all menus for meals, banquets, and cocktail receptions. The reservations coordinator would continually supervise the preparation of all rooms and facilities to be utilized. Finally, a convention coordinator would oversee all aspects of the process. Coordinator Pat Bramlett observed that "Every convention seems to have a quirk that makes if memorable--like misplacing a shipment of convention materials or having more attendees show up than registered, all wanting to fit into a room that is suddenly too small." A single coordinator might handle as many as 125 conventions each year.

The addition of the Convention Center made the Hotel Anaheim's largest self-contained hotel complex and the largest hotel meeting facility on the West Coast. Architects for the Center were again Weber and Nicholson, Los Angeles, with Edward D. Tisch, senior vice president of the Wrather Corporation, as the project director. The project had utilized 800 tons of steel, 4,000 yards of concrete, and 28.5 miles of electrical wire.

On Restaurant Row, El Vaquero Steak House opened in June of 1972. It was decorated in an early-California style. The California Dining Room reopened in June after a major redecoration project. The Fuji Pavilion restaurant opened on the wharf at the marina. With the addition of the new facilities, the Hotel now had a total of seven restaurants and five cocktail lounges.

Fronting Restaurant Row on West Street was the new 2,880 square foot Restaurant Plaza. Designed in an early California motif, it featured a brick and tile patio, fountains, and flower baskets hanging from an elaborate arbor. Outside dining or just cocktails were provided on the new Plaza by El Vaquero.

At El Vaquero (Spanish for "the cowboy") guests enjoyed the combining of the kitchen and the dining areas into one. Patrons were entertained by the cooking process and watched as garnishes were added in full view at wooden work tables. On one side of the restaurant, salads were prepared in large ice bowls. On another side, one viewed soup being prepared in large copper tureens. The decor was that of the olden days of the California ranchos, with exposed rafters overhead and walls of rough-troweled plaster. Chairs were constructed from leather straps and hand-woven Navajo blankets. Illumination was provided by whale oil lamps and candles. Adding to the period decor were historical saddle brands, lariats, spurs, paintings, and land grant documents from the original ranchos of Orange County. Custom made copies of 1840 pots and utensils (in iron, brass, and copper) decorated the walls. Ernest Furstner, vice president of Hotel operations, commented that the restaurant was designed "to transport patrons mentally and physically back to rugged ranch days with wooden tables, tiled and bare planked floors, and large open hearth adobe broiler and oven."

Along with a variety of hearty choices from its menu, El Vaquero's breakfast guests could enjoy selections from a fresh fruit bar. Its luncheon menu included sliced beefsteak on toast with mustard sauce, roast beef hash with poached egg, or broiled halibut steak with pimento butter. Side dishes included corn on the cob, baked potato, or ranch spinach with ham. The dinner menu offered appetizers such as Concido Soup (meat and vegetable) or Ceviche On Ice (fresh scallops marinated in lime juice with olive oil, garlic, and Cayenne pepper). Entrees included a one-pound Vaquero cut New York Steak, Banderilla of Chateaubriand Tips, or Estofado (beef stewed in wine). For dessert, one might have a traditional Spanish pudding (Lemon Flan flamed in rum) or Bunuelos (fried sweet tortilla fritters with Anisette sauce). A wide selection of wines was offered, and only California wines were served at El Vaquero.

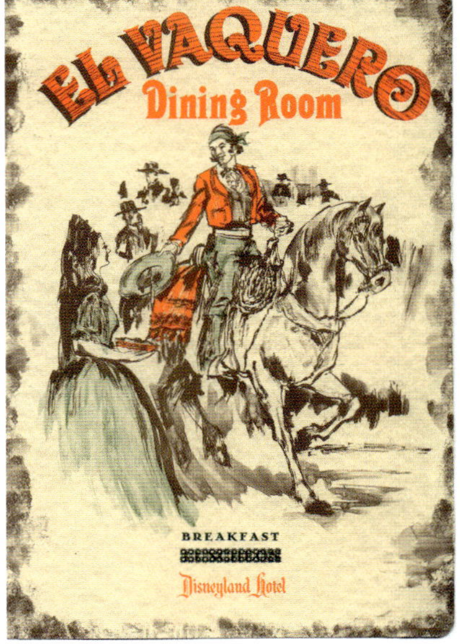

El Vaquero menus.

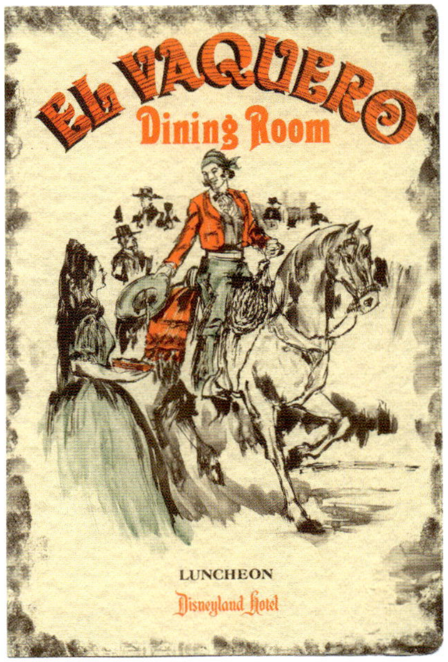

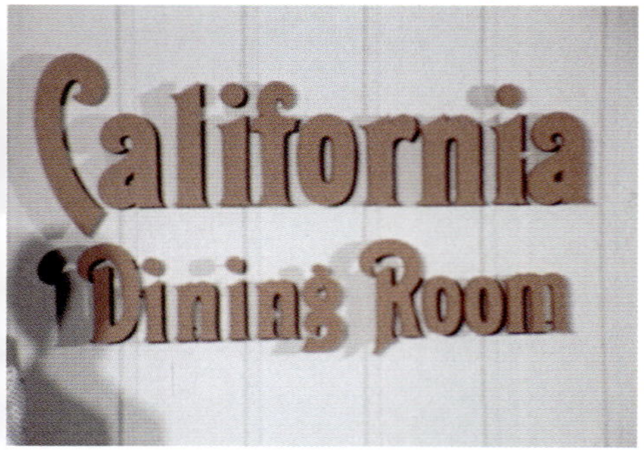

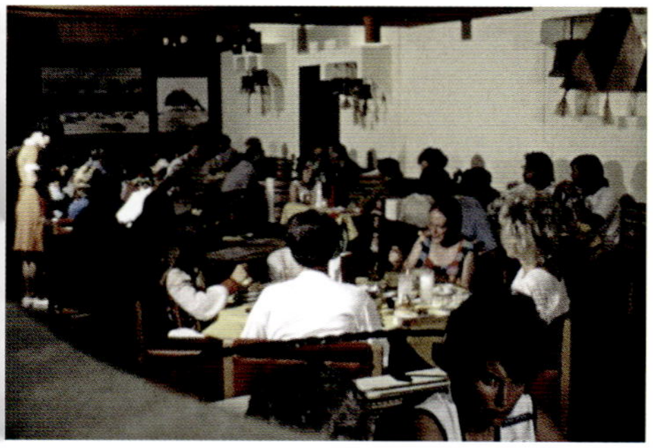

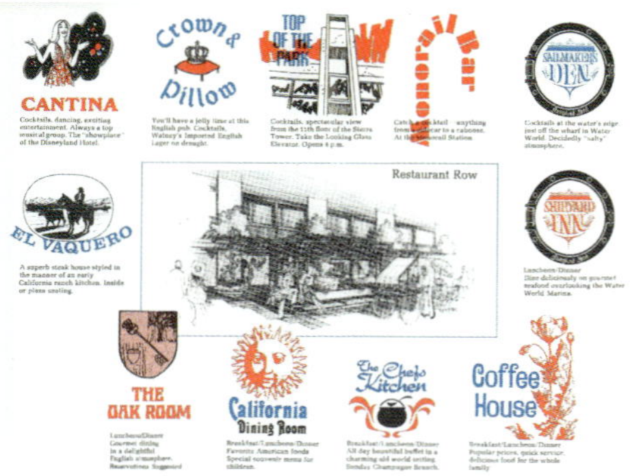

Restaurants at the Disneyland Hotel.

Upon its reopening, the California Dining Room had been redesigned to create a more intimate family atmosphere. Its theme, "the Golden State," was depicted by such artifacts as clusters of hanging ceramic and bronze miniature mission bells and wind chimes, metal weather vanes, and lovely prints of ocean and desert landscapes. The decor emphasized various shades of rust, orange, and plum. Booths were upholstered in heavily woven fabrics of Indian design. Three daily "chef's recommendations" highlighted a new menu. One might find such chef specials as French pancake stuffed with crab meat, fricassee of veal served with rice pilaf, tenderloin tips brochette, roast loin of pork with apricot sauce, Yankee pot roast, or seafood curry. Of its varied selection of salads, the most popular was the Marina Salad. It consisted of chunks of baby tuna, artichoke hearts, olives, string beans, anchovies, little white potatoes, green peppers, tomatoes, celery, and egg, all lightly tossed with an oil and lemon dressing. The renovations of Restaurant Row had been completed again by the two Los Angeles firms: food facility engineers Fred Schmid Associates and architects Weber and Nicholson.

With the opening of the Fuji Pavilion on the wharf at Water World, 2,600 years of traditional Japanese cuisine arrived at the Disneyland Hotel. Operated by the Horikawa Company of Japan and Los Angeles, the outdoor restaurant bore a distinctive logo comprised of three giant flying fish. Its reasonably priced luncheon and dinner menus included such specialties as shrimp tempura, sushi, and sashimi. In the time-honored Oriental tradition, the skill of cooking was surpassed only by the emphasis placed upon the color and shape of the presentation. Beer and soft drinks were available. The Fuji also offered "walk around" specialties that Hotel guests could take with them while exploring the wonders and beauties of the marina area.

The Wrather Corporation, in its annual statement to shareholders, reported that on January 10, 1973, it "and Walt Disney Productions executed an agreement in principle covering the sale by Wrather Corporation to Walt Disney Productions of the stock of the wholly-owned subsidiaries of Wrather Corporation which own and operate the Disneyland Hotel and related facilities." The first step had taken place for the sale of the Hotel to Disney. According to the preliminary agreement, the Wrather company would have received 187,061 shares of Disney common stock and $100,000 in cash. [However, Disney stock took a major beating, slipping to only $40 per share by September of 1973 from its yearly high of $123-7/8 per share. As a result, the Wrather-Disney proposal had to be renegotiated and greatly sweetened by Disney. By June of 1974, that offer had been raised to 189,366 shares of Disney stock and dramatically had been raised to $1.25-million in cash.] The deal was subject to approval of the boards of directors of the two companies, their legal staffs, Wrather shareholders, and several Federal agencies. For various reasons, the deal was never consummated. This may have been the first attempt by Disney to purchase the Hotel.

Guests at the Disneyland Hotel during the summer of 1973 enjoyed a variety of art and craft displays around the marina. Featured were painters, caricaturists, glass blowers, metal sculptors, pottery makers, candle designers, and china painters, all demonstrating their creative talents at the "Art in Action" exhibition. From the late afternoon and far into the evening, free entertainment was provided. A highlight of the evening was the ceremonial lighting of the luau torches around the marina area. Ending the evening were two performances of the Dancing Waters show.

June 18, 1973, witnessed the first usage of a satellite to relay live programming specifically to be cablecast at the other end. Speaker of the House of Representatives Carl Albert, from his office in Washington, D.C., addressed the National Cable TV convention being held at the Disneyland Hotel. Beamed from Germantown, Maryland to the Canadian satellite ANIK-1 (23,000 miles above the equator), it was then relayed to the firm of TelePrompter, Theta-Com and Scientific Atlantic (a Wrather Corporation subsidiary) in Anaheim. The telecast was then sent to the rooftop microwave receiver at the Hotel's TV studio. Finally, it was provided live to the convention and to guest rooms. All this happening in a mere fraction of a second.

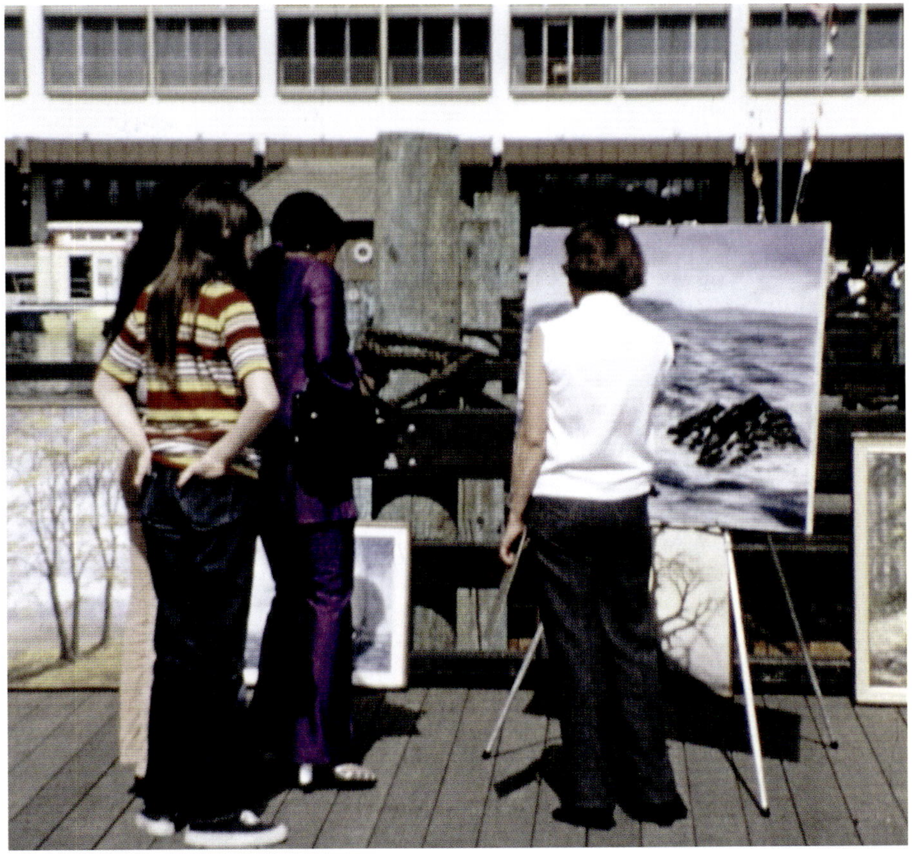

Arts and crafts for sale around the Marina.

Effective January 1, 1974, room rates were as follows: Single (one person) standard $22-26, deluxe $32-40. 2 twins or 2 double beds (two persons) standard $26-32, deluxe $32-40. Deluxe Suites: Triple or Quad $32-40. Studio suite $65. Sitting room with one bedroom $75-85. Sitting room with two bedrooms $100-110. Royal suites $125-175. Crib or rollaway an additional $6.00. After 1974, package deals with flights, rooms and theme park tickets became the norm. Printed material seldom displayed room rates alone.

In the 1974 Wrather Corporation annual report, problems in the U.S. economy and pressures from the Disney company were reflected. Jack Wrather wrote: "As a result of the continuing high rate of inflation and the energy crisis [the gas lines at service stations], 1974 was a difficult year for the hotel industry. In addition, for a substantial portion of 1974 we anticipated that the Disneyland Hotel would be sold to Walt Disney Productions, pursuant to a plan of complete liquidation." It would be more than a decade before the Wrather and Disney companies could reach a purchase agreement. Not deterred by the failed negotiations with Disney, Wrather continued: "In order to maintain Disneyland Hotel as one of the finest hotel complexes on the West Coast, we have undertaken a $1,000,000 program providing for the refurbishing of our garden rooms, many of our dining facilities and other public areas of the hotel." From 1970 through 1974, annual revenues from food and beverage sales had increased from $5-million to $7.2-million. During that same period, yearly revenues from room rentals had increased from $7.7-million to $9.4-million.

Despite continued national economic problems, in the 1975 Wrather Corporation annual report, Jack Wrather stated that the "Disneyland Hotel not only showed a marked improvement in the number of rooms rented, but produced a significant increase in income per occupied rooms." Further, he stated that "We now have on our books the greatest number of pre-sold convention rooms in our 21-year history." Looking to future expansion, he continued: "Studies are now under way to evaluate the feasibility of constructing an additional guest room building on our property. We are also negotiating to acquire a major hotel property in the Disneyland area." In later years,

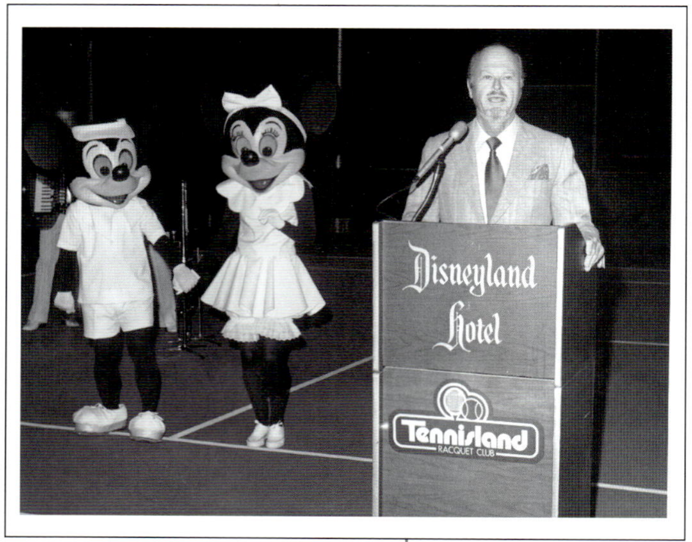

Jack Wrather at Tennisland dedication 1976.

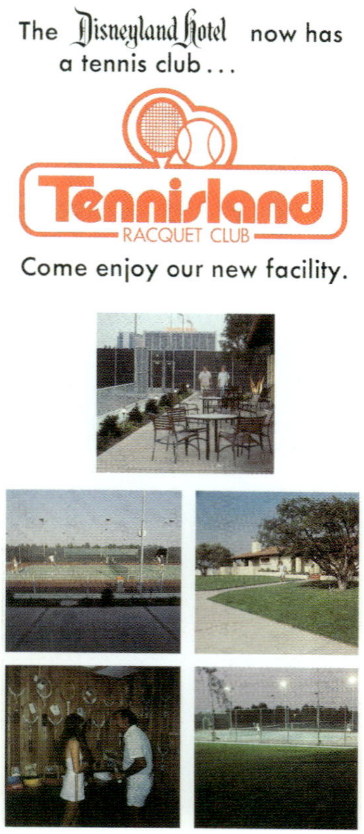

the new construction would be the Bonita Tower and the $8-million purchase would be the nearby 500 room Inn-at-the-Park hotel (formerly the Royal Inn of Anaheim).

Since 1957, millions of families had added to their enjoyment of Disney attractions through free membership in the Magic Kingdom Club. The club offered discounts on Disneyland ticket books, hotel room rates and various other amenities at or around Disneyland. In 1975, Magic Kingdom Club members could get a 2, 3 or 4 night stay at the Disneyland Hotel with deluxe accommodations plus unlimited use of all rides and attractions (excluding shooting galleries) starting at just $48.50 per adult, double occupancy. Another package with similar amenities (staying at Howard Johnson's Motor Lodge) started at just $33.50 per adult. Howard Johnson's was listed as the "Official Host of the Magic Kingdom Club." Junior and child rates were available at substantial savings. Rates were in effect all year long.

The Jungle Cruise added seven new scenes in December of 1976. Gorillas in the Camp featured thirty-one new Audio-Animatronics figures. The total investment in Disneyland had climbed to $168-million. On June 22, Elsie Mae Houck of Tulare, California became the Park's 150-millionth guest.

For 1976, Magic Kingdom Club members could get a package deal (a room for two nights at the Disneyland Hotel plus unlimited use of all rides and attractions each day) starting at just $55.50 per adult, double occupancy. Staying at Howard Johnson's Motor Lodge, similar deals started at $34.50 per adult. Rates were effective all year long.

On November 3, 1976, the Disneyland Hotel held opening ceremonies for Tennisland Racquet Club (located on Walnut Street, north of Cerritos Avenue). Occupying 3.5-acres, it provided ten championship courts (illuminated for night play) and special practice alleys. There was a clubhouse with a full-service pro shop and a resident pro, locker rooms and showers, and a weight and exercise room.

On December 12, 1976, Jack Wrather received the go-ahead to build one of the most modern hotel additions anywhere. But the city's planning commission tacked on an interesting condition to the development. The proposed 13-story tower, to be the third tower in the Hotel complex, would be the tallest structure in Anaheim and would be the maximum height allowed. Under a rule adopted by the city some time previous, no building was permitted to be visible from Disneyland Park. The planners ordered a balloon to be flown at the height of the proposed building to make sure it could not be seen from inside the Park. The concern was that the fantasy atmosphere of Anaheim's main tourist attraction not be disrupted. Architects for the new tower assured the planners contour lines had been drawn and there would be no visual intrusion in the Park. They agreed however, to confirm their paper theories with the balloon test.

The 1977 Wrather Corporation annual report announced an $18-million expansion program, including the third tower building, which would give the Hotel a total of 1,400 guest rooms and suites. [This was the third and final phase of the massive expansion plan announced by Jack Wrather back in 1968.] Included in the expansion plan were a new computerized reservation-registration system, a "space-age" telephone system, enlarged restaurant and bar facilities, remodeled kitchens, and enlarged and redecorated shops and boutiques. Also announced was the $3-million purchase of 21-acres of land contiguous to the original 60-acres leased from Walt Disney back in 1954. Located at the southwest corner of the Hotel, 7.5-acres were designated for additional parking. The remainder of the land was to be studied for future development. That "future development" never took place during the Wrather years.

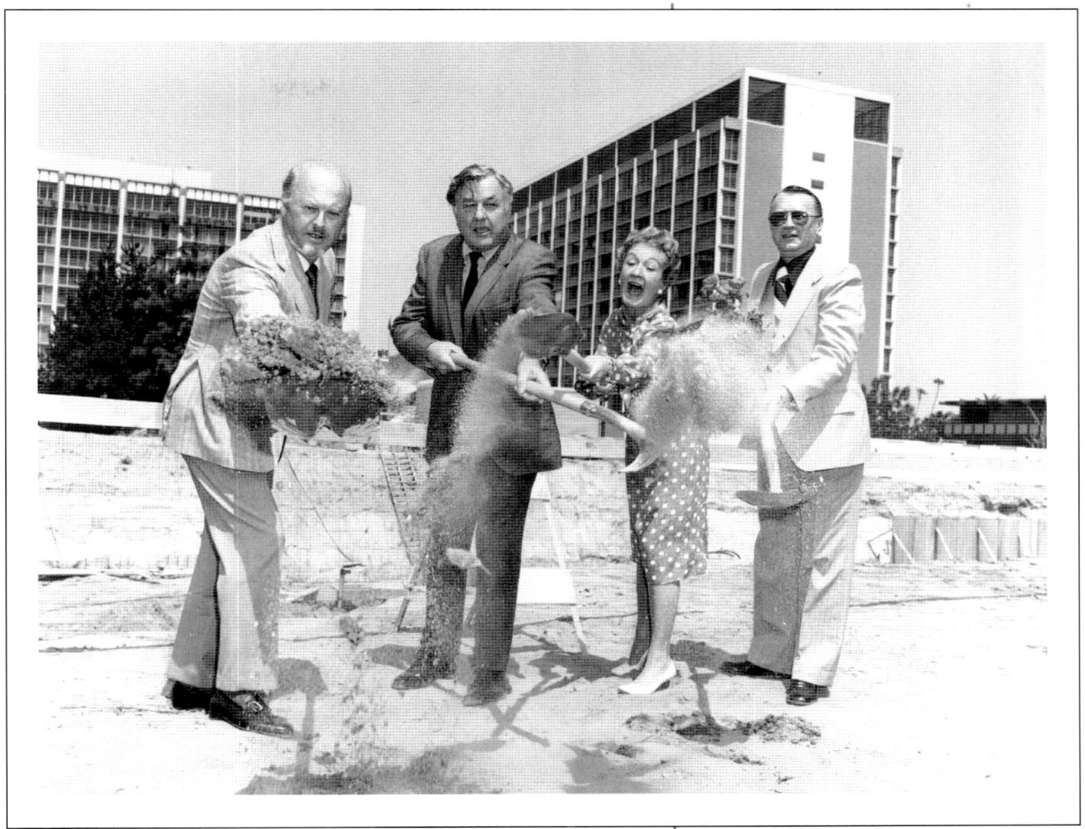

Groundbreaking for the Bonita Tower building.

On March 20, 1977, Jack Sullivan, the Hotel's executive chef, retired after twenty-two years of service. He was the one who had planned the Gourmet restaurant's menu for opening day. Since then, he had skillfully presided over an ever expanding food service at the Hotel, which upon his retirement was the largest food operation on the West Coast. Rolf Jung was named to carry on Sullivan's tradition. Jung (a native of Cologne, Germany) had previously worked at Maxim's in Paris and had been the executive chef for the Marriot Hotel Corporation.

Mickey Mouse turned 50-years-old in 1978. In June the Abominable Snowman took up residence inside the Matterhorn. Including the addition of Space Mountain in May of the previous year, $197-million had now been invested in the Park. On July 25, 1978, it was announced that the Los Angeles Rams were moving to Anaheim, beginning with the 1980 season. A $33-million expansion would enlarge Anaheim Stadium into a 70,500 seat sports complex.

As 1978 began, the Disneyland Hotel took another major step into the "computer age" with the installation of O.D.P. (Online Distributed Processing). Already used at Caesar's Palace, the Flamingo, and the Canadian Pacific Hotel, this was its first use in California. Nineteen individual computer terminals were located throughout the Hotel complex. If one failed, none of the others were affected. The system connected reservations, the front desk, housekeeping, and cashiers

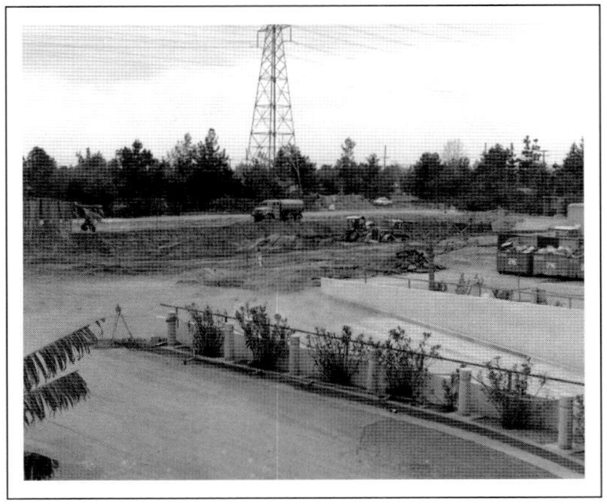

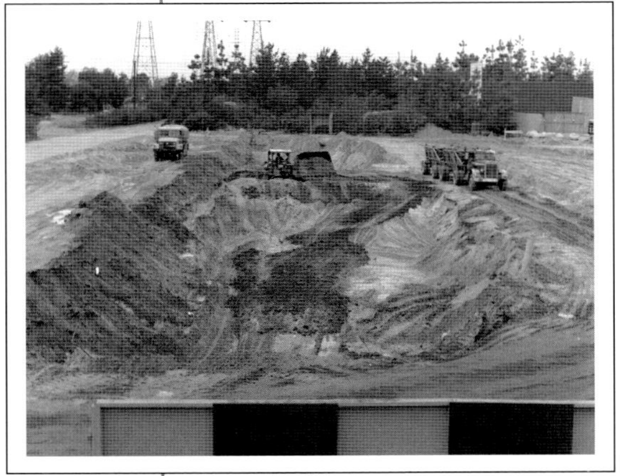

Clearing ground for the Bonita Tower building.

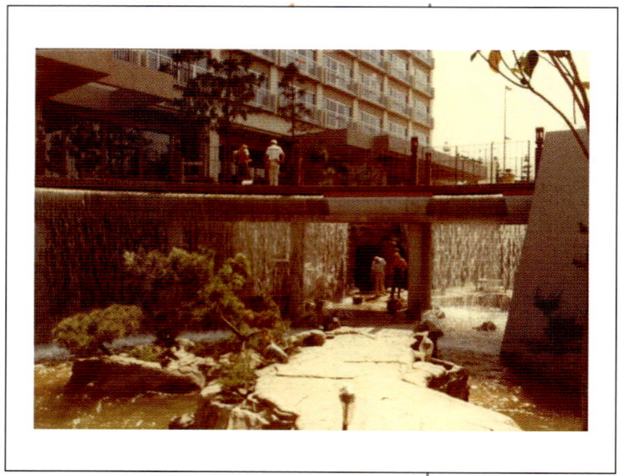

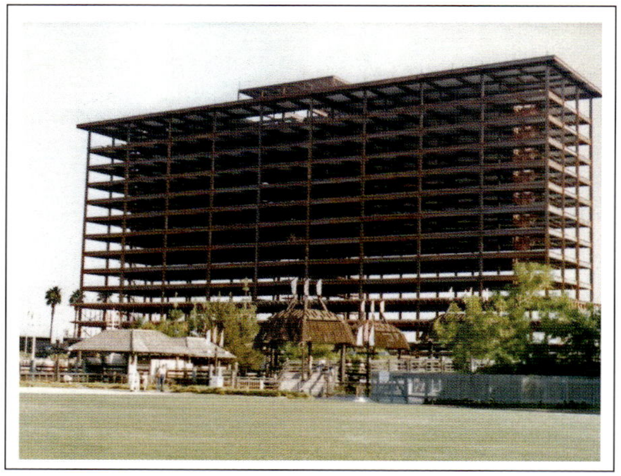

The frame of the Bonita Tower building taking shape. Photograph by Lou Perry; courtesy of Sue Bossert.

at shops and restaurants. Up to 30,000 reservations could be stored, giving the Hotel the ability to better manage its future bookings. The system also made easier and faster the ability to get messages to guests. Each day, housekeeping had a completely updated list of all stay-overs, check-ins, and check-outs. As soon as a room had been cleaned, that information was sent by the system to registration, allowing it to know the availability of rooms. At check-out, O.D.P. displayed a list of all charges: room rate, room service, parking fees, restaurant and lounge charges, etc. Taxes on the guest's bill were automatically calculated. The night auditor's job had been made much easier.

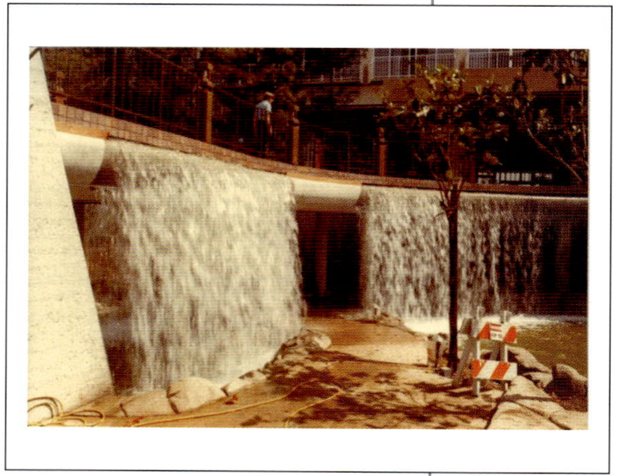

On February 13, 1978, the Employee Cafeteria was opened next to the main kitchen. It was referred to as the "world's friendliest hotel employees" dining room. During the times when full meals were not being served, beverages, sweet rolls, and desserts were available. Hotel employees were charged a nominal amount. Around this same time the California Dining Room was closed, and its space was utilized to enlarge El Vaquero Steak House.

Also on February 13, 1978, the Chef's Table a small, private dining room inside the Hotel's main kitchen was opened. Providing gourmet meals for groups of up to ten guests, the room was designed for "special occasions" (a board meeting, an anniversary, or a wedding party) and was decorated as a formal dining room in a private home. Bonita Wrather had personally selected the room's furnishings and accessories. Menus were individually created by Chef James Boring.

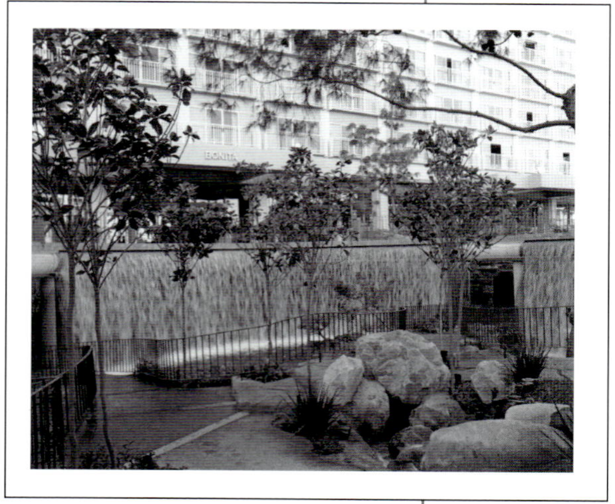

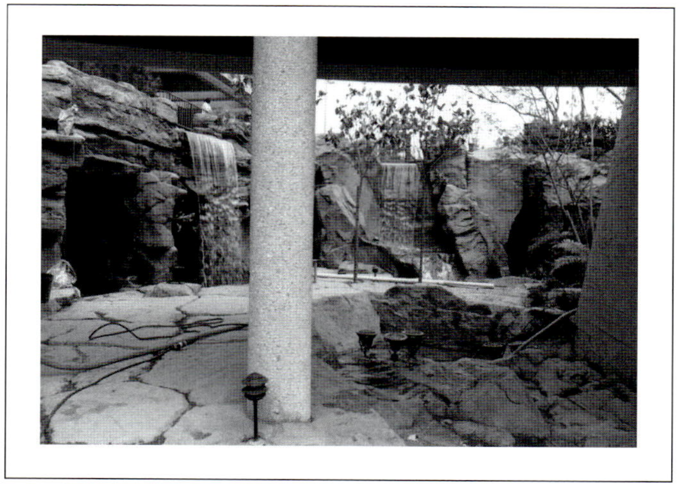

Before their dinner if guests so desired, they were given the "back-of-the-house" tour, personally conducted by Chef Boring. After being greeted in the restaurant's lobby, they were first escorted through El Vaquero, with its exhibit-cooking grill and its salad bar (modeled after a Mexican open-air produce market) being points of interest. Next, in the Chef's Kitchen, Boring would describe to his guests the variety of Mediterranean dishes prepared for this themed restaurant. Following was a tour of the central kitchen's

Construction underway on waterfalls.

various work stations. Here guests learned that in a single day the Hotel could require 250 pounds of ground chuck for hamburgers, 1000 pounds of lettuce, at least 2,000 freshly baked Danish pastries. Also disclosed was that on a daily basis the Hotel's kitchen prepared 35 different types of desserts. Finally, before entering the Chef's Table dining room, the tour stopped at the butcher shop where all of the Hotel's steaks were cut and freshly ground sausage was prepared each day.

Then it was time to enjoy the specially prepared gourmet dinner. It would be served either in the French style (with each guest being served individually) or in the Russian style (family-style, with guests serving themselves from large silver platters placed on the table). Chef Boring personally supervised the meal's service and explained for his guests each course as it was being served. One recent menu had included Consomme Dubonnet, Halibut Mousse with Watercress Sauce, Lemon Ice, Veal Roulade, Oysters, Duxelles, Pommes Dubarry, Chinese Pea Pods, and Grand Marnier Souffle with Fresh Raspberry Sauce. All was complemented with vintage wines from the Hotel's California Wine Cellar.

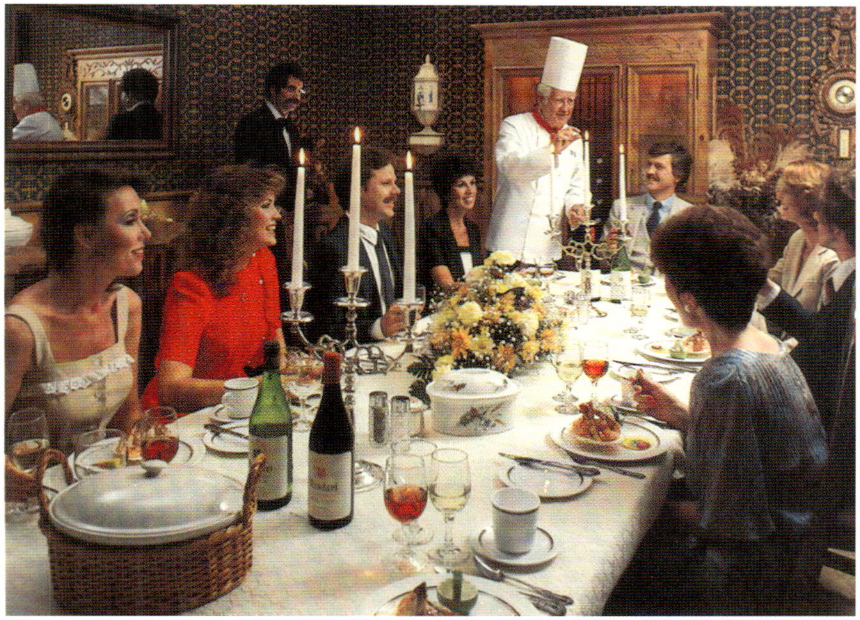

The Chef's Table offered a unique dining experience for Hotel guests.

Chef Boring noted that his "kitchen staff enjoys preparing these special meals. They can express their culinary creativity and present our guests with unique experiences in fine dining." Following the meal, guests frequently honored the chef and his staff with a standing ovation.

In February, the Oak Room Spa at the Marina Tower (previously open only to men) was opened to all. Hotel employees also were granted access for a nominal monthly fee. The spa's manager Ralph Larsen praised the facilities by saying, "The massage tables are the finest I have seen in my forty years in the health business; truly a work of superb cabinetry." Some visitors to the spa would come exclusively for the pleasure of receiving one of the Swedes' famous rose oil massage treatments. The 61-year-old Larsen further commented, "Exercising 10-15 minutes a day, every day, in moderation, is good for us. The secret of staying flexible as we get older is to make our joints move very day."

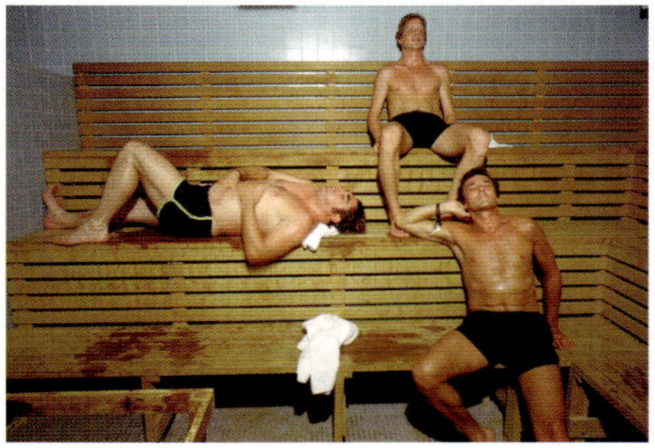

This year saw Bonita Wrather become involved in the redecorating of the Garden Rooms at the Disneyland Hotel. At first, it was just as a hobby. She displayed such talent as an interior decorator that she continued her participation with the refurbishment of the Sierra Tower rooms. As a result of those successful projects, Bonita took over control of the "Decorating Program" for the Hotel. She once stated that decorating was the biggest challenge of her life but that she always came in under budget.

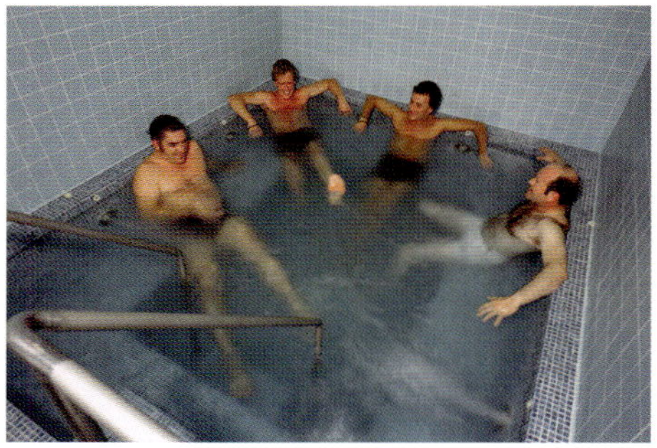

On July 1st, 119 rooms of the newest tower building were opened to guests. By August all the guest rooms of this third tower building were fully opened (although its Grand Opening was not celebrated until the following year). Included were thirty-eight suites with one or two bedrooms. The $18-million, 13-story Bonita Tower (named

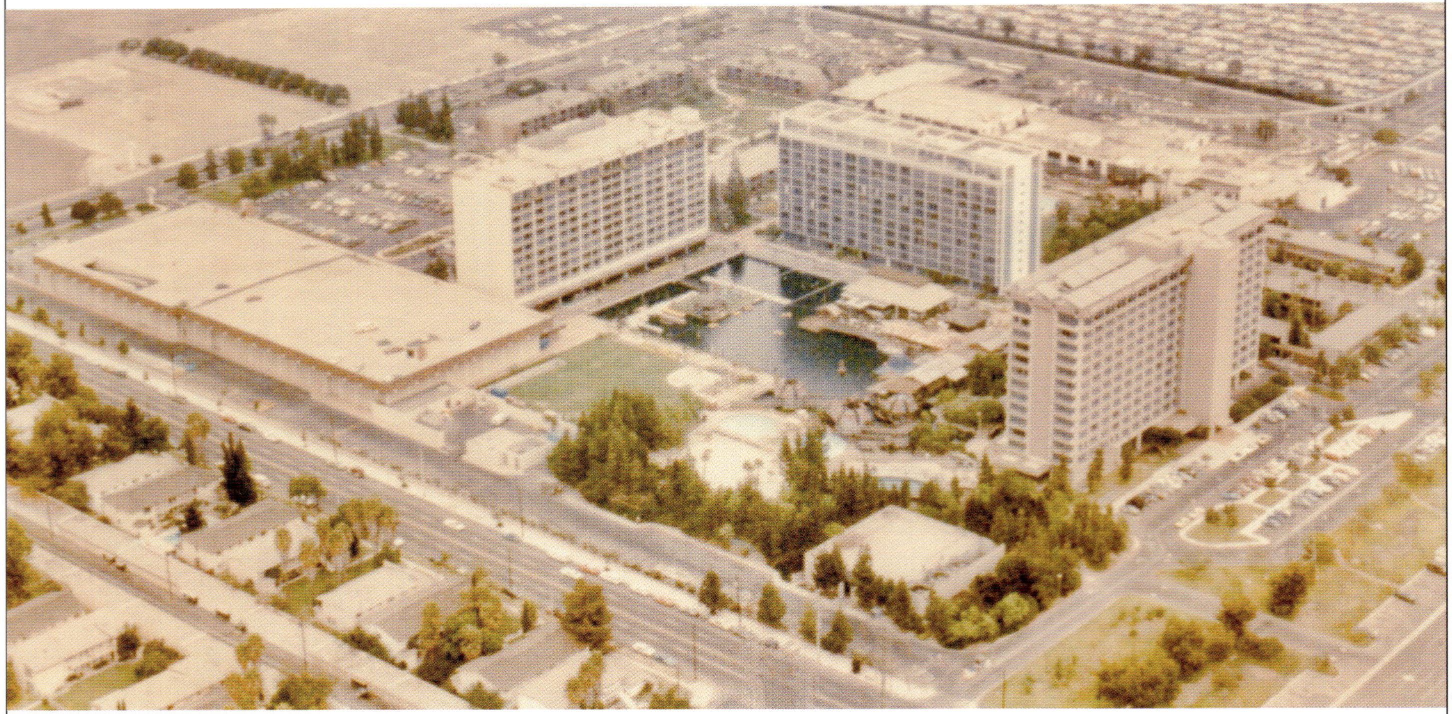

An aerial view of the three towers and grounds of the Disneyland Hotel complex.

after Jack Wrather's wife) became the tallest building in Anaheim. In September, the new Tower's lobby was opened, along with six new meeting rooms (the Santa Rosa, the San Clemente, the Santa Catalina, the Santa Cruz, the Santa Barbara, and the Wrather Board Room). On the lobby level was to be found the Garden Lounge, which overlooked the Dancing Waters and would overlook the Aqua Gardens when opened the following year. This lounge contained a holding (warming) kitchen that allowed for the serving of special breakfasts and buffet lunches for meetings and conventions. The following year, a terrace was added to the Garden Lounge, allowing patrons to enjoy the refreshing evening breezes.

More importantly, the Bonita Tower was the first hotel building in the United States to utilize a solar heating system. Solar panels, installed on the roof, collected the sun's heat, which then heated water in storage tanks. That water was then circulated through the guest rooms. A new laundry-water reclamation system surpassed then current standards in the commercial laundry services. Installed in the basement of the new tower at a cost of $500,000, the facility eventually would supply laundry service for the entire Hotel. The laundry's first supervisor was Pete Kaiserman. The Tower had been designed as an "energy-conscious" structure. This new tower added 367 guest rooms, bringing the total for the Hotel complex to slightly over 1,400 rooms. As with the previous Sierra and Marina Towers, the Los Angeles firm of Weber and Nicholson Associates was the architect for the Bonita Tower.

Other less spectacular changes occurred in 1978 at the Disneyland Hotel. The Shipyard Inn was almost doubled in size and an oyster bar was added. The Sidewalk Cafe at the Coffee Shop was enclosed so as to provide additional dining area that would be available year-around. [In the past, the Cafe had been used only during favorable weather.] El Vaquero was enlarged with seating capacity increased and two new salad bars added. The Chef's Kitchen began a Sunday Brunch, serving over 500 guests. The Hotel installed its own telephone system, ending the dial system and entering the push-button era. A new reservations desk computer system caused several months of problems, but eventually the bugs were eliminated. All hallways in the Marina Tower received new carpets, new vinyl wall coverings, and new lighting fixtures. On Labor Day, the Palm Court lounge in the Marina Tower debuted its new furniture. The Top-of-the-Park lounge was once again refurbished, changing its layout completely and adding a dance floor. [At that time, a name change was contemplated...The Treetop Lounge. Calmer heads prevailed and the original name was retained.] Finally, Tiffy's (a fast food restaurant at the Plaza) was closed when its lease expired on December 31st. After receiving many complaints concerning the quality of its food and service, the Hotel management determined that it was a second-rate facility. Tiffy's had been operated by an outside firm.

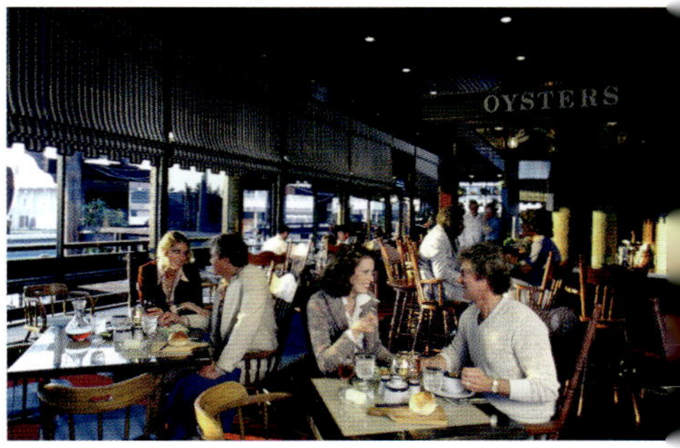

Oyster Bar.

Big Thunder Mountain opened in September of 1979 at the now $206-million theme park. That year Disneyland hosted its first newborn guest when on July 4th, just off busy Main Street, Rosa and Elias Salcedo became the proud parents of Teresa Salcedo (6 lbs., 10-1/2 oz., 19-1/2").

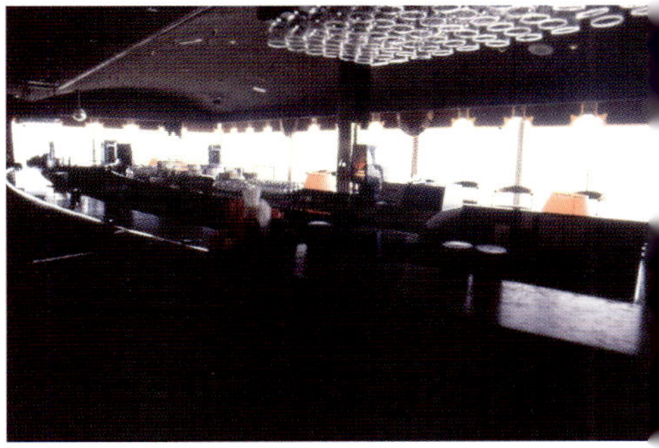

The Top-of-the Park Lounge

1979 Magic Kingdom Club members could now look forward to a new feature of membership. Package deals now including breakfast, lunch and dinner were available. This new service was called the “Gold Key Vacation.” It was billed “Enjoy the most complete way to visit Disneyland. Your personalized “Gold Key” unlocks all the fun and excitement of this exclusive Magic Kingdom Club vacation adventure.” This package included three nights accommodations at the Disneyland Hotel, four days admission and unlimited use of all rides and attractions (except shooting galleries) in Disneyland and all three meals for three days at a variety of fine restaurants in Disneyland and at the Disneyland Hotel. All this for only $235 per adult, double occupancy. Four night stays (minus the meals) staying at the Disneyland Hotel, the Inn at the Park or Howard Johnson’s Motor Lodge with two days admission to Disneyland started at $107 per adult. Similar two and three night packages started at $52 and $79 respectively. These rates were effective January 1, 1979 through December 31, 1979.

In early spring of 1979, the charming Mazie's Pantry, with an outdoor cafe, was added at the Plaza Building shopping center (replacing Tiffy's restaurant), overlooking the Hotel's Olympic-sized swimming pool. [Mazie's was named after Jack Wrather's mother Mazie Cogdell Wrather.] It was a combination of a New York deli and a European sidewalk cafe. Its goal was to provide diners with light and healthy dishes. The interior decor was described as "country casual." Walls were of weathered pine with accents of hand-painted tiles and etched glass panels. The ceiling was decorated with tree branches baring golden leaves. Out-doors, diners relaxed under an orange and yellow canopy. Chef Rolf Jung declared: "We take care to serve the freshest food and to use the best ingredients. Our whole grain bread, baked right here..., is sliced by hand. Our mushrooms are grown in nearby Costa Mesa and delivered fresh every day. And, our Kosher corned beef is flown in from Chicago. It comes in a barrel of spicy brine; we cook it and serve it hot." Home-made soups and sandwiches of all types were featured

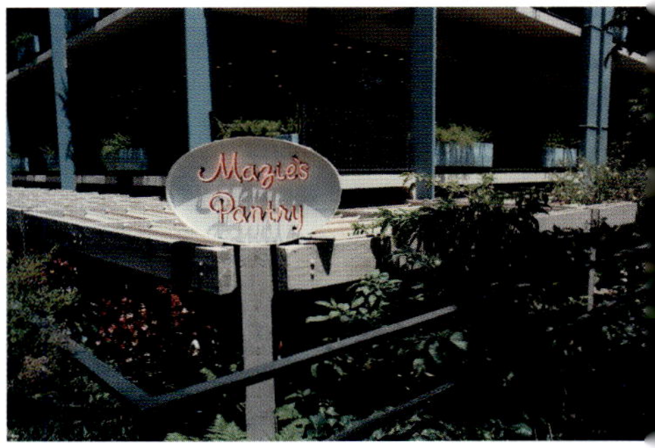

Exterior Mazie's Pantry.

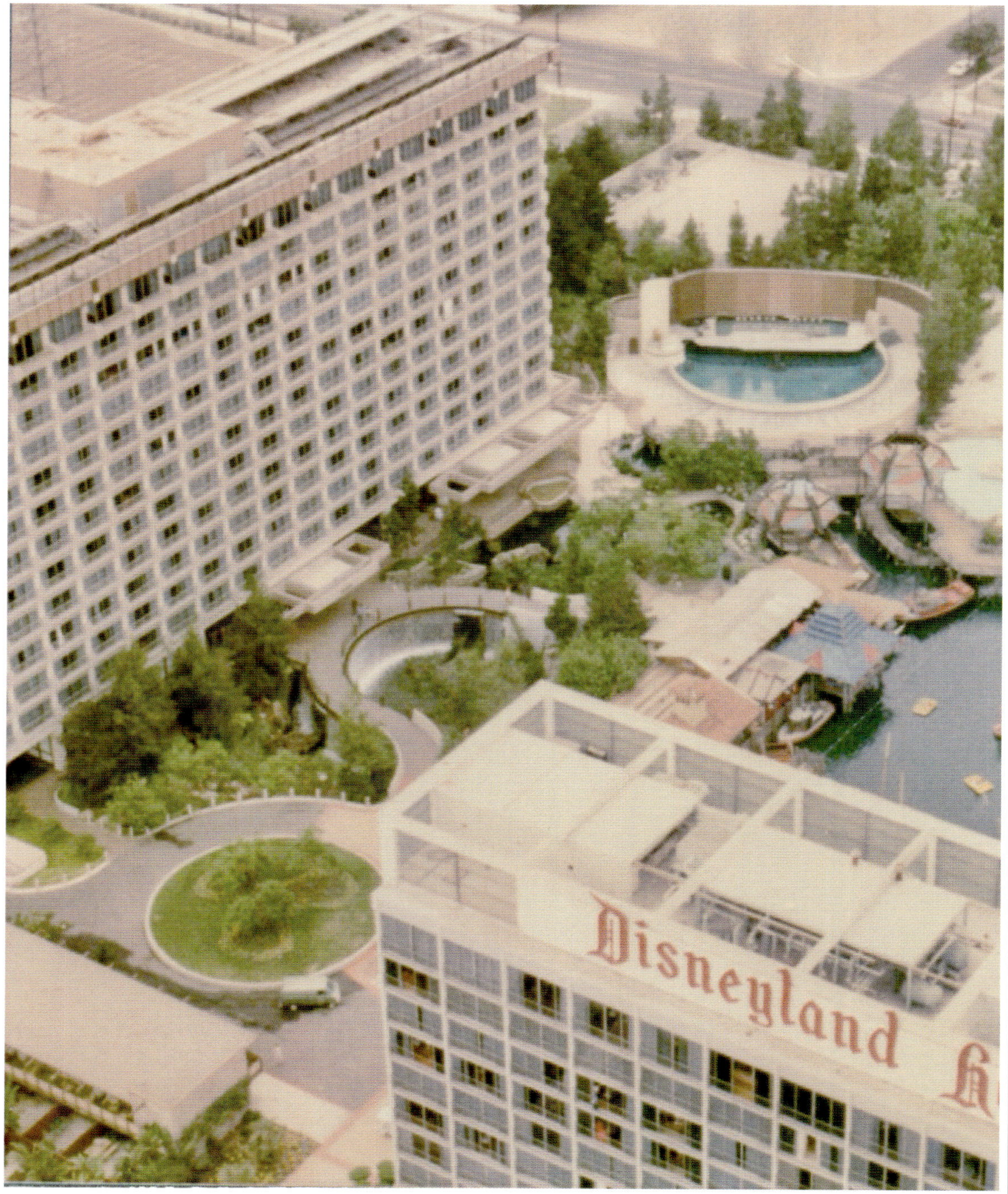

Aerial view showing the new Bonita Tower, Dancing Waters and Horseshoe Falls.

on the menu. A combination plate (available at lunch and dinner) allowed guests to sample several different items. Mazie's special dessert was Chips 'n Chips...a giant, freshly baked chocolate chip cookie, topped with ice cream and hot fudge, and then sprinkled with even more chocolate chips. Originally planned as a 24-hour restaurant, Mazie's was open from 6 a.m. to 2 a.m. and offered a European breakfast for the early risers. [Originally, it had been planned as a health food restaurant to be called The Proud Sprout.]

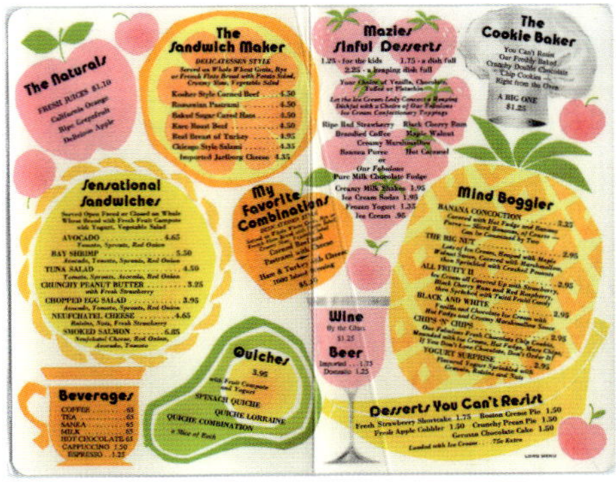

Menu from Mazie's Pantry.

The Disneyland Hotel's Training and Development Department was established in 1979 under the direction of Betty Johnson. Its purpose was to insure that employees provided personalized services to all guests. It further emphasized the importance of teamwork and the maintenance of company standards. All new employees attended orientation meetings, received an employee handbook, and were given tours of all of the Hotel's facilities and grounds. They were instructed in proper grooming, hair care, and personal and cultural awareness. On site training was provided in each particular job skill; and college credits could be earned in three areas of hospitality management through extension courses offered by the North Orange County Community College District. Additional opportunities were provided to learn either Spanish or English as a Second Language. All employees attended semiannual hotel-wide meetings, aimed at keeping everyone up-to-date on changes, plans, and policies. These meetings provided for questions and suggestions from the Hotel's staff members. Wrather Hotels inaugurated its "Managers of Tomorrow" program to provide incentives and to help employees interested in furthering their careers within the company. Director Johnson stated, "We believe our employees set us apart in the hospitality industry. And, no matter where our visitors call 'home,' we know our employees will meet the challenge of making them feel like a part of our 'family' while they are here."

From its beginning, the Hotel had been an international destination. Over the years, various programs had been instituted to better serve the needs of foreign guests. A record was kept of which languages each staff member could speak fluently. Resident Manager David Kerr explained that "we usually can find a staff member to serve as an interpreter when our guests need assistance. We have many employees who speak Spanish, but we also can find someone who speaks Japanese, Persian or even Icelandic." If guests should wish to call Germany, France, Japan, Mexico, etc., they were provided with direct-dialing instruction in their own languages. The Cashier's Desk acted as a currency exchange, providing cash at the current market rate. German marks, Japanese yen, British pounds could quickly be turned into U.S. dollars.

In June, Senor Campos' Taste of Mexico was opened next to the Shipyard Inn on the wharf at the marina. This take-out restaurant offered a menu of Mexican-American fast-food such as tacos and burritos. If patrons wished, they could eat their food while continuing their tour of the marina area, or they could enjoy their meal at patio tables either under the sun or under umbrellas. [Senor Campos' replaced the Fuji Pavilion that had been located there since 1972.]

The Hotel's long time *Check-In* guest magazine was replaced by a glossy, more colorful publication entitled *Kaleidoscope: the In-Room Magazine for the Disneyland Hotel & the Inn at the Park*. Its first issue was summer 1979. In his "Welcome to the Hotel" letter to guests, Frank Bret wrote, "My staff and I have strived to make this hotel better than a home away from home. We want you to feel comfortable enough to kick off your shoes and stay awhile." He continued, "In short, this hotel is an oasis where you can relax and be yourself time after time

Premier issue of Kaleidoscope.

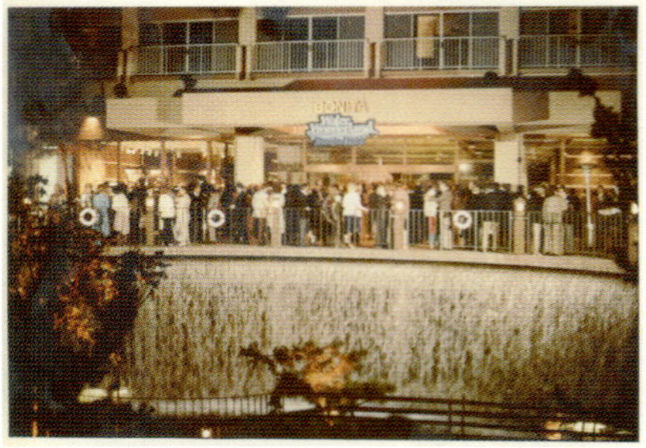

Premiere of Water Wonderland.

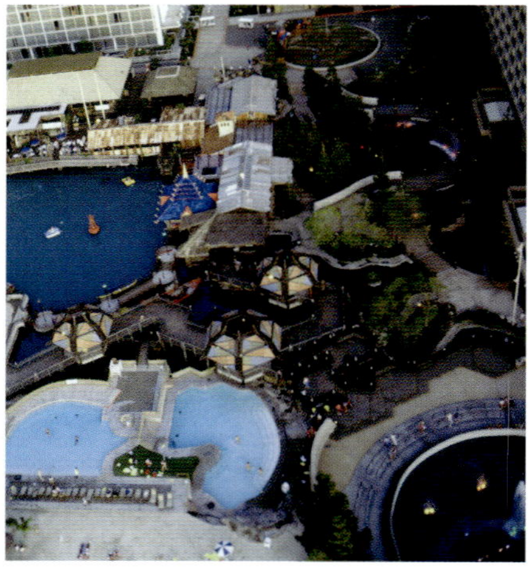

Aerial of Water Wonderland.

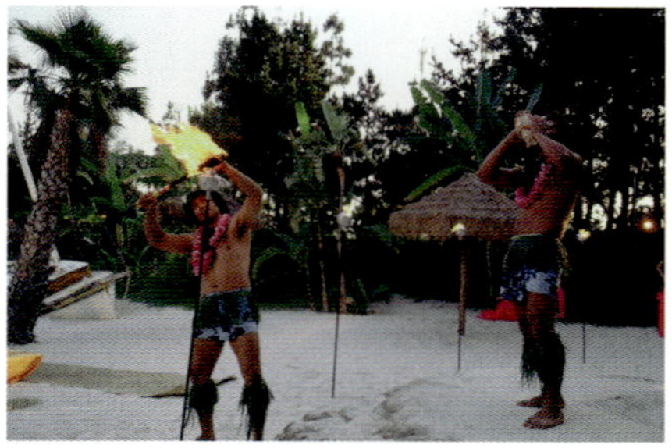

Lighting ceremony.

in a first-class, personal atmosphere. If you don't feel like a king or a queen as you leave us, then we haven't done our job. Please let us know." Its very first cover article concerned the opening of the Hotel's latest attraction, Water Wonderland.

On Thursday, June 7, 1979, the Disneyland Hotel began a four day celebration to herald the opening of Water Wonderland, located in and around the marina area. The first evening's event was called "Celebrity Cruise to Water Wonderland," a red carpet cocktail party for 7,000 specially invited guests, dressed in nautical attire. Guests were provided a walking tour of the new Aqua Gardens (called "Journey to Aquatic Wonders") and a debut of the Still Green laser sculpture show. Guests were entertained by a floating musical revue ("Pacific Terrific") from a barge in the middle of the marina. Included were a Polynesian ceremonial torch lighting, a fiesta of Mexican music, exhibits of Japanese culture, and fireworks. Following was a premiere of the all new Dancing Waters and Lights Fantastic Show. Invited guests then attended the "Captain's Dinner," hosted by the Wrathers, featuring Japanese, Mexican, and Californian cuisine. The dinner ended with "Showtime Around the World," a musical production presented by Cast Members from Disneyland.

Friday, June 8th, was the public premiere of Water Wonderland. Hotel guests were treated to a day at Disneyland. All day ceremonies at the Hotel officially dedicated the various elements of the new attraction. An evening reception was given for Anaheim "friends of the Hotel." As a part of the celebration, at the Inn-at-the-Park, the "California Clambake" was held.

Saturday and Sunday continued the public celebration. Entertainment was provided by Japanese drummers, strolling Mariachis, and Country Western musicians. The "Pacific Terrific" musical revue was encored (and would be performed nightly over the next several summers). The evenings ended with "big band" dancing.

Water Wonderland included a number of new and updated attractions around the marina area and at the base of the newly opened Bonita Tower. In front of the Tower was the new $2-million, four-acre Aqua Gardens. It featured the 165-foot wide, crescent-shaped Horseshoe Falls, the top of which was a bridge for guests of the Bonita Tower to use as a link to the wharf. Also included in this area were a beautifully landscaped rain forest, a series of reflecting pools, and rapids. Finally, there was a fish pond grotto (inhabited by over 400 very expensive Japanese Imperial Koi fish), landscaped in the style of Japanese gardens. While the Aqua Gardens may have had a distinctively tropical atmosphere, in actuality all of the plants, trees, and rocks needed for this new area had been transported only from nearby San Bernardino and the Sierra Mountains.

Each evening at dusk the trumpeting of a conch shell and the beating of a Taiko drum could be heard. Pacific islanders, each wearing a colorful loin-cloth, performed a ceremonial lighting of the propane torches surrounding the marina.

The Dancing Waters show was updated with the installation of a $40,000, twelve-channel Dutko Sound system. Added to the amphitheaters lengthy wall (at a cost of $150,000) was a pulsating fiber-optic mural, entitled Lights Fantastic. Between the three nightly presentations of Dancing Waters, guests of the Hotel were entertained at the marina by an abbreviated version of "Pacific Terrific," emphasizing the cultures of the Pacific Islands.

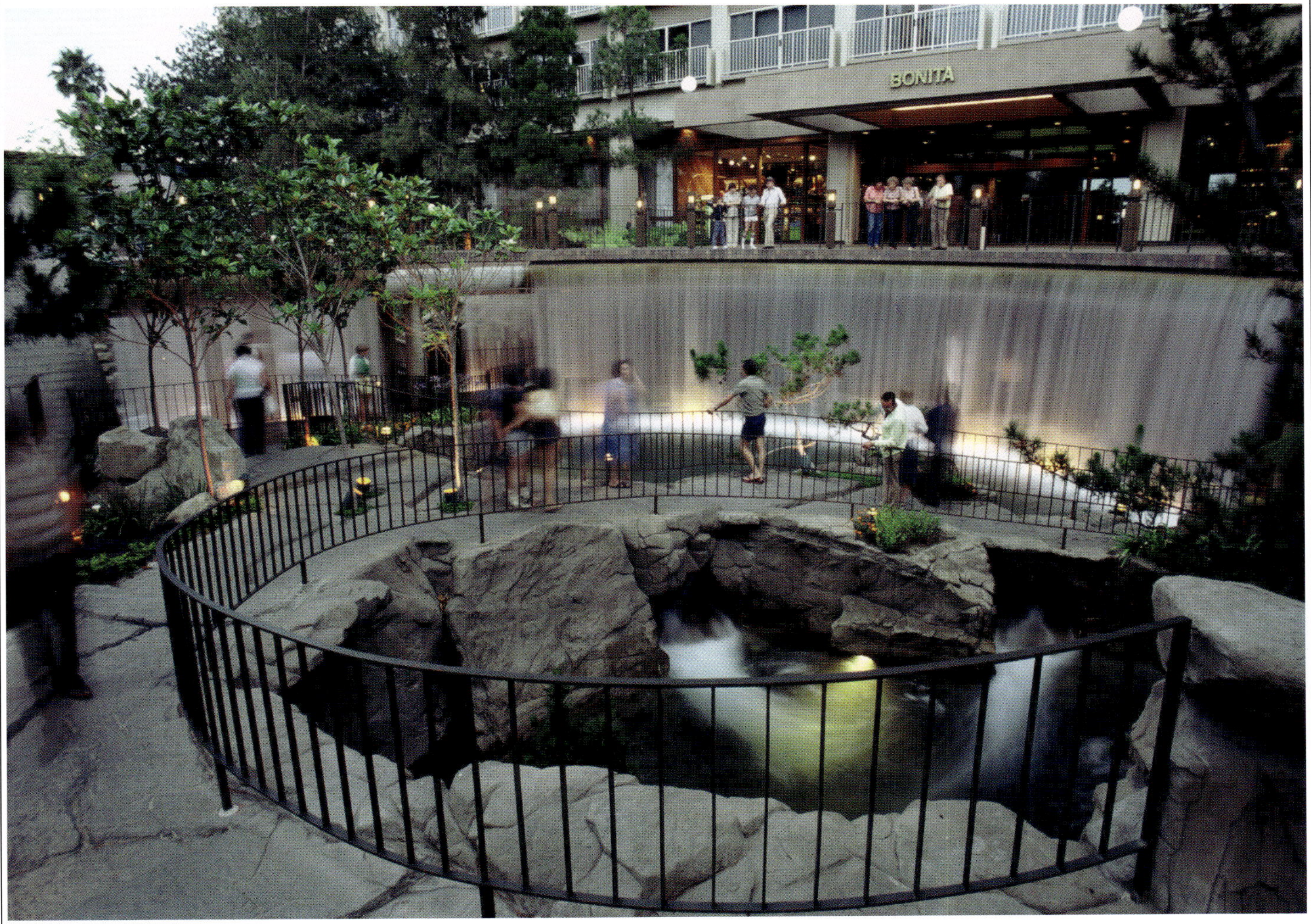

Horseshoe Falls at the all new Water Wonderland.

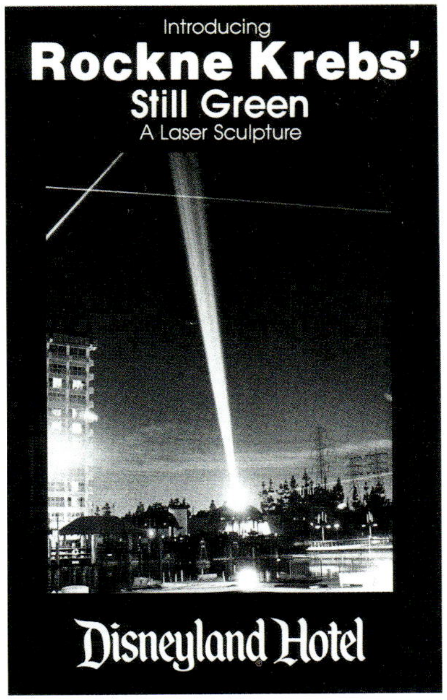

Still Green Laser brochure.

As a part of Water Wonderland, a giant laser sculpture was premiered. Commissioned by Jack Wrather, the laser art was entitled Still Green (a.k.a. Rather Green) by Rockne Krebs, a pioneer in laser art. For its premiere, the Wrathers hosted a dinner party in their private suite at the Hotel, attended by artists, art critics, and museum directors. The praise for Krebs' laser show was lavish. The blue-green laser sculpture was presented nightly and could be viewed from many guest rooms. One argon laser was placed atop the Sierra Tower while another was located on the seventh floor of the Marina Tower, shooting two beams 500 feet across the marina. A third was positioned on the roof of Restaurant Row and shot its beam at a small mirror atop the Convention Center, 700 feet away. Nine small mirrors were placed in various locations around the property. As the laser beam hit a mirror, it

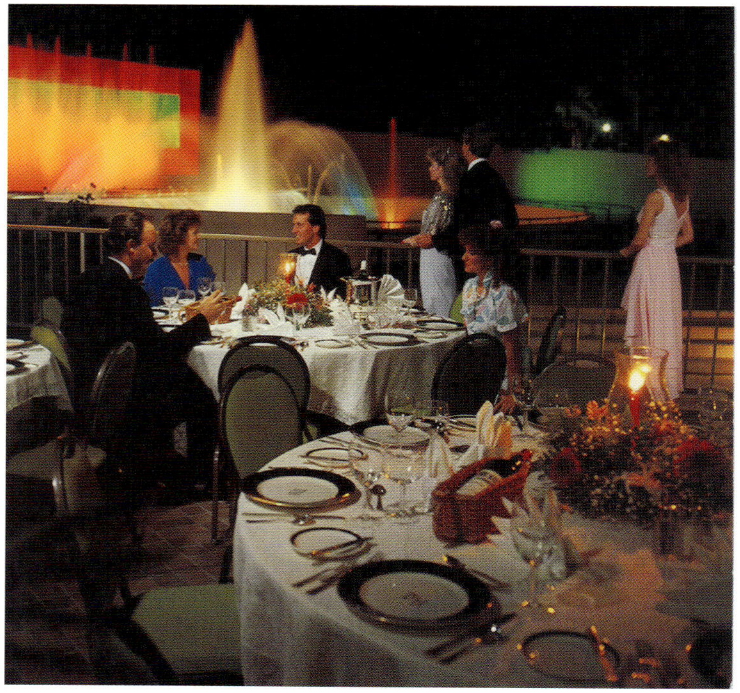

The updated Dancing Waters show.

was redirected to yet another mirror. One beam traveled a half mile to the fifth floor of the Inn-at-the-Park. Eventually, 14 lines of light formed the design of the laser sculpture, covering over 14-million cubic feet of space. Described as a 3-D collage, it was comprised of giant triangles and other unusual geometric shapes. It was so large that no one could view the entire work from one location. Guests walking through the Hotel's property would see an ever-changing configuration of this piece of art. Adding to the sculpture's effects upon the viewer were its reflections in the calm water of the marina and off the charcoal-tinted windows of the three towers. The condition of the atmosphere would also change the sculpture from night to night. Smog, rain, dust, all affected the color and visibility of Still Green.

Concerning his laser creation for the Hotel, Krebs stated that "Still Green is a serious artistic undertaking in the recreation and entertainment milieu, the sort of active urban landscape that is difficult terrain for most art." He added, "A laser sculpture is approachable on so many different levels of visual understanding that the cultural insulation of the museum context is unnecessary." Previously, Krebs' laser sculptures had been featured at the Kennedy Space Center, the Washington Gallery of Modern Art, the Art Institute of Chicago, the Whitney Museum of American Art, the Kennedy Center for the Performing Arts, and other institutions for contemporary art.

In August of 1979, Richard S. Stevens became the new president of the Disneyland Hotel. In one of his first messages to the Hotel staff, Stevens stated: "It is very easy to become complacent when there is a never-ending supply of customers and you enjoy the undisputed 'Number One' role. The challenges therefore become great opportunities for us to show our true capabilities and professionalism. I am very excited about helping all of you in meeting that challenge."

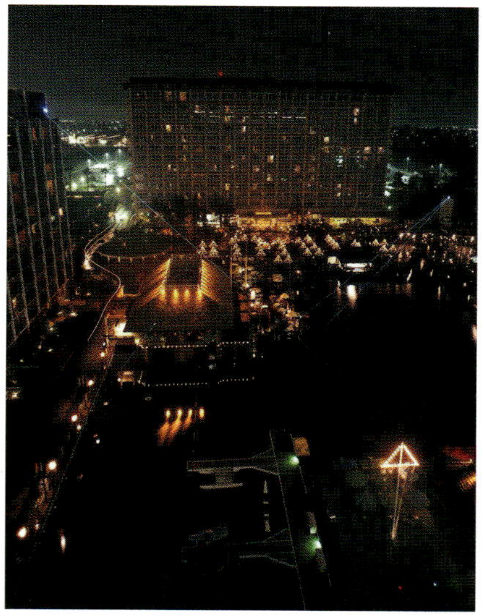

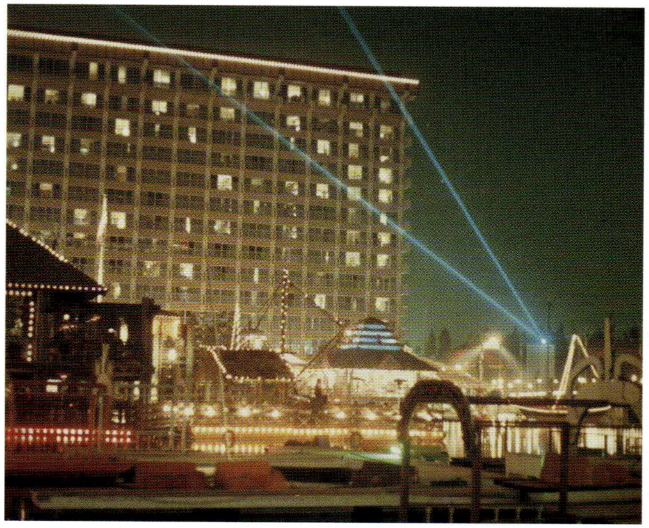

Laser light show at the Disneyland Hotel.

1980-1988

On July 17, 1980, Disneyland celebrated its 25th Anniversary. On December 3rd, ground was broken for Tokyo Disneyland. According to the most recent U.S. Census, Anaheim's population was now 221,847. On August 11th, the Rams football team claimed the enlarged Anaheim Stadium as their new home.

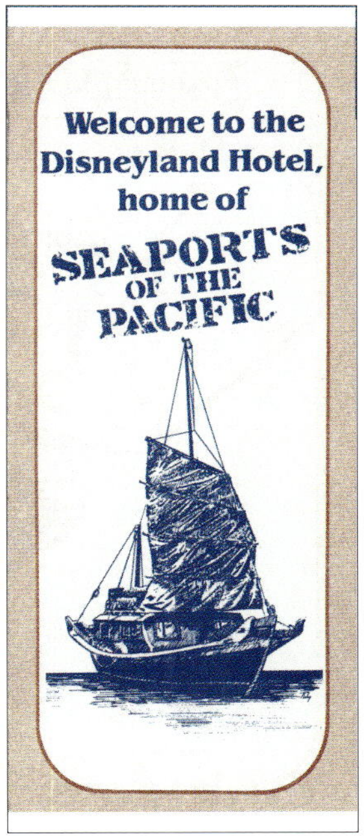

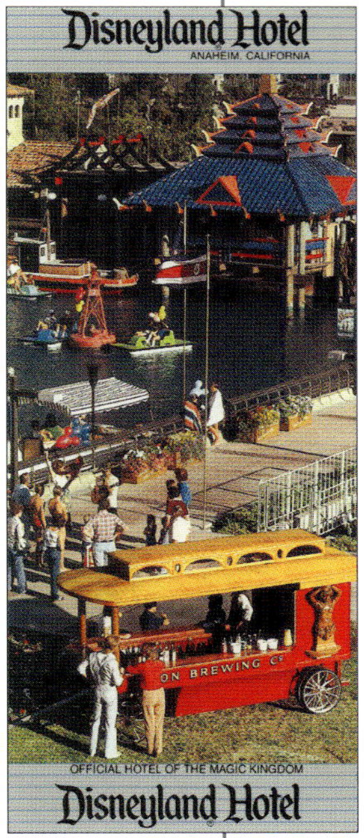

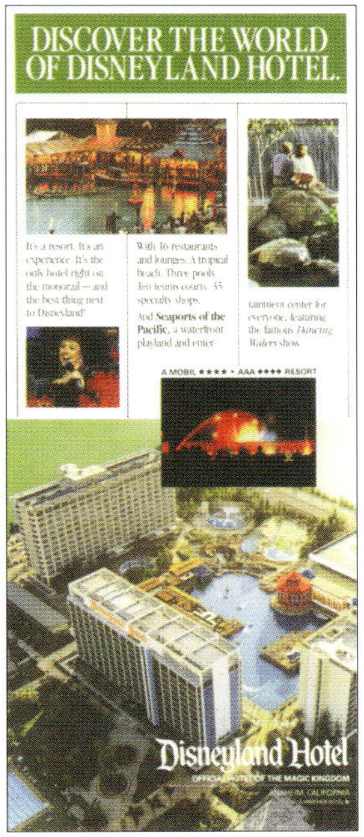

For the summer season of 1980, the 25th Anniversary of the Disneyland Hotel, the Seaports of the Pacific shopping area was added to the marina. Under construction since February, it replaced what had been the artisans market. While WC Construction Division erected the structures, Seaports had been designed by Doug Williamson, Don Williamson, and J. M. Brown Associates (all having worked on set designs for the Laguna Arts Festival). Ed Ettinger, the project's supervisor, explained, "What we've developed is a living theater consisting of those special environments associated with exotic ports of trade in the Pacific Basin." Side by side were an Indonesian pagoda blue tile roof, an Australian weathered tin roof, a Polynesian bamboo roof, and a Latin American red mission-tile roof...a wide variety of colors and textures. Staffed by authentic personnel, the Seaports was a mingling of accents and cultures. In the International Bazaar were to be found an arts and crafts market and shops of imports from the South Seas. Mimes, magicians, and strolling musicians entertained at this international bazaar. Sausalito Sue, a rustic cocktail barge, floated close by on the marina. Entered by means of a wooden ramp, it offered drinks and snacks.

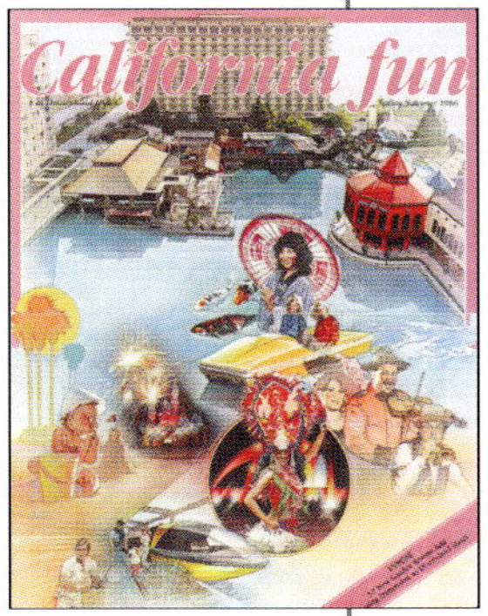

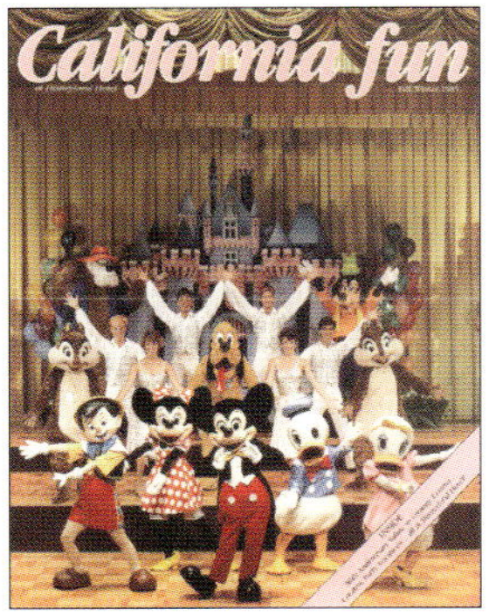

Hotel brochures 1980's.

The restaurant area at the marina by now had become known as the San Francisco Wharf. The California Wine Cellar (specializing in domestic wines) opened at the Seaports of the Pacific. It specialized in 199 premium label wines. At wine tastings, complimentary bread, cheese, and fruit were provided. Guests could purchase their favorite wines, either by the bottle or by the case. Special "gift packs" could be created by personally selecting several varieties of wines to be included. Not far away was to be found Aussie's Pub. The Kangaroo Kick was its special offering; there were twenty-five varieties of imported beer also available. The Pub was short lived and gone by late 1981.

After a $3.1-million redevelopment program, all of the 300 Villa Garden rooms were reopened. The North Gardens were now a combination of executive suites and family units, set in a tropical island landscape. Some of those rooms were redesigned so that they easily could be set up to accommodate small groups (board meetings or planning sessions) of twenty or fewer persons. Each would have its own wet bar and adjoining sitting room. At

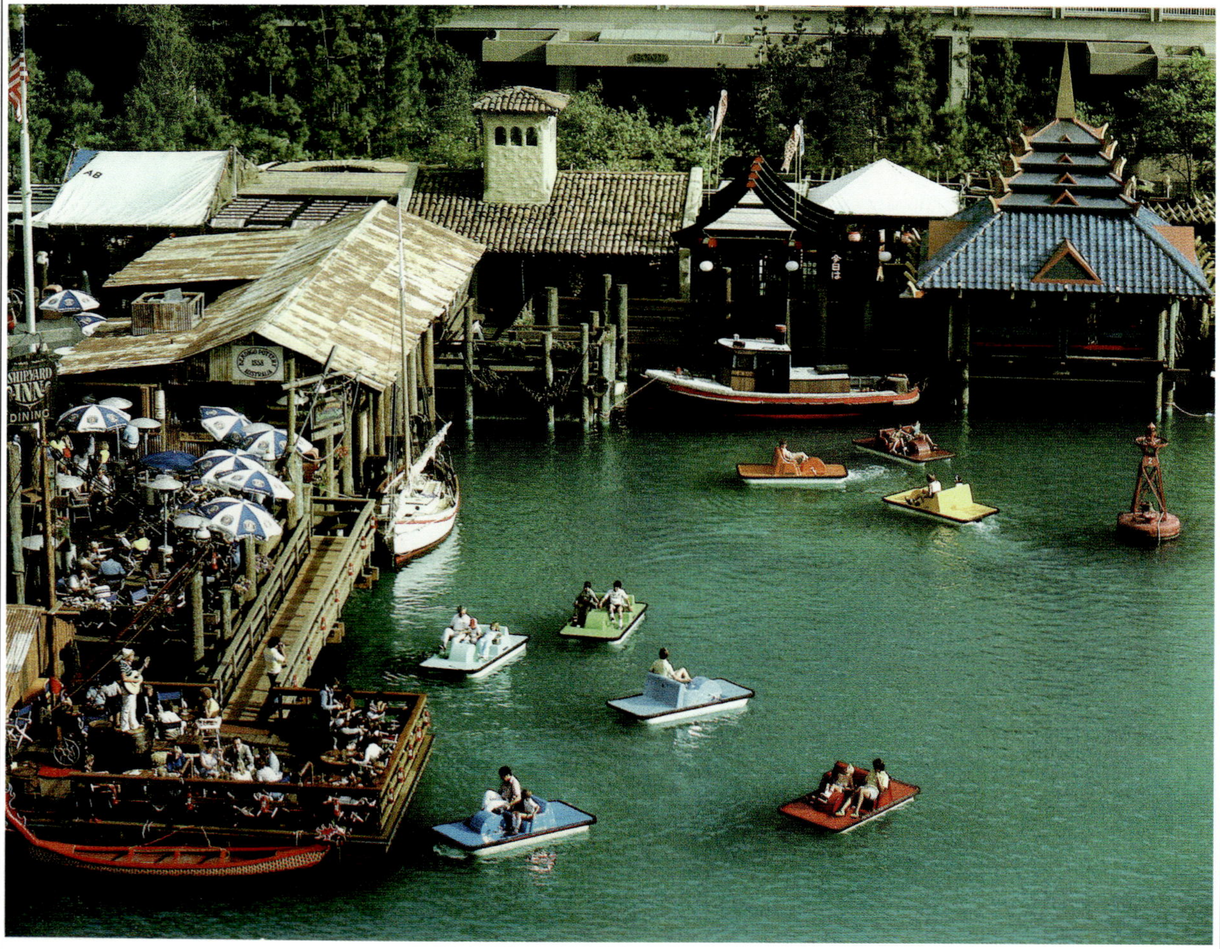

Aerial view of Seaports of the Pacific.

this time, it was projected that the next major development for the Hotel would be the remaining 13.5 acres (from that 21-acre site purchased in 1977) to the south of the Bonita Tower. As stated previously, no development ever took place during the Wrather years of the Disneyland Hotel.

1980 again offered Gold Key Vacations to Magic Kingdom Club members. Identical packages to 1979 were quoted at $260 per adult. Four, three and two night packages (minus meals) were also available starting at $111, $84 and $57 respectively. Additional participating hotels were Hyatt, Grand Hotel and Sheraton Anaheim. Rates were in effect January 1, 1980 through December 31, 1980.

Across the street at Disneyland in 1981, Gert Schelvis of Santa Barbara, California became the 200-millionth Park guest on January 8th.

That year's Wrather Corporation annual report reflected the nation's concerns with the ongoing energy crisis and the economic burdens resulting therefrom. "The hotel began taking steps to reduce lighting cost throughout the 48-acre property in midyear as part of the total energy conservation effort. Replacing existing fixtures and bulbs with new, more efficient equipment resulted in substantial savings. In addition, an energy management control system was installed which significantly reduced electricity usage." Ironically, the nation's troubling inflation rate actually had a beneficial result for the possibility of the Wrather

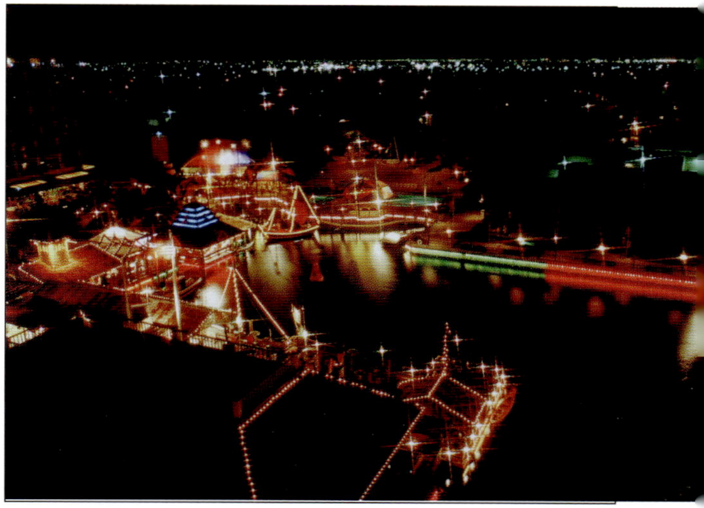

Seaports of the Pacific at night.

company selling the Hotel. In its previous year's annual report, it had been stated that "the Company believes that the market value of the Disneyland Hotel... [Has] increased materially in recent years as a result of inflation and may continue to do so if inflation continues." It would be several more years before any earnest efforts again would be made to sell the Hotel.

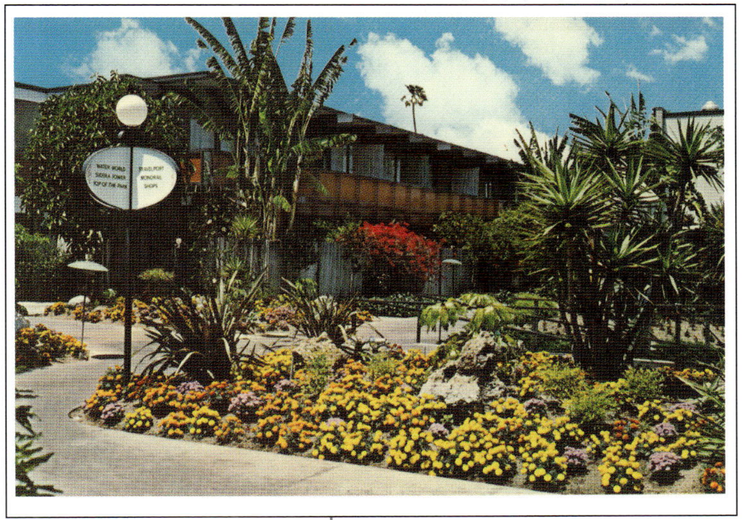

The newly remodeled Villa Garden grounds and rooms.

1981 Gold Key Vacations (with identical package amenities as previous years) were quoted at $275 per adult. Four, three and two night packages were also available (again, minus meals) starting at $135, $102 and $69 respectively. Rates were in effect all year long. The participating hotel list increased with the addition of the Quality Inn, Conestoga Inn and the Anaheim Marriott Hotel.

Almost from its first days, the Disneyland Hotel had made special efforts in hosting wedding parties and honeymooners. Started in autumn 1980 and opened by the spring of 1981, one of the guest room structures in the middle of the North Garden Rooms area had been removed (now five buildings were located here with a total of 106 guest rooms, 26 suites and two conference/hospitality rooms all decorated in an island motif). In its place was a large grassy area, bordered by rose bushes. Winding through the middle of that lawn was a path which led to a bricked, circular patio area, surrounded by yellow roses. In the center, on a red brick platform stood a lovely, white, Victorian-style gazebo with a two-tier green roof. The Gazebo and Rose Garden area had been planned specifically to provide a beautiful setting for weddings and wedding receptions. Also on the grounds, Oriental wedding ceremonies-complete with an authentic rickshaw-could take place on the bridge overlooking the Imperial Koi fish pond at Water Wonderland. Or, after an evenings torchlight ritual highlighted by the “Hawaiian Love Song” on the Hotel’s Papeete Beach, guests could enjoy a luau, beach barbecue or an old-fashioned clambake. Not only did the Hotel have unusual outdoor settings for all occasions, they had beautiful indoor facilities as well. Elegant ballrooms could be decorated in any style and the catering and entertainment could be coordinated for imaginative theme parties, celebrations and receptions. Catering director Gunter Lehmacher stated that "Brides-to-be can let their imaginations soar while our staff of wedding and reception experts take care of the down-to-earth details. "We have 25 years of experience in helping brides select the right setting to suit a theme and budget. And, we are prepared to arrange bridal showers or wedding dinners, photography, flowers, entertainment, hairdressers, limousines, and of course, honeymoon suites and hotel accommodations for the wedding party."

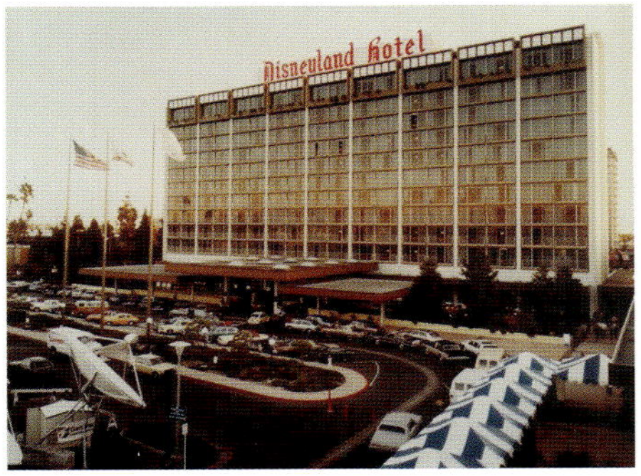

Satellite transmitter at Disneyland Hotel.

By June of 1981, the Hotel's closed-circuit television system had been named Teletour. Because of his great interest in cable and closed-circuit systems, Jack Wrather had hired McCune Audio Visual, Inc. (a nationally respected audio-visual resource center) to expand the Hotel's ability to service conventions, meetings, and guests. Studios were now located atop the Convention Center. Services were available at little or no cost to conventions and meetings since ads from exhibitors, attracted to those events, usually would underwrite the production costs. This expansion of the system now allowed the activities of a convention at the Disneyland Hotel to be cablecast (via telephone lines) to fourteen other Anaheim hotels. The latest improvements even made possible teleconferencing (via satellite) around the country.

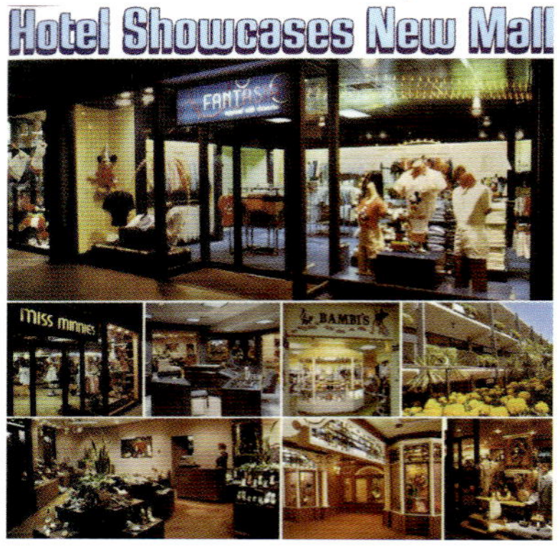

Several new specialty shops debuted in the fall of 1981. *Glass Roots*, specializing in quality glasswares opened in Seaports of the Pacific. *Fantasia*, located on the lower Plaza level featured "apparel with character." Here, you would find a complete range of clothing and accessories for adults, featuring the likeness of Mickey Mouse on each item. Fantasia also carried sportswear, hats and gold jewelry. Jiminy *Cricket's Personal Touch* was located around the corner from *Fantasia* and specialized in gift items of all kinds with each item ready to be personalized with a name on it. Three types of personalizing were available: heat-transfer letters and decals for t-shirts, fancy stitching for hats and engraving for gold and silver jewelry. Next door to *Jiminy's* was *Bambi's*, a "newborn" store that had everything for the well-dressed infant and toddler. Finally, fine jewelry could be purchased at *Kingdom Jewels* located on the upper Plaza level. This shop featured gold, diamond and precious stone jewelry for all budgets. To make shopping easy, these shops were open seven days a week from 8:30 a.m. until 11:00 p.m.

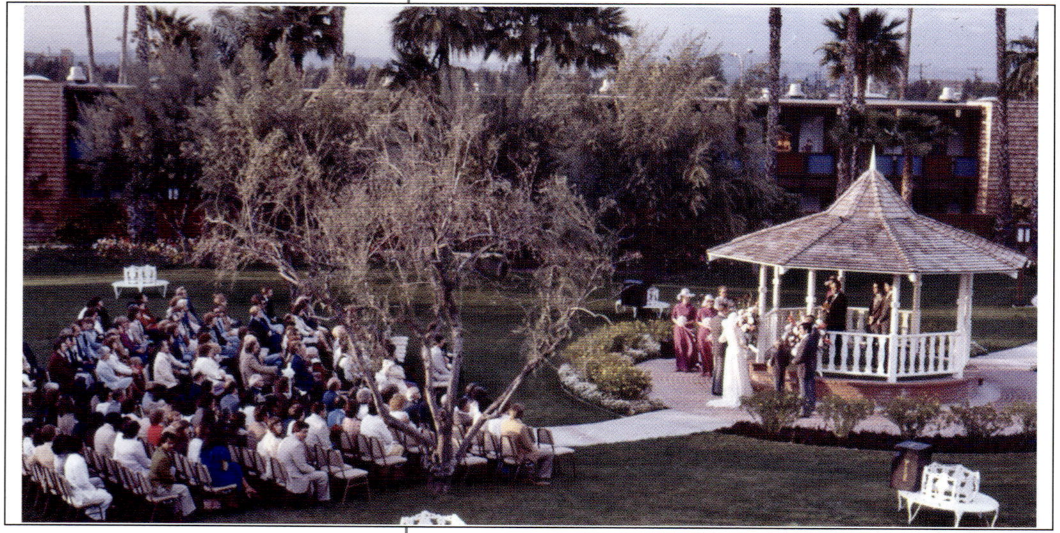

The Gazebo and Rose Garden area.

By late 1981, the Monorail Lounge upstairs at the monorail station had been closed. Opened in November (at ground level in Restaurant Row) was Sgt. Preston's Yukon Saloon. Its name recalled the early television history of Jack Wrather. The goal of this bar was to create a "Gold Rush Days" atmosphere. The interior design and decor was by Singer and Christianson of Beverly Hills. Walls were constructed of old logs and stones; and heavy wood beams crossed the ceiling, seemingly supported by hand-carved totem poles. Indian kayaks were suspended over head; and above the dance floor hung a large Indian tepee. Gathered from antique shops throughout the nation, original Yukon artifacts adorned the walls. An 1836 moose head, a buffalo skin and other trappers' pelts, animal traps, lumberjack saws, snowshoes, and gold panning plates were just some of the items adding to the saloon's authentic atmosphere. Three Frederick Remington oil paintings depicted the Royal Mounted Police and the Alaskan landscapes. Cafe-curtains hung at each window. In the center of the room was an elevated brass-rail bar. Drinks and snacks were served to tables on a thick slab of wood, cut from a tree trunk.

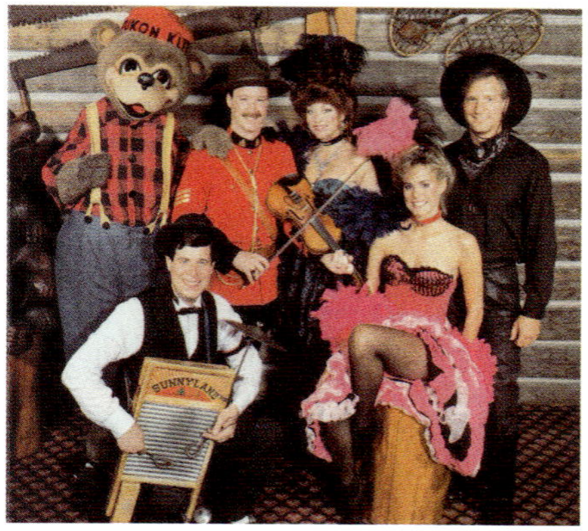

The cast of Sgt. Preston's.

Throughout the evening, the bartenders and the waitresses provided impromptu entertainment, including music hall songs, can-can dances, sketches, slapstick, and jokes. A banjo, a fiddle, and an old upright piano provided the musical accompaniment. Staff member's ID badges bore such colorful names as Sourdough Sam, Pierre Z. Trapper, Payday Polly, Dangerous Dan, Bonanza Babe, Running Bear...to name just a few. The saloon's Madame (hostess) was Klondike Kate. At unscheduled times, she would spin the wheel-of-fortune to determine happy hour or special drink prices. Even Sgt. Preston would make an appearance, wearing his bright red Mounty coat and tall back boots. He was there to keep order among the revelers and to sing a few songs. During the evening, contests were held to determine the "best darned garter grabber," the "hairiest chest," the "hairiest legs," or the best drinker in the house. House Shooters (drinks) included Firewater: a shot of flaming 101 proof green chartreuse and a shot of 151 proof rum; The Frostbite: a shot each of Yukon Jack and Peppermint Schnapps; The Buzz Saw: tequila, sweet and sour, with a splash of 7-Up; and Sgt. Preston's Salute: a 32 ounce mug of beer. Instead of in a lady's slipper, champagne was served in a miner's boot.

By 1982, Orange County was growing faster than any other county in California. Its economy had become the thirtieth largest in the world...ahead of such nations as Denmark, Israel, Egypt, and Portugal. At one time, more than 80,000 acres had been covered with orange groves. By 1982, there were fewer than 8,000 acres of orange trees. Albert Wolf, a descendant of the original German settlers of Anaheim, stated that "Orange County is becoming swarmed over with people, cars, houses, and office buildings. Pretty soon the only orange trees you'll be able to see will be in museums. We'll have to change the name from Orange County to People County." Mayor Don Roth of Anaheim (population, 225,000) stated, "Agriculture is going by the wayside. That's progress. Land here is too valuable to be used for agriculture." In 1982, agricultural land in the county sold for between $3,000 and $6,000 per acre. An acre of land that was zoned for business sold for between $150,000 and $500,000. In 1960, Orange County's population had been 500,000...by 1982, it had grown to 2.2-million.

In June of 1982, Passports replaced Ticket Books at Disneyland. On October 1st, EPCOT Center opened in Florida. At the Disneyland Hotel in June, the Off-Road Raceway (remote control model dune buggies) was added just to the south of the Sierra Tower. The system was manufactured and installed by Thola Productions of Laguna Hills, California, who would later create the Queen's Berth tugboats. By June, Michael Bullis had become the new general manager at the Hotel.

Due to Disneyland now using Passports instead of ticket books, Gold Key Vacation packages were no longer offered in 1982. Five night packages started at $181, four night packages started at $149, three night packages started at $114 and two night packages started at $77-all prices were per adult, double occupancy. The Jolly Roger Inn was added to the list of participating hotels. Rates depended on which hotel was selected and were in effect all year long.

In the fall of 1982, Walt Disney Productions in conjunction with Westinghouse Broadcasting (Group W)) announced the Disney Channel, a 16-hour-a-day pay cable service dedicated to programming for children and the entire family. Group W and Disney initially committed $100 million to program development for the project. Service debuted in April of 1983.

In 1982, remodeling and renovation projects at the Hotel and several additions in the area of entertainment cost over $10-million. During the year, the Hotel experienced a drop in the number of guests; due to increased prices, profits increased substantially over the previous year.

Magic Kingdom Club package rates for 1983 were as follows: five night packages $339 to $655, four night packages $305 to $527, three night packages $229 to $395 and two night packages $153 to $265. These rates were quoted for a family of four with the higher rates applied to the Disneyland Hotel. New, budget minded hotels (at the low end of the rate amount) included the Concord Inn, the Anaheim Park Motor Inn, the Anaheim

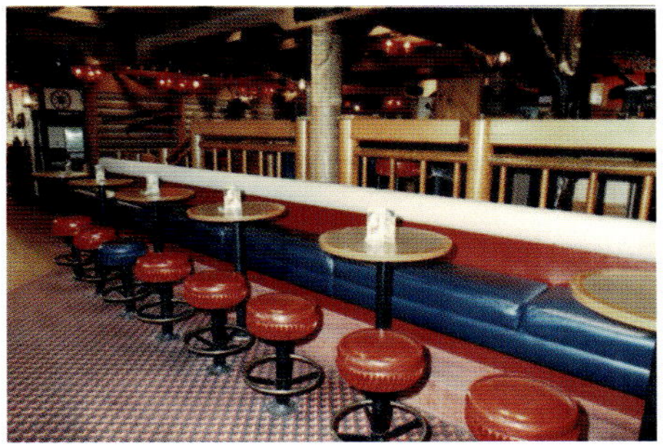

Interior & exterior views of Sgt. Preston's.

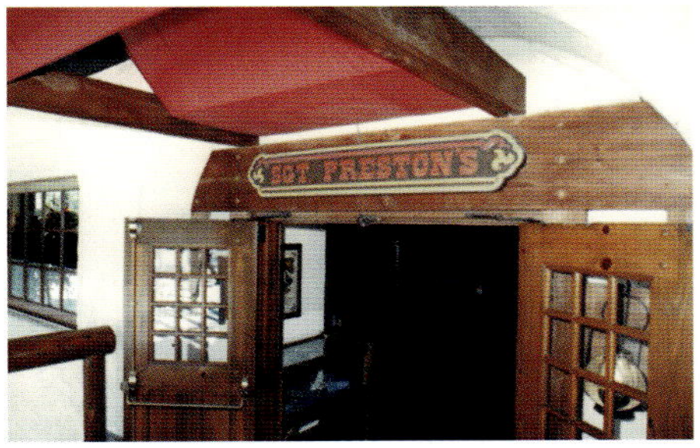

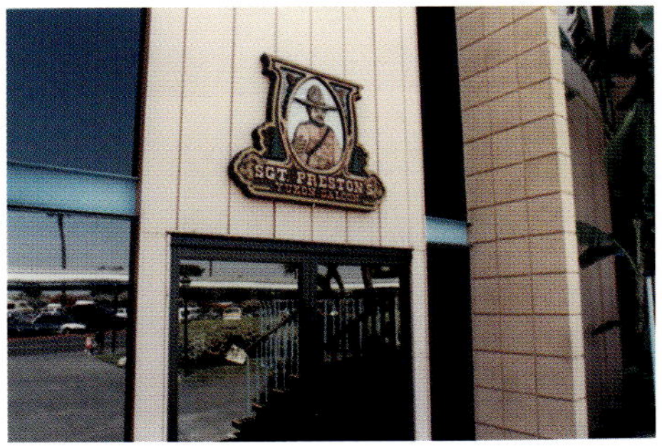

International Inn and the Ramada Inn. Substantial reduced rates were available in the off-season April 4 through May 16 and September 6 through December 15.

In December, the Atari Adventure was opened below water level of the marina. It contained 63 state-of-the-art video games. Access was at the dock in front of the Marina Tower at the north end of the marina. A year before, the marina had been drained to allow for the construction of the game room's walls. This was only the second such Atari video game room in the nation. The room's manager, Dick Reynolds stated: "It is probably the best looking game room in the entire United States." The room was dimly illuminated by hundreds of tiny lights. The plush decor included deep pile red carpet, accented with brass railings. The room was open from early morning until midnight. Above the video room, private parties could be booked on the dock. Cocktail parties, receptions, and other "special" events took place in a Las Vegas theme.

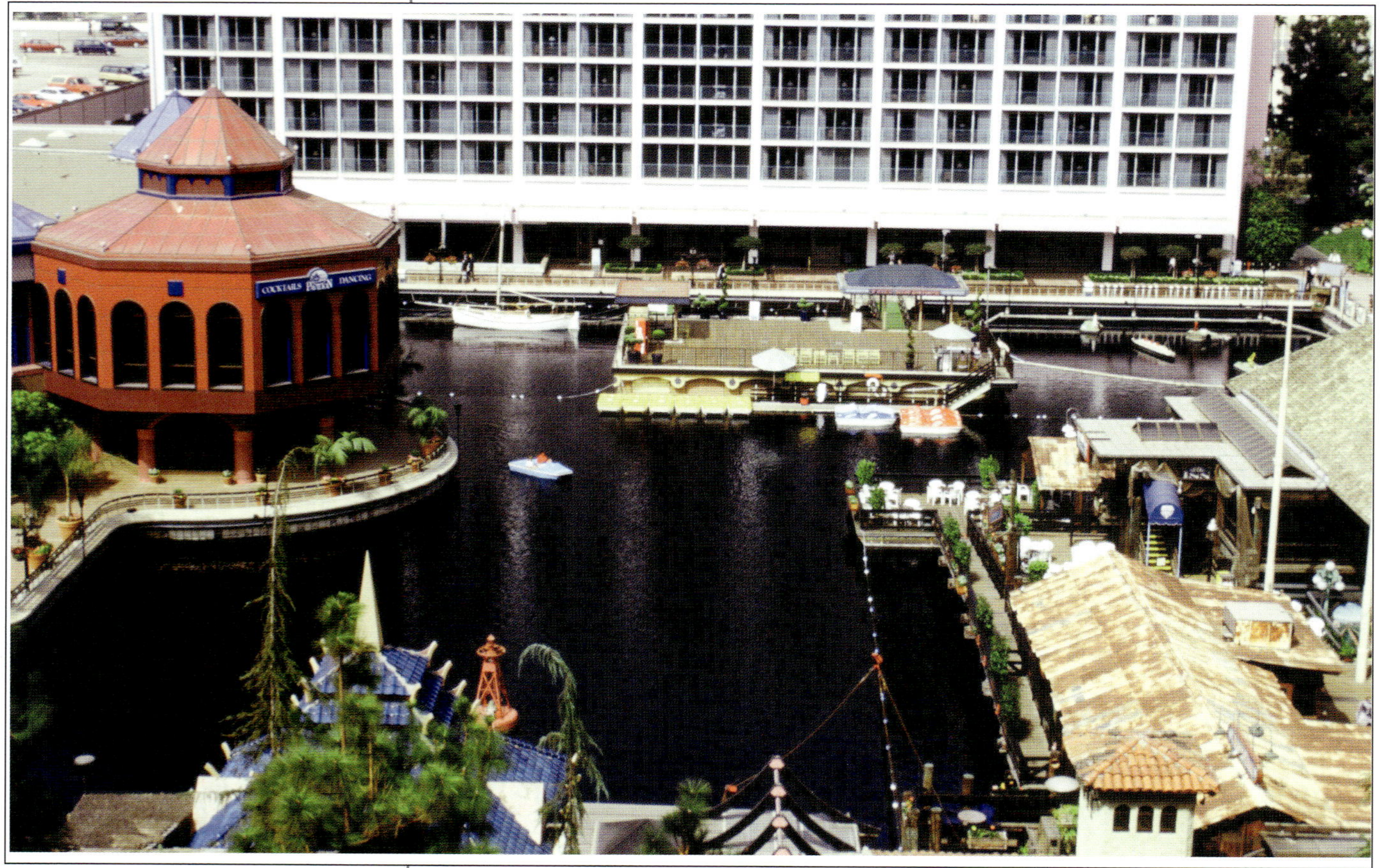

Aerial view of the Marina and Pavilion Lounge.

On April 15, 1983, Tokyo Disneyland was opened. On May 25th, the New Fantasyland was opened at Disneyland. Across the street at the Hotel, as part of a $14-million expansion plan, the meeting and convention facilities' total floor space was increased to 160-thousand square feet (becoming the largest convention resort in all of southern California). Also added and connected to the Convention Center were two distinctive restaurants and two new lounges.

In April, refurbishing of the Bonita Tower began. This was a continuation of an on going program begun in 1980 to redecorate and upgrade all of the Disneyland Hotel's 1,121 rooms and suites.

Opened on July 1st, at the base of an octagonal-shaped structure at the southeast corner of the Convention Center, the Italian themed Caffe Villa Verde offered a wide selection of homemade pasta dishes. The restaurant had a 280-seat capacity on the inside and a sidewalk patio providing service for an additional forty persons. Outside, over-looking the marina, patrons dined while seated on wooden benches and chairs. Inside, the kitchen pantry provided a display of freshly prepared breads, pastries, and pastas. Here one could enjoy homemade ice cream while surrounded by an authentic Italian tile decor. The restaurant was highlighted by brick archways, stucco walls, and Italian tile accents.

Located next to the Caffe Villa Verde was the newly opened Top Brass Lounge. Directly above that restaurant, on the second floor of the tri-level complex was the new Pavilion Lounge. Entered by means of a wide, tall flight of stairs from the marina area, the lounge was opened nightly for cocktails and dancing. Overlooking the illuminated marina, the Pavilion also provided a thrilling view of the Park's "Fantasy in the Sky" fireworks display and a spectacular view of the Hotel's Dancing Waters show and the Still Green laser sculpture display.

The second (more formal) restaurant was opened on July 20th. Located next to the Caffe Villa Verde and to the rear of the Convention Center's southeast corner, Granville's Steak House (using Bonita Wrather's maiden name) was a first class restaurant, seating one-hundred patrons. Granville's celebrated the finest of Americana regional cuisine. Vegetables were served family-style. An interesting and novel feature of the menu allowed a diner to sample two of the regional specialities of the house by ordering two half-entrees on the same plate.

A twenty-two day strike highlighted 1984 at Disneyland. A two-year freeze in wages and cuts in fringe benefits were rejected by 1,800 of the Parks' employees. The Country Bear Christmas Show premiered in November. After several bitter battles to save the company from hostile take-over attempts, Michael D. Eisner and Frank G. Wells became the new management team of Walt Disney Productions on September 23, 1984. This major change at Disney was partially orchestrated by Roy E. Disney (Walt's nephew and the son of Roy O. Disney, co-founder of the company). The installation of new management would lead to increased efforts to acquire the Disneyland Hotel.

Magic Kingdom Club package rates for 1984 were as follows: five night packages $429-$681, four night packages $343 to $543, three night packages $255-$405 and two night packages $169 to $269. These rates were quoted again for a family of four. Lower rates were available during the off-season. Luxury hotels were listed as The Disneyland Hotel and the Anaheim Marriott. Dollar-wise (budget) hotels added were the Town and Country Inn, Zaby's Motor Lodge, Sandman Inn and the Stardust Motel.

At the Disneyland Hotel, things also had become a little more raucous in March of 1984. For its gala Saint Patrick's Day Grand Opening, Sgt. Preston's Yukon Saloon had been expanded and renamed Sgt. Preston's Yukon Saloon and Dancehall, debuting the lively Sgt. Preston's Yukon Follies (reminiscent of the 1890's gold rush days). For this twice nightly revue, over 300 seats were available. Guests were entertained by the antics of Dapper Dan, Klondike Kate, Yukon Jack, and a dancing bear, named Yukon Klem. The expansion had doubled the Saloon's size by incorporating those areas formerly occupied by the Oak Room and by the Crown and Pillow. There was a bigger stage and an improved lighting system to showcase the nightly entertainment. The new and larger bar area included kitchen facilities, allowing snacks to be served that would compliment the drinks and the entertainment provided at Sgt. Preston's. The expanded facility also provided a dance area for late night patrons. [On May 25, 1992, Sgt. Preston's Yukon Follies would be replaced by the Neon Cactus lounge.]

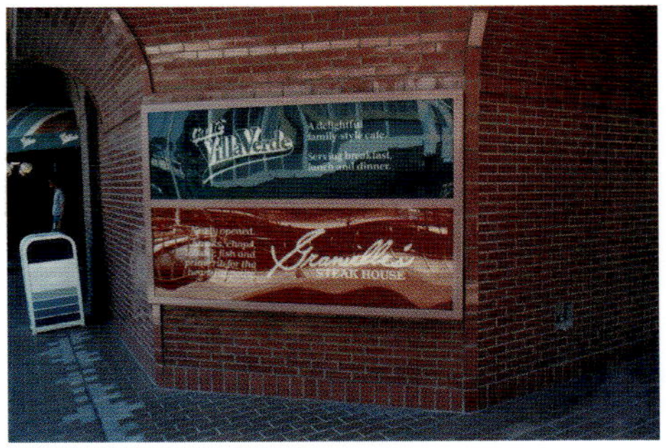

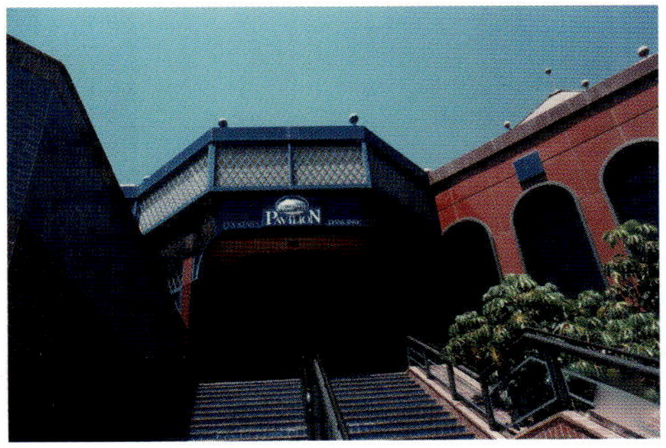

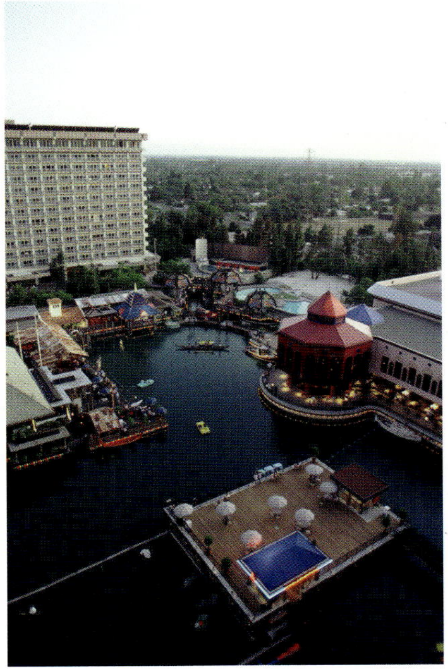

New features for 1983 at the Disneyland Hotel

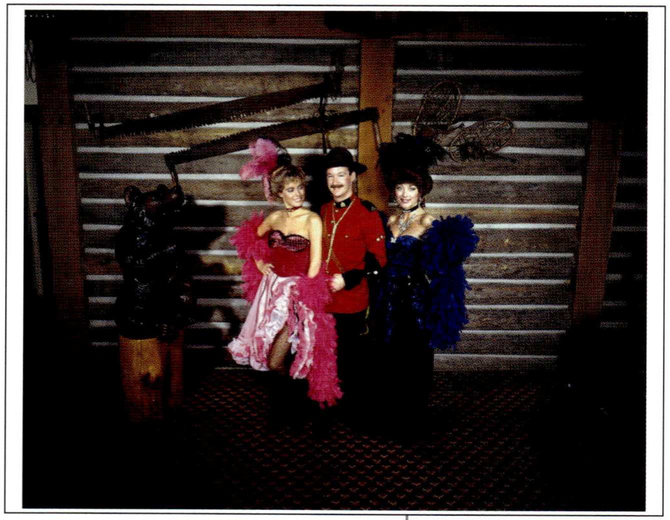

The cast of Sgt. Preston's Yukon Follies stage show.

By May of 1984, the Hotel's West Street entrance had undergone a major facelift. This multi-million dollar remodeling project was aimed at improving the appearance of the eastern entrance to the Hotel. One of the first steps in the renovation of the Plaza area had been the relocation of the Airport Service Bus Terminal, thereby improving the traffic flow for both vehicles and Hotel guests. The terminal was moved from its previous location on the first floor beneath the monorail station to the far south end of the West Street parking lot. Covered waiting areas, a small ticket office, and pick-up/drop-off zones were all part of this new terminal. The project would not be completed until November.

A beautiful pedestrian area with lush landscaping was added in the area where visitors arrived and departed the Hotel on Disneyland trams. Officially named the Monorail Plaza, the new facade of the buildings had a Victorian theme and was decorated in bright blues and reds. Three porticos were designed to resemble those to be seen on the Convention Center's expansion roof. A quaint clocktower was added to the Plaza area so as to give the area a Disneyland Main Street theme.

At the marina, the Queen's Berth was launched. Located in the northeast corner, it consisted of twenty-two remote control tugboats that could be maneuvered around an exact scale model of the *Queen Mary* ocean liner. Nearby in the North Sierra Tower, a refurbishment of its 150 rooms had been completed by early summer. In June, renovations also were completed on the Hotel's four deluxe suites.

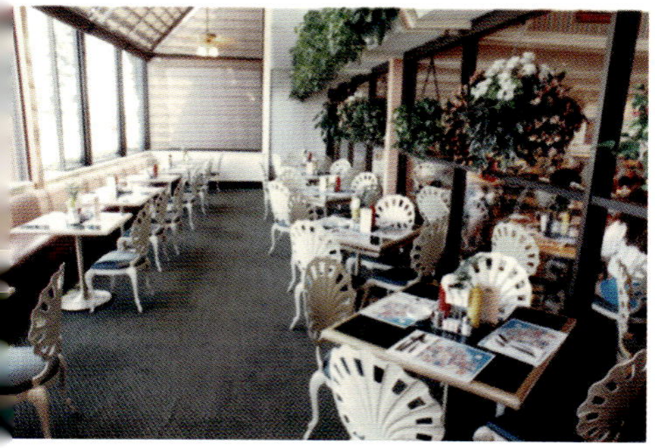

Coffee Shop atrium.

By September, the Coffee Shop had received an extensive facelift. A beautiful domed ceiling, a picturesque atrium, and a redesigned terrace for outdoor dining had been added to the restaurant. At the same time, both the 11,250 square foot Embassy Ballroom and the 9,200 square foot Magnolia Room were remodeled and redecorated. Redecoration of the entrance lobby and the main staircase to the second floor convention/banquet area was included in this project.

December of 1984 witnessed the continuation of the many honors that the Hotel had received during its nearly three decade history. For a second year in a row, the Hotel received the Mobil Four Star rating and for the fourth straight year, the Automobile Club Four Diamond rating was received. Meetings and Conventions Magazine honored the Hotel with its Gold Key "for excellence in its meeting facilities, food and beverage service, accommodations and guest services." Corporate Meetings and Incentives Magazine declared that the Disneyland Hotel was one of the "Ten Best Hotels for 1984 for Excellence."

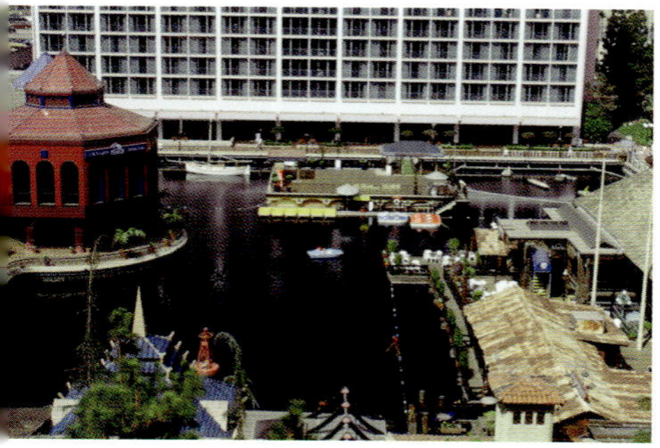

Queen's Berth upper right.

By early 1984, Disney was facing some bad times. Two hostile attempts had been made to take-over the company. Ray Watson (Chairman of the Board) had suggested to Ron Miller (CEO, but only for a few more months) that acquisitions were a way to help protect the company. At that time, several possibilities were discussed, among them were ABC television and the Wrather company. On Wednesday, June 6, 1984, Watson met with Jack Wrather. Having recently fallen into ill health, Wrather finally relented. However, before negotiations could begin, Wrather passed away in November.

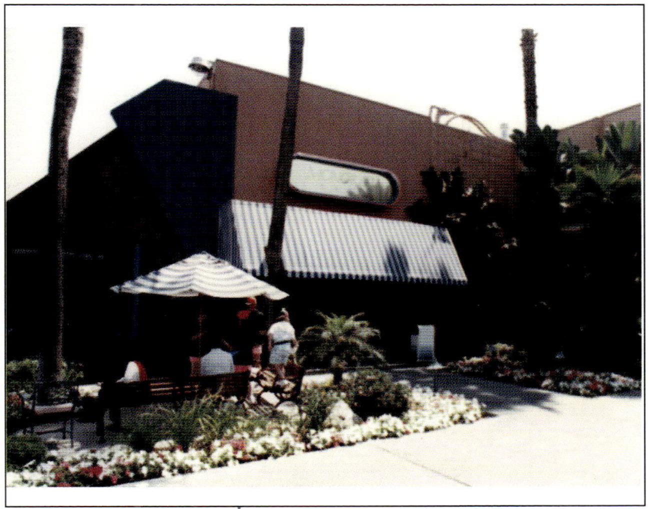

At Disneyland on August 24, 1985, Brooks Charles Arthur Burr became the 250-millionth guest of the Park during its thirty year history. Starting January 1st, the Disneyland Gift-Giver Extraordinaire Machine began an actual countdown of each guest walking through the Park's turnstiles. Gifts and prizes (ranging from a Disneyland one-day passport all the way to a brand-new Cadillac Sedan de Ville) were awarded to guests arriving corresponding to the magic number "30." That same year, "year-'round, 7-day operation" began. Videopolis had been opened in June. On December 5th, the City of Anaheim celebrated the 30th Anniversary of Disneyland with Skyfest, the release of more than 1-million helium filled balloons, nearly tripling the previous entry in the Guinness Book of World Records. The event took place on the 84th birthday of the Park's founder, Walter Elias Disney.

Magic Kingdom Club package rates for 1985 (again quoted for a family of four) were as follows: five night packages $382 to $694, four night packages $306 to $556, three night packages $230 to $418 and two night packages $154 to $280. The summer season was listed as June 1 to August 31 when higher rates were applicable.

The next year in mid-1986, the Coffee House (originating in the earliest days of the Hotel) was renamed the Monorail Cafe. In January of that same year, the newly landscaped Oriental Gardens area was opened. Above the Pirates of the Caribbean at the Park, the Disney Gallery was opened. The Gallery area had originally been designed and decorated as a private apartment complex for the Disney family but was never been completed or utilized as such. The premiere display at the Gallery was "The Art of Disneyland: 1953-1986," showcasing conceptual artwork, designs, and models created during the planning of and the expansions of the Park over a period of more than three decades. This exhibition was the first time that most of those creative works of art had been seen by the public. In February, the Country Bear Vacation Hoedown premiered; and in September, the 3-D film Captain EO premiered at Disneyland. In 1987, the Mark V monorail trains debuted with fiberglass bodies, improved suspension, and computer controls.

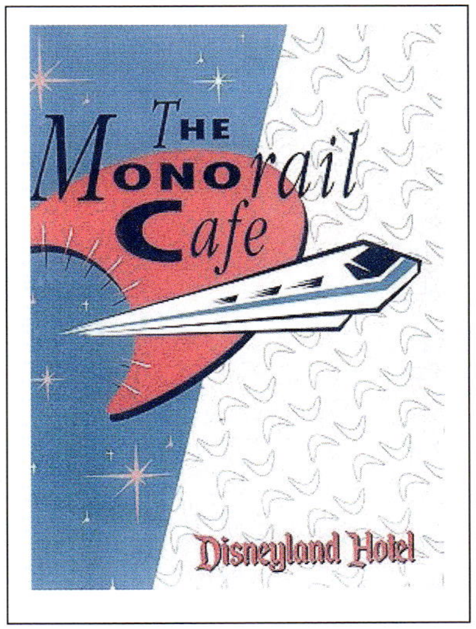

The Monorail Café opened in 1986.

Walt Disney always had been extremely grateful to Jack Wrather for aiding him in 1954 when money ran short and Walt could not build a hotel across the street from his Park. In his time, Walt would never hear of any suggestions to attempt to gain ownership of the Disneyland Hotel or to renegotiate the 99-year lease on the property. Some years after Walt's death in 1966, the Disney company began numerous attempts to purchase control of the Hotel. For many years, the Wrather company resisted all such offers.

Future attempts were rejected by the new management at Wrather but fortunes were changing for the Corporation. Due to declining profits, the Wrather company had been forced to sell off its oil and gas holdings, and eventually it was forced to sell off the rights to its old television series.

Looking toward the possibility of eventually selling the Disneyland Hotel, the Wrather Corporation retained the firm of Hospitality Valuation Services, Inc., based in New York and well respected as "hotel appraisers, ana-

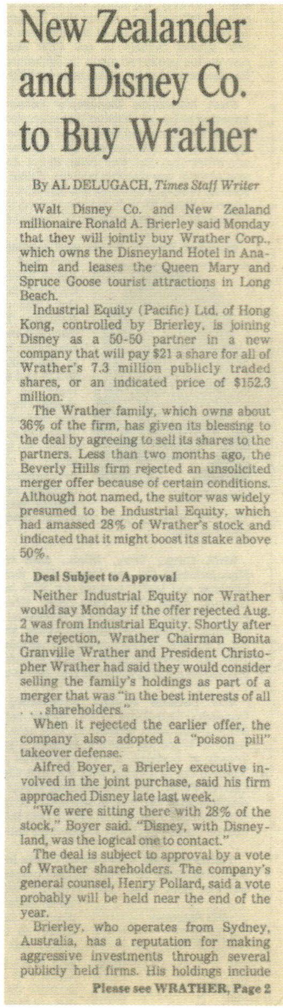

New Zealander and Disney Co. to Buy Wrather

By AL DELUGACH, *Times Staff Writer*

Walt Disney Co. and New Zealand millionaire Ronald A. Brierley said Monday that they will jointly buy Wrather Corp., which owns the Disneyland Hotel in Anaheim and leases the Queen Mary and Spruce Goose tourist attractions in Long Beach.

Industrial Equity (Pacific) Ltd. of Hong Kong, controlled by Brierley, is joining Disney as a 50-50 partner in a new company that will pay $21 a share for all of Wrather's 7.3 million publicly traded shares, or an indicated price of $152.3 million.

The Wrather family, which owns about 36% of the firm, has given its blessing to the deal by agreeing to sell its shares to the partners. Less than two months ago, the Beverly Hills firm rejected an unsolicited merger offer because of certain conditions. Although not named, the suitor was widely presumed to be Industrial Equity, which had amassed 28% of Wrather's stock and indicated that it might boost its stake above 50%.

Deal Subject to Approval

Neither Industrial Equity nor Wrather would say Monday if the offer rejected Aug. 2 was from Industrial Equity. Shortly after the rejection, Wrather Chairman Bonita Granville Wrather and President Christopher Wrather had said they would consider selling the family's holdings as part of a merger that was "in the best interests of all . . . shareholders."

When it rejected the earlier offer, the company also adopted a "poison pill" takeover defense.

Alfred Boyer, a Brierley executive involved in the joint purchase, said his firm approached Disney late last week.

"We were sitting there with 28% of the stock," Boyer said. "Disney, with Disneyland, was the logical one to contact."

The deal is subject to approval by a vote of Wrather shareholders. The company's general counsel, Henry Pollard, said a vote probably will be held near the end of the year.

Brierley, who operates from Sydney, Australia, has a reputation for making aggressive investments through several publicly held firms. His holdings include

Please see WRATHER, Page 2

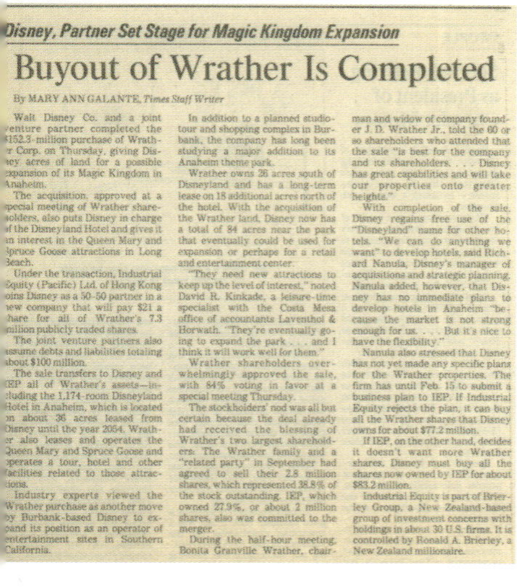

Disney, Partner Set Stage for Magic Kingdom Expansion

Buyout of Wrather Is Completed

By MARY ANN GALANTE, *Times Staff Writer*

Walt Disney Co. and a joint venture partner completed the $152.3-million purchase of Wrather Corp. on Thursday, giving Disney acres of land for a possible expansion of its Magic Kingdom in Anaheim.

The acquisition, approved at a special meeting of Wrather shareholders, also puts Disney in charge of the Disneyland Hotel and gives it an interest in the Queen Mary and Spruce Goose attractions in Long Beach.

Under the transaction, Industrial Equity (Pacific) Ltd. of Hong Kong joins Disney as a 50-50 partner in a new company that will pay $21 a share for all of Wrather's 7.3 million publicly traded shares.

The joint venture partners also assume debts and liabilities totaling about $100 million.

The sale transfers to Disney and IEP all of Wrather's assets—including the 1,174-room Disneyland Hotel in Anaheim, which is located on about 36 acres leased from Disney until the year 2054. Wrather also leases and operates the Queen Mary and Spruce Goose and operates a tour, hotel and other facilities related to those attractions.

Industry experts viewed the Wrather purchase as another move by Burbank-based Disney to expand its position as an operator of entertainment sites in Southern California.

In addition to a planned studio-tour and shopping complex in Burbank, the company has long been studying a major addition to its Anaheim theme park.

Wrather owns 26 acres south of Disneyland and has a long-term lease on 18 additional acres north of the hotel. With the acquisition of the Wrather land, Disney now has a total of 84 acres near the park that eventually could be used for expansion or perhaps for a retail and entertainment center.

"They need new attractions to keep up the level of interest," noted David R. Kinkade, a leisure-time specialist with the Costa Mesa office of accountants Laventhol & Horwath. "They're eventually going to expand the park . . . and I think it will work well for them."

Wrather shareholders overwhelmingly approved the sale, with 84% voting in favor at a special meeting Thursday.

The stockholders' nod was all but certain because the deal already had received the blessing of Wrather's two largest shareholders: The Wrather family and a "related party" in September had agreed to sell their 2.8 million shares, which represented 38.8% of the stock outstanding. IEP, which owned 27.9%, or about 2 million shares, also was committed to the merger.

During the half-hour meeting, Bonita Granville Wrather, chairman and widow of company founder J. D. Wrather Jr., told the 60 or so shareholders who attended that the sale "is best for the company and its shareholders. . . . Disney has great capabilities and will take our properties onto greater heights."

With completion of the sale, Disney regains free use of the "Disneyland" name for other hotels. "We can do anything we want" to develop hotels, said Richard Nanula, Disney's manager of acquisitions and strategic planning. Nanula added, however, that Disney has no immediate plans to develop hotels in Anaheim "because the market is not strong enough for us. . . . But it's nice to have the flexibility."

Nanula also stressed that Disney has not yet made any specific plans for the Wrather properties. The firm has until Feb. 15 to submit a business plan to IEP. If Industrial Equity rejects the plan, it can buy all the Wrather shares that Disney owns for about $77.2 million.

If IEP, on the other hand, decides it doesn't want more Wrather shares, Disney must buy all the shares now owned by IEP for about $83.2 million.

Industrial Equity is part of Brierley Group, a New Zealand-based group of investment concerns with holdings in about 30 U.S. firms. It is controlled by Ronald A. Brierley, a New Zealand millionaire.

lysts, [and] consultants." The 229-page final report was received by Wrather's chief financial officer Roy Rawis on April 5, 1986 and was immediately stamped "CONFIDENTIAL." Having "conducted an inspection of the site and improvements" and having "analyzed the hostelry market conditions in the Anaheim area," the appraisers concluded that the Hotel's fair market value was $173.6-million. However, taking into consideration the Hotel's outstanding debts, the purchase figure was adjusted to $144.8-million, plus the assumption of $28.8-million in debt.

By the middle 1980's, many areas of the Disneyland Hotel were in need of refurbishment. Sid Bass, a major stockholder in the Disney company at that time, pointed out that "Whether you own it or not, when people aren't impressed with the hotel, you'll be the [one] getting the blame." The new management at Disney now made the acquisition of the Disneyland Hotel a major goal.

A much bigger concern developed for Disney in June of 1987 when the news became public that Industrial Equity (a New Zealand firm controlled by Ronald Brierley, a corporate raider) had purchased 28-percent of Wrather and that it intended to purchase at least 50-percent of Wrather. The greatest danger for Disney was that another company (and a foreign company) might gain control of the Disneyland Hotel and control over the right to use the "Disney" name on other hotels in the Southern California area.

Disney's next offers to Wrather to purchase the remainder of the company were refused as being too low. To prevent Wrather from selling to someone else, Disney reminded the company that the monorail's leasing contract was soon due for renegotiation. The unstated threat was that Disney could make the Hotel less desirable to a potential buyer by increasing the leasing cost of the monorail to an exorbitant amount, making it unlikely that anyone else would desire to purchase it.

The monorail "threat" caused great concern inside the Wrather company. At the time, plans were being formulated to build an exhibit hall on the acres Wrather had added in 1977 on the southern boundary of the 60-acres originally leased from Disney. CEO Chris Wrather was concerned "that the unresolved Disneyland Hotel monorail agreement could be a source of difficulty in connection with the refinancing of [a] loan" to allow that future construction. The Disney strategy seemingly had complicated any plans that Wrather might have had to sell to a third party and any plans for further development of the Hotel's property.

Next, Disney approached the New Zealand firm with the proposition of a joint buy-out of Wrather. After months of negotiations, on September 27, 1987, Disney and Industrial agreed that each would become 50-50 owners (with the one major stipulation that Disney would have total control over the Disneyland Hotel and its other Anaheim properties). That deal cost Disney $76-million. Six months later, Disney purchased Industrial Equity's 50-percent of Wrather for an additional $85-million. In the end, the total deal to gain control of the Disneyland Hotel had cost the Disney company $161-million, plus the assumption of $89-million of Wrather debts.

In January of 1988, thirty-three years after the original groundbreaking, the Disneyland Hotel became a portion of the entertainment empire that Walt Disney had founded.

The Disneyland Hotel had grown from 104 guest rooms and a smattering of amenities into a major tourist facility with well over a thousand guest rooms, varied dining and shopping experiences, and a full range of convention and meeting facilities. The Hotel also helped to introduce a futuristic mode of rapid transit in the form of the monorail. Thanks to Walt and Jack's belief in following their dreams, Anaheim had grown to become a major international recreation, convention and travel destination. Jack Wrather's master plan guided the Disneyland Hotel through three decades of innovative development, while contributing to the growth of Anaheim and Orange County and supporting his friend's dream of Disneyland. From a mere 87 rooms in 1954, the city now offered over 18,000 guest accommodations. From a town of only 881 in 1876, it had grown into a major city of over a quarter million. What had appeared to be a questionable area for development in the early 1950's had been turned into one of the most dynamic economic areas in the United States. A very large portion of that change and growth had been stimulated by a man with a mouse and a Texas wildcatter.

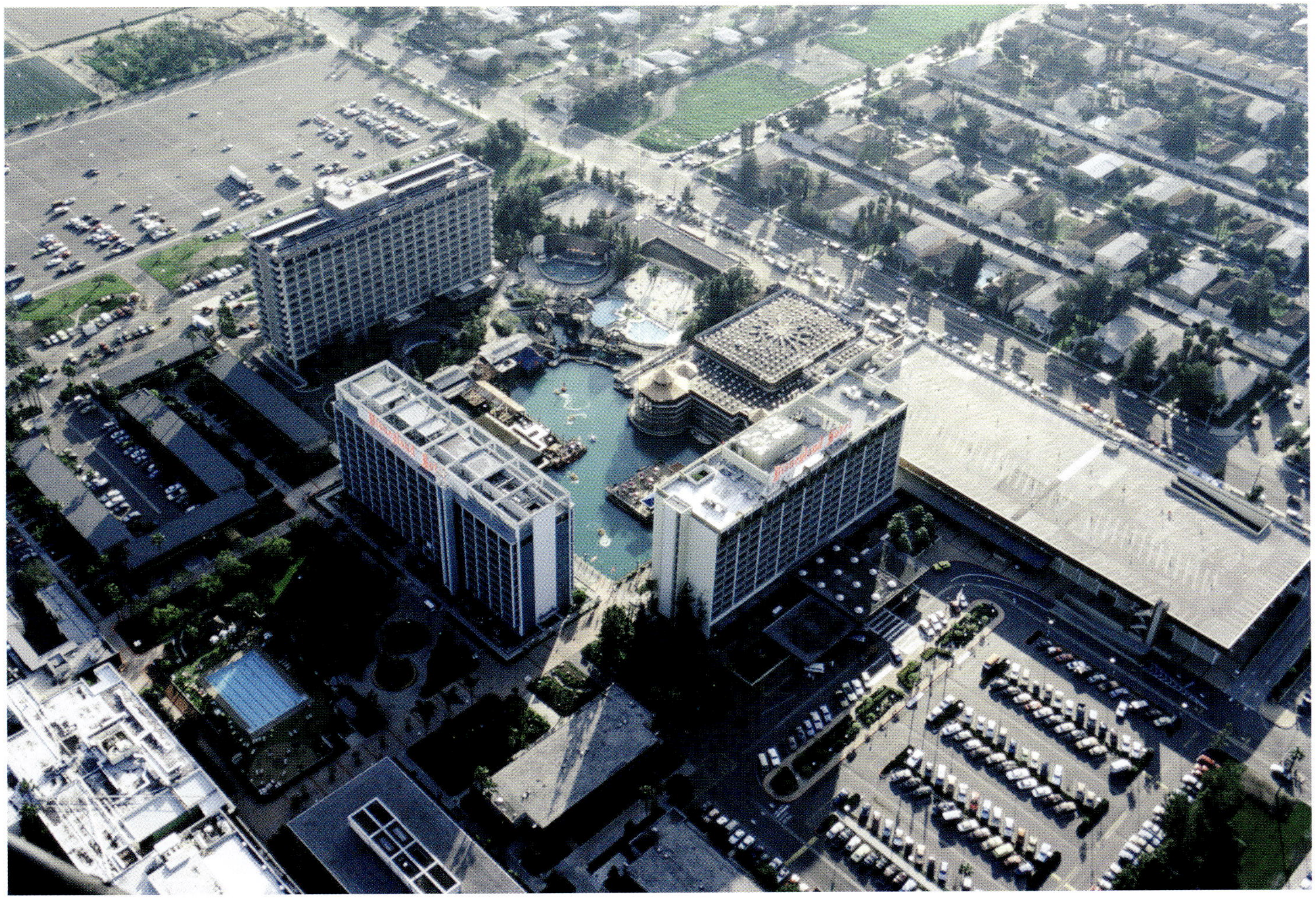

AN EPILOGUE

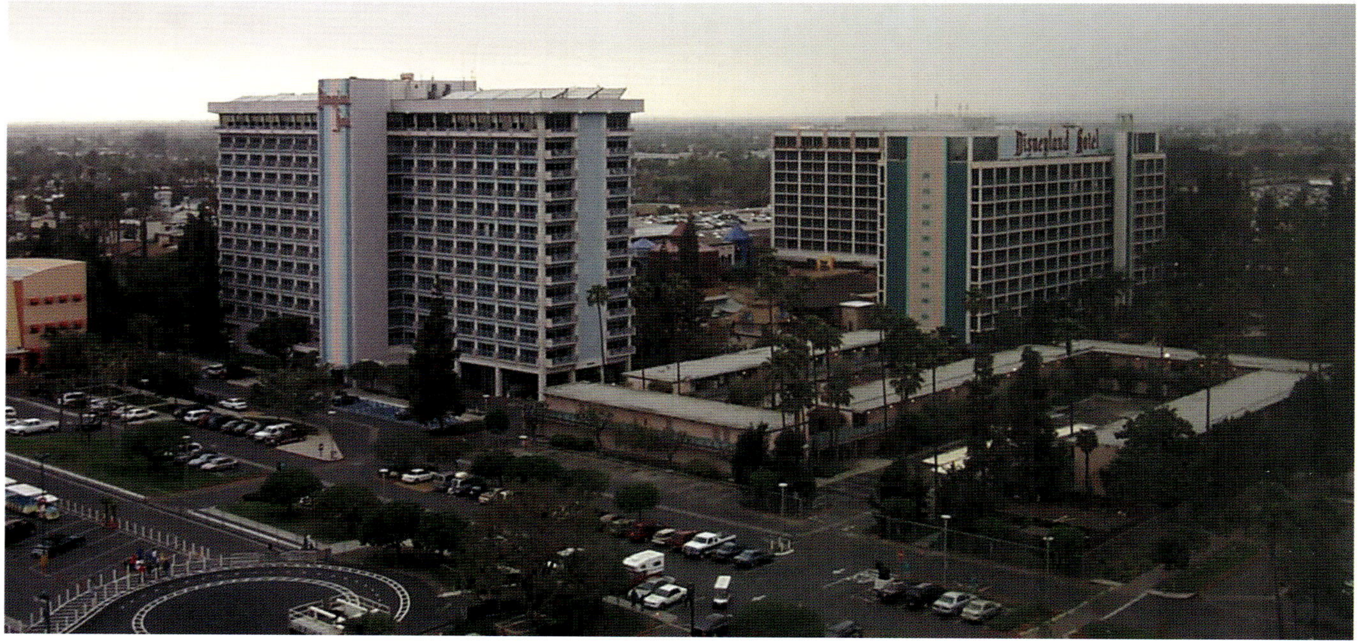

Near the end for the original five guest accommodation structures dating back to 1955.

Beginning in 1999, eleven years after the Walt Disney Company had acquired ownership of the Disneyland Hotel, entire portions of the oldest sections of the Hotel were demolished. As is too often the case, the "old" must give way for the "new." Disney was in the process of turning a major section of Disneyland's old parking lot into a new theme park (Disney's California Adventure) and adding a new hotel (Disney's Grand Californian Hotel). On the remainder of the old parking lot a lavish shopping, dining, and entertainment area (Downtown Disney) was being constructed. To accommodate some of this new development, the oldest buildings of the Disneyland Hotel had to give way.

The "wrecking ball of progress" fell first upon all of the two-story guest room structures in the Northeast section of the Disneyland Hotel. Dating to the Hotel's opening in 1955, the five southern guest room structures (later to be known as the Oriental Gardens) were then demolished. As a result, the Disneyland Hotel was reduced to 990 guest rooms. This was the least number of guest rooms available since before the addition of the second tower building at the beginning of 1970.

Next, the Hotel's lengthy, two-story structure along West Street also had to go. The site of the Gourmet and the long-time popular Coffee House (and all of the area that had been developed into Restaurant Row by 1970), ceased to exist. Anaheim's first ballroom, the Embassy Room, was also gone. Gone too were the Olympic size pool, the Monorail Cafe and the Plaza Complex building. With all this now gone, a great deal of the earliest history of the Wrather years would be lost. Even West Street itself would cease to exist when it was official designated Disneyland Drive. [The Hotel's address now would be changed to 1150 Magic Way (a new road farther to the north). The portion of West Cerritos Avenue that had run in front of the Hotel's Marina Tower was completely eliminated.] What Jack Wrather had affectionately referred to as his "little motel in the middle of the orange grove" soon became a mere memory.

Replacing Restaurant Row...a twelve theatre multi-plex. Replacing the Plaza Building shops...a sports bar. And replacing the South Garden Rooms...a parking lot.

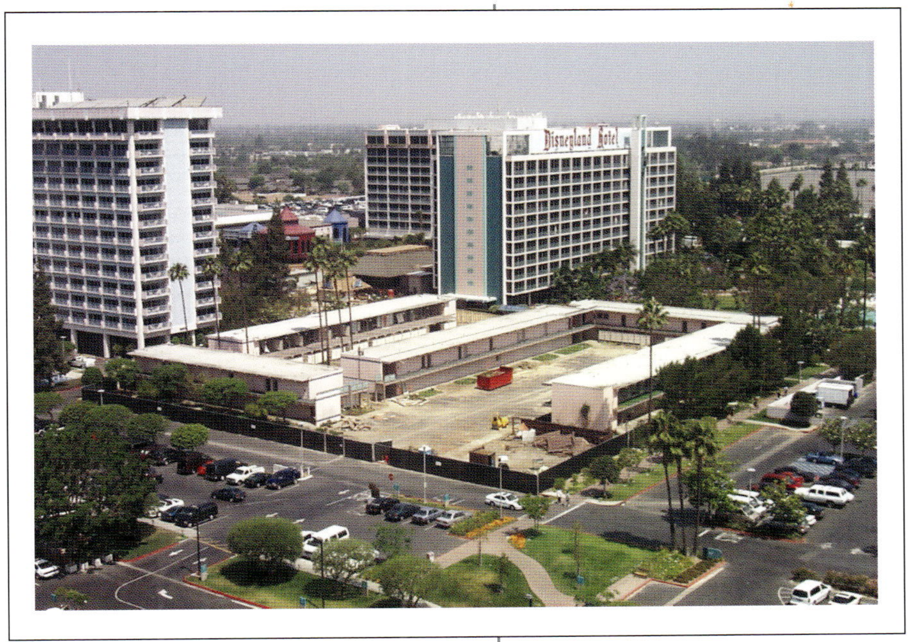

Fenced for demolition June 1999.

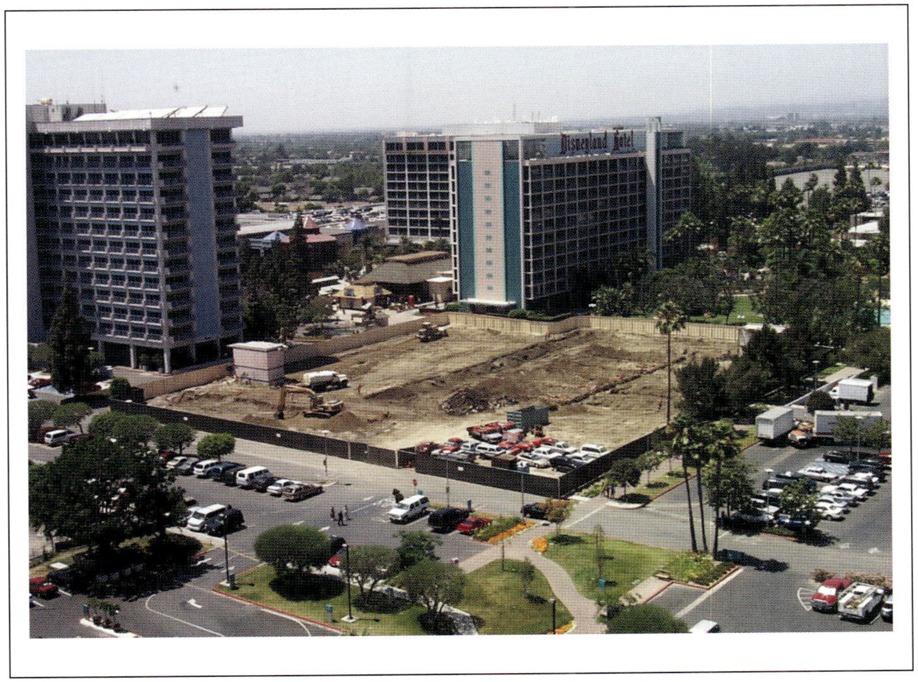

Demolished and leveled...

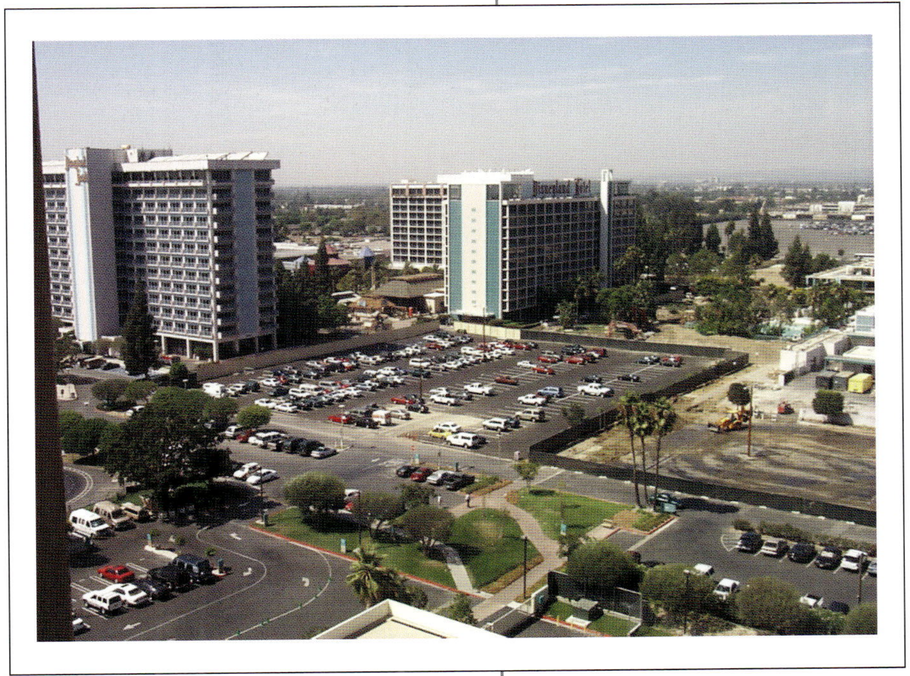

...and paved over into a parking lot.

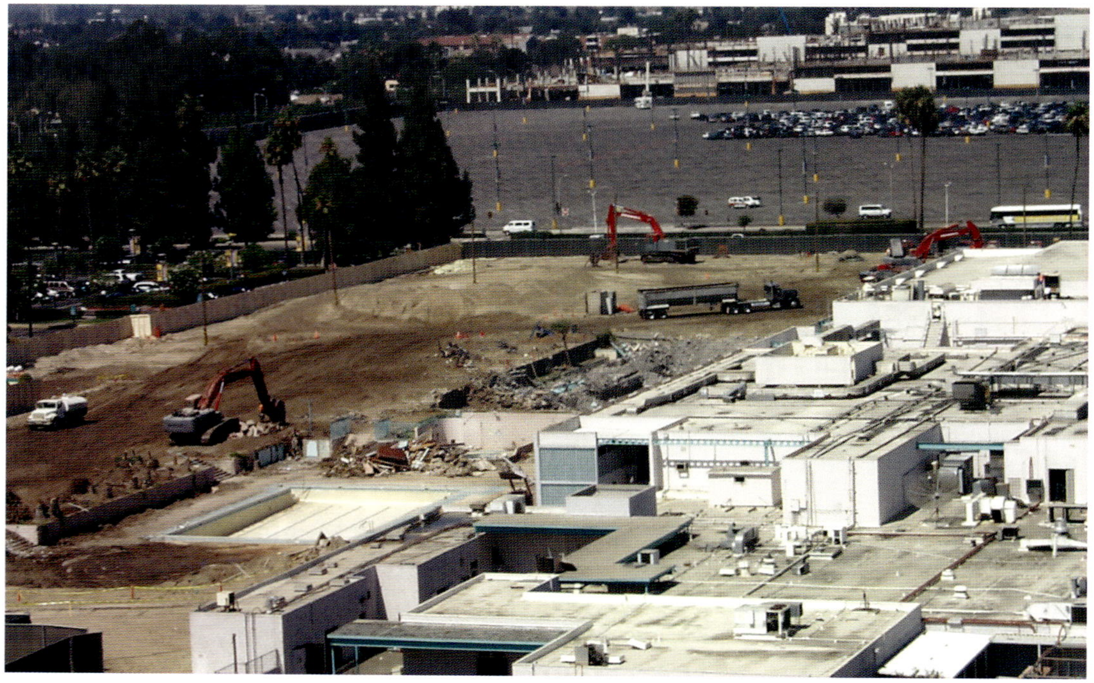

Demolition underway on remaining structures.

The only structure to survive this onslaught of expansion was part of the second story of the Monorail Station (that had welcomed its first train load of passengers in 1961). That building was significantly remodeled and reopened to monorail service in 2001.

In 1999, in a matter of a few short months, most of the Hotel's earliest history was erased...paved over and landscaped. As Joni Mitchell's 1970 hit song so aptly put it: "*Don't it always seem to go / That you don't know what you've got 'til it's gone / They paved paradise and put up a parking lot.*"

For the millions of Hotel guests, who over the years have received numerous pleasures, great joy, and lasting memories from the Wrathers' meticulous care in planning and untiring efforts to continually improve the Disneyland Hotel, a great deal of thanks and gratitude is extended.

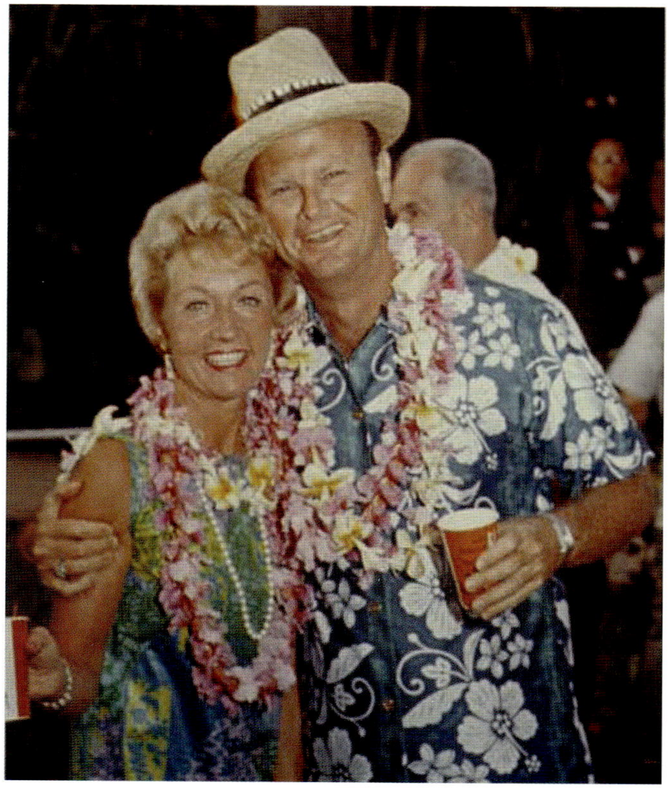

Jack and Bonita Wrather.

Bonita Granville Filmography

Bonita Granville appeared in fifty-six feature films during her acting career. Over a two decade period, she worked at most of the major studios in Hollywood. Following is a complete listing [*movie title,* (studio), character played] of her acting credits:

1932

Westward Passage (RKO)...young Olivia Allen (age 9)

Silver Dollar (Warner Brothers)...Liddy

1933

Cavalcade (Fox)...young Fanny Bridges

Little Women (Warner Brothers)...Amy's classmate

Cradle Song (Paramount)...uncredited bit part

1934

Anne of Green Gables (Allied Artist)...uncredited girl

A Wicked Woman (MGM)...girl on train, scenes deleted

The Life of Vergie Winters (RKO)...young Joan Winters

1935

Ah, Wilderness! (MGM)...Mildred Miller

1936

These Three (United Artists)...Mary Tilford

Song of the Saddle (Warner Brothers)...young Jen

The Plough and the Stars (RKO)...Mollser Gogan

The Garden of Allah (United Artists)...girl in convent

1937

Maid of Salem (Paramount)...Ann Goode

Call It a Day (Warner Brothers)...Ann Hilton

Quality Street (RKO)...uncredited Isabella playing piano

It's Love I'm After (Warner Brothers)...Gracie Kane

1938

Merrily We Live (MGM)...Marian Kilbourne

Beloved Brat (Warner Brothers)...Roberta Morgan

(aka *A Dangerous Affair* and *A Dangerous Age*)

White Banners (Warner Brothers)...Sally Ward

My Bill (Warner Brothers)...Gwendolyn Colbrook

Hard to Get (Warner Brothers)...Connie Richards

Nancy Drew, Detective (Warner Brothers)...Nancy Drew

1939

The Angels Wash Their Faces (Warner Brothers)...Peggy Finnegan

Nancy Drew, Reporter (Warner Brothers)...Nancy Drew

Nancy Drew, Trouble Shooter (Warner Brothers)...Nancy Drew

Nancy Drew and the Hidden Staircase (Warner Bros.)...Nancy Drew

1940

Forty Little Mothers (MGM)...Doris

Those Were the Days (Paramount)...Martha Scroggs

(aka *At Good Old Siwash* and *Good Old Schooldays*)

The Mortal Storm (MGM)...Elsa

Third Finger, Left Hand (MGM)...Vicky Sherwood

Escape (MGM)...Ursula

(aka *When the Door Opened*)

Gallant Sons (MGM)...Kate Pendleton

1941

The People vs. Dr. Kildare (MGM)...Frances Marlow

(aka *My Life Is Yours*)

The Wild Man of Borneo (MGM)...Francine Diamond

Down in San Diego (MGM)...Betty Haines

H.M. Pulham, Esq. (MGM)...Mary Pulham

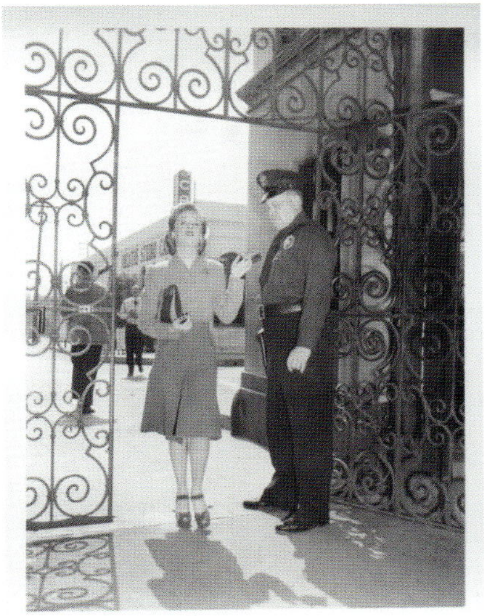

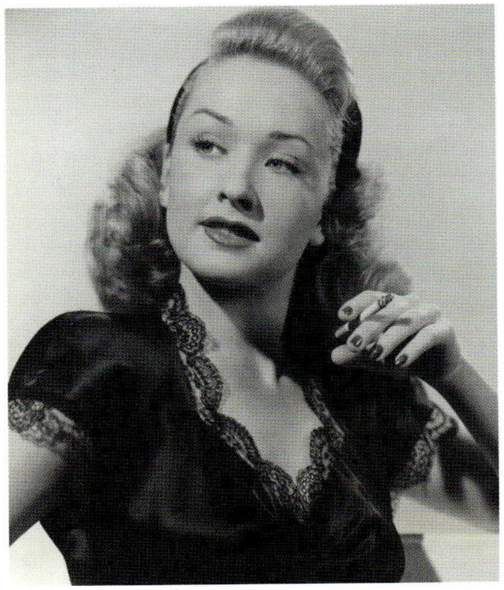

1942

Syncopation (RKO)...Kit Latimer

The Glass Key (Paramount)...Opal Madvig

Now, Voyager (Warner Brothers)...June Vale

Seven Miles from Alcatraz (RKO)...Anne Porter

1943

Hitler's Children (RKO)...Anna Muller

1944

Song of the Open Road (United Artists)...Bonnie

Andy Hardy's Blonde Trouble (MGM)...Kay Wilson

Youth Runs Wild (RKO)...Toddy

1945

Senorita from the West (Universal)...Jeanne Blake

1946

The Beautiful Cheat (Universal)...Alice
(aka *What a Women!*)

The Truth About Murder (RKO)...Chris Allen
(aka *The Lie Detector*)

Breakfast in Hollywood (United Artists)...Dorothy Larson
(aka *The Mad Hatter*)

Suspense (Monogram)...Roni

1947

Love Laughs at Andy Hardy (MGM)...Kay Wilson
(aka *Uncle Andy Hardy*)

The Guilty (Monogram)...Estelle Mitchell and Linda Mitchell

1949

Strike It Rich (Allied Artists)...Julie Brady

1950

Guilty of Treason (Eagle Lion Classics)...Stephanie Varna
(aka *Treason*)

1956

The Lone Ranger (Warner Brothers)...Welcome Kilgore

1981

The Legend of the Lone Ranger ...cameo appearance

Bonita Wrather Television Appearances

1951

February 20, *Armstrong Circle Theatre*, "That's Simons Girl"

March 5, *Lux Video Theatre,* "Not Guilty--Of Course"

October 11, *Gruen Guild Playhouse,* "Hit and Run"

October 15, *Somerset Maugham TV Theatre,* "Masquerade"

November 15, *The Schaefer Century Theatre*, "One Strange Day"

1952

May 31, *The Schaefer Century Theatre*

1955

May 20, *Schlitz Playhouse of Stars,* "Sentence of Death"

July 17, *Dateline Disneyland* (brief interview)

1956

February 9, *Climax!*, "The Fifth Wheel" (playing herself)

1957

March 7, *Lux Video Theatre*, "One Way Passage"

May 22, *The United State Steel Hour*, "Shadow in the Sky"

1958

March 3, *Studio One*, "The Fair-Haired Boy"

1965

May 9, *Lassie*, "Lassie's Teamwork"

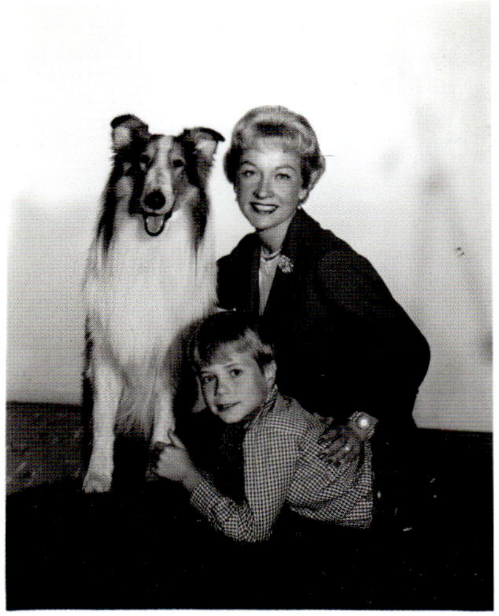

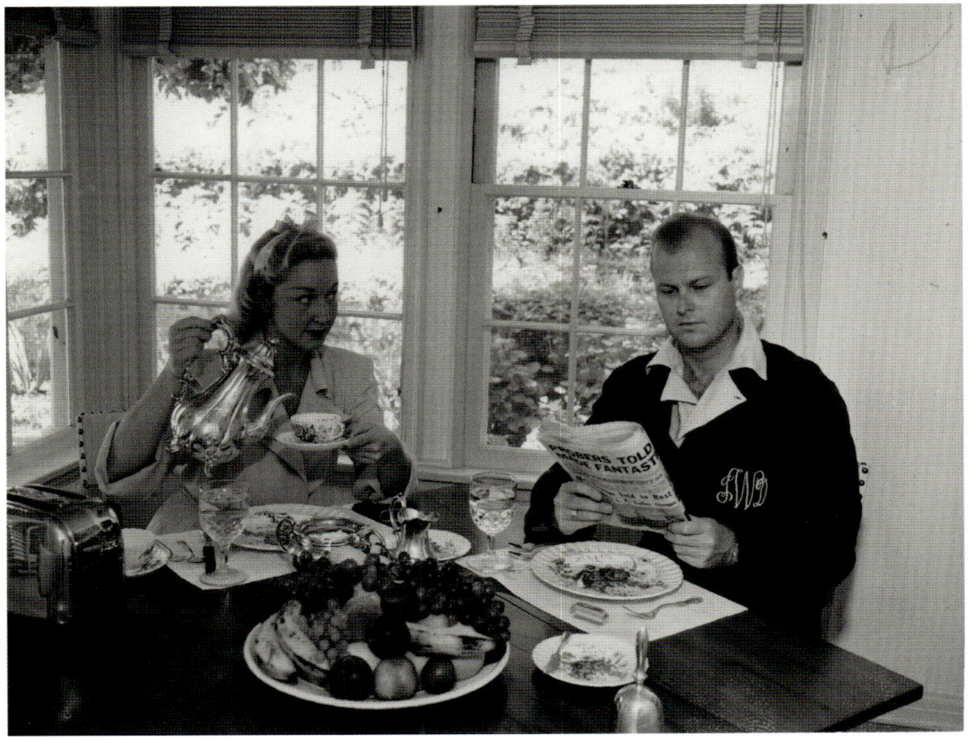

THE DISNEYLAND HOTEL: A Timeline

The Wrather Corporation Years (1955-1988)

1955

March 18 - Groundbreaking, officiated by Jack & Bonita Wrather and Anaheim Mayor Charles Pearson

July 17 - Dateline Disneyland, live telecast of Grand Opening of Disneyland (Wrathers interviewed)

October 5 - Hotel opened, 104 rooms in five 2-story buildings

October 5 - Mr. & Mrs. Robert Arnone of Inglewood, CA became Hotel's first guests

October 5 - Little Gourmet restaurant opened in converted ranch house at southeast corner of Hotel's property

Olympic-size swimming pool built (heated and illuminated)

1956

February 15 - Gourmet restaurant opened on West Street (with second floor banquet hall)

February 15 - Coffee Shop/Coffee House opened

February 15 - Round-the-World Lounge opened

August 25 - Hotel's Official Grand Opening; Administration Building complex opened on West Street

Coral Swim Club added to pool area

North Garden Rooms added with 96 rooms

1959

Garden Room structure added

1960

Two more Garden Room Structures added from 1960 to 1961

Hotel now had over 300 rooms

1961

June 11 - Disneyland monorail connected to Hotel's Monorail Station on West Street (press preview on May 25)

Two more Garden Room structures added

Miniature golf course, 50-tee driving range, 18-hole, and golf course added on 40-acres (golf course removed in 1971 for addition of marina and Marina Tower)

November 28 - Embassy & Magnolia Rooms banquet halls officially opened above West Street shops and restaurants (included Orange County's first ballroom) (Magnolia replaced the original banquet hall above the Gourmet)

1962

September - Sierra Tower North opened, 11-story with 150 rooms (Orange County's first high-rise building). Hotel now had over 450 rooms

Fall - Top-of-the-Park lounge opened on top of Sierra Tower

Monorail Lounge/Bar opened at Hotel's Monorail Station (closed in late 1981)

1963

Sidewalk Cafe opened next to Coffee House

1965

Summer - Coffee Shop/Coffee House doubled in capacity (later known as Coffee House Restaurant)

Summer - Gourmet restaurant remodeled

October 5 - Hotel's 10th Anniversary

1966

June - Sierra Tower Annex opened with 150 rooms

(Hotel now had 616 guest rooms)

Six new conference rooms added (Sierra Tower's first floor)

November - Plaza Building shopping complex opened

1968

August - Wrather, Corp. purchased Gourmet Restaurants, Inc.

Crown and Pillow Pub opened adjoining Oak Room

1969

California Dining Room replaced the Gourmet restaurant

Shipyard Inn & Sailmaker's Den lounge opened (closed January 3, 1999 and replaced by Hook's Pointe & Wine Cellar on April 8, 1999)

1970

January 12 - Oak Room Health Spa opened (later called Disneyland Hotel Health Spa) in Marina Tower

January 15 - Marina Tower (319 rooms) opened, with new lobby on Cerritos Avenue (contained Palm Court Lounge)

Spring - Jack & Bonita Wrather dedicated 3.5-acre Water World marina

May - Dancing Waters show amphitheater opened

June - The Cove opened (late named Papeete Beach)

June 15 - Vacationland opened (recreational vehicle park)

Restaurant Row opened on West Street with Country Kitchen (in 1973 became Chef's Kitchen and in 1990 became Goofy's Kitchen). Oak Room opened to the public for dinner (since early 1960's had been a private men's luncheon club).

Blum's restaurant opened in Plaza Building (later replaced by Tiffy's fast food restaurant)

Molly Malone's Fish Market opens at the marina

1971

Original lobby building (on West Street) became Travelport

1972

June - El Vaquero Steak House added to Restaurant Row

June - California Dining Room redesigned (closed in 1978 and its space became part of El Vaquero)

September - Convention Center (with Exhibition Hall and Marina Ballroom) opened at cost of $7.2-million (Grand Opening ceremonies on November 9th)

Fuji Pavilion restaurant opened at the marina (replaced in 1979 by Senor Campos' Taste of Mexico)

1976

November 3 - Tennisland Racquet Club held opening ceremony

1978

February 13 - Employee Cafeteria opened (later called Pier 1717)

February 13 - Chef's Table opened (small private dining room for special groups and occasions)

July & August - Bonita Tower opened, 13-story, 367 rooms (first U.S. hotel with solar heating system), $15-million

August - Hotel now had over 1,400 rooms

Garden Lounge opened in Bonita Tower

1979

Spring - Mazie's Pantry/Restaurant (cafe-style) opened at Plaza Building (replaced Tiffy's fast food restaurant)

June 7 - Water Wonderland playground opened

June 7 - Aqua Gardens, with 165-foot waterfall & Koi fish pond, opened

June 7 - Still Green laser sculpture premiered

June - Senor Campos' Taste of Mexico opened on marina (next to Shipyard Inn)

1980

Seaports of the Pacific shopping, dining, and entertainment area opened on the marina

Hotel's 25th Anniversary

California Wine Cellar opened at Seaports of the Pacific on the marina

Villas opened (executive suites & family units)

Fall - Mandarin Lounge/Bar opened (replaced Palm Court Lounge in Marina Tower)

Fall - Sausalito Sue Bar opened (floating barge on marina)

1981

November - Sgt. Preston's Yukon Saloon opened on Restaurant Row

1982

June - Off-Road Raceway opened (remote control model dune buggies)

1983

Meeting and convention space expanded to 160,000 square feet (Southern California's largest convention facility)

July 1 - Caffe Villa Verde opened (became Stromboli's Ristorante on May 12, 1995)

July 20 - Granville's Steak House opened

July - Pavilion Lounge opened (second floor, Convention Center)

July - Top Brass Lounge opened (next to Caffe Villa Verde)

1984

March - Sgt. Preston's Yukon Saloon enlarged and renamed Sgt. Preston's Yukon Saloon and Dancehall

March - Sgt. Preston's Yukon Follies stage show premiered

Queen's Berth added to marina (22 remote control tugboats)

1986

January - Oriental Gardens opened in front of Sierra Tower

Mid-year - Monorail Cafe opened (formerly the Coffee Shop/Coffee House) and closed August 6, 1999

1988

January - Walt Disney Company acquired the Wrather Corporation, thereby obtaining ownership of the Disneyland Hotel

BIBLIOGRAPHY

Andrek, Mary. "The Disneyland Hotel Story: Boomtown," *Kaleidoscope: the In-Room Magazine of Disneyland Hotel and Inn at the Park*, summer 1980, pp. 15-17.

Andrek, Mary. "The Disneyland Hotel Story: Into the '80s," *Kaleidoscope: the In-Room Magazine of Disneyland Hotel and Inn at the Park*, autumn 1980, pp. 12-14.

Andrek, Mary. "The Disneyland Hotel Story: The Wildcatting Years," *Kaleidoscope: the In-Room Magazine of Disneyland Hotel and Inn at the Park*, spring 1980, pp. 5-8.

"Another Attraction for Seaports," *Focus: For Employees of the Disneyland Hotel*, January-February, p. 1.

Black, Geoff and Brett Colson; Myrtle Davidson Malone, ed. *Dreams to Reality: A Profile of Modern Day Anaheim*. (Houston: Pioneer Publications, Inc., 1993).

Bright, Randy. *Disneyland: Inside Story* (New York: Harry N. Abrams, Inc., Publishers, 1987).

Broggie, Michael. *Walt Disney's Railroad Story: The Small-Scale Fascination That Led to a Full-Scale Kingdom* (Pasadena, CA: Pentex Media Group, 1997).

California Misadventure, part I, on Jim Hill Media website. http://www.jimhillmedia.com/legacy/index.htm?../articles/ archive.0005-3.1.htm~contentFrame

Disneyland guidebooks (1955 through the mid-1980's...under various titles such as *Walt Disney's Disneyland Pictorial Guidebook* and *Walt Disney's Guidebook to Disneyland*)

*Disneyland Hotel Check-In (*guest monthly and/or bi-monthly magazine, various editions from the mid-1960's through the early 1970's).

The Disneylander: The Magazine for Disneyland Employees (various issues from 1959 to 1961).

Disneyland Holiday Magazine (various issues from 1957 and 1958).

The Disneyland Hotel (employee handbook, 1989).

Disneyland Hotel (various guest brochures, pamphlets, and news releases from 1955 through the 1980's).

Disneyland Hotel (various postcards from 1955 to the present).

Disneyland Line (various issues of the Disneyland employees' monthly magazine from 1961).

Disneyland: The First Quarter Century (sold at Disneyland, 1979).

Disneyland: The First Thirty Years (sold at Disneyland, 1985).

Flower, Joe. *Prince of the Magic Kingdom: Michael Eisner and the Re-Making of Disney* (New York: John Wiley & Sons, Inc., 1991).

Fulton, William. "Bonita Granville Wrather: Salvaging the Empire That Jack Built," *California Business*, February 1986, pp. 24-30.

Bruce Gordon and David Munford. *Disneyland, the Nickel Tour: A Postcard Journey through a Half Century of the Happiest Place on Earth* (Santa Clarita, CA: Camphor Tree Publishers, 2000).

Grover, Ron. *The Disney Touch: ABC and the Quest for the World's Greatest Media Empire* (Chicago: Irwin Professional Publishing, 1997).

Grover, Ron. *The Disney Touch: How a Daring Management Team Revived an Entertainment Empire* (Homewood, IL: Business One Irwin, 1991).

The Handbook of Texas Online website, Jack Wrather biography.

http://www.tsha.utexas.edu/handbook/online/articles/view/

WW/fwr18.html

Holliss, Richard and Brian Sibley. *The Disney Studio Story* (New York: Crown Publishers, Inc., 1988).

The Internet Movie Database website. http://www.imdb.com

Kaleidoscope: The In-Room Magazine for the Disneyland Hotel & the Inn at the Park (guest quarterly magazine, various editions from summer 1979 through the mid-1980's).

Libman, Gary. "Bonita Wrather Fills Void with Devotion to Business," *Los Angeles Times* (Monday, February 18, 1985), pt. iv, pp. 1, 12.

Maltin, Leonard. *The Disney Films*, 4th ed. (New York: Disney Editions, 2000).

Maltin, Leonard. *Leonard Maltin's Movie Encyclopedia: Career Profiles of More Than 2,000 Actors and Filmmakers, Past and Present* (New York: Penguin, 1995).

Marling, Karal Ann (ed.). *Designing Disney's Theme Parks: The Architecture of Reassurance* (New York: Flammarion, 1997).

The Museum of Broadcast Communications website, Jack Wrather. http://www.museum.tv/archives/etv/W/htmlW/wratherjack/wrat her-jack.htm

Remembering Bonita Granville website, biography and photos. http://members.tripod.com/~classicfilmfan/bg/index.html

Shannon, Leonard. *Disneyland: Dreams, Traditions, and Transitions* (Disney's Kingdom Editions, 1994).

Smith, Dave. *Disney A to Z: The Updated Official Encyclopedia* (New York: Hyperion, 1998).

Stein, Jeannine. "My Style: Bonita Wrather in Conversation with Jeannine Stein," *Los Angeles Herald Examiner* (Monday, December 2, 1985), pp. B1, B5.

The Story of Disneyland (first Park guide book, Disneyland, Inc., 1955).

Taylor, John. *Storming the Magic Kingdom: Wall Street, the Raiders and the Battle for Disney* (New York: Alfred A. Kroft, Inc., 1987).

Thomas, Bob. *Building a Company: Roy O. Disney and the Creation of an Entertainment Empire* (New York: Hyperion, 1998).

Thomas, Bob. *Walt Disney: An American Original* (New York: Hyperion, 1994).

Vacationland Magazine (various issues from 1958 to 1966).

Walt Disney Productions Annual Report (for fiscal year ended October 2, 1954).

Watts, Steven. *The Magic Kingdom: Walt Disney and the American Way of Life* (Boston: Houghton Mifflin Company, 1997).

Wrather Chatter (various copies of the company's bi-monthly publication to employees).

Wrather Corporation Annual Report (various shareholder reports from the 1960's through the 1980's).

"Wrather Corp.'s Last Roundup," *Business Week*, 29 September

1973, p. 68.

Acknowledgments...

A special thanks is due to Dave Smith, Becky Cline and staff at the Walt Disney Archives in Burbank, California. Many very helpful suggestions and much valuable information was provided during the creation of this book.

To Dave Lay at Disneyland Resorts, your help has been greatly appreciated. You went out of your way in helping with this project.

A very special thank you to Marcia Pera at the Disneyland Hotel for making that call to Tony.

Thanks Mike Conners for your wonderful stories and information.

Also, many thanks to the Staff of the Charles Von der Ahe Library at Loyola Marymount University in Los Angeles, California Dr. Errol Stevens, Neil Bethke, Dr. William C. Stalls. Access to the *Jack and Bonita Wrather Papers* was extremely helpful to this publication.

Thank you to Mr. Ryan Bowman for his wonderful website on Bonita Granville Wrather.

To Mr. Bret Colson, thank you for your valuable suggestions as well as your book "Dreams to Reality." It is a must reading for anyone interested in the history of Anaheim, California.

Molly & Christopher Wrather for your amazing benevolence.

Dean W. Barickman-thank you so much for your input. It was greatly appreciated.

Dave Bossert for the wonderful privilige of working with you..